WEEPING BRITANNIA

Weeping
BRITANNIA

Portrait of a Nation in Tears

THOMAS DIXON

OXFORD
UNIVERSITY PRESS

OXFORD

UNIVERSITY PRESS

Great Clarendon Street, Oxford, OX2 6DP,
United Kingdom

Oxford University Press is a department of the University of Oxford.
It furthers the University's objective of excellence in research, scholarship,
and education by publishing worldwide. Oxford is a registered trade mark of
Oxford University Press in the UK and in certain other countries

© Thomas Dixon 2015

The moral rights of the author have been asserted

First Edition published in 2015

Impression: 1

Published in the United States of America by Oxford University Press
198 Madison Avenue, New York, NY 10016, United States of America

British Library Cataloguing in Publication Data
Data available

Library of Congress Control Number: 2015931966

ISBN 978-0-19-967605-7

Printed in Great Britain by
Clays Ltd, St Ives plc

For Caleb Dixon

CONTENTS

V. FEELINGS

LIST OF ILLUSTRATIONS

'Therefor to wepe come lerne att me.'
De Arte Lacrimandi
*c.*1500

I Am a Rock

Willliam Martin was serving as a captain in the British military police in Brunei in 1945 when he was taken captive by the Japanese and interned in the Kuching prisoner of war camp. His captivity was relatively uneventful until he made the mistake of throwing a pair of trousers over a wire fence to a fellow captive—a soldier with only a loin-cloth to cover him. Taken before the assistant commander of the camp for his charitable misdemeanour, Captain Martin was punched and kicked; a bayonet was repeatedly jabbed into the flesh of his feet; one guard smashed his face with the butt of a rifle, closing his left eye, making his nose bleed, and lacerating his mouth; after a few minutes in a cell he was taken out again and used by the guards for ju-jitsu practice. He was then made to stand on the edge of a drain, thrashed on the thighs with the flat of a bayonet, and told to weep. He refused to do so, at which his Japanese tormentor knocked him into the ditch and jumped on his chest. Captain Martin recalled: 'I felt my ribs go.' After being thrown back into his cell, barely conscious, Martin sat with his head in his hands. One of the camp guards again asked him if he was weeping. He replied, 'No Britisher ever weeps.'[1]

It would make a wonderful tear-jerking scene in a movie—a classic example of that genre of cinematic moment that invites us to cry over someone not crying. A 1950 Mass Observation question asked the panel of participants whether they cried at the movies. As we shall see, men and women had very different tastes in weepies, but those men who had seen active service were particularly moved by scenes of heroism in films about explorers, adventures, or the war. In fact, in the light of what we know about the habits of mid-twentieth-century British men, I imagine Captain Martin would have wept both when reunited with his loved ones after his release from Kuching, and subsequently when watching movies at his local cinema. The semi-privacy of the cinema, and an identification with the fictional stories dramatized there, provided just the opportunity that even the most resolute of Britishers needed to shed tears in the post-war years.[2]

'No Britisher ever weeps.' It is a great piece of rhetoric, and I am not literal-minded enough to take Captain Martin posthumously to task for the factual inaccuracy of his claim, either as a historical statement, or as a sociological generalization. I am sure that William Martin himself, in a more reflective moment, would have recalled the tears shed by important figures in British history including Boadicea, Richard the Lionheart, Prince Hal, Lady Jane Grey, and George IV, as narrated in Henrietta Marshall's popular children's history book *Our Island Story*.[3] He would have recalled, no doubt, some private tearful moments from his own childhood and family experiences too. But none of this is to the point. At that moment in Kuching prison camp, William Martin represented the British Empire. With blood streaming from his nose, a black eye, a ringing in his ears, and the searing pain of his broken ribs, he knew he must show no weakness. To refrain from weeping, especially when tauntingly ordered to do so by a 'Jap' prison guard, was to prove the strength and superiority of the British character. Martin's account of his experiences, given at the War Crimes trial of his captors after the end of the conflict, ends with the observation that after his refusals to dissolve into tears, the guards suddenly left him alone. William Martin had won their grudging respect, as well as the psychological show-down.

How things have changed since 1945. No Britisher ever weeps? It now seems as though we do little else. We live under the almost unchallenged reign of emotion. American talk-shows led the way in the 1980s, followed by their British equivalents. The new religion of *Oprah* centred on confessional conversations, with celebrities and everyday folk sharing their feelings—and their tears—guided by TV psychologists, on hand to teach millions of viewers the new catechisms of emotional intelligence (and to sell them their books). Looking back, and wondering when the tide of tears turned in modern Britain, people remember the England footballer Paul Gascoigne and the Prime Minister Margaret Thatcher both publicly weeping in 1990, but most of all they think of the outpouring of grief over Princess Diana in 1997. Many people at the time thought this was unwarranted, inappropriate, even hypocritical. But millions joined in.[4]

And now, for some years, by far the most successful television programmes have all been sob-fests. Talent shows, reality shows, singing shows, dancing shows, baking shows, and shows about our bodies, clothes, lifestyles, pets, and children: all of them have been turned into tear-jerkers. Last night, to take just one example, I watched on television the final episode of a reality series called *Educating Yorkshire*. It used the story of a teenage boy called Musharaf, with a terrible stammer, and his inspirational teacher, Mr Burton, to rerun the plot of the weepy movie about George VI, *The King's Speech*, in the context of an English GCSE oral exam in a Dewsbury academy. The climax saw Musharaf find his voice, gain his hoped-for C-grade, and give an inspiring speech to the whole school on his last day there. Boys, girls, and teachers dissolved into tears in response (although it was a relief to see at least a few of them giggling). I looked at Twitter: it was awash—the nation was Tweeping and Twailing.[5]

I am a sucker for this kind of thing myself. Even though I was watching Musharaf's speech through the quizzical spectacles of a historian with a professional interest in the phenomenon, only too aware of the narrative and emotional techniques being deployed, I could not help welling up. And I will refrain from embarrassing myself by listing the many other things that have made me cry in films and television over the years. I grew up in Britain after the age of the stiff upper lip had ended—an era of nearly a hundred years, running roughly from the death of Charles

3

Dickens in 1870 to the death of Winston Churchill in 1965, and at its zenith during the First and Second World Wars. Throughout my own lifetime, upper lips have been slackening. In the 1980s and 1990s, people spoke about 'new men' being in touch with their feelings, as well as taking great care over their grooming, and I always wholeheartedly embraced the former if not so much the latter. My initial interest in the histories of weeping, Britishness, and the stiff upper lip stemmed from a curiosity about my own mixed inheritance as a weepy Britisher.

Some people, especially those born while Churchill was still alive, find the new touchy-feeliness of British life slightly disgusting. They call it 'emotional incontinence'. The phrase, with its origins in the psychiatric literature of the late nineteenth century, implies that a similar shame should attach to a public stream of tears as to a public stream of urine.[6] In 2010, the journalist and broadcaster Joan Bakewell expressed her shock at all the sobbing and hugging in the fiftieth-anniversary edition of the soap opera *Coronation Street*. This sort of 'emotional incontinence', she said, 'would have shocked older generations' who espoused stoicism rather than sentimentalism.[7] A year later, the comedian Jo Brand made a television documentary about public weeping. She was against it, saying that crying should be reserved for very rare occasions, and then take place in private.[8] Online comments responding to the programme proved she was not alone. One remark came from someone calling himself—and I speculate here about gender—*Algol6o* (the name of a kind of computer language). *Algol6o* wrote: 'If you need to blub, go into the bog and do it privately. Small children and effeminate foreigners might be expected to do otherwise but any Briton over the age of 8 should have self-control.' It is another sign of the sensibilities of our own age that this remark was later removed from the BBC website for being offensive to other users.[9] Perhaps Alexander Pope's poem lampooning Joseph Addison's celebrated sentimental play *Cato: A Tragedy* would also have been deleted. It described a woman responding to Addison's drama with copious urine

4

rather than the expected fashionable tears of eighteenth-century sensibility: 'But while her Pride forbids her Tears to flow | The gushing Waters find a Vent below.'[10]

Whether you look on the recent changes in the emotional style of British life with the contempt expressed by *Algol60*, with passionate enthusiasm, or with stoical indifference, you might feel that it is a phenomenon worth exploring and explaining. That is what *Weeping Britannia* sets out to do, showing how, when, and why a supposedly universal human phenomenon—the shedding of tears—came to be seen as unBritish and, in the process, recovering some of the thoughts, feelings, and experiences of tearful men and women from all parts of the British Isles over the last 600 years. British tears have been more plentiful, and have had many more meanings and functions, than the limited modern framework of the 'stiff upper lip' versus 'emotional incontinence' would suggest. In fact, it was the extreme restraint that peaked in the mid-twentieth century, rather than the tearful sensibilities that flourished both before and afterwards, which marked an aberration in our national history. In earlier times we were a nation of proficient, sometimes virtuosic weepers. We are only now gradually recovering from a lengthy period of militarized, imperialistic nationhood. The stiff upper lip had its purpose in the Kuching prisoner of war camp, and had served the same purpose during Britain's emergence as the world's greatest empire, in the Victorian and Edwardian eras. But that era is just one part of a much longer and more interesting historical story. That longer history includes British piety, enthusiasm, pathos, and feeling, as well as the now infamous British restraint, itself a thing of many layers and stages, including reactions against both Roman Catholicism and the French Revolution.

It was in 1965 that the American singer-songwriter Paul Simon wrote 'I Am a Rock'.[11] It is not a song about Britishness, but its attitude of defiant isolationism encapsulates one element of what was most pathetic (in both senses) about the stiff upper lip. The lyrics include the line 'I have no need of friendship; friendship causes pain', concluding, 'And a rock feels no pain; And an island never cries.' The imperial British prided themselves on exactly this. It was an attitude well adapted to an island nation, surrounded by a sea of foreign tears. The British, for a time, had tried to embody their own geographical characteristics, inhabiting not only dry islands, but dry-eye lands. But by 1965 there were signs of change, beyond the music of Paul Simon. The death of Churchill created an opportunity finally to enter a truly post-war age. The first forerunner of the Notting Hill Carnival took place that year, representing a new kind of British exuberance, and the anthropologist Geoffrey Gorer published a book entitled *Death, Grief and Mourning in Contemporary Britain*, lamenting the continuing repression of healthy expressions of grief. There was a growing sense that the stiff upper lip might have been good on the battlefield but was not appropriate for peacetime, and could cause physical and emotional forms of illness.[12]

One good reason, then, to explore the history of tears is to explode some myths about British national character. Another is to free our minds from certain psychological limitations in the present. Delving into the records of weeping in earlier times reveals a crowded mass of exotic experiences, and interpretations of them, next to which our own emotional lives seem meagre and conventional. The intensity of feeling, extremity of expression, and depth of moral and religious commitment involved are all unfamiliar to us. We may still go to the theatre to watch Shakespearian tragedies, although the responses of modern audiences are pretty tame, but there are other phenomena, such as witch trials, public hangings, and revivalist sermons preached on hillsides to crowds of tens of thousands, which violently moved our ancestors, but which have never touched us.

This is also a matter of intellectual history. Our beliefs about our bodies and minds are themselves constituents of our emotional experiences. For example, at various times, people have believed their feelings to be the movements of sinful passions through fallen flesh; the interplay of four basic physiological 'humours'; divinely designed mechanisms regulating thought and behaviour for virtuous ends; useless relics of the behaviour of pre-human evolutionary ancestors; the leaking out of repressed childhood traumas; the unhealthy build-up of stress hormones. Each of these beliefs constitutes not a different interpretation of the same basic experience, but rather the basis for a drastically different kind of subjective experience. These beliefs produce distinct emotions, not just distinct ideas. Thinking and feeling develop through time together.[13]

Since the publication in 1872 of Charles Darwin's influential book on the subject, *The Expression of the Emotions in Man and Animals*, we have tended to think of crying as one of a set of basic expressions—part of a universal language of emotion. But to interpret weeping as the standard outward expression of individual sadness is to overlook its true nature, complexity, and significance. Darwin himself rightly noted that tears could not be neatly associated with any single mental state. They can be secreted 'in sufficient abundance to roll down the cheeks,' he wrote, 'under the most opposite emotions, and under no emotion at all'.[14] Tears have historically been shed in many different circumstances, individually and collectively, in joy as well as grief, in resignation or rebellion, at momentous public ceremonies and in the most private moments. Tears can signify despair or determination, weakness or strength, rage or compassion. They can be produced by sensations, memories, and thoughts, as well as by strong emotions. So, when we cry over a film, a piece of music, or an event in our lives, we are doing something much more than showing that we are sad. A tear is a universal sign not in the sense that it has the same meaning in all times and all places. It is a universal sign because, depending on the mental, social, and narrative context, it can mean almost anything.[15]

Tears are produced when our soggy spongelike bodies are gripped, and then squeezed, by a powerful set of ideas, often in narrative form. This is one of the many things that appeals to me about weeping as a subject for historical study: the resulting story is simultaneously one of bodies, of ideas, and of narratives, because a tear is simultaneously a secretion and a signifier. At one level, weeping seems to be on a par with vomiting, sweating, sneezing, or farting—a bodily reflex, an excretion—even a sort of waste disposal. And even the lowly fart has proved itself amenable to enlightening historical investigation.[16] Yet tears exist on a much more exalted level, too. They are alone among bodily fluids in being objects of admiration, considered not only immaculate but deeply meaningful, even as vehicles of the divine. The tear is the Virgin Mary of bodily secretions, a snowflake on the dung-heap of human excreta.[17] The status of the tear as a venerated excretion is only one of the paradoxes of weeping, which, as we shall see, has been believed to be involuntary, healthy, sincere, pious, intellectual, and manly, yet also theatrical, pathological, hypocritical, blasphemous, emotional, and effeminate.

Three important aspects of weeping are lost in thinking of it as a mere physiological expression: the intellectual, the interactive, and the imaginative. As William Blake put it in 1803, 'A tear is an intellectual thing.'[18] The philosopher Jerome Neu, who adopted Blake's phrase as the title of his book, encapsulates this in the slogan: 'We cry because we think.'[19] It is particular beliefs about the world, rather than mere physiology, that turn on our tears, and it is their intellectual and moral nature that has led many theorists over the centuries to deny that animals can shed real tears. Weeping is not only a form of embodied thought, but it is also a social activity. From infancy onwards, tears are strongly associated with attachment and separation and so are not best thought of as expressions of individual emotion, but rather as a kind of liquid social bond.[20] Historically too, weeping has been a social, public activity of a piece with other such activities, including praying, preaching, and repenting; thinking, reading, and writing; acting, singing, and spectating; meeting, marrying, and mourning. The intellectual and social dimensions of tears are most powerfully accessed through imaginative stories, especially those told and listened to collectively. So, the next time you are sitting on the sofa quietly sobbing over *The King's Speech* or *Educating Yorkshire*, you should be aware that a complex, shared, unconscious, intellectual narrative is running its course down your cheeks. If this seems an odd thought to you now, it will hopefully seem less so after you have read the rest of this book.

So, *Weeping Britannia* is intended to be more than a museum of tears (although it is that too). It aims to anatomize, reconstitute, even reanimate, and feel once more, the experiences of tearful individuals, and those who witnessed them, in earlier historical periods. Of course it is impossible to access directly the subjective experiences of the dead. It is also impossible to take part in their actions or think their thoughts, but that does not prevent us from attempting political or intellectual histories. We do what we can, without believing our attempts at historical mind-reading will be flawless. And since even our own minds, and those of our loved ones, can be opaque, to say the least, in the face of our attempts at understanding, the challenge of teasing out the emotional lives of those who lived and died centuries ago is of a different order, but not a different type, from the challenges we face every day in trying to imagine the unseen thoughts and feelings behind the observable words and deeds of ourselves and others. In both the contemporary and the historical cases, we enter into the emotional lives of others via their words, beliefs, and actions. In what follows, the method I have often adopted has been to juxtapose first-person accounts of tearful experiences with more reflective writings, whether in the form of literature, philosophy, science, or journalism, setting out theoretical and moral ideas about weeping in the period in question. The theory, experience, language, and ethics of weeping have co-evolved across the centuries. They have left their marks in historical documents of all kinds, from spiritual memoirs to working-class autobiographies, Shakespearean tragedies to newspaper advice columns, philosophical tracts to reality television programmes, private letters to parliamentary debates, Romantic poems to postmodern tweets. Within those documents, we find evidence not only of emotions that elicited tears, but also of those second-order emotions—of pleasure, sympathy, admiration, or disgust—elicited by the spectacle of emotional tears.

It would not be possible to recover something as personal and emotional as weeping through a dry account of events and ideas alone. For that reason, this book is structured in a way that allows the particular experiences of individuals to bring to life a broader narrative of large-scale social, religious, cultural, and intellectual changes. I have tried to create a portrait (rather than, say, a sociological survey or a statistical analysis) of a nation through a series of lachrymose miniatures—a string of twenty historical teardrops. The men and women whose tears populate this story include some of the most influential individuals in British history: Oliver Cromwell, George III, Queen Victoria, Winston Churchill, and Margaret Thatcher. But many everyday folk, forgotten celebrities, and even fictional characters such as Titus Andronicus and Little Nell, are also represented. *Weeping Britannia* delves into the histories of love, grief, religion, crime, sex, madness, medicine, patriotism, literature, theatre, cinema, and music to discover how and why people have been moved to tears in Britain since the end of the Middle Ages. Some of those whom we might have expected to be the most stoical and restrained were often publicly moved to tears, including soldiers, lawyers, judges, prime ministers, lord chancellors, and even an executioner. Major religious and political upheavals in our national past, such as the Reformation, the English Civil War, the French Revolution, the rise and fall of the British Empire, and the legacy of the Second World War all permanently changed the meanings of tears and ideas of the British as a nation.

The secularization of Britain, which started in earnest in the nineteenth century, and reached a new level during the mid-twentieth, removed

from public life one of the great contexts for the production and interpretation of tears. In the contrast between the moist eyes of earlier
centuries and the dry ones of the twentieth, we can see also the contrast
between Christian sensibility and a more secularist stoicism, inspired by
the imperial philosophies of the ancient world. The tears of Jesus, the
Virgin Mary, and Mary Magdalene (whose weeping marked the English
language through the creation of a new word to describe it, 'maudlin')
had previously been everyday moral and emotional examples. It is
appropriate, then, that the first of our twenty tearful historical moments
should involve a late medieval woman whose violent religious sobbing
took her all the way from King's Lynn to Jerusalem, and back again.

I. PIETY

1

Looking for Margery

Mother, miller, brewer, and mystic, Margery Kempe was an extreme weeper. Thanks to the survival of her remarkable *Book*, the earliest surviving autobiography in English, we can still hear Margery's distinctive voice six centuries later. Hers was the voice of one crying in the wilderness—or at least crying in King's Lynn—and not just crying but roaring and sobbing, sometimes even changing colour and falling down as she wept. Margery was born around 1373, the daughter of the Mayor of Lynn (as the town was then known). She married a local brewer, ran unsuccessful brewing and milling businesses, and bore fourteen children, suffering a bout of madness after the birth of the first, before a series of visions converted her to a religious way of life. Her boisterous style of devotion was characterized by the gift of tears—dramatic, loud, and frequent—a gift that many, including Margery herself, had reason to wish she had never received. Margery's autobiography, rediscovered in the 1930s, is the tale of a woman upstaged by her own tears.[1]

It was clear to me from an early stage in my investigations into the history of British weeping that Margery should be my starting point: the *fons et origo* of English tears, a noisily bubbling spring. I have not come across any other historical figure whose life has been so utterly deluged and defined by tears. So I got on a train to King's Lynn in search of the spirit of Margery. Today, the town still contains well-preserved buildings from the medieval and early modern periods, including a guildhall, a prison, a priory, and the ruins of a Franciscan friary. But as I hunted for the street on which Margery and her husband lived and brewed, all I found was a branch of Argos and a modern shopping centre. Along Paradise Road and Paradise Parade, many of the windows were boarded up. Past Times had closed down. A display of Santa-style red and white lingerie illuminated the window of Ann Summers, with a poster captioned 'Oh, oh, oh!' A festive negligée was not a gift one would normally associate with Margery Kempe, I reflected. Probably a hair-shirt would be more apt. But it was not entirely inappropriate either. Margery's book includes stories of her sexual as well as her spiritual adventures, including an occasion when she planned an illicit encounter with a man after evensong.[2] Having decided against sharing this observation with the Ann Summers staff, I pressed on towards St Margaret's church, where Margery worshipped and wept in the fourteenth and fifteenth centuries.

As it started to rain heavily, I recalled an occasion in Margery's book when a fire in Lynn had threatened to destroy the church. Margery prayed and wept all day until a miraculous fall of snow, like mysterious frozen tears, doused the flames, saved the church, and earned Margery the gratitude of the town.[3] Was this downpour, from which I now sheltered inside that same church, a sign to me from Margery, I wondered, as I struggled to find any record of her life inside St Margaret's. The medieval parts of the building are overlain by the extensions, ornamentation, and statuary of many generations. Behind the altar is a huge carved and painted wooden screen—a piece of high Victorian medievalism—on which a golden crucified Christ is flanked by some of the Fathers of the early Church. These theologian-saints, including Augustine, Ambrose, Gregory, and Jerome, were the originators of the theology of tears which Margery learned via the devotional texts of her own time, read aloud to her by her spiritual mentors. These were books teaching the devout both how to think and how to feel. They had titles like *The Fire of Love*, *The Ladder of Perfection*, and *The Pricking of*

Love.[4] The image of pricking is a very important one in the theology of tears. The three traditional source of tears were devotion, compassion, and compunction. The last of these literally meant a kind of pricking or piercing (the etymology is the same as for 'puncture'), showing that the soul of the believer had been pierced, as Christ's side was pierced by a spear. Compunction, along with faith and baptism, was one of the three key ingredients of salvation, and the sign of its presence was a flow of tears.[5]

Continuing my tour of St Margaret's, I eventually discovered a mini-exhibition about Margery that I had previously missed, and learned a little more about her life in Lynn. As I signed the visitors' book and prepared to leave, my attention was caught by the comments left by others. Several visitors described the church as 'nice', one as 'very clean and tidy'. Several messages were about deceased loved ones. One, in a child's hand, read 'i miss my granny and auntie'. But what most struck me were the frequent references to peace and quietness: 'Thank-you for the peace and tranquillity'; 'Calm, light and inspiring'; 'Peaceful and calming'; 'Thank you for the peace and stillness inside this church'; 'Peaceful haven'; 'Delightful, quiet and impressive'. All this stillness and calm did not feel like the noisy world of Margery Kempe at all. Margery would have experienced St Margaret's as a bustling and noisy centre of medieval town life. Today it had become a haven of stillness, reflection, and nostalgia set apart from the business of modern existence: a spiritual Past Times.

But a couple of entries in the visitors' book got closer to Margery's world. One complained of a 'bad-tempered organist' who 'nonetheless makes beautiful sounds', and another stated, 'Came to pray—but was too noisy with workmen and women.' This sense of difficult and noisy individuals disrupting the spiritual lives of others—as well as the reference to beautiful music—suggests at least some thin threads of connection with the woman described in a comprehensive study of tears as the all-time 'weeping champion' of recorded history.[6] So I made my own entry in the visitors' book–'Thomas Dixon. Historian. Looking for Margery'–dashed through the rain to a pizza restaurant opposite, reopened my copy of *The Book of Margery Kempe*, and continued my search.

The *Book* is a story of mishaps and struggles, and of Margery's determination to use her divine gifts to overcome the many obstacles she encounters. Central among those gifts is her copious weeping. Although Margery shed holy tears in volumes possibly never matched before or since, such tears were part of an established apparatus of medieval piety, imported from northern Europe, and centred on two figures: the mourning Virgin, known variously as the *Mater Dolorosa*, the weeping Mary, or the Lady of Pity; and her wounded, suffering, crucified, and bleeding son, Jesus Christ. In Margery's day, a carved or painted *Pietà*, showing a mourning, sometimes weeping, Virgin Mary cradling her son's corpse, would have been found in almost every church in England. Songs of Marian devotion such as the 'Stabat Mater' and the 'Salve Regina' are among the most important sources of the western tradition of tears, including the image of this world as a 'vale of tears'.[7]

Although Margery's tears were the products of a world of painted icons, wooden virgins, and plaster saints, she was none of these things. More Wife of Bath than Mother of God, Margery's wailing, like everything else in her life, has an endearingly down-to-earth, sometimes ridiculous quality to it.[8] If the *Book* is ever turned into a film, it should be called *Carry On Crying*. While Christ had entered Jerusalem triumphantly on a donkey, when Margery attempts to re-enact the feat on her pilgrimage, she almost falls off her donkey from crying so much over the joy and sweetness of the moment.[9] Even one of the rare miracles attributed to Margery has a rough and undignified aspect to it: she 'miraculously' survives a large lump of wood and masonry falling on her head.[10] The religious path, for Margery, is littered with impediments. She struggles, for instance, to persuade her husband to cease demanding sex with her, after her conversion. On one occasion he even pesters her for sex by the side of the road, on a hot summer afternoon, during a pilgrimage in the English countryside.[11] Contemporary records show that Margery's husband had other failings too, being punished on one occasion for breaking the rules governing the price and quality of the beer he sold, and on another for the quite baffling offence of 'filling the common fleet with dung'.[12]

Even among the pious, Margery made enemies. A visiting preacher in Lynn, not used to all the noise, banned Margery from the church for her incessant wailing, which was interrupting his sermons. 'I wish this woman were out of the church', he said, 'she is annoying people.'[13] The Church authorities suspected Margery of heresy, accusing her of being a member of the proto-Protestant 'Lollard' movement which gave a prominent role to laypeople, including women; denied the right of the Church to ordain a special priesthood; and encouraged the reading of the Bible in the vernacular. This over-confident and spiritually assertive married woman, a member of no religious order, who had the effrontery to tell clergymen how to behave and what to believe, had the air of a Lollard about her. In Leicester, the Mayor accused Margery of being 'a false strumpet, a false Lollard, and a false deceiver of the people'. There is no doubt that Margery's life was in danger because of this association.[14] The first Lollard to be burnt for heresy, in 1401, was William Sawtry, who had been a priest in Lynn. The highest ranking of the Lollards, Sir John Oldcastle, was found guilty both of heresy and of treason, and was executed in 1417.[15]

When on her trip to the Holy Land, Margery cut a striking figure, dressed all in white, frequently in tears. Her appearance attracted adverse comment both from locals, who were astonished by this noisily sobbing English woman, and from her fellow pilgrims, who, on Margery's account, 'were most annoyed because she wept so much and spoke all the time about the love and goodness of our Lord'. Some said they would not continue to travel with her even for a hundred pounds. Margery was ruining their trip with all her heavy religious talk of Christ, love, sin, and suffering, and her ostentatious weeping.[16] The completion of this pilgrimage, regardless of the views of her companions, was a remarkable achievement. Margery's journey from northern Europe was arduous, dangerous, and took months to complete. It involved crossing the Alps, taking a galley from Venice to Haifa, and finally riding from there to Jerusalem, all under the protection of a band of crossbowmen. Very few medieval women had the necessary resources, independence, and courage to make such an expedition. Margery travelled without her husband, and received the protection of a series of clergymen who chaperoned her during different parts of her journey, and mediated in the constant disputes between Margery and her annoyed travelling companions. Returning from Jerusalem via holy sites in Assisi and Rome, Margery arrived back in Norwich some time after Easter in 1415, around eighteen months after she had set out.[17]

It was during her visit to Jerusalem in 1414 that Margery's tears reached a new level. It was from this moment that she developed her characteristic 'roaring' and 'crying out'.[18] When she was shown, as tourists and pilgrims still are on tours today, the holy sites where 'our Lord had suffered his pains and his Passion', Margery 'wept and sobbed as plenteously as though she had seen our Lord with her bodily eyes suffering his passion at that time'. And when she came to Mount Calvary, the site of the crucifixion itself, Margery could not stay standing, or even kneel, but 'writhed and wrestled with her body, spreading her arms out wide, and cried with a loud voice as though her heart would have burst apart'. From this time on, including after her return to England, Margery was prone to regular fits of what she variously calls 'weeping', 'crying', and 'roaring'. When trying to suppress her cries, she could turn a livid blue and then 'the colour of lead'. Even the sight of a male baby or a handsome young man could set Margery off, reminding her of her

Lord's incarnation in the male human form. Seeing a man whip a horse could get her roaring, conjuring for her the image of the flogging of Christ. Margery herself interpreted these physical outbursts as signs of her holy thoughts and feelings: the effects of 'the fire of love that burned so fervently in her soul with pure pity and compassion'. Others thought they were the effects of a wicked spirit, a kind of illness, or too much wine.[19]

Margery had always been prone to tears, both before and after she started to succumb to these bouts of holy roaring. At various points in her *Book*, Margery records shedding tears of sorrow at her own sins and unkindness to others; of grief when her husband coerces her into sex; of compassion for those in poverty and distress; of lamentation over the sinfulness of the world in general and of specific individuals; of despair at the world and desire for heaven; and of transcendent aesthetic feeling.[20] In one of her earliest religious visions, Margery recalled that, as she lay in bed with her husband at night, she 'heard a melodious sound so sweet and delectable that she thought she had been in paradise'. Margery jumped out of bed and exclaimed, 'Alas that ever I sinned! It is full merry in heaven.' The heavenly music was more beautiful than any earthly equivalent and, whenever Margery heard 'any mirth or melody' afterwards, she 'shed very plentiful and abundant tears of high devotion, with great sobbings and sighings for the bliss of heaven, not fearing the shames and contempt of this wretched world'.[21]

Margery Kempe's autobiography is a priceless record of the meaning of weeping for one English woman in the High Middle Ages. In many respects Margery was utterly exceptional, but her experiences can still reveal something of practices and attitudes of the mercantile and religious folk of fifteenth-century England among whom she lived. Margery took established social customs of shedding tears in mourning, compassion, and religious devotion, and extended them far beyond their usual limits. Her weeping was a performance, a public act which brought her a great deal of attention and of criticism. It was not her tears themselves that were controversial, but the excessive and provocative manner in which she performed them.

I confess that I can sympathize with Margery's critics, including her companions on her travels, and the visiting preacher at the church of St Margaret's, Lynn. Her constant sobbing and wailing, accompanied by pious religious preaching, must have been, frankly, annoying. Anyone today who finds public weeping ostentatious, embarrassing, or self-righteous should just be thankful that they do not have Margery Kempe for a neighbour or colleague. We read that the Archbishop of York on one occasion asked Margery irritably, 'Why do you weep so, woman?', to which Margery replied, 'Sir, you shall wish some day that you had wept as sorely as I.'[22] Another clergyman, trying to comfort the sobbing Margery, tells her, 'Woman, Jesus is long since dead.' Margery replies, 'Sir, his death is as fresh to me as if he had died this same day, and so, I think, it ought to be to you and to all Christian people.'[23] Although these self-righteous retorts must surely have irritated her critics even more, it is hard not to admire her self-assurance and defiance in the face of those male clergy who sought to impose their authority on her by stemming the flow of her tears.

Accounts of the lives of male clergy themselves show that weeping was a spiritual activity not confined to female mystics. It was standard for bishops to weep as they celebrated mass, and tears were an expected accompaniment to the private prayers of the clergy too. Thomas Becket and Francis of Assisi were both notably tearful. After celibacy became the rule for all clergy, sources record nocturnal emissions of tears as holy men wept and wrestled with the demon of lust, alongside other sins and sufferings, in the privacy of their bedchambers, mimicking the exclamation of David in the Psalms: 'I am weary with my groaning; all the night make I my bed to swim; I water my couch with my tears.'[24] Holy tears took their place in the religious art, literature, and devotions of the period alongside other spiritualized bodily fluids, including the milk of Mary, venerated at

Walsingham, or the holy blood at Hailes Abbey.[25] The Abbaye de la Trinité, Vendôme, advertised amongst its relics one of the tears of Jesus, shed over the grave of Lazarus, and placed in a bottle by an angel. In fact, at least eight different French churches claimed to possess such a tear.[26]

One way in which Margery's tears were typical was that they were a response to the pain and passion of Christ which, during the High Middle Ages, became the primary focus of a kind of affective meditation widely practised by both laypeople and those in religious orders. Passion plays, poetry, and paintings all dramatized the sufferings of the human Christ in order to teach the faithful how to feel. One of the earliest examples of the genre was a twelfth-century text by Aelred of Rivaulx, dedicated to his sister, entitled *Rule of Life for a Recluse*, which set out the correct emotional responses to the story of the passion. At one point, Aelred instructs his reader:

> draw near to the cross with the Virgin Mother and the virgin disciple, and look at close quarters upon that face in all its pallor. What then? Will your eyes be dry as you see your most loving Lady in tears? Will you not weep as her soul is pierced by the sword of sorrow? Will there be no sob from you as you hear him say to his mother, 'Woman, behold your son,' and to John, 'Behold your mother'?[27]

Similarly, a late medieval poem written in Middle English, but with the Latin title *De Arte Lacrimandi*, is written in the voice of the Blessed Virgin mourning over her son. Its refrain is 'Therfor to wepe come lerne att me'.[28]

Visual images could reinforce such textual lessons. St Francis was reputed to have gone blind from the extent of his weeping, over many years. His extreme and compassionate response to the suffering of Christ was first triggered by a painted crucifix, from which Christ seemed to speak to him, leaving him trembling and in tears.[29] Northern European painters of the fifteenth century such as Rogier van der Weyden and Dieric Bouts pioneered striking depictions of Christ, his mother, and Mary Magdalene with tears very visibly coursing down their cheeks.

Some of the images of Christ show him with a crown of thorns and bloodshot eyes, the tears and blood mingling on his face.[30] A late fifteenth-century work that, for me, captures the essence of the extreme religious crying of Margery Kempe particularly well is Niccolò dell'Arca's sculpted collection of figures, showing the mourning Marys lamenting over the dead Christ, in the church of Santa Maria in Bologna (Figure 1). This is visceral weeping, with the emphasis not so much on the shedding of tears as on the act of crying out in lamentation. It is weeping that you can hear as well as see: proper, unrefined, medieval roaring of the kind for which Margery became famous. Margery might even have encountered devotional sculptures like dell'Arca's during her visits to Bologna, Venice, Assisi, and Rome, a few decades before this work was made.[31]

In medieval devotional aids, whether visual or verbal, we find recognition of an essential fact about crying: it is something that needs to be learned. There is such a thing as the 'craft of wepyng'.[32] The affective devotion of the High Middle Ages, which embodies this insight, is sometimes described as Franciscan in its origins, and although there were various and earlier sources, the figure of St Francis captures the spirit of what was involved: compassion for all of humanity, encouraged by meditation on the painful passion of the human Christ, and extending to sympathy with the sufferings of the whole creation.[33] According to one legend, St Francis on his deathbed remembered to thank his donkey for carrying him through his ministry; in response, the donkey wept.[34] As we shall discover in later chapters, weeping animals were not so unusual in medieval and early modern Europe.[35] The funeral of Francis was an occasion for much public, contagious weeping. The Pope himself delivered the eulogy, in tears, and as a list of all the miracles of the saint was read out, according to one account, one of the cardinals, 'a man of mighty and penetrating intellect' and piety, 'discoursed of them with sacred utterance, bedewed with tears', and this in turn brought more vehement sobs and sighs from the Pope, who 'poured forth streams of

Figure 1. Niccolo dell'Arca's late fifteenth-century representation of the mourning Marys, in the church of Santa Maria in Bologna. Jenny Audring/Flickr.

tears', setting off all the other prelates and the people, who accordingly 'bedewed' their clothes with floods of tears.[36] We can be pretty sure that Margery did some bedewing too, when she visited Assisi en route from Jerusalem to Rome nearly 200 years later.[37]

So, although Margery had many critics, some of whom claimed her weeping was insincere, put on, or pathological, ultimately she received a sympathetic hearing when it mattered, because her piety was in tune with the officially sanctioned spirituality of her times. When Margery visited another female mystic, Julian of Norwich, she received reassurance that her uncontrollable crying was an authentic sign of the divine, of which she should not be ashamed: tears of compunction, devotion, and compassion were signs that the Holy Ghost was in her soul, Julian told Margery.[38] In her encounters with archbishops, Margery received approval too. She met with Thomas Arundel, Archbishop of Canterbury, in his garden at Lambeth Palace before her pilgrimage to the Holy Land. Arundel listened sympathetically to Margery's description of her gift of weeping, and said he was glad that the Lord had revealed himself in this way.[39] It was Arundel who would also preside over the trial of Sir John Oldcastle for heresy. It is recorded that time and again, 'with tears running down his face' the Archbishop urged Sir John to give up his heretical beliefs and return to the unity of the Church, but to no avail. On 14 December 1417, Oldcastle was drawn, hanged, and burned.[40]

Oldcastle's execution was among the first fruits of what would become the violent harvest of the Protestant Reformation. The break from Rome saw monasteries dissolved and icons smashed, devotional paintings white-washed and figures of Mary burned like heretics. The world of weeping so colourfully inhabited by Margery Kempe would be suppressed, and differences would be painfully drawn out between acceptable and unacceptable kinds of tears under the new dispensation. It was not only institutions, doctrines, and liturgies that were to be reformed, but also bodies, emotions, and sensations: the whole physiological life of the nation.

2

Marie Magdalen's Funeral Teares

Weeping is a universal human response to death from which the British have occasionally tried to exempt themselves. The anthropologist Geoffrey Gorer published a study of *Death, Grief and Mourning in Contemporary Britain* in 1965 which, as I noted above, complained of the denial of feeling and repression of grief as pernicious national characteristics. Today there is no shortage of weeping over the departed, whether our own loved ones or public figures. Even in the twenty-first century, however, British culture retains a strong strand of suspicion towards displays of emotion in general, and funeral tears in particular. Observers found fault with the Chancellor of the Exchequer George Osborne in 2013 for shedding tears at the funeral of Margaret Thatcher. He was accused variously of insincerity, false sentiment, and a twisted moral compass. The maudlin mass grieving for Princess Diana back in 1997 provoked an even stronger anti-emotional backlash, and her young sons were admired for their dry eyes at her funeral.[1]

British opponents of public weeping embody an element of anti-Catholicism still inhabiting our mixed-up national unconscious half a millennium after the Protestant Reformation. That painful and partial transition to a new form of national religion permanently changed how people mourned in Britain, what they felt about their tears of grief, and how they responded to the crying of others. These changes are documented in the lives and writings of the preachers and poets of the time.

The result was a culture in which certain forms of weeping, especially those associated with Catholic rituals of penitence and mourning, were branded as excessive, effeminate, and ineffectual. The tears of Mary Magdalene were an emblem of all that was being rejected (see Figure 2 for one early sixteenth-century visual representation). One of the most interesting tracts on weeping of the sixteenth century was called *Marie Magdalen's Funeral Teares*. This short book, published anonymously in 1591, was written by an English Catholic living in hiding, Robert Southwell. Southwell describes Mary's tears of mourning as the cause of Jesus' decision to raise Lazarus from the dead. Then, addressing Mary Magdalene directly about her tears at the tomb of Jesus, he writes, 'Thy weeping was for a man, and thy tears have obtained Angels.'[2] The ability of earthly tears of mourning to have such heavenly results was exactly what was at issue in this era. After the Reformation, tears no longer obtained angels.

Figure 2. *The Magdalen Weeping*, Workshop of Master of the Magdalen Legend, *c.*1525. © 2014. Copyright The National Gallery, London/Scala, Florence.

Southwell was born in 1561 and grew up in Norfolk in a converted Catholic priory. His grandfather had acquired the property when acting as one of Henry VIII's visitors for the suppression of monasteries in the 1530s. The spirit of Catholicism lived on in young Robert. Such was his early affinity with the Church of Rome that his parents teased him with the nickname 'Father Robert'. Nominally Protestant, but living within the material and spiritual architecture of a recent Catholic past, Southwell embodied the religious ambivalence of sixteenth-century England. After training in France as a Jesuit, Southwell returned to Elizabethan England as a Catholic missionary, bearing in earnest the joking title of his childhood. In 1592, he was betrayed by a member of the family who were concealing him. After two-and-a-half years of solitary confinement and torture he was put on trial. Being a Catholic priest was, in itself, defined as an act of treason and the verdict was never in doubt. In February 1595, at the age of 33 (traditionally the age of Christ at his crucifixion, as Southwell himself pointed out), he was sentenced to death. Contemporary accounts noted his cheerful demeanour at Tyburn, even as he dangled half-alive from the noose in his final seconds, doing his best to make the sign of the cross. Such was the sympathy of the crowd and officials that the full sentence—including being cut down and disembowelled alive—was not carried out. Instead the hangman mercifully pulled on Southwell's legs to hasten his death, before beheading the corpse, and holding it up before a subdued crowd. The dead body of Father Robert was then butchered in the approved manner, being first 'bowelled' and then 'quartered'.[3]

Robert Southwell is remembered today as the leading exponent of the literature of tears that flourished at the end of the sixteenth century and the beginning of the seventeenth. His poems included 'The Vale of Tears' and 'St Peter's Complaint', the latter inspired by the bitter, remorseful tears of Peter after denying Jesus. Southwell's works were widely known, and their influence can be traced in Shakespeare as well as in Anglican religious poetry of the early seventeenth century by Aemilia Lanyer, George Herbert, and John Donne.[4] The culmination of his prose writings was *Marie Magdalen's Funeral Teares*. The composite figure of Mary Magdalene in Catholic tradition was based on several accounts of weeping women mentioned in the Gospels: the sister of Lazarus who weeps over her dead brother, the sinful woman who anoints Jesus's feet with her tears (often seen as a prophetic act anticipating the embalming of Jesus's corpse), and the Mary who weeps at the empty tomb and is the first person to see the risen Jesus.[5] As Southwell put it: 'For as shee watched to finde whom shee had lost, so shee wept for having lost whom shee loved.'[6] He thus contributed to an existing tradition celebrating Mary Magdalene as an exemplary and tearful mourner.[7] The posthumous dismembering of Southwell by the English crown was one more symbol of the evisceration of the Catholic religion, including its mourning practices.

Henry VIII declared himself supreme head of the Church of England in 1534. Scotland's formal break with Rome came in 1560 and, after a turbulent period in which a Catholic monarch (Mary, Queen of Scots) ruled over a Protestant people, James VI succeeded to the Scottish throne in 1567. At the death of Elizabeth I, in 1603, James VI of Scotland additionally became James I of England, unifying the crowns and styling himself 'King of Great Britain and Ireland' until his death in 1625.[8] It is to James that we owe one of the great texts produced by the Reformation. The translation of the Bible (including well over a hundred references to weeping and tears) into English authorized by the Protestant King James was completed in 1611, and it still bears his name. People could now read (or have read to them) accounts of the mourning tears of David over his son Absalom, of Jesus over Lazarus, and of Mary Magdalene over Jesus, all in their own language.[9]

Pre-Reformation mourning involved wailing over the body, the rending of clothes and hair, the kissing of the corpse, and the shedding

of plentiful tears.[10] The Catholic way of death, which persisted in
Ireland long after the Reformation, despite British colonial attempts to
enforce Protestantism, offered a much more intimate relationship with
the corpse, before, during, and after the funeral service.[11] Southwell's
treatise on Mary Magdalene's tears emphasized that she sought out
Christ's corpse in the tomb, wishing to be with his physical remains as
her 'chiefe comfort'.[12] Associated with a physical proximity between the
living mourners and the dead body were beliefs about the connection
between the actions of the bereaved and the spiritual destiny of the
deceased. Acts of mourning were believed to speed the progress of the
departed soul through purgatory, a place for the purging and cleansing
of sins, as the soul was prepared for its final heavenly resting place.
Funeral tears could help to wash clean the departed soul. The state of
purgatory was a spiritual lavatory, in the literal sense of that word.
Margery Kempe, in her marathon crying sessions, would sometimes
weep an extra hour specifically for the souls in purgatory, and in
Southwell's poetry tears are portrayed as having the power to wash
out the stains of sin.[13]

The practice of wailing over the corpse was especially marked in
Catholic Ireland, where it was associated by English colonizers with
both heathenish religion and political rebelliousness. In the sixteenth
and seventeenth centuries, English visitors wrote with astonishment of
the 'howlings and barbarous out-cryes' that accompanied the body to the
grave.[14] In the case of more well-to-do families, the wailing was performed by hired mourners. The shrieking of these women, resembling
'hags or hellish fiends', was cited by English writers as the source of a
proverbial phrase, 'to weepe Irish', meaning 'to weepe at pleasure, without
cause, or griefe' in the manner of a paid mourner.[15] Irish mourning was
compared to that of Spaniards, Africans, and pagans.[16] English observers
would continue to be astonished by the nature of Irish mourning in the
eighteenth, nineteenth, and twentieth centuries. A Victorian work on

keening, using the practice to illustrate the 'history, manners, music, and superstitions' of the Irish, quoted from John Wesley's diary about his shock at witnessing the 'Irish howl' at a funeral in County Cork in 1750. Wesley described how four paid female mourners, set up by the grave, let out a 'dismal inarticulate yell'.[17] English newspapers reporting on the burials of victims of the 'Bloody Sunday' massacre in Derry, Northern Ireland, in 1972, noted not only the abundant tears of the women in black who 'stumbled after the coffins, calling the names of the dead', but also their howling laments: 'Wailing women collapsed at gravesides in an overwhelming display of grief.'[18] Such practices, depicted by Protestants as characteristically Catholic, had persisted for a time beyond the Reformation in parts of England too. In 1590 in Lancaster, Protestant reformers denounced the 'manifold popish superstition' still displayed by locals whose rituals including kissing the corpse, jangling bells, and 'wailing the dead with more than heathenish outcries'.[19]

One part of the Protestant answer to these 'popish' tendencies was to rewrite the rituals and liturgies of the Church of England, including the burial service. This was achieved by Thomas Cranmer during the six-year reign of the child-king Edward VI, who had succeeded his father Henry VIII in 1547. Cranmer oversaw a series of intensive reforms that turned the Church of England into a definitively Protestant body. This included passing the Act of Uniformity in 1549 (which in theory more than practice applied to Ireland as well as to England and Wales) and producing a new Book of Common Prayer.[20] Cranmer's prayer-book, still much loved by Anglican traditionalists, was an important document in the reforming of mourning practices. The corpse was now moved outside the church to distance the living from the dead, and excessive funeral tears were banished along with it. The emphasis of Cranmer's burial service is on the justice of God and faith in the power of Christ to save sinners. It offers a brutal realism about death—'Man that is borne of a womanne hath but a shorte time to lyve and is full of misery: he cometh up and is cut downe lyke a flourre'—combined with a transcendent hope for resurrection. The priest gives 'hearty thankes' to God 'that it has pleased thee to deliver thys our brother out of the myseryes of this sinneful world', and expresses the hope that soon all the faithful will be raised up in God's kingdom. Tears feature rarely in the Book of Common Prayer, and then only as signs of contrition in sinners preparing for communion, or in the texts of psalms. By contrast, the Sarum Missal (the most widely used Catholic rite in England prior to the Reformation) includes an entire votive mass designed to draw forth 'abundant rivers of tears', and several references to the tears of sinners having the effect of assuaging the anger of God.[21] The Protestant aspiration to keep tears contained within the private domain was embodied, incidentally, in Thomas Cranmer's behaviour as well as his liturgical reforms. It was said of Cranmer that he never allowed his demeanour to reveal his feelings in public but 'privately, with his secret and special friends, he would shed forth many bitter tears, lamenting with the miseries and calamities of the world'.[22] Archbishop Cranmer, it would seem, was a pioneer of the view that if you really have to cry, you should do it in private.

According to Cranmer and his fellow reformers, funeral tears were not only blasphemous but also ineffective. They were blasphemous because they displayed a lack of faith in God's power and justice, and an inflated sense of the ability of the individual to influence the divine plan. They were ineffective because salvation was granted only by the supreme power and mercy of God. The doctrine of purgatory was rejected as unbiblical and corrupt, and the metaphysical power of the mourner's tears to promote the spiritual well-being of departed loved ones was at a stroke reduced to nil.[23] In the 1550s, Matthew Parker, a future Archbishop of Canterbury, preached the funeral sermon for the German reformer Martin Bucer. Parker stated bluntly that to mourn for the dead was to show a lack of faith in the resurrection. It was not only 'unseemly and wicked', but also 'womanish', 'childish', and 'beastly', Parker said, 'to use any howling or blubbering' for the departed in the manner of the 'heathen'. Such concerns persisted into the seventeenth century. One clergyman was still complaining in 1612: 'It is a wonder to see the childish whining we now-adayes use at the funeralls of our friends. If we could houl them back again, our Lamentations were to some purpose; but as they are, they are vaine and in vain.'[24]

Of course Protestants continued to shed tears, at funerals as well as in other aspects of their lives, religious or otherwise. It is recorded that at the funeral of one Dr Whitaker at Cambridge University in 1595, for instance, the Vice Chancellor's sermon had been 'pathetically preached' and 'the spring-tide of his weeping stopped his preaching'.[25] Nonetheless the sixteenth century had seen funeral tears acquire a powerful new set of negative associations: with popery, with paganism, and with primitive Irish keening. This perspective on earlier mourning rituals gives us, incidentally, a glimpse of how much worse things could have been at Lady Thatcher's funeral in 2013. At least George Osborne did not break out in a keening lament and insist on opening the coffin to kiss the old lady's corpse. A tear down the cheek is nothing in comparison to some of the extremes of pre-Reformation Catholic mourning. But it shows how persistent is the Protestant reaction in our country that even one funeral tear can still cause a national outcry.[26]

The reformation of tears also had an impact beyond behaviour at funerals. Catholics and Protestants wept differently; and they thought and wrote about weeping differently. The Reformation instigated a general recalibration of the tear ducts. At the most impressionistic level, there was a difference of emotional tone. Indulgent Catholic expressiveness was replaced by uptight Protestant astringency. John Calvin attacked the crocodile tears encouraged by the papist practice of confession. For him, a matter as sacred as spiritual penitence could not be judged by a flow of tears: 'We have taught the sinner not to look on his compunction or on his tears but to fix both eyes solely on the mercy of God.'[27] A turbulent encounter between Mary, Queen of Scots, and the reformer John Knox in 1563 also captures this contrast between the Catholic and Protestant types. Mary was furious with Knox for his public criticism of her possible marriage with a foreign Roman Catholic. Angrily sobbing, she demanded to know what it had to do with him. Knox replied:

> I never delighted in the weeping of any of God's creatures; yea, I can scarcely well abide the tears of mine own boys, when my own hands correct them, much less can I rejoice in your majesty's weeping: but seeing I have offered unto you no just occasion to be offended, but have spoken to the truth, as my vocation craves of me, I must sustain your majesty's tears, rather than I dare hurt my conscience, or betray the common-wealth by silence.[28]

That sense of visceral discomfort with tears—something that could scarcely be tolerated—along with the pious claims to plain-speaking, biblical purity, and simple, unadorned worship, were a part of the Protestant spirit.

Weeping was central to several aspects of Catholic religion, including affective meditation on the passion of Christ, the cultivation of pity through the example of the Blessed Virgin, and the display of compunction by the penitent sinner, as well as prayerful lamentations for the souls of the dead. Tears were, therefore, directly associated with three of the most Catholic of Catholic institutions: the cult of the Virgin, the practice of confession, and the doctrine of purgatory. Furthermore, in the Catholic worldview, tears could do things. They had real, spiritual consequences for the souls of the penitent on earth as well as for the wept-for departed. For the Protestant, both the domain and the power of tears were reduced. Weeping became primarily a solitary act of grief over sin rather than a collective act of mourning.[29] The attitude is perhaps best expressed in Jesus' saying, as he carried his cross towards Calvary, addressing the women who wailed and lamented behind him: 'weep not for me, but weep for yourselves.'[30] In these words, it is as if we can hear the voice of a Protestant reformer reproaching excessively tearful Catholics.

After the Reformation, tears of penitence could no more achieve salvation for oneself than they could help the soul of another towards heaven. Rather, they showed that God was at work. Thus, in his 1601 poem 'The Blessed Weeper', Nicholas Breton wrote of God:

> He cleans'd my soule, From all my filthy sinne:
> And with my teares, did wash it cleane againe[31]

George Herbert and John Donne also contributed to the poetry of tears in the early seventeenth century. Neither was averse to tears, but both painted them in the proper Protestant proportions. Weeping for one's own sins was allowable, but not necessary. What was truly required was an inward change of heart, not an outward display of grief. Signalling this very significant change of emphasis, Herbert wrote that 'repentance is an act of the mind, not of the body'.[32] John Donne's 1623 sermon on the text 'Jesus wept' similarly emphasized that the 'right use of teares' was in inward sorrow for sin, whether or not one was of a lachrymose nature: 'a soule that can poure out it self into these religious considerations, may be a weeping soule, though it have a dry eye.'[33] This was a Protestant picture, with tears as secondary signs of inward God-given sorrow, rather than as effective outward acts of penance or supplication. The figure of the weeping Protestant, praying alone in bedroom, field, or saddle, was a vehicle for the power of God and a sign to others of his mercy.

As always, when faced with a choice between two alternatives—in this case Catholic sentimentality or Calvinist severity in the matter of tears—the Church of England ultimately chose both. The literature of tears of the Counter-Reformation and the reformers' denunciations of excessive and idolatrous weeping both fed into seventeenth-century Anglican culture. The Anglican clergyman Thomas Playfere preached on the text 'weep not for me, but weep for yourselves' in 1595. He explained the first half of the text, using other biblical passages, as well as the Stoic philosopher Seneca, as a warning against immoderate tears for the dead. The risen Jesus' question to Mary Magdalene, 'Why weepest thou?' could also be read in this way, as a rebuke to all tearful mourners. Turning to the second half of the text, the admonition to 'weep for yourselves', Playfere took up the figures of Mary Magdalene and St Peter as exemplars of appropriate weeping and lamentation over sin, even using the imagery of the power of tears to wash away sin, and approving of the use of tears in both prayer and preaching.[34] Indeed, tears were among the standard responses to sermons aimed for by Protestant as much as by Catholic preachers. The seventeenth-century Protestant visionary and prophet Anna Trapnel recalled that in her youth she 'ran from Minister to Minister, from Sermon to Sermon', hoping to be moved to the point of weeping, 'and if I had not shed some tears in a Sermon, then I went home full of horror, concluding my self to be that stony ground Christ spake of in the parable of the sower'.[35]

In summary, Thomas Playfere said in 1595, 'A man can never love himselfe aright, if hee do not sometimes weepe in repentance, nor his neighbour, that doth not sometimes weepe in preaching, nor God that doth not sometime weepe in prayer: so that wee must not bee like the Stoickes which were never moved, then wee shall weepe too little.'[36] This was not the Catholic way of devotional tears and mournful howling, but the Anglican *via media lacrimosa*: not too much and not too little. Aemilia Lanyer was one of the first women to publish original poetry in English. Her *Salve Deus Rex Judaeorum*, published in 1611, was an extended reflection on the passion of Christ in which the tears of the mourning Marys and the daughters of Jerusalem were positively valued as instructive acts of faith from which men should learn.[37] John Donne's sermon on 'Jesus Wept', while taking the Protestant line on tears doctrinally, was full of praise for the power and importance of tears, when properly used, and of the importance of the human affections from which they arose: 'Inordinateness of affections may sometimes make some men like some beasts; but indolencie, absence, emptinesse, privation of affections, makes any man at all time, like stones, like dirt.'[38]

We still have, in our everyday language of feeling, a word which is a living relic of Reformation controversies about tears. The term 'maudlin', deriving from the name of Mary Magdalene, and first used in the early seventeenth century, means an excessive, sentimental, womanish, insincere, and quite possibly also drunken form of tearfulness.[39] Reports of Irish wakes of this period included the allegation that the funeral service was preceded by boisterous all-night drinking sessions, and the 'maudlin' weeping drunkard became a recognized comical character.[40] So, when we denounce certain forms of tearful sentimentality as 'maudlin' today, we are using the language of those early modern Protestants who bequeathed to us, along with a revulsion for excessive public grief, a view of weeping at once more passive and more private than the Catholic traditions it replaced. The Reformation of tears had changed them from outward communal signs, produced as parts of rituals of devotion, confession, and mourning, with the power to cleanse the souls of the dead and to change God's mind, to inward and private experiences of the power of God to change one's own heart.[41]

3

Titus Andronicus: Ha, Ha, Ha!

The 1590s was a wet decade. The English musician and composer John Dowland wrote one of its most popular pieces, a pavan entitled 'Flow my tears', which became a hugely popular song. The weepy numbers continued to flow from Dowland's lute in the following years, including 'Go Cristall Teares' and 'I Saw My Lady Weep', culminating in 1604 with his *Lachrimæ, or Seaven Teares Figured in Seaven Passionate Pavans*, setting to music, in turn, old tears, new old tears, sighing tears, sad tears, forced tears, a lover's tears, and true tears.[1] Dowland, also a Catholic, did for music what Southwell was doing for the poetry of tears. On the stage, a vogue for revenge tragedies by playwrights such as Thomas Kyd and Christopher Marlowe provided another lachrymose outlet as the Elizabethan age and the sixteenth century approached their endings.[2] Swimming with these cultural currents was a brilliant poet and playwright, a distant cousin of Robert Southwell, whose histories and tragedies were performed on the English stage for the first time in the early 1590s: William Shakespeare.

Shakespeare's first tragedy was also the first of his plays to be printed (see Figure 3).[3] It staged bloody scenes of death and dismemberment, providing a fictional counterpart to the fate of those like Southwell who were publicly hanged, beheaded, and disembowelled in the Elizabethan era. First performed in the early 1590s, *The Lamentable Roman Tragedy of Titus Andronicus* is a revenge play of astonishing violence: bowels, limbs,

THE
MOST LA-
mentable Romaine
Tragedie of Titus Andronicus:

As it was Plaide by the Right Ho-
nourable the Earle of *Darbie*, Earle of *Pembrooke*,
and Earle of *Suffex* their Seruants.

LONDON,
Printed by Iohn Danter, and are
to be fold by *Edward White* & *Thomas Millington*,
at the little North doore of Paules at the
figne of the Gunne,
1594.

Figure 3. Title page of *Titus Andronicus*, the first of Shakespeare's plays to be printed. By permission of the Folger Shakespeare Library.

heads, hands, and tongues are lopped and hewn. Virtually all the protagonists end up dead, many of them killed in the space of a few lines in a
final blood-soaked show-down. Playgoers in search of gore and tragedy
certainly got their money's worth. Hamlet, Prince of Denmark, is Shakespeare's most famous melancholic, but as an all-out woeful weeper, Titus
Andronicus, the Roman general, is hard to beat.[4]

The tears in *Titus Andronicus* provide a microcosm of early modern
weeping, reflecting the revival of ancient Greek and Roman medical,
philosophical, and literary texts during the Renaissance.[5] Shakespeare's
play brought back to life for his audience classical ideas about sorrow,
catharsis, stoicism, and pity. The manifest failures of weeping as staged in
Titus Andronicus support the idea that the late sixteenth century was a
time of crisis in the history of tears: a crisis which, for some, could be
alleviated but, for others, deepened further by the performance and
consumption of stage plays themselves. Immersing ourselves in the wet
world of Titus Andronicus, reading the text of the play alongside Renaissance medical theories about the 'humours' of the body, can return us to
that moment of crisis. The politics and performance of tears would
remain controversial in the ensuing decades, both before and after the
closure of the London playhouses in 1642, in the period of the Civil War.[6]

In the time of Shakespeare, there was no connection between being
English and not crying, if anything quite the reverse. The English people
had a reputation not for restraint but variously for sweatiness, drunkenness, meat-eating, anger, violence, simple-mindedness, and melancholia.
A manual of health, *The Touchstone of Complexions* by the Dutch physician Levinus Lemnius, compared the bodily temperaments of the
nations of Europe, ranking the English a notch below the Italians, in
terms of the overall quality of their temperament. Lemnius described
the English as 'of body lusty and well complexioned', having
'somewhat thicke spirits', and 'high and hauty stomackes', with a tendency towards grudges and rages—the summary printed in the margin

reads: 'Englishmen and Scottes have greate stomacks & angry'. The same author considered the English people unsophisticated in their studies of humanity and the 'exquisite arts'; these were, it seemed, thick spirits in more ways than one.[7] The Catholic writer Thomas Wright, in his book on the *Passions of the Minde* in 1601, agreed that the English had a reputation in Europe for being simple. Wright thought that those from hotter climates, like Spaniards and Italians, learned how to conceal their passions, but that the ingenuous English, unwisely, wore their hearts on their sleeves.[8]

Not just simple and lusty, but sweaty too, the English were especially susceptible to the *sudor Anglicus*, a sweating sickness which spread across the Continent during the sixteenth century. Lemnius reported that 'the English sweat' was brought on by a rich diet and wet weather. The English were renowned for their love of beef 'wherewith they cramme themselves very ingluviously, even as the Germanes and Netherlanders doe with drinke'. The melancholy-inducing weather was famous too: 'the ayre with them is troubled, cloudy and many tymes with foggie dampes overcast.' The enthusiastic consumption of wine and spirits would have seen the grudging, angry, sweaty natures of the English taking on the characteristics of the drunkard: maudlin, violent, and melodramatic, in some cases 'contentious and brawling', in others 'weeping, howling and heavy couraged'.[9] The melancholic, the drunkard, the stage-actor, and the theatre-goer were all inclined towards excessive expressions of their feelings, including both laughter and tears. Melancholia, dubbed *The English Malady* by Dr George Cheyne in 1733, was in its infancy as a national trait in the sixteenth and seventeenth centuries.[10] John Dowland's Latin motto was *Semper Dowland, semper Dolens*: always Dowland, always miserable.[11]

Weeping, for early moderns, was, like urinating, sweating, bleeding, or vomiting, an 'expression' in the literal sense of a squeezing out.[12] This is one of the origins of our modern idea of weeping as a kind of emotional incontinence.[13] In Renaissance medicine, tears were a kind of 'excrement': a liquid distilled from the blood, spirits, humours, or vapours, produced by the heart or brain, and pressed out through the eyes. For Timothy Bright, writing his *Treatise on Melancholy* in 1586, tears were 'the brain's thinnest and most liquide excrement'.[14] Robert Burton, in his *Anatomy of Melancholy*, in 1621, described sweat and tears within a similar humoral system. The principal humours, or fluid parts of the body, were blood, phlegm, choler, and melancholy. 'To these humours,' Burton noted, 'you may add serum, which is the matter of urine, and those excrementitious humours of the third concoction, sweat and tears.' I must say, incidentally, that in the whole history of ideas about weeping I have come across no more wonderful phrase for tears than 'excrementitious humours of the third concoction'.[15]

In Renaissance drama and medicine, as in the modern critic's cliché, 'I laughed, I cried', bodily responses to comedy and tragedy sat cheek by jowl.[16] One of the reasons that passion plays were banned during the Reformation was that the custom had arisen of interspersing the sacred drama with bawdy comic interludes, such as knockabout scenes between Noah and his wife—a kind of biblical Punch and Judy. The suppression of passion plays, mourning rituals, and the cult of the Virgin Mary, along with the less successful attempt to eradicate such pagan festivities as the celebration of Christmas, New Year, and May Day, created a need for new ways for people to learn how to laugh and cry. This need was met by the tragedies and comedies put on by commercial theatres from the 1570s onwards.[17] People could now purchase tears, whether of sympathy, sorrow, or laughter, as desirable commodities purveyed by troupes of players. Over-the-top weeping was one of the techniques employed by clowns to produce laughter, and medical writers perceived an underlying connection between the two. Laughter and weeping were generally believed to be uniquely human reactions, and in cases of extreme emotion, the two could become confused.[18] This is exactly what occurs at the pivotal moment of *Titus Andronicus*. Confronted with his sons' heads and his own severed hand, Titus does not weep but laughs: 'Ha, ha, ha!'[19] Before this, Titus has been a prolific and eloquent weeper. Afterwards he is dry-eyed, and deranged. As a medical and philosophical case study, *Titus Andronicus* offers some intriguing lessons.[20]

The central event of the play is the rape and mutilation of Titus' daughter Lavinia, modelled on the ancient story of the rape of Philomela, as told by Ovid.[21] Lavinia's assailants—the sons of Tamora, queen of the Goths—having killed Lavinia's husband, rape her, cut out her tongue and lop off her hands, all with the approval of their monstrous mother, the queen. Titus' sons are framed as the murderers of their sister's husband. Lavinia is left deformed, both morally and physically: 'mangled' is how her uncle describes her.[22] She cannot speak, she cannot write, and, although her eyes can still shed tears, their meaning is even harder to read than usual. Titus' brother Marcus finds Lavinia in her mutilated state, and brings her to her father saying:

> Titus, prepare thy aged eyes to weep,
> Or if not so, thy noble heart to break:
> I bring consuming sorrow to thine age.[23]

Marcus here offers Titus a choice—tears or heartbreak—consistent with the prevailing medical doctrine that tears could relieve mental suffering, and a failure to weep could cause disease.[24] What follows is a familial inundation of Andronicus tears. When a reference to her two brothers, whom Lavinia alone knows to be innocent, produces tears on her cheeks, Marcus ponders, 'Perchance she weeps because they killed her husband, Perchance because she knows them innocent.' Tears are depicted, in terms reminiscent of the religious literature of the period, as 'martyred signs' and as 'orators', the latter an image also used by Robert Southwell in *Marie Magdalen's Funeral Teares*.[25] Titus' grief proves contagious, his son Lucius exhorting him, 'Sweet father, cease your tears, for at your grief, See how my wretched sister sobs and weeps.' Marcus offers Titus a handkerchief to dry his eyes, which is rejected as it is already drenched in Marcus' own tears. Lucius then proffers his own soggy napkin to his weeping sister.[26]

Having poured out his woes for the mangled Lavinia, Titus is persuaded by the evil Moor Aaron to cut off his own hand as a ransom for the safe return of his sons. On his knees, the one-handed Titus begs, 'If any power pities wretched tears, To that I call.' Marcus is the voice of reason, telling his brother to calm down: 'do not break into these deep extremes', 'let reason govern thy lament'. This elicits a bitter self-justification from Titus, rejecting the idea that there is any reason to be found in his miseries, or even in life itself. He depicts his own tears as elemental forces of nature, describing himself as the sea and the earth; Lavinia as the sky, or 'welkin', and the wind:

> I am the sea; hark, how her sighs do blow!
> She is the weeping welkin, I the earth:
> Then must my sea be moved with her sighs;
> Then must my earth with her continual tears
> Become a deluge, overflow'd and drown'd;
> For why my bowels cannot hide her woes,
> But like a drunkard must I vomit them.[27]

That final image of a drunken vomiting out of woes reinforces the notion of tears as a kind of bodily excretion, and one associated with melancholy and with alcohol. This moment is the high water mark of Titus' epic, meteorological weeping. Shakespeare identifies tears with all the seasons and all the waterworks of nature: streams, rivers, and oceans; showers, storms, and life-giving rain. The Andronicus weather is foggy, damp, and overcast. Lavinia and Titus at different points refer to their 'tributary tears' of mourning, alluding simultaneously to tributes to the dead and to natural rivulets—an image suggesting streams feeding into swelling, larger rivers of collective woe.[28] Lavinia is described as a pure spring, muddied by her rape, and Titus' grandson is described both as a 'tender sapling' and a 'tender spring', 'tender' here having the sense both of youthful and moist. Titus tells the boy, 'thou art made of tears'.[29] According to standard physiological theories of the day, children, women, and old men were all more naturally prone to tears.[30] Women, in particular, were thought of as 'leaky vessels', whose tears flowed from them alongside other fluids, including maternal milk and menstrual blood.[31]

So, *Titus Andronicus* offers a portrait of what Robert Burton would later call 'the liquid or fluent part of the body'.[32] It portrays tears as powerful natural forces, connecting humanity to the elements, through their bodily fluids. George Herbert's poem 'Grief', published in 1633, exploits the parallels between tears and other natural water sources in a similar way. It begins:

> O Who will give me tears? Come all ye springs,
> Dwell in my head & eyes: come clouds, & rain:
> My grief hath need of all the wat'ry things,
> That nature hath produc'd.[33]

In René Descartes's treatise on the passions of the soul we find a physical rationale for all these identifications of tears with natural aquatic processes. For Descartes, sweating, weeping, and raining were not just metaphorically but literally the same things: instances of vapours, in the body or in the air, being converted into water. So, when weeping eyes are described as 'rainy' in *Titus Andronicus*, Descartes, at least, would not have read that as a metaphor.[34]

The stage direction that follows the speech in which Titus declares 'I am the sea' and 'she is the weeping welkin' is simple and chilling: *Enter a Messenger, with two heads and a hand*. The mocking return of Titus' hand as a rejected ransom, along with the heads of his executed sons, is the final blow. This is when the crying stops. The sponge has been squeezed dry. Marcus, who had previously counselled Titus to govern his passions, sees this as an invitation to give vent to the tempest. 'Ah, now no more will I control thy griefs,' Marcus says. 'Rend off thy silver hair, thy other hand Gnawing with thy teeth.' 'Now is a time to storm.' As there is no response, Marcus asks 'Why art thou still?' When Titus' reaction does come, it is that horrid laugh: 'Ha, ha, ha!' Marcus protests: 'Why dost thou laugh? It fits not with this hour.' Titus replies: 'Why? I have not another tear to shed.'[35]

From this moment, Titus weeps no more and, pretending to be mad, sets out to exact his clear-eyed, dry-eyed revenge on Tamora and her sons. Titus lures the sons to their doom in a piece of weird and macabre clowning, which ends with him slitting their throats, making them into a pie, and serving it to their mother at a feast of death at which he also kills Lavinia, 'her for whom my tears have made me blind'.[36] Surely, then, Titus is not pretending to be mad, but is mad. His dry eyes show not that he has stoically mastered his sorrow but that his sorrows have mastered him. Titus, a man whose 'sorrows are past remedy', has made the transition from sadness to madness, following a pattern set out in the medical textbooks of the day, including Timothy Bright's *Treatise of Melancholy*, which was probably known to Shakespeare, judging from the texts of both *Hamlet* and *Titus Andronicus*.[37]

Bright articulated the standard view that weeping was an expression associated with melancholy and sorrow, but only in their moderate forms. With Aristotle, Montaigne, and Descartes, Bright taught that in extreme sorrow, the tears dried up.[38] This was a dangerous condition that could lead to madness, or even death. Bright wrote that when grief is too extreme it 'ravisheth the conceite, and astonisheth the heart'. Tears were natural to a 'mediocritie of that passion' but in great extremity, 'sorrow being converted into an astonishment, the senses ravished, and benumed therewith, the teares are dryed up or stayed', to be replaced sometimes instead with the 'voydaunce of urine, & ordure'.[39] Although this last suggestion of alternative excretions is not explored in any of Shake-speare's stage directions, in other respects this sounds like an exact description of Titus Andronicus. Bright explains how the same calamitous event can first produce 'abundance of weeping' and 'brookes of teares' but then 'drieth them all up, through destruction of the minde, and stupiditye as it were of the hearte'. Titus' tears and their cessation provide a textbook example of the progress of the early modern passions. First his sorrows gush forth in tributaries and rivers, culminating in his declaration 'I am the sea'. But then, as his passionate sorrow intensifies with the presentation of the heads of his two sons, he says: 'I have not another tear to shed.' His understanding ravished, his heart made stony and stupid, and his mind destroyed: this is the effect of inordinate sorrow on Titus Andronicus.

It is the extremity of his grief that seems to be his final undoing, and so perhaps Titus should have listened to the advice of his more stoical brother, Marcus. Although classical literature contained plenty of examples of weeping heroes, it was still common to accuse tearful men of weakness and effeminacy.[40] In Shakespeare's own works, examples include the condemnation of Coriolanus for being a 'boy of tears' and of Romeo for his 'blubbering and weeping'. 'Art thou a man?', Friar Laurence asks the tearful boy: 'Thy tears are womanish.'[41] Tears are repeatedly shown, in Titus Andronicus, to impair the functions of the rational mind. On more than one occasion tears choke or interrupt an attempt at articulate speech.[42] Tears function as signs and symptoms of strong passions, which in turn were widely conceived as diseases of the soul. Thomas Wright, in his 1601 work on The Passions of the Minde, wrote that there were three main consequences of inordinate passions: 'blindness of understanding, perversion of will, and alteration of humours; and by them, maladies and diseases'.[43]

In The Lamentable Tragedy of Titus Andronicus, then, audiences were delivered a clear set of warnings about tears. Although Titus is an eloquent defender of the power of tears as part of the meteorology of the

mind, and even his stoical brother can find a place for tears as a proper
and healthy response to death and adversity—'tributary tears' as well as
tears of joy meet with approval—ultimately Titus' grief, expressed in
floods of tears, becomes inordinate, leading him to madness and, indirectly, death. *Titus Andronicus* is a play full of tears, and yet, time and
again, the tears don't work. When Tamora pleads with Titus for the life of
her son Alarbus (as depicted in the Peacham Drawing, Figure 4), when
Lavinia begs Tamora to prevent her rape, and when Titus petitions the
Roman tribunes for the lives of his sons, the tears fail.[44] Tears and pity
should function together in an economy of feeling: grief being exchanged
for mercy through the shared currency of tears. I grieve, I weep; you
weep, you show mercy. Instead the invariable result of tearful supplication in *Titus Andronicus* is a dismembered body: Alarbus disembowelled,
Lavinia mutilated, Titus' sons beheaded. By the final scenes of the play,
the tears have dried up, and all hope for pity has gone.

The closing two lines make it plain that this has been a drama about
the failure of pity. As the 'ravenous tiger' Tamora's corpse is thrown to
the beasts and birds, Lucius says:

> Her life was beastly and devoid of pity
> And being dead, let birds on her take pity.[45]

Pity, piety, and *pietà* (the iconic representation of the Virgin Mary
mourning her son) all derive from the same Latin word.[46] So, does
Shakespeare's play reveal a hidden sympathy with his cousin Robert
Southwell, and a nostalgic yearning for a pre-Reformation world of
Marian devotion and tearful Catholic religion? Probably not. The final
resolution of the play does centre around what looks very much like a
pre-Reformation act of mourning for the dead, including the family
kissing Titus' corpse and shedding tears on his blood-stained face.[47] On
the other hand, the drama could equally be read as a Protestant sermon
on the powerlessness of tears to change God's mind, since it shows so

Figure 4. The Peacham Drawing: the only surviving contemporary illustration of a Shakespeare play. © Reproduced by permission of the Marquess of Bath, Longleat House, Warminster, Wiltshire, Great Britain.

insistently that supplicatory weeping is in vain. What is most obviously missing from the repertoire of tears in Shakespeare's first tragedy, however, is anything resembling penitence, compunction, or repentance. And, in the absence of those, it is hard to see how any kind of Christian economy of tears, Catholic or Protestant, can be discerned. The play testifies to a crisis in tears, but not to a religious resolution.[48]

The final tears of the final act of *Titus Andronicus* belong to the young boy, Titus' grandson. The boy's father Lucius, Titus' only remaining son, addresses the child in words that are surely also addressed over his head to the theatre audience beyond, and perhaps even to us:

> Come hither, boy, come and learn of us
> To melt in showers.[49]

Throughout the play, tears have provided a sympathetic bond between Titus and his family. With Titus dead, the Andronici wish to teach their youngest member, and Shakespeare perhaps to teach his audience, of the power of tears to tie families and societies together in what Titus has earlier called a 'sympathy of woe'.[50] The boy tries to say some words of farewell to his departed grandfather, but is overcome:

> O Lord, I cannot speak to him for weeping,
> My tears will choke me if I ope my mouth.[51]

What Shakespeare presents his audience with here is a task: somehow to learn to weep without becoming morally and mentally deranged, without going blind, without losing the power of speech, without resorting to the old pieties. More importantly he provides them with an activity through which to make the attempt: the collective witnessing of a classical tragedy.[52]

Partly thanks to Shakespeare, gathering in theatres and weeping over tragedies started now to become a part of the English national character. The extent of both violence and weeping on English stages and among English theatre-goers was remarkable to foreign visitors during the eighteenth century. The French, for instance, had a very different theatrical tradition, which did not include Shakespeare in its repertoire until the nineteenth century. The Abbé Le Blanc, in a series of *Letters on the English and French Nations* published in 1747, expressed astonishment and revulsion at *Titus Andronicus* in particular, summarizing the action of the play, including the bloody and tearful aspect of Lavinia from the third act onwards, and apologizing to his readers for its horrific nature. 'What a scene of blood and slaughter is here! How could a man imagine such a spectacle as this! And how fierce must the temper of those people be, who could amuse themselves at the representation of it!' The same author noted that the English were particularly moved by dramatic characters losing their minds, ideally 'a beautiful young lady, whose misfortunes have turn'd her brain'. These were the scenes, he noted drily, at which the English weep most plentifully.[53]

The English Shakespeare scholar Edward Capell, writing in 1783, celebrated the genius of *Titus Andronicus*, noting that readers of the play, 'if they are not without feelings, may chance to find themselves touch'd by it with such passions as tragedy should excite, that is—terror, and pity'. Two hundred years after its composition, people in Britain were still learning how to feel, and how to weep, through their collective and individual responses to the story of Titus Andronicus. Among the play's qualities, Capell mentioned one line in particular as having 'something great in it even for Shakespeare'. The line in question? Titus's response to the severed heads and hand: 'Ha, ha, ha!'[54]

4

The Actor, the Witch, and the Puritan

It is something of a surprise to learn that Oliver Cromwell, the leader of the Roundheads in the Civil War, the man who defeated the royalists, signed King Charles I's death warrant, and ruled as Lord Protector from 1653 until his death in 1658, was a great weeper. 'Old Ironsides' was a man driven by a fierce religious vision, a fanatic, thinking of himself as a puritan Moses, leading his people out of exile. Tolerant towards other Protestant sects, but brutal in his repression of Catholicism, the Lord Protector's defining traits were his military acumen, ruthless leadership, and puritanical drive.[1] Cromwell is the archetype of the English puritan— a severe and humourless figure whom we might imagine to be emotionally repressed and contained, even the bearer of a British stiff upper lip. But this is an element of British national identity we need to rethink. A puritan would not often be caught smiling, let alone laughing, but he saw plenty to weep about, in the sins of others and himself. Cromwell wept in private as well as in public. It was said that, on one occasion, praying in private with great ardour and vehemence, 'the tears were forced from him with such abundance as to run under the closet door'. To understand Cromwell's tears, we need to re-examine the place of male and female tears in various parts of the public sphere in the seventeenth century.[2]

Before looking at the political history of tears in the Civil War period, it is useful to notice two fundamental contradictions, each of which animates that history. We could term these 'the actor's paradox' and 'the witch's dilemma'. The actor's paradox is the fact that tears are supposed to be the ultimate hallmarks of heartfelt emotion, yet they are also the stock in trade of professional fakers. In weeping, we are all actors, and when observing the tears of others we become the audience. As performers we hope our tears will seem spontaneous and authentic; as observers, we may suspect friends, lovers, family members, or colleagues of a touch of theatricality when they weep. The experience of witnessing on-stage tears, and sometimes responding with one's own, in the early modern theatre, brought home this perplexed relationship between truth and falsehood in the matter of weeping.[3]

The witch's dilemma is the Catch-22 of femininity and tears, which is still with us today: women who weep are accused of being weak and manipulative; those who don't are called hard-hearted, callous, unfeminine, a bitch, or a witch.[4] The witch's dilemma is premised on an entirely self-contradictory set of ideas, depicting weeping simultaneously as a loss of control over one's emotions and also an act of cold and deliberate manipulation. The witch's dilemma, a long established annoyance for modern women, was potentially fatal for those women who were hanged as witches in the sixteenth and seventeenth centuries, partly because of their alleged inability to weep. So, in the early modern figures of the actor (usually known as a 'player' in this period), the witch, and the puritan, we find three archetypes which we continue to use to think about our own and others' tears. These archetypes were honed during the Civil War period, as pamphleteers and controversialists turned to the worlds of religion and the theatre to evaluate tears shed in the political arena.

In *Hamlet*, the melancholic protagonist muses on how 'monstrous' it seems for another character, the Player, with pale face, broken voice, and distracted aspect to force tears from his eyes over the fate of Hecuba in the story he is relating of the fall of Troy. Hamlet asks in annoyance, 'What's Hecuba to him, or he to Hecuba, That he should weep for her?'[5] The audience here is asked to commiserate, and quite possibly to weep over, the 'real' woes as performed by the actor playing Hamlet as opposed to the fictional ones that brought forth artificial tears from the fictional actor, played by a real-life actor, re-enacting a narration of a pseudo-historical story, by a mythological character, Aeneas. The stream of simulation seems endless, like a low-tech early modern version of *The Matrix*.[6] As the audience look through their own tears at the on-stage weeping, are any of the tears or feelings real? A phrase of John Donne's comes to mind, used by him in a different context, but with an apt double meaning in this one: 'tears are false spectacles.'[7]

A further element of pretence was added when the female characters were played by boy actors. The boy playing Desdemona in a touring performance of *Othello* in 1610 moved the audience to tears with his unusually piteous rendition of a corpse. An elegy to the boy actor Walter Clun referred to how he had used 'polished words', 'woman's dress', and 'seeming sorrow' to make audiences weep at a fiction as if it were the truth.[8] Similarly, when the first audiences wept over the plight of Lavinia in *Titus Andronicus*, then they did so ostensibly in sympathy with a boy actor pretending to be a mutilated and defiled woman in the midst of a horrific family revenge in ancient Rome. What was Lavinia to them, or they to Lavinia? At least some playgoers reflected on the strangeness of all this at the time. The essayist Thomas Browne wrote that in real life he did not weep for his own troubles but that, at the theatre: 'I weep most seriously at a Play, and receive with a true passion, the counterfeit griefs of those knowne and professed impostures'.[9] Did tears like Browne's, sharing in a sympathy of woe with actors simulating the feelings of non-existent people, suggest an admirable capacity for compassion or a pathological susceptibility to unreal, dangerous, and effeminate passions? Anti-theatrical polemicists like

Stephen Gosson in the 1580s and William Prynne in the 1630s were quite sure it was the latter.

Gosson was the son of an immigrant carpenter from the Low Countries and a Kentish grocer's daughter. He grew up in lodgings above his father's shop in Canterbury, and attended the cathedral school, run by Matthew Parker, the Archbishop of Canterbury. Parker, who had preached against the 'womanish' and 'beastly' 'howling or blubbering' of the papists during the 1550s, arranged for Gosson to receive a scholarship to study at Oxford.[10] Gosson went up to Oxford in the 1570s but never completed his degree, possibly for a lack of funds, but embarked on a varied career as a writer, tutor, and clergyman, including a period where he seems to have acted as a spy for Queen Elizabeth's principal secretary, Francis Walsingham. This is the most plausible explanation of the otherwise inexplicable fact that Gosson registered at the English College in Rome in 1584. This was a Jesuit training establishment for Catholic missionaries, and there is no other sign that the Anglican Gosson ever had any Catholic sympathies. Robert Southwell lived and worked at the English College at exactly this time, and so it is possible that one of the individuals on whose activities Gosson reported back to Walsingham was the author of *Marie Magdalen's Funeral Teares*. Gosson does not seem to have become a puritan himself, even though his anti-theatrical views place him at the more severe end of the Protestant spectrum. Spy or otherwise, the lucrative church livings that Gosson landed later in his career suggest he had become very well connected in establishment circles.[11]

It was after an early, abortive attempt to write a romance for the stage, entitled *The Ephemerides of Phialo*, that Gosson decided to turn his energies instead to the campaign against playgoing. His most influential publication on the subject was entitled *Playes Confuted in Five Actions*, and was published in 1582. Gosson was the first writer to point out that a biblical injunction against cross-dressing could be applied to boy actors playing female roles. In the midst of various other rules in the book of Deuteronomy, including a very sensible reminder of the necessity of building a parapet to prevent people falling off one's roof, the relevant verse reads: 'The woman shall not wear that which pertaineth unto a man, neither shall a man put on a woman's garment: for all that do so are abomination unto the Lord thy God.'[12] This became a standard reference for later writers. Among Gosson's other objections was his view that plays dangerously stirred up strong affections, which were 'naturally planted in that part of the minde that is common to us with brute beastes'. Tragedies were especially harmful: 'The beholding of troubles and miserable slaughters that are in Tragedies, drives us to immoderate sorrow, heavines, womanish weeping and mourning, whereby we become lovers of dumpes, and lamentation, both enemies to fortitude.' Attending playhouses in order to weep over fictional miseries, then, risked stoking up animal feelings, weakening the character, and tipping oneself over into immoderate and harmful sorrow.[13]

William Prynne was a prolific polemicist, publishing over 200 pamphlets on a range of religious and political issues from the puritan point of view from the 1620s onwards. His major anti-theatrical work, however, can hardly be called a pamphlet. This thousand-page diatribe, published in 1633, was entitled *Histriomastix: The Player's Scourge, or Actor's Tragedy*.[14] Overheated and endlessly repetitive, this humourless compendium is documented with countless notes, authorities, biblical quotations, and footnotes, expanding in tiny text, much of it in Latin, across the foot and margin of each page. Prynne notes, depressingly, that although Jesus wept, he never laughed, and suggests that those guilty of attending comedies should rather weep over their sins than laugh at the performance: 'weeping is a pricking of the heart, laughter a corruption of manners.'[15]

Trying to read *Histriomastix* is like listening to the pub bore. Prynne was obsessed with sex. On one occasion Samuel Pepys found himself stuck next to Prynne at a dinner, during which Prynne took out of his pocket a collection of accounts of the lustful activities of thirty nuns who had been ejected from an English convent.[16] The central argument of *Histriomastix* is simple: 'That all popular, and common Stage-Playes, whether Comicall, Tragicall, Satyricall, Mimicall, or mixt of either (especially as they are now compiled, and personated among us) are such sinfull, hurtfull, and pernitious Recreations, as are altogether unseemely, and unlawfull unto Christians.' Prynne exercised himself with the effeminacy and sexual immorality associated with the performers of plays and their audiences, so-called 'play-haunters'. He argued that female actors were 'notorious, impudent, prostituted Strumpets', while the use of boy actors dressing up in women's clothes was even worse: 'a preparative, an incendiary, not only to sundry noysome lusts, to speculative, to practicall adultery, whoredome, and the like: but even to the most abominable unnaturall sinne of Sodom.' Prynne goes on to list all those nations and professions known to be addicted to sodomy, each with its own footnoted authority, including, of course, 'Cardinals, Popish Bishops, Abbots, Priests, Friers, Monkes'.[17] And yet, when it suited his purposes, Prynne was quite happy to cite the decrees of the Catholic Church in his support, including one enacted by the reforming Cardinal Carlo Borromeo in 1565 banning passion plays because of the bawdy and profane performances they had become associated with and stating that the story of the passion instead must be 'learnedly and gravely declared by the preachers in such sort, as that they may stirre up piety and teares in the auditors (which are the most profitable fruites of sermons)'. Tears stirred up by sermons were profitable, those produced by plays were part of a dangerous world of passion and incontinence.[18]

Histriomastix has been described as a crime against literature. More importantly for Prynne, it was interpreted as a crime against the crown.[19] King Charles I and his Catholic wife, Queen Henrietta Maria, were both keen playgoers, and devotees of Shakespeare. In 1633, the same year that

Prynne's work was published, the king and queen enjoyed a performance of *The Taming of the Shrew* at their court. That play includes a scene in which a nobleman wishes his page boy to weep, as part of an elaborate deception, and comments that if the boy does not have 'a woman's gift' of being able to 'rain a shower of commanded tears', then an onion in a handkerchief will do just as well to 'enforce a watery eye'. The queen may have been familiar with such tricks, since she was known to have acted in stage plays herself.[20]

In these circumstances, Prynne's description of all female actors as known whores was certainly a mistake. His book was offensive to the crown for other reasons too, many of them relating to Prynne's puritan theology and his opposition to King Charles's Archbishop, William Laud. As a result, Prynne was convicted of sedition in 1633, and again in 1637. His punishments included having his ears cut off (just trimmed the first time, hacked off barbarically the second), his nose slit, and the initials 'S.L.' (for 'seditious libeller') branded on his cheeks.[21] The cases of Gosson and Prynne show how judgements about the moral and religious effects of plays were serious political matters, with playwrights and actors increasingly seen as the pets of royalists and aristocrats. Prynne remained in prison until 1640, when his sentence was overturned by the Long Parliament. Within two years the puritans had the upper hand: the theatres were closed and the Civil War had begun.

The rending apart of the body politic, including the removal of its head, during the period between 1642 and the restoration of the monarchy in the person of Charles II in 1660 was a tragedy on an epic scale, played out across the three kingdoms of England, Scotland, and Ireland.[22] One of the ways that the hatred, violence, and distrust of the period were staged was through the spectacle of witch trials. Fearful communities looked for scapegoats and sometimes found them in the figure of the witch: a woman (or occasionally man) in league with the devil using preternatural powers to do harm to her enemies. One of the signs of a true witch was the inability to shed tears. Witches were sometimes known as purveyors of natural remedies within their communities, but were also suspected of darker powers, including the ability to transmute themselves into the forms of animals, and to cause illness and death. During the Civil War period, the accusation of witchcraft often had religious and political connotations. Some witches were accused of popish superstition, and others of sedition and disloyalty. The biblical text 'Rebellion is as the sin of witchcraft' took on a new resonance as witchcraft and warfare together threatened both Church and Commonwealth.[23] The visionary prophet Anna Trapnel, who had spent her youth seeking out sermons to make her weep, now became a famous public figure who, in tearful, ecstatic visions and trances (one of which lasted twelve days), denounced Cromwell as the Antichrist. She found herself accused of witchcraft as well as sedition.[24]

In the context of a witch trial, weeping or not weeping could be a matter of life and death. Witch-finding handbooks such as King James's *Daemonologie*, published in 1597, and the medieval *Malleus Maleficarum*, stated that a witch could not weep, even when ordered in the name of Christ to do so by a witch-hunter.[25] The category of the witch is an important one in the history of tears—an archetype of inhuman dryness. According to early modern sources, others who were deemed ill natured because of their inability or unwillingness to weep included Stoics, Vikings, the Swiss, tigers, bears, wolves, and werewolves.[26] The witch was a sort of anti-Mary Magdalene figure. While the Magdalene was a voluptuous sinner, all too womanly and passionate, overflowing with ingenuous feminine fluidity, from her love for Jesus and her compassion and penitence, the witch was old, deceitful, and desiccated: hard of heart and dry of eye.[27]

At the trial of the octogenarian cunning woman Ann Bodenham in Salisbury in 1653, two women were examined: a maid who claimed she had been bewitched by Bodenham, and who shed tears as the verdict against the old lady was read out, and Bodenham herself who was found guilty of all sorts of extraordinary acts of devilry, including turning herself temporarily into a dog, a lion, a bear, or a wolf. The account of the case by Edmond Bower described Bodenham additionally as 'a woman much addicted to Popery, and to Papistical fancies'. Yet she lacked the Catholic's ability to shed tears. Bower wrote that Bodenham would 'make a noyse as if she wept' but that under close observation 'she was never seen to let fall a tear'. The moral of the case for Bower was 'those that will rebelliously harden their hearts against God, shall be judicially hardened by him'. Bodenham's punishment from God for spiritual rebellion was her dry and hardened nature; her earthly punishment for her dry eyes was death by hanging. Bower noted that 'this Witch could not shed one penitential tear, though thereby she might have been reprieved from death'.[28] In reality, though, if old Ann Bodenham had managed to squeeze out a few tears at her trial, they would more likely than not have been met, as were other tears shed by alleged witches, with the claim that these were not true tears revealing a contrite inner nature, but rather a mere pretence turned on and off at will. This is the witch's paradox, an insoluble conundrum for women who are subjected to it. Tears are false spectacles, yet dry eyes are signs of inhumanity.

So, while weeping too much was to risk seeming childish, womanish, and 'player-like', not weeping at all was even worse.[29] As one Oxford preacher asked in a sermon delivered to members of both houses of parliament in 1644, 'who but Witches or Tygers could see their deare native Country fainting like the Saviour of it, under such a bloudy sweat as now it lies in' without shedding tears over its torments?[30] Both in person and in print, those involved in the Civil War were accordingly free with their tears. In 1646, Richard Crashaw, an Anglican poet who later converted to Catholicism, published his poem about Mary Magdalene entitled 'The Weeper', including two lines about the Magdalene's eyes later described by the Victorian writer Edmund Gosse as perhaps the worst in all English poetry: 'Two walking baths; two weeping motions; Portable & compendious oceans.' There was an endless supply of this sort of thing to be found in hundreds of other religious and political tracts of the times, and Gosse could have found even worse examples.[31] The clergyman John Featley wrote the longest work of the period on tears, published in 1646: over 700 pages of soliloquies, prayers, and devotions on the themes of weeping, the afflictions of women, and the Civil War, comparing the distress of the nation to that of the Israelites in Egypt. The imagery of the title page (Figure 5) suggested that tears were both a divine and a feminine gift. In terms of the politics of tears, Featley hedged his bets by dedicating *A Fountaine of Tears* to both king and parliament.[32] Other tearful titles published around this time included a pamphlet entitled *Loyalties Tears: Flowing After the Blood of the Royal Sufferer,* and a weekly periodical called *Mercurius Heraclitus, or, The Weeping Philosopher, Sadly Bemoaning the Distractions of the Times,* which promised its readers 'true News from wet Eyes, sad Hearts and perplexed Minds'.[33]

King Charles I wept at several key junctures during the Civil War, including when giving his assent to the execution of his friend and ally the Earl of Strafford, the Lord Lieutenant of Ireland, under pressure from parliament in 1641; when parting from his wife Henrietta Maria at Dover as she was forced into exile in 1642; and when agreeing in 1648 to see the bishops of the Church of England abolished and replaced by a more radical, Presbyterian structure.[34] One of the bestselling books of the whole period was published in 1649 a few days after the execution of the king. Entitled *Eikon Basilike,* meaning 'Portrait of the King', it purported to record the meditations and prayers of the king himself in the final weeks of his life. The cover carried an engraving showing the king in tears and at prayer (Figure 6). Here Charles was a Christlike man of sorrows, looking upon his enemies, as Christ had looked upon Jerusalem, weeping with compassionate grief. Like Christ, the Charles of *Eikon*

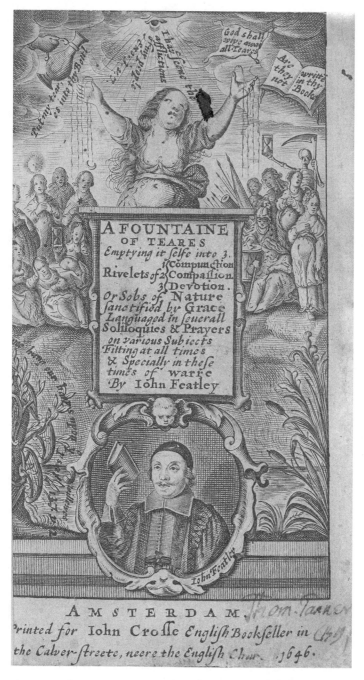

Figure 5. Title page of John Featley's *A Fountaine of Teares* (1646). The
Bodleian Libraries, the University of Oxford: Tanner 12.

The Explanation of the EMBLEME.

Ponderibus *genus omne mali, probris; gravatus,* *Vixq; ferenda ferens,* Palma *ut* Depressa, *resurgo.*	Though clogg'd with weights of miseries Palm-like Depress'd, I higher rise.
Ac, velut undarum Fluctus Ventiq; *furorom* *Irati Populi* Rupes immota *repello.* Clarior è tenebris, *cœlestis stella, corusco.* *(Victor et æternùm-felici pace* triumpho.	And as th'unmoved Rock out-brave's The boistrous Windes and rageing waves: So triumph I. And shine more bright In sad Affliction's Darksom night.
Auro Fulgentem *rutilo gemmisq; micantem,* *At curis* Gravidam *spernendo* calco Coronam.	That Splendid, but yet toilsom Crown Regardlessly I trample down.
Spinosam, *at ferri facilem, quo* Spes mea, Christi *Auxilio. Nobis non est* tractare molestum.	With joie I take this Crown of thorn, Though sharp, yet easie to be born.
Æternam, *fixis fidei, semperq;-beatam* *In Cœlos oculis* Specto, *Nobisq; paratam.*	That heav'nlie Crown, already mine, I View with eies of Faith divine.
Quod Vanum *est, sperno; quod* Christi Gratia *præbet* *Amplecti studium est.* Virtutis Gloria *merces.*	I slight vain things; and do embrace Glorie, the just reward of Grace.

Τὸ Χῑ οὐδὲν νῑκησε τὴν πόλιν, οὐδὲ τὸ Κάππα.

Figure 6. Frontispiece to *Eikon Basilike* (1649), engraved by William Marshall. The Bodleian Libraries, the University of Oxford: Vet.A3.E.316.

Basilike tells his followers to weep not for him but for themselves. The image of the tearful martyr-king became a rallying point for royalists. John Milton wrote a reply on behalf of the Commonwealth entitled *Eikonoklastes* (the image-breaker), complaining that the rhetoric of *Eikon Basilike* would 'catch the worthless approbation of an inconstant, irrational, and Image-doting rabble'. The religious conflicts between Catholics and Protestants of the previous century echoed loudly in such exchanges.[35]

In the same year that Ann Bodenham was condemned as a witch, Oliver Cromwell shed tears as he delivered a lengthy and impassioned theological and political oration at the opening of parliament. Later that year, in December 1653, he declared himself Lord Protector. In the tradition of King David, not to mention King Charles, Cromwell was a man of tears. The recollections of family, supporters, and opponents all testify to his tears, both public and private. Male tears in the political arena in this period of European history were relatively common, especially at moments of crisis and drama, but Cromwell took this to a new level. For his opponents, Cromwell's ostentatious blubbering was just one more confirmation that the man could not be trusted. The Leveller leader Richard Overton, who feared that Cromwell sought to set himself up as a new form of royalty, wrote, 'You shall scarce speak to Cromwell about anything but he will lay his hand on his breast, elevate his eyes, and call God to record, he will weep, howl and repent even while he doth smite you under the first rib.'[36] A pamphlet advocating the assassination of Cromwell appeared in 1657, entitled *Killing No Murder*. The author, sarcastically referring to Cromwell as 'his Highness', listed the traits that he shared with other tyrants, including a pretence of piety and religious zeal displayed, in Cromwell's case, by a mastery of 'prayers and tears'. Achieving his aims 'more by fraud than force' Cromwell had fooled many by being 'fluent in his tears, and eloquent in his execrations'; he was endowed with 'spungy eyes, and a supple conscience'.[37]

The royalist poet and playwright Abraham Cowley, when a student in Cambridge, had written a comedy to mark the visit of the 11-year-old Prince Charles, for whom it was performed during a visit to the town in 1642. The play, entitled *The Guardian*, lampooned the extremism and hypocrisy of the puritans, and sought to entertain the young prince with familiar comical ideas about women manipulating men with their tears: 'Nothing's at their command, except their tears, And we frail men, whom such heat-drops entice.'[38] When the monarchy was restored, eighteen years later, after the death of Cromwell and the collapse of his regime, the prince who had seen Cowley's play became King Charles II. After the theatres reopened, *The Guardian* was revived on the London stage. At the same time, in one of his political tracts, Cowley looked back on Oliver Cromwell's tears themselves as part of a theatrical performance, writing that by his 'hypocritical praying, and silly preaching, by unmanly tears and whining' Cromwell initially passed himself off as pious and well-meaning. In the end, however, people saw through Cromwell's weeping as a piece of stagecraft: 'His very actings of Godlinesses grew at last as ridiculous, as if a Player, by putting on a Gown, should think he represented excellently a Woman, though his Beard at the same time were seen by all the Spectators.'[39] How pleased the royalist playwright Cowley must have been at the irony of denouncing a puritan in these terms, as an unmanly, cross-dressing player, and an unconvincing one at that. On the national stage as well as in the theatre, to resort to womanly 'heat-drops' was always to risk such charges.

II. ENTHUSIASM

Stop, Gabriel!

Every period in British history was more tearful, and more approving of tears, than the middle decades of the twentieth century, the heyday of the stiff upper lip.[1] We have already encountered plenty of examples of tears as effective pious and political performances in the medieval and early modern periods. However, as we enter this second phase of the story of British tears, we are approaching the zenith of national lachrymosity. The five decades from the 1740s to the 1780s witnessed unprecedented enthusiasm, sensibility, sentiment, and emotion. The Reformation and Civil War were long enough past for fears of Catholicism, sensuality, theatricality, and hypocrisy to have faded. The Stoicism favoured by some seventeenth-century intellectuals, and the extremes of early Protestant severity were losing their authority and all sorts of public figures, from preachers and philosophers to actors and painters, embraced a new culture of feeling, in which a range of religious thoughts and moral virtues could be both taught and expressed through tears.[2]

I have chosen the term 'enthusiasm' to stand for this whole period, as it captures the heat and passion involved better than some of the rather more limp alternatives, like 'sentiment' or 'sensibility'. All these terms were used by contemporaries at the time, and 'enthusiasm' was very often a pejorative term used by those wishing to warn against the dangers of giving free rein to strong emotion.[3] Historians have established that there were deep Christian roots to this cultural turn, and that the grass-roots religious revivals experienced on both sides of the Atlantic shared in many of the same features that were hallmarks of the more refined and literary cult of sensibility, including the promotion of moral respectability and literacy, as well as the prominence given to sighs, tears, trembling, and weeping. Both also made a particular appeal to the interests of women. The Methodist John Wesley published sentimental novels and poems himself, while the resemblance between George Whitefield's performances and those of the most celebrated actors of the age was widely noted at the time.[4]

If you wanted to get a taste today of what it might have been like to be among the enormous crowds preached to by George Whitefield in the eighteenth century, then you could do worse than to go to a football match. Ideally it should be the last game of the season, and with one or both of the teams on the verge of promotion or relegation. Crying is guaranteed, as is the fact that the television coverage of such matches will include lingering shots of the tear-streaked faces of men, women, and children. In April 2013, for instance, Cardiff City were promoted to the Premier League, re-joining the top division for the first time in fifty years. Cardiff's famously emotional and volatile forward, the Cardiff-born international Craig Bellamy, burst into tears at the final whistle, telling reporters afterwards, 'We deserve to go up, there's no doubt about it.' At the other end of the same division, just across the Severn Estuary, and at the same moment, there were tears of despair among fans of Bristol City who were relegated.[5]

Such scenes are repeated across the British Isles on the final weekend of each football season, as fans tearfully face the prospect of the footballing equivalents of heaven or hell, salvation or damnation, election or repro-bation. These footballing tears, shed by open-air crowds of thousands of 'fans' (the shortened modern form of 'fanatics'), are the descendants of mass open-air religious experiences of an earlier period.[6] The leaders of the Methodist movement in the eighteenth century were criticized for their 'fanaticism' and 'enthusiasm'. For some of these critics, Methodism was just another kind of Puritanism, for others it was another kind of popery. In either case, it was undoubtedly a religion of the heart. The Methodists pioneered open-air preaching to audiences of thousands of ordinary working men and women, gathered in fields and on hillsides, hearing biblical stories, singing hymns, and weeping. Here we find one of the ancestors of modern mass tearful responses to both sporting events and pop music.[7]

The revivalism of the eighteenth century is instructive for another reason too. According to a vague, schematic version of the history of ideas, perhaps only dimly and semi-consciously accepted by anyone, the seventeenth and eighteenth centuries saw the birth of something called the 'Age of Reason' or the 'Enlightenment', during which old superstitions and religious ideas were rooted out by the discoveries of science and secular philosophy. Clever rational people like us, the story goes, were created *ex nihilo* all over Europe, to wag their fingers at credulous peasants, priests, astrologers, and witch-hunters. This self-aggrandizing myth of the 'Enlightenment' was constructed by some of the participants in the scientific and philosophical life of the period itself. Although it bears some relation to actual developments, including the founding of early scientific societies which aimed to study nature independently of religious or political interests, it is clearly pretty hopeless as a general characterization of the early modern, or indeed any other period. An early Fellow of the Royal Society, Walter Charleton, combined several of these interests together. He wrote an influential book in 1674 on the *Natural History of the Passions*, including the latest physiological theories of weeping in relation to the heart, the brain, and the newly discovered lachrymal glands. One of his previous works had been entitled *The Darkness of Atheism Dispelled by the Light of Nature*, setting out what would become standard theological arguments about the power of

rational and empirical studies of the natural world to supplement revelation and scripture as sources of knowledge of God. The so-called 'Age of
Reason' was also an age of ostentatious weeping, violent passions, religious revivals, and the persistence of feelings and beliefs of a kind which,
according to the cartoon version of intellectual history, were jettisoned in
the 1660s.[8]

Even that most hard-headed of Enlightenment sceptics, the Scottish
philosopher David Hume, believed that reason, far from being supreme,
was and ought only to be the slave of the passions.[9] Hume is rightly
remembered as someone who doubted the teachings of Christianity, but
his construction of a philosophy of feeling, sympathy, and passion is another
reminder of the inadequacy of received ideas either about the 'Age of
Reason' or, for that matter, about dour Scots. Hume was one of a generation
of thinkers, including the economist Adam Smith, who put moral sentiments and human feeling at the heart of their social philosophies.[10]

According to an anecdote that circulated after Hume's death, the great
philosopher once heard the revivalist Methodist preacher George Whitefield (pronounced 'Whitfield') giving a sermon in Edinburgh. Whitefield
was widely admired as a performer. The most famous actor of the age,
David Garrick, was supposed to have said that he would willingly give a
hundred pounds to be able to say 'Oh!' like George Whitefield.[11] The
encounter in Edinburgh between the pre-eminent preacher and the pre-
eminent philosopher of the age embodies in a single vivid episode a
meeting between two of the great forces of British life and thought at this
time. This was a moment when enlightenment met enthusiasm. Hume
was reported to have listened to 'the latter part' of one of Whitefield's
sermons, his enthusiasm for the preacher not having been quite sufficient
for him to arrive on time, and to have said afterwards, 'He is the most
ingenious preacher I ever heard. It is worth while to go twenty miles to
hear him.' Hume reported that at the climax of the sermon, Whitefield,
after a solemn pause, told the congregation, 'The attendant angel is just

about to leave the threshold, and ascend to heaven. And shall he ascend and not bear with him the news of one sinner, among all this multitude reclaimed from the error of his ways?' At this point Whitefield stamped his foot and lifted his eyes and hands to heaven. Hume recalled that 'with gushing tears' Whitefield shouted, 'Stop, Gabriel! Stop, Gabriel! Stop, ere you enter the sacred portals, and yet carry with you the news of one sinner converted to God.' The preacher's description of the saviour's dying love to sinful men then reduced the whole assembly to tears, although I suspect that there were at least a couple of dry eyes on that particular occasion.[12]

In the league table of all-time great British weepers, George Whitefield is edged into second place only by Margery Kempe.[13] Whitefield's sermons elicited copious tears not only from the hundreds of thousands of men and women who heard him preach, on both sides of the Atlantic, but also from himself. John Collet's contemporary painting of Whitefield preaching in the open air (Figure 7) shows him holding a handkerchief. Another contemporary observer wrote: 'I hardly ever knew him go through a sermon without weeping, more or less, and I truly believe his were the tears of sincerity. His voice was often interrupted by his affection.' The same witness continued: 'I could hardly bear such unreserved use of tears, and the scope he gave to his feelings, for sometimes he exceedingly wept, stamped loudly and passionately, and was frequently so overcome, that for a few seconds, you would suspect he never could recover.'[14] Whitefield used to comment upon the tears of his hearers. During one sermon, preached in a field, in which he retold the biblical story of Abraham and Isaac with huge pathos, Whitefield told his hearers, 'I see your hearts affected. I see your eyes weep.' Another time he told a congregation: 'Your tears and deep attention are an evidence, that the Lord God is amongst us of a truth.'[15]

At the start of his career, as a young man in his twenties, Whitefield embarked on a series of outdoor sermons to coal miners at Kingswood

Figure 7. John Collet's eighteenth-century depiction of George Whitefield preaching. Private Collection/Bridgeman Images.

near Bristol. 'My bowels have long since yearned toward the poor colliers', he noted in his journal, 'who are very numerous, and as sheep having no shepherd.'[16] Contemporary estimates put the size of the crowds he drew at up to 20,000.[17] Whitefield noted that 'The first discovery of their being affected, was, to see the white gutters made by their tears, which plentifully fell down their black cheeks, as they came out of their coal pits.'[18] For Whitefield himself, preaching and weeping were physically demanding. The former slave Olaudah Equiano observed that when Whitefield preached he sweated 'as much as I ever did while in slavery'. Another source claimed that after his sermons, which were often two hours long, Whitefield would vomit copiously, including bringing up blood, before he was able to speak again. Whitefield's converts were sometimes carried from the field, like corpses, poleaxed by the Holy Spirit. At one meeting in America in 1740, five people were actually killed in the crush to hear Whitefield. In all, Whitefield made thirteen crossings of the Atlantic during his lifetime, as well as undertaking numerous preaching tours in England, Wales, Scotland, and Ireland. It is estimated that he preached over 18,000 sermons during his career; all or almost all of them included tears. That is a lot of weeping.[19]

George Whitefield grew up in a Gloucester pub called the Bell Inn, run by his stepfather. As a schoolboy, he enjoyed making speeches and acting, including dressing up to play the female roles in plays. As an Oxford student, Whitefield discovered his vocation, meeting John and Charles Wesley and joining their 'Holy Club' in 1733. This became the core of the Methodist movement, which sought to effect a renewal in the religious life of the nation, reacting against the perceived laziness, world-liness, decadence, and corruption of the clergy of the established Church. Ultimately it was John Wesley who emerged as the leader of the inter-national Methodist movement, but in the early years Whitefield was an equally important figure. In the late 1730s it was Whitefield who pion-eered open-air preaching as a spiritual tool to reach the neglected souls of the labouring poor. Initially Wesley shared the established view that this was an improper, possibly even unlawful activity. However, it had clear biblical precedents, as well as having been practised by both Catholic and Protestant preachers of earlier centuries, and when Wesley saw the impact Whitefield was having, he soon became an enthusiastic outdoor evangelist himself.[20]

Whitefield and Wesley were explicit in their condemnations of the clergy and hierarchy of the Church of England, but stopped short of formally separating. By the end of the eighteenth century, however,

Methodist chapels, communion services, baptisms, and burials constituted what were clearly rivals rather than revivals in relation to existing
institutions. A defining feature of Methodism, along with outdoor
preaching, and the simple, direct appeal to the hearts and feelings of
working people, was its use of hymns, including many written by John
Wesley's brother Charles. In this respect, the Methodist revival represented a departure from the traditional Protestant suspicion of music as
an excessively sensual means of spiritual devotion.[21] Finally, Methodist
meetings and publications were also opportunities to make money,
whether to fund schools and orphanages or for the Methodist mission
itself. The mid-eighteenth-century Methodist movement in Britain, along
with the religious renewal or 'Great Awakening' in America, thus laid the
foundations for a range of later institutions, from the Salvation Army to
the 'Televangelism' of the twentieth and twenty-first centuries, of which
one character in a Woody Allen film observed, 'If Jesus came back, and
saw what's going on in his name, he'd never stop throwing up.'[22]

A satirical print published in 1760 entitled *The Scheming Triumvirate*
grouped Whitefield with the sentimental novelist Laurence Sterne and
the actor-manager Samuel Foote together as a group of money-making
hucksters.[23] For all three, tears were part of a commercial transaction,
and Whitefield was quite unabashed about this dimension of his endeavours, saying that 'the devotion and business of a Methodist go hand in
hand'. The support of the Countess of Huntingdon was crucial to the
later stages of Whitefield's British endeavours. He wrote to her, of
the elevated social connections she could open up to Methodism, that
the 'prospect of catching some of the rich in the gospel net is very
promising'. 'Tears trickle from my eyes,' he told his wealthy patron,
'whilst I am thinking of your Ladyship's condescending to patronize
such a dead dog as I am.'[24] The initiatives for which this tearful old
dog raised money were, even by the standards of the time, morally
suspect. A school for black children set up in America was a slave

institution, funded by planters and slave-owners. Whitefield was an enthusiastic defender of the institution of slavery as consistent with the Bible. Techniques of spiritual discipline used in Whitefield's various schools included keeping children up crying and praying all night, as well as beating them and tying them up if they proved resistant to this form of education.[25] Nonetheless, for many years, Whitefield's mission was a huge financial success, especially in America, where Whitefield was the most famous individual and by far the bestselling author of the first half of the 1740s. His main American publisher, the printer, politician, and Founding Father Benjamin Franklin, was not the only one to turn a weeping profit from the weeping prophet.[26]

Surviving memoirs by Methodist lay preachers and other converts in this period are written in a formulaic way, with recollections of an early life of sin, drunkenness, and lewdness, followed by a dramatic, agonizing, and tear-filled conversion, interpreted as a change of heart, a rebirth to new life, and a sign of membership of God's elect. Despite their conventional structure, these accounts offer glimpses into the lives of those who felt the appeal of Wesley and Whitefield. In 1745, Sampson Staniforth, a 25-year-old soldier from Yorkshire, was stationed in Ghent during the War of the Austrian Succession. It was the middle of the night and he was standing sentinel at a dangerous post. His memoir recalls that as soon as he was alone he kneeled down and 'determined not to rise, but to continue crying and wrestling with God, till He had mercy on me'. Staniforth writes that he cannot recall how long he was in this agony but that he looked up to heaven and saw a vision of Jesus on the cross: 'At the same moment these words were applied to my heart, "thy sins are forgiven thee." My chains fell off; my heart was free. All guilt was gone, and my soul was filled with unutterable peace.'[27] John Haime also fought in the British army in the 1740s. His spiritual state fluctuated between despair over his sinfulness, accompanied by bitter cries and tears, and moments of divine relief, also marked by tears, but now of love and ecstasy.[28] Haime's experience was typical. Methodism was premised on a simple and dramatic contrast between sin and salvation, both of which were occasions for tears. When John Wesley preached in York in May 1753, on the text 'Let us come boldly to the throne of grace, that we may obtain mercy, and find grace to help in time of need', one of those present recorded: 'I never saw a congregation so affected. Most of the people were in tears, some for joy, some from a sense of their sins.'[29]

Methodism attracted both men and women, but the latter were in the majority, including an aptly named Irishwoman and her mother, Miss Teare and Mrs Teare, with whom Whitefield once had breakfast at their home in Athlone.[30] Another female convert was Mary Saxby, born in 1738 in London, the daughter of a silk weaver and his wife. After Mary's mother died, she was brought up by an uncle, who sent her to the school set up by Whitefield's followers at the Moorfields Tabernacle in London. Young Mary ran away from home and spent the rest of her life itinerant and more or less destitute, among gypsies and labourers, and occasionally in the workhouse or prison, making money by singing ballads and selling items of drapery and haberdashery. She was partially deaf, and had ten children by a drunken and unreliable husband, six of whom died before her.[31]

Saxby is known to us through her posthumously published *Memoirs of a Female Vagrant, Written by Herself.* The memoirs centre around a Methodist conversion story. Saxby's addiction to 'obscene jests, filthy ribaldry, and profane swearing' is overcome by the unmerited grace and the 'bleeding, dying love' of her saviour, through the agency of Methodist preachers and a neighbour who recommends a book by the seventeenth-century minister Joseph Alleine. Saxby finds that Alleine's *Alarm to Unconverted Sinners* exactly describes her spiritual situation, 'and before I had read many lines, I was bathed in tears'. Her account goes on: 'This book, the Lord was pleased to make of singular use to my soul; for many a time have I laid it before me, and wept, and prayed in bitterness of soul, because I feared that I was unconverted. Oh, how did I long, yea pant and breathe to be converted! Sometimes a gleam of hope broke in; at other times, gloomy fears prevailed.' In Alleine's book, Saxby would have read such advice as, 'The true penitent's tears are indeed the wine that cheereth both God and man' and, using an image that became a favourite among Methodists, 'Thou must strive to enter, and wrestle with tears and supplications, as Jacob, if thou meanest to carry the blessing.'[32] When Mary Saxby's moment of conversion comes, it is at a prayer meeting with a Methodist preacher: 'He then went to prayer; and the Lord was pleased to give him such a spirit of supplication, that there was not a dry eye in the room—though several very wicked people were present.'[33]

As the image of wrestling suggests, weeping for Methodists was not only often an outdoor activity, but also an athletic one. The spiritual struggles involved were ones that gripped, shook, and convulsed the body. John Haime's memoir narrates the bodily exertions involved in being torn between the worlds of sin and salvation, his every throb of spiritual suffering or release marked by wrestling and weeping. On one occasion, seeking mercy from God in a church, Haime wrote, 'I fell down before the Lord, with bitter cries and tears, till my strength failed me, and it was with difficulty I could walk out of the room.'[34] Others combined bodily and spiritual wrestling even more literally, including the Welsh woman Marged ferch Ifan, the only person in the *Oxford Dictionary of National Biography* whose occupation is given as 'harpist and wrestler'. Ifan was also a blacksmith, boat-builder, and the greatest hunter of her time, as well as a Methodist. She was reputed, even at the age of 70, in the 1760s, still to be the best wrestler in Wales.[35]

So, Methodism attracted miners and mill hands, soldiers and singers, and at least one wrestling harpist. Many of these individuals were drawn from communities with a history of dissent from the Church of England. In the seventeenth century, such communities had produced their own weeping prophets in figures like Anna Trapnel, and her associate the Welsh independent minister Vavasor Powell, as well as James Nalton in Yorkshire and Joseph Alleine in Wiltshire, whose book would later convert Mary Saxby. Nalton and Alleine were both puritan ministers ejected from the Church of England after the Restoration of the monarchy. Drawing on these puritan, dissenting, and independent religious traditions, Methodism was particularly successful in the south-west of England, in northern industrial towns, and in Wales, where the Calvinistic version favoured by Whitefield flourished.[36]

One of the leading Welsh Methodists was Daniel Rowland. A nineteenth-century historian of the Methodist movement wrote that Rowland's thunderous preaching 'kindled the fervid Welsh with enthusiasm'. Ardent 'shoutings' and weeping broke out from the thousands who assembled to hear him. Rowland was an imposing figure, 'gigantic in body', and known as the 'angry cleric' for his passionate denunciations of sinners. Crowds would be moved to 'tears and convulsive sobs, followed by cries of *Gogoniant*, (Glory!) and *Bendigedi* (Blessed!)'. These cries 'ran through the multitude like a contagious fever'. One of Rowland's converts, when trapped on the roof of a building being swept away in a flood, facing his imminent death by drowning still praised God, shouting '*Gogoniant! Gogoniant!*' Prior to his conversion to Methodism, Rowland was reputedly a lax and 'godless' establishment clergyman. An example of this godlessness was the fact that after preaching his Sunday sermon, Rowland would descend from the pulpit to join in the 'Sunday athletic games of his parishioners'. This included playing football: an unseemly and frivolous activity for a man of God at any time, but especially on a Sunday.[37]

After his conversion, Rowland's angry preaching, urging the labouring poor of Wales to give up their sinfulness, lewdness, drunkenness, and immorality, met with violent opposition as well as enthusiastic support. In one case his opponents set up a rival assembly to attract potential converts away from his preaching. This particular assembly took the form of football-playing and wrestling, and it is not the only recorded instance of Methodism and football entering into direct competition with each other. In 1820, a group of Methodists in Yorkshire tried to disrupt the annual football match between the villages of Preston and Hedon by preaching, praying, and singing hymns on a nearby hill.[38] The fact that football and Methodism were explicitly offered as alternative Sunday activities for the working communities of the eighteenth and nineteenth centuries serves to reinforce the point that these were activities fulfilling similar functions, creating social bonds through shared physical activities linked to moral and religious narratives. In the contest between Methodism and football, football eventually won. During the twentieth century, the communal singing and weeping of the Methodists and their ilk now migrated from prayer meetings on hillsides to football matches in stadiums. The tears were transposed rather than dried up. After the rise and fall of eighteenth-century sensibility, of Victorian pathos, and of the stiff upper lip, George Whitefield and Daniel Rowland would eventually be replaced by Paul Gascoigne and Craig Bellamy.[39]

6

Four Hundred Pounds to Cry

When it comes to feats of sensibility, I am no slouch. My lachrymal glands respond quite readily not only to events in the lives of myself and others, but also to novels, films, concertos, symphonies, operas, soap operas, and—now getting more embarrassing—TV talent shows, political speeches, and the triumphs and disasters of Wimbledon and the Olympics. But I have never cried—have never come remotely close to crying—over a painting. As far as I am concerned, anyone who has done so must be a virtuoso of fine feeling in possession of a quite exceptional capacity for aesthetic sensitivity. I do know these tender souls exist, however, thanks to the American art historian James Elkins who took out advertisements requesting accounts of such experiences when he was researching a book on the subject. Despite the fact that Leonardo da Vinci once wrote that a painter might move people to laughter but never to tears, Elkins received over 400 replies describing tearful responses to paintings.[1] These formed the starting point for his book on the subject, which ranges across the history of art from a thirteenth-century Japanese depiction of a waterfall, via Dutch devotional images, the Italian Renaissance, French sentimentalism, and German Romanticism, to Picasso's *Guernica*, and the abstract expressionist works of the American painter Mark Rothko, which Elkins found were by far the most wept over twentieth-century paintings. Rothko commented in 1957, 'The people who weep before my pictures are having the same religious experience I had when I painted them.'[2]

In all of this research, what James Elkins did not find, or at least did not write about, was a single instance of anyone weeping over a painting by a British artist. This is not especially surprising. Post-Reformation British culture was not a hospitable environment for sentimental pictures. Religious iconography, Catholic sensuality, and false ideas about the power of tears were all highly suspect in the eyes of Protestants. This was partially changed by the fashion for feeling which swept across Europe during the middle decades of the eighteenth century. This phenomenon—often known as the 'cult of sensibility'—was shaped especially by up-and-coming, consumerist, city-dwellers who sought to mark themselves out as educated, refined, and virtuous in a way which was not dependent on their family, religious, or political connections. In theory, at least, this was a democratic trend, based on shared human feelings. The lachrymose spirit of the Christian and classical traditions was distilled into new containers: sentimental novels, tragic plays and operas, and even some paintings became the vessels of the temporarily much-vaunted quality of 'sensibility'.[3]

The most famous tear-jerking canvas of the eighteenth century was *Young Girl Weeping Over her Dead Bird*, painted by the French artist Jean-Baptiste Greuze and admired by sighing, swooning, and sobbing salon-goers in the 1760s. This is a classic image of sensibility, showing a young woman of indeterminate age, her head in her hand, her gaze sorrowfully directed downwards, where her pet canary is expired, flat on its back, garlanded with flowers and foliage.[4] By modern standards, the sentimentality is stomach-churning. Even Elkins, whose book is a celebration and defence of tearful responses to art, struggles to find anything good to say about the Greuze girl. The picture makes him queasy; it is 'precious, cloying, effusively sentimental, and weirdly artificial', not to mention 'slyly sexual'.[5] For my own part, I find it hard to take the picture seriously since it reminds me so much of Monty Python's 'Dead Parrot' sketch. I can almost hear the young girl complaining exasperatedly to the pet shop owner, 'This is an ex-canary'.

Despite the fact that this kind of sentimental work was associated more with French and Italian artists, there was at least one eighteenth-century British painter, the most accomplished and versatile visual artist of his age, in fact, who set out to produce, through the medium of oil on canvas, the kind of tearful response that was becoming commonplace in response to novels of sensibility, and had long been produced by the stage. The result was an extraordinary painting of a weeping woman, which became the focus of an ugly controversy, marring the painter's final years. It was William Hogarth's 1759 painting *Sigismunda Mourning over the Heart of Guiscardo* (Figure 8).

William Hogarth had achieved huge success documenting his age through satirical prints and moralizing paintings, as well as producing

Figure 8. William Hogarth, *Sigismunda Mourning over the Heart of Guiscardo* (1759). © Tate, London 2014.

remarkable portraits and grand historical canvases. Images such as *Gin Lane* are famous for their portrayal of the seediness of the London streets, while Hogarth's various print series, including *The Four Stages of Cruelty* and *Industry and Idleness*, offered to teach moral lessons through tragi-comic observations of the progress of individuals in careers of virtue or vice. As a painter, Hogarth's most lasting success was probably the *Marriage à la Mode* series, unmasking marriage among the well-to-do as a financial transaction, its authenticity constantly undermined by the venality and sexual immorality of all involved.[6]

Hogarth himself was not innocent of some of the vices he satirized, including pride, vanity, and the love of money and fame. His decision to shift his attentions temporarily from producing laughter to producing tears was triggered by an auction in 1758 at which a painting attributed to the then fashionable sixteenth-century painter Correggio, depicting *Sigismunda With the Heart of Guiscardo*, fetched the astonishing sum of just over £400. Hogarth was right in doubting the attribution to Correggio (in fact the *Sigismunda* sold in 1758 was by Francesco Furini), and had in any case long been animated by a hatred of those 'connoisseurs' who swooned over 'old master' paintings by the likes of Correggio or Guido Reni, while failing to appreciate the merits of contemporary works by, for instance, William Hogarth. When the 'infinitely rich' Sir Richard Grosvenor approached Hogarth shortly afterwards to commission a painting from him, rashly telling the artist he could choose his own subject and name his own price, Hogarth saw an opportunity to prove that he could out-Sigismunda any old master, and he set about producing his own version of the image that had recently sold for a small fortune. The result was a highly accomplished and striking painting, and a public relations disaster.[7]

Among his rather garbled handwritten autobiographical notes, Hogarth recorded that 'my whole aim was to fetch Tear from the Spectator my figures was the actor that was to do it. Sigismunda grieve over her lovers heart.' In other words, Hogarth conceived of his central figure, Sigismunda, as an 'actor', who would, he went on, 'touch the heart' of viewers through their eyes, as the player on the stage touched the audience through their ears, with the result in both cases being tears. Hogarth noted that he had seen many people shedding involuntary tears at a tragedy, but that he had never seen the same phenomenon produced by a painting, and nor had anyone else he knew. To achieve this unprecedented aesthetic response to a painting was the challenge Hogarth set himself.[8] A theoretical treatise on aesthetics published in 1730 confirmed that the power of painting to produce tears was thought to be less than that of poetry or drama. The author wrote, of the superior power of poetry, 'I mean that Power which every Day we see that a moving Poem or a Tragedy have of drawing Tears from the Eyes; which we do not, or least very rarely see done, by the Sight of the finest Painting.' The same author went on to consider the question of whether a series of fifty paintings, each one depicting the next image in a tragic story, might not have an equal ability to produce tears, but still concluded that such a series could never have the power that 'one single moving Scene in a Play has to draw Tears from the Eyes' by affecting the passions and acting on the imagination.[9] Another influential aesthetic theorist of the period, Lord Kames, placed the viewing of a moving historical painting above reading prose, but below witnessing the performance of a tragedy, in ranking its ability to 'extort tears'.[10]

Unlike Mark Rothko's paintings, which achieve their tearful effects by offering the viewer an intense but entirely abstract aesthetic encounter, Hogarth sought to produce tears through a visual image which suggested to the viewer a very particular tragic narrative. The tale of Sigismunda and Guiscardo can be traced back to Boccaccio's fourteenth-century *Decameron*, and was known to British readers through John Dryden's version, published in 1700 in his final work, *Fables Ancient and Modern*.[11] The story concerns a king, Tancred, and his daughter, the young widow

Sigismunda, whom he forbids to remarry. Sigismunda nonetheless falls in love with Guiscardo, who is in the service of the king. The lovers are discovered by the king, who is possessed by an intense, apparently almost incestuous jealous passion towards his daughter. The king kills Guiscardo, rips out his heart, and sends it to his daughter Sigismunda in a golden goblet. Sigismunda has previously berated her father for weeping like a woman, and vows instead to die like a man, without a tear. Confronted with the heart of her lover, however, she weeps, before pouring poison over the bloody heart, and drinking the fatal mixture from the goblet. Her final tears are restrained and dignified. In Dryden's version, Sigismunda's tears are silent, like a 'sober shower of rain': 'Mute, solemn sorrow, free from female noise, Such as the majesty of grief destroys.' It is this mute, sober, moment of tears, as Sigismunda holds the open goblet in her hand, touching the heart of her murdered lover (or husband in Dryden's version, which included a hasty marriage), that Hogarth sought to capture in his painting for Sir Richard Grosvenor, entitled *Sigismunda Mourning over the Heart of Guiscardo*.[12]

There is no doubt that Hogarth took time and pain over his *Sigismunda*. A maidservant in the household recalled that Hogarth's wife Jane, in tears of grief for her recently deceased mother, had been the model for *Sigismunda*. Several friends and critics saw the painting while it was being painted, and one of these said, 'I never saw a finer resemblance of flesh and blood, while the canvas was warm, I mean wet.'[13] Fleshly, bloody, warm, and wet—this was not quite what Sir Richard Grosvenor, for one, was expecting. He imagined he had commissioned a lightly moralistic comedy of manners; what he got was a bloody melodrama, dripping with bodily fluids. Grosvenor didn't like it, and refused to pay Hogarth the £400 he asked. Grosvenor said, 'I really think the performance so striking and inimitable, that the constantly having it before one's eyes would be too often occasioning melancholy ideas to arise in one's mind, which curtains being drawn before it would not diminish in the least.' The reference to curtains suggested that the picture was in the same category as either religiously or sexually dangerous images which could not be openly viewed in polite company. In response, Hogarth composed, with the help of a more literary friend, some lines of rather bitter poetry about the fate of his picture, scolding art connoisseurs for their obsession with Raphael, Rubens, and Guido Reni and telling them that art should be judged not by comparison with old masters but in its relation to nature and to human feeling: 'These are the height of mimic skill. The heart to pierce, the fancy fill.' That image of a pierced heart has echoes of the medieval idea of tears of compunction. Then, in reference to Grosvenor's comment that the picture filled his mind with melancholy thoughts, Hogarth's poem went on:

> These are the Painter's truest test,
> And these Sir Richard's self confess'd.
> Nay; 'tis so moving that the Knight
> Can't bear the figure in his sight?
> And who would tears so dearly buy,
> As give four hundred pounds to cry?[14]

It was not only Hogarth's patron who didn't like the picture. The critics didn't like it, and the public didn't like it. When the painting was displayed at the Society of Artists' exhibition in London in 1761, Hogarth, paranoid about criticisms, posted a man to listen in secret to the comments of viewers and to write them down. After a few days of this, Hogarth withdrew the picture from the exhibition in a fit of vanity and rage.[15]

Hogarth's autobiographical notes included the claim that his *Sigismunda* had succeeded in its aim—'I have more than once seen the tear of sympathy trickle down the cheek of a female, while she has been contemplating the picture'—but what are more evident than sympathetic tears in the historical record are sniggers of derision.[16] After its withdrawal from the exhibition in 1761, hostile published criticisms of the picture soon followed. These flowed from the pens of Horace Walpole (Gothic novelist, art critic, and son of the former Prime Minister Robert Walpole), John Wilkes (a rising politician who opposed the policies pursued by the young George III's Prime Minister, the Earl of Bute), and Charles Churchill (a satirist and an associate of Wilkes). Hogarth found himself on the wrong side of these well-connected figures, both aesthetically and politically.

Walpole described Sigismunda, in a letter to George Montagu, as 'a maudlin whore tearing off the trinkets that her keeper had given to her, to fling at his head'. He later published very similar comments in his *Anecdotes of Painting in England*, although replacing 'maudlin whore' with 'maudlin strumpet' and adding that the feeling of disgust raised by the woman's 'vulgar expression' (that is, her bold and red-eyed stare, which Walpole suggested showed a mixture of sexual defiance, rage, and drunkenness) was intensified by her fingers which were 'bloodied by her lover's heart that lay before her like that of a sheep's for her dinner'.[17] Contrasting Hogarth's rendition unfavourably with the versions of Sigismunda offered by both Dryden and Furini, Walpole complained that it conveyed none of the 'sober grief, no dignity of suppressed anguish, no involuntary tear, no settled meditation on the fate she meant to meet, no amorous warmth turned holy by despair'; in short none of the virtues of sensibility that should have been in evidence. The tears were of the wrong kind: ostentatious, deliberate, and defiant rather than mute and involuntary. Walpole had made some of these comments in person to Hogarth while the painting was still warm and wet in his studio, with the result that the version that survives lacks some of the features about which Walpole complained. The fingers are no longer bloody, and Sigismunda is no longer about to rip off a necklace to return to her father (or her 'keeper' in Walpole's scenario).[18]

Walpole's central contention, then, was that Hogarth had set out to paint the sober grief of a virtuous, if rebellious, daughter and had given the world a picture instead of a drunkenly sobbing rejected prostitute. The phrase 'maudlin whore' encapsulated exactly the same sentiment as Grosvenor's reference to hanging the canvas behind curtains; this was a picture redolent of sexual licence, Catholic religiosity, or both. We have already seen that the term 'maudlin' had become established as a short-hand both for the piously penitent weeper of Catholic tradition, Mary Magdalene, and the undignified tears of drunkenness.[19]

John Wilkes, once a friend of Hogarth's, now turned against him, for political reasons, and used *Sigismunda* for the purpose. In his political periodical *The North Briton*, Wilkes wrote that the figure of Sigismunda was not even human and that if she resembled anything on earth it was Hogarth's 'own wife in an agony of passion; but of what passion no connoisseur could guess'.[20] Charles Churchill, having praised Dryden's version of the tale as one that could call forth grief from even a Stoic, and compassion from a heart of steel, turns to Hogarth's rendition:

> But O, how much unlike! How fall'n! how chang'd!
> How much from Nature, and herself estrang'd!
> How totally depriv'd of all the pow'rs
> To shew her feelings, and awaken ours,
> Doth Sigismunda now devoted stand,
> The helpless victim of a Dauber's hand.[21]

A print produced as part of the long-running feud between Hogarth and Churchill included an image of Hogarth as a cross between a jackal and a lion in front of a painting covered by a curtain, which reads, 'This Curtain Hangs Here to preserve from Vulgar Eyes the Beauty of the inestimable Picture representing a Harlot blubbering over a Bullock's Heart; Painted by Willm. Hog-Ass.'[22]

As his first biographer noted, once Hogarth's opponents had dis-covered 'his parental partiality for Sigismunda', they were able to 'wound the artist in his most vulnerable part', and 'they mangled her

without mercy'.[23] Hogarth wrote in his autobiographical notes that these
attacks came at a time when his health was at its worst, in a kind of 'slow
feaver', and that they could not fail to hurt 'a feeling mind' such as his. In
fact they continued up to the time of his death in 1764, three years after
he had withdrawn *Sigismunda* from the Society of Artists' exhibition.[24] It
had marred the final years of his life, and had given Hogarth, if no one
else, a tragedy to cry about.

So, what was really wrong with Hogarth's painting? Why was it
described as maudlin and disgusting, while the Greuze girl was considered graceful and dignified? As is so often the case when trying to
understand the reception of a work of art, literature, philosophy, or
science, a large portion of the answer is to be found not in the work
itself, but in its author's persona and politics. In this case, Hogarth was
well past his prime as an artist, had a lifetime's accumulated professional
and personal enmities, and some newly formed political ones too. His
opponents saw an opportunity to humiliate Hogarth, and they took it.
But there were various reasons why Hogarth's picture provided his
opponents with ready ammunition. It is rarely the case that the most
profoundly moving works of art are those that have been created with the
express intention of making the audience cry. Weeping, like happiness, is
most likely to be achieved when approached indirectly. As consumers of
art, we tend to be hostile and suspicious towards works (whether they be
novels, songs, movies, or TV adverts) that seem to have been designed
with the sole intention of making us cry.[25] Hogarth's approach was too
direct and too literal minded. He wanted to prove that a painting could
touch people's hearts and make them weep as he had seen women doing
at a tragedy; so he painted a picture of a woman touching a heart and
weeping, at the culmination of a tragedy.

In the end, though, it came down to sex. The reception of Hogarth's
Sigismunda is part of the history of British attitudes to sex as well as to
the public expression of feeling. Dryden's Sigismunda had been mute,

solemn, sober, contained, and stoical. One cannot imagine Hogarth's figure in those terms and, as we have seen, that failure put critics in mind of foreign, Catholic sensualism. The critical response could be summed up as, 'No sex please, we're British'. Greuze's allusions to sexuality were indirect and veiled, and to be expected, from a Frenchman. In the Hogarth painting, although to a modern viewer it might look pretty restrained, the bodily passion is all too visible. The sexual directness of the gaze is combined with a finger touching the almost pulsing, red flesh of her lover's organ with a finger that, in the first version at least, was wet with his vital juices. When I first started reading works by art historians about sentimental paintings of this period, I thought they were all obsessed with sex. But I can now see that the images themselves, and the critical responses to them, provide plenty of reasons for thinking in this way.[26]

Walpole said of *Sigismunda Mourning over the Heart of Guiscardo* that 'Hogarth's performance was more ridiculous than anything he had ever ridiculed'.[27] At the same time that Hogarth was working and reworking *Sigismunda*, he produced two versions of a print ridiculing Methodism, the first version entitled *Enthusiasm Delineated* (Figure 9).[28] These depictions of overheated preachers and their immoral, hypocritical, and delirious congregations included the weeping figure of George Whitefield at the lectern. In the first version, Whitefield's closest hearers include a handcuffed, penitent thief whose tears were being bottled by Christ, evoking a phrase addressed by the Psalmist to God: 'Thou tellest my wanderings: put thou my tears into thy bottle: are they not in thy book?'[29] The Christ figure is farting, in allusion to the Methodist idea of the Holy Spirit as a 'heavenly wind', and next to him a nobleman slides his hand inside a young woman's dress as she lets a large, phallic wooden icon fall down in front of her.[30]

Hogarth's *Enthusiasm Delineated* sought to associate the allegedly pious tears of enthusiasm with credulity, superstition, Roman Catholicism, bodily incontinence, and sex. It carried in visual form the message

Figure 9. William Hogarth, detail of *Enthusiasm Delineated* (unpublished, *c.*1760–2). © The Trustees of the British Museum.

of George Lavington, the Bishop of Exeter, in his treatise *The Enthusiasm of Methodists and Papists Compared*, in which he stated that excesses of the spiritual and the carnal affections were often closely allied, and that some of 'the warmest and most enthusiastic pretenders to the love of God' entertained a violence of passion for their neighbours that was 'not quite so spiritual'.[31] A barometer in one corner of Hogarth's image, protruding from an excited 'Methodist's Brain' (in which art historians have perceived both male and female genital organs), measures the spiritual temperature of the congregation in terms including 'love', 'lust', 'ecstasy', 'convulsions', and 'madness'.[32] Here, Hogarth was saying, were people weeping like crazy, suffering, it would seem, from a kind of lachrymose nymphomania.

The playwright Samuel Foote, creator of the character 'Dr Squintum', the most famous spoof of George Whitefield, contrasted enthusiasm in divinity with enthusiasm in the arts. The former he described, in the same terms as Hogarth's print, as a kind of 'religious phrensy' that 'mistakes the dictates of an inflamed imagination, the vapours of a troubled brain' for the effects of divine inspiration. Artistic enthusiasm, on the other hand, was something quite different, involving 'that effort of genius, that glow of fancy, that ethereal fire' which transports the artist to a creative state of 'Promethean heat', which can be expressed through the literature of a Milton, the paintings of a Raphael, or 'the comic pencil of a Hogarth'.[33] Hogarth, like Foote, would have seen a world of difference between the frenzied tears of Whitefield and the tears represented and elicited by the ethereal fire burning in the eyes of *Sigismunda*. The reception of his painting, however, suggested it was not so easy to maintain this distinction. What was offered to the world as an emblem of dignified sensibility could be interpreted instead as an expression of feverish passion. For her detractors, *Sigismunda* embodied the wrong kind of enthusiasm.

In his will, William Hogarth stipulated that his wife was not to sell his prized painting for less than £500. As a result, *Sigismunda* remained unsold. The publisher John Boydell eventually purchased the work for much less, and displayed it in his Shakespeare Gallery in London, a fitting location for Hogarth's attempt to capture the power of a stage tragedy within the frame of an oil painting.[34] During the nineteenth century, *Sigismunda*'s fortunes improved, including finally fetching the price Hogarth had hoped for. In July 1807, *The Morning Post* reported that 'The celebrated Picture of Sigismunda was sold at Christie's, on Saturday last, for Four Hundred Guineas; a proof that the transcendent merit of our great Hogarth in this piece, is now justly viewed, free from the envy and malignity that once laboured to depreciate it.'[35] In 1870, the painting was included in an exhibition of 'Old Masters' at the Royal Academy in London, including works by both continental and British artists. Hogarth's *Sigismunda* was hung alongside works by Rubens and Rembrandt, da Vinci and Titian, as well as a domestic scene by Jean-Baptiste Greuze, and Sir Joshua Reynolds's portrait of the greatest producer of theatrical tears of the later eighteenth century, Mrs Sarah Siddons, depicted as the tragic muse. According to the reviewer in the *Pall Mall Gazette*, it was only Hogarth, among British painters, who had come close to emulating the methods and results of the great Italian masters, whose influence over artistic tastes he had so much decried. His *Sigismunda* may have been of a 'repulsive subject' and 'dramatically overstrained', but the reviewer thought that as a piece of painting it was direct, forceful, simple, and 'altogether masterly' in a way that had not been matched even by Reynolds or Gainsborough.[36]

Nine years later, *Sigismunda* was bequeathed to the nation, and was immediately put on display in the National Gallery. On Monday 2 June 1879, it was estimated that over 16,000 visitors were in the gallery, and the new Hogarth was the centre of attention.[37] A few years later, the art critic Lionel Johnson wrote of a recent experience at the National Gallery, which 'would have enraptured poor Hogarth'. Johnson had seen two men 'of rusty and ragged appearance' standing in front of *Sigismunda*. One said to the other, 'We've been through the whole show, and I say it's the best of the lot. Look at the woman's eyes!'[38]

7

The Man of Feeling

The Edinburgh lawyer and writer Henry Mackenzie's novel *The Man of Feeling*, featuring a sensitive hero named Harley who weeps in sympathy with beggars, prostitutes, orphans, and lunatics, was published in 1771, at the peak of a wave of literary sensibility.[1] It remains the most famously tear-soaked text not only of the sentimental genre, but in all of English literature. From the 1740s to the 1780s, sentimental novels like this were all the rage. Samuel Richardson, Laurence Sterne, Sarah Fielding, Fanny Burney, and others produced the goods for a growing literary marketplace, as increasing numbers of men and women acquired the means, education, and inclination to entertain and edify themselves with these portable narrative performances. For the first time, it was to works of prose fiction, as well as to religion, drama, and poetry, that people turned in large numbers in search of lachrymal exercise. Sentimental tales, sometimes presented in the form of a fictional correspondence or supposedly discovered fragments of manuscripts, could be read, and wept over, in solitude, or in semi-private groups of family and friends. This kind of reading and weeping was new, and became a recognized characteristic of eighteenth-century culture.[2] It was just one part of a world of moral weeping which extended from condemned criminals to their judges, chaplains, and executioners, and from philosophers, preachers, and philanthropists to prostitutes, forgers, highwaymen, and thieves.

One of *The Man of Feeling*'s most admiring readers was the poet Robert Burns, who was moved to tears by Shakespeare and the Bible, as we shall see, as well as by Mackenzie, and also on one notable occasion by a painting. While Greuze had painted a girl crying over a dead bird, and Hogarth a woman mourning her dead lover, other artists tried to fetch a tear with images of dead soldiers, often being mourned by a wife, a child, and sometimes, for good measure, a dog.[3] It was one such image that moved Robert Burns to tears in Edinburgh, during a social gathering in early 1787. The encounter, at the home of the recently retired Professor of Moral Philosophy, Adam Ferguson, was later recalled by Sir Walter Scott, at the time only a teenager.[4] Burns was in his late twenties, and apparently ill at ease: the 'heaven-taught ploughman' mixing with university-taught professors.[5] Burns's attention was taken, Scott wrote, by a print by Henry Bunbury entitled *Affliction*, 'representing a soldier lying dead in the snow, his dog sitting in misery on the one side, on the other his widow with a child in her arms'. Beneath this image were some lines by the clergyman-poet John Langhorne describing the woman:

> Bent o'er her babe, her eye dissolved in dew,
> The big drops, mingling with the milk he drew,
> Gave the sad presage of his future years,
> The child of misery baptized in tears.[6]

Burns was 'much affected' by the poem and Bunbury's print, 'or rather the ideas which it suggested to his mind'. Whatever the exact sentiments conjured up, their effects were observable on Burns's cheeks: 'He actually shed tears.'[7] A couple of years later, a high-art version of Bunbury's print was produced, also inspired by those lines from Langhorne, and with similar effects. This was an oil painting by Joseph Wright of Derby, entitled *The Dead Soldier*, displayed at the Royal Academy in 1789.[8] A friend of Wright's, William Hayley, wrote, 'I and all the lovers of painting with whom I have conversed, since my return to town, consider his pictures this year as the very flower of the Royal Exhibition. His dying soldier made me literally shed tears; his moon-light enchanted me.'[9]

Burns 'actually shed tears', Hayley 'literally shed tears'. Even in the era of sensibility and enthusiasm, it could be remarkable to be moved to tears—especially by a painting—and especially when the weeper was male. The idea that there was something feminine about tears was never entirely erased. This period produced no paintings that I know of depicting young men weeping over dead birds or deceased lovers (although James Barry did produce a painting of King Lear weeping over the body of Cordelia, in 1774).[10] But a more intense effort was now made, in both theory and practice, than had ever been exerted before, to produce and to praise the 'manly tear'—a phrase coined in a poem by Gilbert West in 1739, setting the tone for what was to come.[11] Henry Mackenzie's creation, Harley the man of feeling, became the archetypal producer of such tears, which were interpreted as signs of virtue, tenderness, and humanity.

Harley is a man of means, but not of the world. A fragmentary discovered manuscript narrates his various encounters with more worldly sorts, some of them virtuous but unfortunate, others downright criminal. They include a card-sharp, a misanthropic philosopher, a reformed prostitute and her father, and an old soldier with his orphaned grandchildren. When he can, Harley helps these people, bestowing gifts of money and property along with his trademark tears. Visiting Bedlam, he encounters a young woman from a good family whose lover, sent away by her father, has died. The effects of grief, combined with revulsion from the elderly man her father now proposes she should marry, have driven the young woman mad. Having heard her story, Harley gives it the 'tribute of some tears'. The woman responds, in language echoing earlier humoral theories of the body: 'I would weep too, but my brain is dry; and it burns, it burns, it burns!' The woman, wearing a ring given to her by her dead lover, wildly and plaintively holds her hand out to Harley; 'he pressed it between both of his, and bathed it with his tears.' Astonished and moved to pity by this woman's tale of woe, Harley gives a couple of guineas to the asylum keeper, saying, 'Be kind to that unfortunate.'[12] The episode concludes in the usual way: 'He burst into tears, and left them.' A later chapter, in which Harley grieves with the old soldier's grandchildren at their parents' grave, concludes with even more extravagant sensibility: 'The girl cried afresh; Harley kissed off her tears as they flowed, and wept between every kiss.'[13]

Modern readers, including academics whose job it is to make sense of the literature of the past, have found Harley pretty hard to take.[14] The most common response lies somewhere between embarrassment and mild disgust. But *The Man of Feeling* was one of the bestselling books of the 1770s, reprinted in dozens of editions in both Britain and America.[15] One reviewer declared that any reader 'who weeps not over some of the scenes it describes, has no sensibility of mind'.[16] It touched the families of prime ministers and tenant farmers alike. Lady Louisa Stuart, the daughter of the Earl of Bute, recalled *The Man of Feeling* arriving in her household, 'my mother and sister crying over it, dwelling upon it with rapture!' Stuart herself, only 14 and 'not yet versed in sentiment', had a 'secret dread I should not cry enough to gain the credit of proper sensibility'.[17] Robert Burns was only 12 when the book came out, but had already begun his education in both literature and sensibility. Three years earlier, Burns and his family had been visited in their farmhouse one evening by young Robert's tutor John Murdoch, who read to them from *Titus Andronicus*, which he had brought with him as a present, along with an English grammar. The tragedy dissolved the whole family into tears, and Robert was so distressed by the account of Lavinia's mutilation that he said that if Murdoch left the book, he would burn it. The tutor said he 'liked to see so much sensibility' in a young lad.[18]

Fifteen years later, during the lively meetings above a pub of a secret society, the Tarbolton Bachelors' Club, Burns engaged in thinking, drinking, and philosophizing about feeling. At this time he became a devoted reader of *The Man of Feeling*, carrying his copy around with him constantly, until it fell to pieces.[19] Burns wrote to Murdoch, the tutor who had made him cry with *Titus Andronicus*, that his favourite authors were now all 'of the sentimental kind', including Henry Mackenzie, Laurence Sterne, and the poet William Shenstone, and describing *The Man of Feeling* as 'a book I prize next to the Bible'. These sentimental works, he went on, were for him 'the glorious models after which I endeavour to form my own conduct'.[20] The manly tear signified both sensitivity to the world and a kind of sorrowful detachment from it. Recall that at the end of his encounter in the asylum, Harley burst into tears 'and left them'.

In France, Denis Diderot, in a tribute to the novels of Samuel Richardson, wrote, 'Come, fellow men and learn from him how to reconcile yourselves with the evils of this life. Come and we will weep together over the unfortunate characters in his fictions, and we shall say, "If fate strikes us down, at least honest folk will also weep for us." '[21] As the aspirations of Burns and Diderot to apply the lessons of sentimental literature to their own lives make plain, the manly tear was not confined to novels. The correspondence, memoirs, legal records, newspapers, sermons, and pamphlets of the period all bear witness to the new volume and visibility of male tears. Even the figure of the Stoic sage became a tearful sentimentalist, thanks to an essay by David Hume.[22] Novels such as *The Man of Feeling* were both mirrors and motors of changing codes of behaviour. Tears produced by philanthropists, politicians, condemned criminals, lawyers, judges, clergymen, audiences at executions, and on at least one occasion the executioner too, were the currency in a new economy of feeling. Tears flowed in the same old channels as money and power.

In theory, the manly tear was a gesture arising from a universal love of humanity, with radical egalitarian potential, as we shall see in Chapter 8. In reality, however, or at least in British reality, it tended to reinforce the existing paternalistic social order, with the wealthy giving tears along with charitable donations, and expecting tears of gratitude in return.[23] These wet transactions were meant to show how the social order was held together by bonds of affection. The resigned weeping of a sensitive but powerless figure like Harley was hardly a call to revolution. In *The Man of Feeling*, violent action, or indeed almost any action other than alms-giving, is rejected in favour of gentle teardrops. Despite the fact that Robert Burns sometimes aligned himself with the political radicals of the 1790s, his own social philosophy can be at least partially inferred from his tearful appreciation of this kind of writing. In 1790 Burns was moved to a flood of 'honest tears' by a story in Mackenzie's periodical *The Lounger* which romanticizes the enduring doglike affection of a servant for his high-handed master.[24] A few years earlier, Burns had got his mother's servant woman Elizabeth Paton pregnant (she later gave birth to a daughter), but without offering to marry her.[25] Burns was tried by the local church elders and forced to pay a fine. Burns described this in his poem 'The Fornicator': 'With rueful face and signs of grace, I pay'd the buttock-hire.' Burns probably later paid for his sexual incontinence with tears as well, especially when reading in *The Lounger* about 'the attachment and regard to which the faithful services of our domestics are entitled'.[26]

In *The Man of Feeling*, Harley encounters a penitent sexual fornicator, whose position was not entirely unlike that of Elizabeth Paton. The character Harley meets is a woman reduced to prostitution by a rakish seducer. Harley discerns virtue in the woman's tears and rewards her with money and by helping to reconcile her with her father, as well as with the obligatory shower of tears.[27] The figure of the penitent prostitute, and of Mary Magdalene, her moral and religious archetype, continued to provide occasions for tears beyond the realms of fiction. The Magdalen Hospital for Penitent Prostitutes had opened in London in 1758. One of its supporters, the merchant and philanthropist Jonas Hanway, wrote a tract arguing for the value of the institution on both economic and moral grounds. The hospital, Hanway thought, could also be a factory, making carpets for export to Persia and Turkey, while the women, once suitably reformed and married off, could become mothers to the next generation of workers, soldiers, and sailors. These economic benefits were to be arrived at via donations, which accompanied exchanges of tears. Hanway asked his readers, 'Can he, whose heart is not steeled to the impulse of humanity, forbear to sympathise in *tears of forgiveness*, with *tears of real repentance?*'[28] In a sermon about charitable institutions in 1762, during which orphaned charity-girls were arrayed before the congregation, John Langhorne—the author of the lines under the Bunbury print that moved Burns to tears—addressed the children directly: 'Yes, ye poor daughters of sorrow! born to no hope but the humanity of your fellow-creatures, your own miseries shall plead your cause—your own unhappy circumstances shall excite compassion in every *gentle* breast, shall call forth the tear from every *tender* eye, shall open every *generous* hand to contribute to your relief.' Tears could open wallets, so Langhorne invited his congregation to 'indulge the sweetest of all passions, *the tender delight of pity!*'[29] The memoirs of the eighteenth-century impersonator, beggar, and trickster Bampfylde Moore Carew similarly confirm that money flowed reliably when the tears of the beggar, the alms-giver, or ideally both, were in full stream.[30]

The flamboyant high-society clergyman William Dodd understood this too. Dodd was known as the 'macaroni parson'—a 'macaroni' being someone who had returned from their European travels devoted to all the latest continental fads and fashions. Dodd was the chaplain of the Magdalen Hospital, where he would display dozens of singing, sobbing, alluringly penitent ex-prostitutes as part of the Sunday service. According to Horace Walpole, Dodd preached 'entirely in the French style, and very eloquently and touchingly'. In a sermon to the president and governors of the Magdalen Hospital, Dodd asked his hearers to look at the lovely creatures before them, to imagine their previous sinful lives, to witness these women's 'flowing tears of penitence and remorse', and to feel delight in their own hearts. Dodd's performances achieved the desired results—tears and money.[31]

Those for whom doe-eyed orphan girls or prostitutes made good were not strong enough stuff could witness performances of even greater pathos and tearfulness by attending public hangings at Tyburn. The narrator of *The Man of Feeling* comments that in observing 'the effects of the stronger passions' we all become philosophers, and that 'it is perhaps amongst the spectators at Tyburn that the most genuine are to be found'.[32] Samuel Johnson's friend and biographer, the Scottish lawyer and writer James Boswell, made a particular habit of attending public executions, sometimes also meeting with the condemned just before they met their maker. For Boswell this was indeed an opportunity to experience and observe strong passions, most notably his own transports of terror and pity.[33]

Perhaps the only published genre that could rival either Methodist memoirs or sentimental novels for unremitting tearfulness was *The Ordinary of Newgate's Accounts*. These popular publications were moralistic potted biographies of criminals executed at Tyburn, written by successive holders of the post of prison chaplain (known as the 'Ordinary') at Newgate between the 1670s and the 1760s.[34] The courtroom and the scaffold had long provided opportunities for tears to be shed by prisoners, advocates, judges, juries, and onlookers. On one particularly dramatic occasion, after the failed Jacobite rising of 1745, even the executioner wept bitterly, asking for forgiveness, before decapitating the rebel Earl of Kilmarnock, whose gentlemanly and Christian demeanour 'drew Tears from thousands of the Spectators'.[35] Five years later it was the same executioner, John Thrift, who dispatched a notable figure, James MacLaine, a dandyish highwayman who had, according to the chaplain's account, shed many tears during his trial, inducing women in the public gallery to follow suit. MacLaine very courteously robbed Horace Walpole, among many others, and featured, in skeletal form, on the wall of the dissecting chamber, in the last of William Hogarth's admonitory series on *The Stages of Cruelty* in 1751.[36]

In general, the tears in the Newgate narratives fell into three categories: tears shed by convicts in fear of their death; tears of true penitence shed by condemned criminals as signs of a contrite heart, often accompanying a final confession of guilt; and tears of pity wept by those who witnessed the criminals' final moments. Only the first category were met with a measure of disapproval, and all these tears were interpreted within a Christian framework of sin, penitence, and the hope for divine forgiveness. During the seventeenth century, chaplains were more likely to impress upon convicts, in the proper Protestant spirit, the insufficiency of tears and sighs alone, as signs of true penitence, unless accompanied by an inward conversion.[37] These sorts of warnings became less frequent in the eighteenth century, and tears became a routinely expected part of the convict's final hours, to the extent that some of the condemned needed reassurance if they found themselves dry-eyed in the final moments. A highwayman called William Piggot, anxious to prove his repentance, told the Ordinary in 1721 that, although he was truly penitent, 'it was not easily in his Power to weep, nor had he ever remembered himself to shed a Tear; except once, since he was in the Condemned Hold at the final parting with his little Son.'[38]

For the most part, however, tears were produced as expected and desired. On 28 April 1760, Robert Tilling, a 23-year-old domestic servant from the north-east of England, was hanged for robbing his master. Tilling was visited by Methodists in the days before his execution, one of whom subsequently preached and published a sermon on the 'remarkable conversion' of Tilling to Methodism. He reported that he had found Tilling 'in a very spiritual and sweet Frame; quite broken in Spirit and melted into Tears' while meditating on the words of John's Gospel.[39]

The Ordinary's account of Tilling's execution ends by noting, with a touch of disapproval, that immediately before he was hanged, Tilling, now behaving as a true Methodist, 'prayed in the hearing of the people with a loud voice for about twenty minutes', telling his listeners, as part of a prophetic oration urging repentance, 'My dear brethren, I could weep over you with a flood of tears, as our Lord wept over Jerusalem.'[40] A few years later, the condemned men were Jonathan Dennison, aged 26, and John Swift, a young lad of barely 15. Both were both hanged for offences of theft. Young Swift's distraught father was 'weeping and wringing his hands', while his son 'returned tear for tear'. The Ordinary recounted that 'the multitude were greatly affected at the sight, many turned away and dropt a tear, unable to bear the sight with a dry unconcern'. The teenage boy tried to give a speech warning others to 'take warning by him', and to keep the commandments and obey their parents, 'but was at a loss for words, and broke afresh into tears'.[41] This scene would not have been out of place in a sentimental novel. Events at Tyburn were seen through the dewy eyes of sensibility.

The most sensational and sentimental of all these scenes at Tyburn occurred in 1777 when the two condemned malefactors were a young man called Joseph Harris who had held up the Islington coach, robbing a gentleman of two guineas and seven shillings, and a clergyman convicted of forging a bill of exchange, purportedly from the Earl of Chesterfield, for over £4,000. Harris and his stricken father exchanged agonized tears in much the same manner as John Swift and his father in 1763. The clergyman was none other than the macaroni parson, Dr William Dodd, whose voluptuous lifestyle had finally caught up with him. During his final days Dodd asked to be visited by the Methodist leader John Wesley. The Newgate chaplain recorded much praying and weeping. On his final morning, Dodd's composure was remarked upon and observers at both Newgate and Tyburn were moved to tears by his plight and his religious exhortations. Very large numbers saw Dodd's ending, and many wept, perhaps thousands of people, although it may have been hard to tell whose cheeks were wet with tears and whose with rain, as there was a downpour just before Dodd and Harris were hanged. Dodd apparently expressed the wish that the reformed prostitutes from the Magdalen Hospital could have been there to sing the twenty-third Psalm.[42]

Some have suggested that the tears of sentimental novels like *The Man of Feeling*, and of the cult of sensibility in general, expressed a new, secular social philosophy of the kind set out by great figures of the Scottish Enlightenment such as David Hume and Adam Smith, who placed great emphasis on the roles of sympathy and the moral sentiments. One study of eighteenth-century sensibility explains it as the product of a 'popular demand for a new set of ideas with which to account for human nature and order society, beyond the explanations given by Christian dogma'.[43] When Robert Burns shed his tears on the carpet of Adam Ferguson's drawing room in 1787, he was indeed weeping in the company of the associates and intellectual successors of Hume and Smith. And yet we should recall Burns's comment that *The Man of Feeling* was a book that he prized 'next to the Bible', another repository of disconnected and tearful narratives and parables.

The whole gestural vocabulary of weeping, kissing, and falling on each other's necks, characteristic of Mackenzie's writing, has biblical sources, including the reconciliations between Jacob and Esau, and especially that between Joseph and his brothers in the book of Genesis, which moved James Boswell to tears when he read it: 'And he fell upon his brother Benjamin's neck and wept, and Benjamin wept upon his neck. Moreover, he kissed all his brethren, and wept upon them.'[44] And of course there are New Testament parallels too, including the tears of Peter, and of Mary Magdalene, which are alluded to in *The Man of Feeling*. The whole book could be summarized as embodying St Paul's injunction to 'weep with them that weep'. Mackenzie and Burns were purveyors of a melancholy, biblical, sorrowful kind of enthusiasm, and a faith that the power of God, rather than political or economic forces, would ultimately wipe away all tears.[45]

The highest model for the manly tear was the divine example of Jesus, whose tears were preached upon with greatly increased frequency during the eighteenth century as part of an argument against Stoicism and in favour of humanity and tenderness.[46] Jesus' tears over the grave of Lazarus had previously been an awkward topic for Protestant preachers. John Donne was highly unusual among seventeenth-century Anglican clergy, perhaps unique, in preaching on the text 'Jesus wept' (John 11: 35).[47] The idea that Jesus could be subject to the power of human passions, and even worse that he might blubber and howl over a dead body, like a Catholic, was an unwelcome one. But this changed during the eighteenth century. From Richard Steele's *Christian Hero* in 1701 to the writings of the clergyman, headmaster, and prolific essayist Vicesimus Knox in the 1780s and 1790s, there was a consensus that the tears of Jesus, both over Lazarus and over Jerusalem, were marks of tenderness and compassion which should be seen as a divine pattern for those who would imitate Christ. This was the view of Henry Mackenzie, who wrote a story contrasting a tearful clergyman, unashamed of his feelings, with an insensible philosopher modelled on David Hume.[48] Jesus wept, it was agreed, not only out of pity for the family of his friend Lazarus, but also in sorrow at the depraved state of humanity, and the reign of death brought about through the Fall.[49] The conclusion, as Vicesimus Knox would put it, was that Providence intended the lachrymal glands for use: 'Jesus himself wept and thus for ever hallowed the briny fountain.'[50] There was even a sermon preached to King George III on the subject, early in his reign in 1762, by William Mason, who preached that the 'sacred fountains' of Christ's tears were not of private grief, but 'generous, social, sympathetic tears'.[51] The message was clear: Jesus of Nazareth was the original man of feeling.

8

The French Revolution

Three moments in British history contributed more than any others to the idea that tears were something foreign to these islands. The first was the Reformation, which bequeathed to us the idea that religious sobbing, especially at funerals, was sensual, self-indulgent, blasphemous, and Catholic.[1] We shall see in later chapters that the third and final factor was the process of building a global empire in the nineteenth century, during which religious, military, and scientific forces combined to distinguish the tearless Brits from their primitive subjects.[2] The second of the three moments, coming between the ages of Reformation and empire, was an event that marked the beginning of the end for the age of 'enthusiasm': the French Revolution. The violence and tragedies of the French Revolution elicited tearful reactions of sensibility and pity among its most prominent British commentators. Of these, the tears shed by the radical feminist and revolutionary sympathizer Mary Wollstonecraft in Paris in 1792, when she witnessed Louis XVI on the way to his trial for treason, are among the most interesting. But before we can understand them, there are several elements in the historical, political, and cultural drama that need to be explained.

The French Revolution was a major event in British history. It led to a quarter-century of warfare between Britain and France, ending with Wellington's defeat of Napoleon at Waterloo in 1815. This period of military struggle against a country with revolutionary, then imperialistic ambitions, underpinned by a mixture of its old Catholic faith and a terrifying cult of Reason, all attached to a culture of sentimentalism and violent political passion, provided ample materials for a newly intense bout of anti-French feeling, with lasting effects. The perceived differences between British and French ideals were crudely summed up in an image entitled 'The Contrast, 1792: Which is Best?' by Thomas Rowlandson, identifying Britain with religion, morality, lawfulness, industry, and happiness, while the French Revolution involved atheism, anarchy, equality, madness, idleness, and misery. Note that the dangerous notion of 'equality' was on the mad, miserable French side of the comparison.[3]

In terms of British politics, sympathy with or antipathy to the ideals and outcomes of the revolution became a touchstone of opinion during the 1790s, with radicals who supported the new concepts of human rights and democracy coming under increasing pressure as events in France took turns for the worse, and even worse.[4] The fall of the Bastille in July 1789 and the freeing of the political prisoners it held, followed by the declaration of the rights of man by the new government, had promised to inaugurate an era of enlightened constitutional government. But it soon became clear that the revolution had unleashed more than just a lot of lofty ideals. With those ideals came bloodthirsty violence directed against the property and persons of the aristocratic *ancien régime*. With aristocrats and clergymen hanging from lamp-posts in Paris, the government became increasingly authoritarian. The guillotine accounted for the dispatch of many and various enemies of the revolution, numbered in their thousands, with ever greater rationality and efficiency. The bloody 'Reign of Terror' overseen by Maximilien Robespierre during 1793 and 1794 extinguished any remaining embers of sympathy for the revolution glowing in the hearts of most British radicals. The victims of the guillotine included not only the king and queen, Louis XVI and Marie Antoinette, but ultimately Robespierre himself.[5]

Who would not weep at such a spectacle, especially in the age of sensibility? Many did, on both sides of the political debate, but the problem was that the culture and style of sensibility was fast going out of fashion and, in many quarters, even being blamed for the French Revolution itself.[6] During this period the idea emerged, among anti-sentimentalists, that to shed tears of sympathy for the suffering of others was not only potentially childish and effeminate, but that it was something foreign too. As one commentator put it, crying was a dangerous fashion that had been imported from the French.[7] But how did the literature of sensibility get connected with Robespierre's bloody regime? How could consuming soppy novels and saccharine paintings be supposed to lead to the mass killing of aristocrats and the tearing down of all the traditions of Church and state?

This connection was made, at the time and subsequently, in terms of a shared intellectual parentage. The cult of sensibility and the French Revolution were portrayed as siblings, the bastard offspring of Jean-Jacques Rousseau. The radical Genevan philosopher's name became synonymous with a worldview of sentiment, romanticism, and natural rights.[8] This 'new morality', alleged to have provided the form and fabric of guillotines and cambric handkerchiefs alike, elevated sympathetic feeling with the sufferings of others above all other virtues, including obedience, rationality, reflection, and restraint. This philosophy taught that sympathetic feeling was something natural, an inborn virtue in all men and women. Robespierre, in a speech delivered at the height of the Terror, endorsed these ideas. He spoke of virtue as a 'natural passion', something that could be testified to equally by all 'feeling and pure souls'. Virtue was that 'tender, irresistible, imperious passion, torment, and delight of magnanimous hearts, that profound horror of tyranny, that compassionate zeal for the oppressed', which extended also to a love for one's country and a 'sublime and sacred love for humanity'. 'You feel it at this moment burning in your souls,' Robespierre told the members of the French assembly, 'I feel it in mine'.[9]

The endorsement of the new philosophy of feeling by a figure such as Robespierre, who was to become the arch-villain of subsequent accounts of the revolution, tainted the whole movement. Critics could now point to France as a practical demonstration of what they had been arguing for some decades: that a philosophy of feeling and sympathy, while it might sound very pious, could not, on its own, lead to a balanced and just political system. It was a dangerously subjective, emotive philosophy. Who was to say exactly which feelings were to be trusted? While Robespierre thought he felt virtue burning in his soul, others suspected otherwise. For Thomas Carlyle, looking back some decades later, this revolutionary feeling was identified with something more sinister, yet equally intangible. 'It is the Madness that dwells in the hearts of men. In this man it is, and in that man; as a rage or as a terror, it is in all men.'[10] Seen in this light, the culture of sensibility, with its sympathetic beggars, penitent prostitutes, and dying animals, no longer seemed such a harmless form of moral schooling for nice young ladies and men of feeling. Instead, here was a pathway to a disordered morality of unrestrained passions and political anarchy. The rivers of tears which had flowed through the literature of sensibility had now become the rivers of blood which flowed out of the French Revolution. A Victorian edition of Henry Mackenzie's *Man of Feeling* included a satirical 'Index to Tears (Chokings, etc., not counted)', which ran to forty-seven cases, inviting readers to laugh rather than cry over the book. The introduction described the novel as a rehearsal of the 'false sentiment', borrowed from Rousseau, which had led directly to the revolution. This was a decidedly French book, to be disowned and laughed at by later generations of British readers. Although it should be added that the publishers of that 1886 edition included in the endpapers an advertisement for cambric handkerchiefs, just in case.[11]

The follies of sensibility were encapsulated, for its critics, in the excessive displays of feeling bestowed upon patently unworthy recipients,

including paupers, drunkards, lunatics, criminals, democratic revolutionaries, philosophers, and dumb brutes. The image of a young woman
weeping over an ailing or deceased animal, especially a lap-dog or pet
bird, once the acme of sentimental refinement, became an icon of a
deranged morality. Sterne's *Sentimental Journey* had included a famous
scene of mourning over a dead donkey, which now became infamous.[12]
Connecting this episode to broader cultural and intellectual currents, one
twentieth-century critic memorably pronounced in all earnestness: 'The
opposition between neo-classicist and Rousseauist is indeed symbolized
in a fashion by their respective attitude towards the ass.'[13] The most
famous symbol of the zoophilic sympathy of the period was, of course,
a French production that we have already encountered: Greuze's girl
weeping over a dead bird. This painting embodied all the components of
the cult of sensibility and its associated morality: the idealization of the
feminine and the sentimental, the exploration of affectionate connections
between humanity and the natural world, and the hint of something
deeper, darker, and more passionate.[14]

At the centre of the British debate about the French Revolution was the
philosopher and politician Edmund Burke. Burke's political sympathies
in the 1770s had been progressive and liberal, supporting the Americans
in their war for independence from British rule. His friends and allies
included the Whig opposition leader Charles James Fox. Burke and Fox
were to be divided permanently, however, by their differences over the
French Revolution. Tears were shed on all sides of the British debate
about the revolution: by Burke as he wrote his famous treatise on
the subject, by Fox on the floor of the House of Commons, and by
Wollstonecraft in Paris in 1792. Although all the participants in this
debate were steeped in the sensibility of their upbringing, all could see
that the tide had turned against this kind of display. So they found
themselves attacking each other for shedding the wrong kind of tears,
in the wrong way, in response to the wrong people and events. The most

influential political figures of the period thus tried, but generally failed, to disown their disreputable sentimental sides.

Burke's *Reflections on the Revolution in France*, published in 1790 at a time when the excesses of the revolution, including the executions of the king and queen, were still some way off, nonetheless denounced the revolution's tendency to mob-rule, and warned of worse to come. The unfolding of events in the following years lent an air of prescience and authority to Burke's pronouncements, but when they were published they seemed unduly pessimistic. They also displayed an excessive sympathy with the French royal family and the associated aristocratic hierarchies and traditions. In a famous passage, Burke recalled his experience of setting eyes on Marie Antoinette in the 1770s, before she was queen: there 'surely never lighted on this orb, which she hardly seemed to touch, a more delightful vision'. Marie Antoinette had been 'glittering like the morning star, full of life, and splendour, and joy'. Burke contrasted this vision of royal loveliness with the spectacle of an armed and ugly Parisian mob dragging the queen and king back from Versailles to their residence in Paris in October 1789. 'Oh! What a revolution!' Burke exclaimed, 'and what a heart must I have, to contemplate without emotion that elevation and that fall!' Burke wrote that he would have thought a nation of honourable men would leap to the queen's defence. 'But the age of chivalry is gone,' he lamented, replaced by an age of rational economists and calculators: 'Never, never more, shall we behold that generous loyalty to rank and sex, that proud submission, that dignified obedience, that subordination of the heart' which characterized true freedom, true 'manly sentiment', and 'chastity of honour'.[15]

Critics and satirists pounced on Burke's eulogy of Marie Antoinette and his nostalgia for chivalry. This was mere 'stuff'; it was affected and sentimental 'foppery'. Burke replied, in one private letter, that the passage was sincere, and that the contrast between the queen's former splendour and her current humiliation had indeed drawn genuine tears from him as he wrote, which had 'wetted my paper'.[16] Radical replies were forthcoming while Burke's tears were still wet on the page. Mary Wollstonecraft lambasted him for weeping over the queen while caring nothing for the plight of the sick, the poor, and the enslaved: 'Such misery demands more than tears—I pause to recollect myself, and smother the contempt I feel rising for your rhetorical flourishes and infantine sensibility.'[17] The bestselling revolutionary firebrand Tom Paine wrote in similar terms, accusing Burke of conjuring up theatrical scenes to produce 'through the weakness of sympathy, a weeping effect'. In weeping over royalty, while forgetting the victims of their absolute power, 'He pities the plumage, but forgets the dying bird.'[18] Burke was crying in the wrong way over the wrong objects; for deposed rulers rather than oppressed peoples. The radicals agreed that to shed these tears over royalty was to display an unnatural and perverted sensibility; these were the kind of tears shed by a degenerate European aristocracy, whose passing Burke mourned, and whose effete, sexually ambiguous, and insincere kissing and weeping was lampooned by a 1790 cartoon by Isaac Cruikshank satirizing Louis XVI's affected new-found love of his people, one of whom declares, 'I'll furnish tears to drown the king.'[19]

Burke's hostility to the French Revolution and its British supporters also gave rise to the most dramatic tearful episode ever to unfold on the floor of the House of Commons. On 6 May 1791, during a dull late-night debate about the administration of government in the British territory of Quebec, Edmund Burke took the opportunity to pass comment on the perversion of principles evident in the government of France, and to ridicule those in Britain, including his colleague Charles James Fox, who had held up the revolution as a monument to human wisdom. Fox was distraught to find himself denounced and deserted by his friend and mentor. Newspapers the next day reported that Fox, in responding to Burke, 'suddenly burst into tears' and, speaking with difficulty 'in a strain of sublime pathos', said that he would not so easily give up on a friendship of twenty-five years.[20] Many reports of the incident were admiring of Fox's display, interpreting his tears as signs of goodness of heart and strength of personal attachment. But this weeping Whig was also a gift for satirists. One visual artist, William Dent, showed Fox crying like a baby who had lost his father.[21] Isaac Cruikshank had Fox weeping so copiously that a boy with a bucket, himself moved to tears, was needed to try to mop up the spillage, while Fox declared, 'Ah well a day my poor heart will almost Break. 25 years Friendship & use me thus. Oh–Oh– Edmund–!!!' (Figure 10).[22] Several newspapers carried a satirical squib entitled 'How to Cry!' purportedly by a junior MP seeking advice on the most apt moments and methods for the deployment of parliamentary sobs as a technique for passing legislation. The author wrote: 'I conceive, Sir, and almost with tears in my eyes, that this crying fashion has been

Figure 10. Isaac Cruikshank, *The Wrangling Friends, or Opposition in Disorder* (1791). © The Trustees of the British Museum.

imported from the French, who, in this whole business of the Revolution, have shown themselves great masters of stage effect.'[23]

So, was this the wrong kind of crying too? While Burke's tears allegedly displayed unnatural sympathies for a degenerate aristocracy, Fox's were described as babyish and affected—a mere French fashion. Even though there were tears on all sides of this debate, it was certainly Fox and the revolutionary sympathizers who appeared more inclined to tearful responses and who ultimately became associated with all that was wrong with tearful, French sensibility. Major John Cartwright, a veteran campaigner for parliamentary reform in Britain, wrote that in seeing 'many millions of my fellow creatures suddenly redeemed from a cruel servitude', by the events of the French Revolution, 'my heart leaped with joy, and the tear of ecstatic gratitude to the Disposer of events, glistened in my eye'.[24] By 1798 the association between sensibility and revolution had become entrenched. Another Cruikshank image, this time marking the triumph of Nelson over Napoleon in the naval Battle of the Nile that year, showed Fox as a crocodile, wearing a revolutionary cockade, shedding tears for the French.[25] In the same year, James Gillray produced a complex allegorical image to accompany a poem in the *Anti-Jacobin* entitled 'New Morality'. The poem mocked the 'child of nature' who had been taught by Rousseau to weep first for the 'crush'd beetle' and 'the widow'd dove'; secondly for the sufferings of the guilty; and only finally for family, friends, king, and country. Gillray's illustration depicted 'Sensibility' as one of the three unappealing muses of the revolutionaries, weeping, as ever, over a dead bird.[26]

Although there is ample evidence that the manly tear was still widely shed, in public as well as private, and often approved of, weeping was regularly depicted as a feminine, as well as a foreign, activity. That tears were potentially effeminate had been a standard view for centuries, and with the discrediting of male sensibility, it came to the fore again. Women had been the primary audience for novels of sensibility. In visual representations, the figure of sensibility was always female.[27] The char-acterization of women as soft and snivelling sentimentalists, moved to tears by dead birds but clueless about proper politics, was becoming one of the most powerful tools for their cultural and political exclusion. It had long been alleged that women could produce tears at will in order to manipulate men. The shock expressed by the novelist Fanny Burney when she witnessed her friend Sophy Streatfield producing tears on command on one occasion in 1779, however, suggests it was far from a common ability. Burney observed that Streatfield's face was not con-torted or 'blubbered' but remained 'smooth and elegant' and that 'she was smiling all the time' as the tears rolled down her cheeks. Another woman present at this impromptu performance thought that Streatfield's 'tearful eyes, and alluring looks' along with her beauty and 'softness', would 'insinuate her into the heart of any man she thought worth attacking'.[28]

It was against this background that Mary Wollstonecraft took up her pen in the 1790s to launch her career as a political polemicist through her response to Burke in 1790, *A Vindication of the Rights of Men*, and the next year her most famous work, one of the founding texts of feminism, *A Vindication of the Rights of Woman*. Mary Wollstonecraft had a mixed relationship with sentiment and sensibility during her short career as an author. Her own early publications included fiction that was sentimental in genre, albeit unconventionally so. In 1789 she produced, under a male pseudonym, 'Mr Cresswick, Teacher of Elocution', an educational anthology of literary extracts: *The Female Reader: or, Miscellaneous Pieces in Prose and Verse, Selected from the Best Writers, and Disposed Under Proper Heads, for the Improvement of Young Women*. The selections for this improving work include sentimental stories by authors such as Henry Mackenzie, along with poems, extracts from conduct books, and all the most tearful biblical stories, including the reconciliation of Joseph with his brothers (featuring much kissing and crying), Jesus' tears over the grave of Lazarus, and St Paul's lachrymose departure from his friends in the book of Acts. This was a veritable handbook of religious and moral weeping. It seemed that young women were to be improved primarily via the exercise of their lachrymal glands, and that they were to learn, like Robert Burns, to prize sentimental literature 'next to the Bible'.[29]

But this educational pot-boiler did not reveal the true voice of Mary Wollstonecraft as it was to emerge in her influential political writings. It was a very different Wollstonecraft who chided Burke for his tears and his 'infantine sensibility', and who mercilessly denounced her fellow women for allowing themselves to be reduced to the sentimental, coquettish, ornamental playthings of men. She would have hated Sophy Streatfield's party trick. Wollstonecraft's exhortation to womankind was to become more masculine; to develop in themselves the powers of reason; and to instil in themselves and their daughters rational virtue and virile restraint rather than weakness and sensibility.[30] Wollstonecraft was as fierce as any critic of the philosophy of feeling in denouncing the fine lady 'who sheds tears for the bird starved in a snare' and who 'takes her dogs to bed, and nurses them with a parade of sensibility', while neglecting her children and maltreating her servants.[31] Wollstonecraft's writings after 1789 reveal her awareness of the need for radicals to distance themselves from the discredited culture of sensibility. Samuel Taylor Coleridge, similarly, attacked the 'effeminate and cowardly selfishness of sensibility' as exemplified by the weeping female reader: 'She sips a beverage sweetened with human blood, even while she is weeping over the refined sorrows of Werther and Clementina.'[32] It was as an exponent of a bracing moral rationalism and a defender of the equal political rights of all men and women that Mary Wollstonecraft arrived alone in Paris, a successful 33-year-old author and single woman, to witness the unfolding of the revolution at first hand.[33]

Wollstonecraft's letters at this time include an account of one of her most vivid experiences, shortly after her arrival in France. The date was

26 December 1792. Wollstonecraft caught a glimpse of Louis XVI in his carriage being taken to his trial for treason; a trial which would lead to his execution early the following year. She wrote to her friend and publisher Joseph Johnson of what she saw:

> About nine o'clock this morning, the king passed by my window, moving silently along (excepting now and then a few strokes of the drum, which rendered the stillness more awful) through empty streets, surrounded by the national guards, who, clustering round the carriage, seemed to deserve their name. The inhabitants flocked to their windows, but the casements were all shut, not a voice was heard, nor did I see any thing like an insulting gesture.—For the first time since I entered France, I bowed to the majesty of the people, and respected the propriety of behaviour so perfectly in unison with my own feelings.

The terrible stillness, the deathly thud of the drum, like a heartbeat about to be stopped, the mute Parisians surging forward but contained, for the moment, silently, by their windows: this, Wollstonecraft wrote, was in unison with her feelings, themselves held back within their bounds like the majestic people of Paris. But the containment was temporary:

> I can scarcely tell you why, but an association of ideas made the tears flow insensibly from my eyes, when I saw Louis sitting, with more dignity than I expected from his character, in a hackney coach going to meet death, where so many of his race have triumphed. My fancy instantly brought Louis XIV before me, entering the capital with all his pomp, after one of the victories most flattering to his pride, only to see the sunshine of prosperity overshadowed by the sublime gloom of misery.[34]

That night she could not sleep, tormented by images of staring eyes and bloody hands. No wonder Mary Wollstonecraft was perplexed. The radical scourge of the 'infantine' Burke, the rational woman who mocked the hypocrisy of fine ladies, was now weeping herself over yet another dying bird: the French monarchy in the person of Louis XVI. Always a thinker, Wollstonecraft tried to interpret the tears as they dried on her cheeks. The tears were produced not by mere feelings but by 'ideas'; they did not reveal sensibility but flowed 'insensibly'. Nonetheless, the historical narrative which gripped Mary Wollstonecraft that morning and, in a way that she could not explain, squeezed tears out of her, was exactly that which had filled the eyes and wetted the paper of Edmund Burke as he wrote his panegyric to the fallen splendour of the French royal family two years before.

On all sides of the French Revolution debate, then, people attacked their political opponents for producing the wrong kind of tears: unnatural, artificial, perverse. Yet still, they wept. For future generations, weeping was now tainted: an activity for effeminate foreigners, conjuring up sentimental pictures of dead birds on the one hand, and bloody images of dead Frenchmen on the other. And many who still wanted to weep would, like Mary Wollstonecraft, reinterpret the activity as the end-point of a train of ideas rather than feelings. As her fellow radical William Blake would write in a poem in the early years of the next century, 'A tear is an intellectual thing.'[35]

One version of the transition from sensibility via revolution to restraint can be traced through the career of Helen Maria Williams. Williams's own weeping 'at a tale of distress' had inspired a Wordsworth sonnet in 1787.[36] Three years later, she wept over the glories of the French Revolution, as she described the 'sublime spectacle' of the festival of federation in her *Letters written in France in the Summer of 1790*. Williams reported that crowds of women held up their infants in their arms and 'melting into tears, promised to make their children imbibe, from their earliest age, an inviolable attachment to the principles of the new constitution'. Williams herself was not indifferent to this spectacle: 'I acknowledge that my heart caught with enthusiasm the general sympathy; my eyes were filled with tears; and I shall never forget the sensations of that day.'[37] Two years on from her first revolutionary enthusiasm, in a second volume of *Letters from France*, Williams was no longer captivated by a feeling of common humanity with the French. Now she perceived an important difference in national manners:

> You will see Frenchmen bathed in tears at a tragedy. An Englishman has quite as much sensibility to a generous or tender sentiment; but he thinks it would be unmanly to weep; and, though half choaked with emotion, he scorns to be overcome, contrives to gain the victory over his feelings, and throws into his countenance as much apathy as he can well wish.

Williams concluded that 'We seem to have a strange dread in England of indulging any kind of enthusiasm.'[38] The idea of 'national character' would not have its heyday until the nineteenth and twentieth centuries, but there are hints, like this one, of developing beliefs about the emotional styles of different nations during the eighteenth century, and specifically about the inexpressiveness of the English. In 1759, for instance, the Scottish philosopher and economist Adam Smith contrasted the 'emotion and vivacity' of the French and Italians with the phlegmatic Englishman who, 'having been educated among a people of duller sensibility', was less likely to indulge in 'passionate behaviour' such as public weeping. Smith wrote at a time when the sentimental vogue had started to make itself felt on British shores, and he himself approved of the trend. Smith preferred frank and sincere Europeans, who gave expression to their natural feelings, to those he described as the deceitful and barbaric 'savage nations' who 'smother and conceal the appearance of every passion'.[39] Smith would not have approved of the feigned apathy of Williams's English theatre-goer.

So, while Helen Maria Williams was not the first to suggest a contrast between British dullness and continental extravagance in the matter of emotional expression, her observation in 1792 was a milestone nonetheless. It is the earliest statement I have found identifying the repression of tears and the active masking of feeling, rather than a more general quality of phlegmatic dullness, as a national characteristic among Englishmen.

It is no coincidence that it came in the immediate aftermath of the French Revolution, by way of contrast with the uncontained French, and at a moment of backlash against the culture of sensibility, nor that it concerned the appropriate response to tragedy. The British were gradually learning their lesson: unchecked tears of sorrow and compassion could lead to madness, as they had for Titus Andronicus, or to bloody terror, as they had for the French.

In this way, the revolution in French politics led to a discernible shift, if not something as foreign as a revolution, in British manners. The fifty years leading up to 1789 had witnessed the undoubted heyday of British tears, generously dispensed in religious, artistic, moral, and political arenas. In the eighteenth century, weeping had been much more than what it would later become, for some, a mere 'expression of emotion'. It was a moral and religious activity; something to be cultivated, tutored, practised, learned, performed. To shed a tear could signify the violent and sudden transition of one's soul from one state to another; it could be an act of lamentation over the sins of the world and the reign of death; or it could be a token, tendered in sympathy and compassion, for the sufferings of another. In all these cases, tears in the eighteenth century had about them a suggestion of enthusiasm; they could be signs of feeling, of fervour, even of fanaticism. For most of the century, in Britain, the admirable warmth and humanity discerned in the act of weeping seemed to outweigh the anxiety that a shower of tears could signal the beginning of a torrent of unrestrained passion. As we have seen, that changed during the final decade of the century, as British political writers sought to distance themselves from the French fashion for tears, sensibility, and revolution. However, it would still be nearly another century before the 'stiff upper lip' mentality would take shape and take hold. There was plenty of Georgian and Victorian pathos to live through before then. It was not yet time to throw out the cambric handkerchiefs.

III. PATHOS

9

The Sanity of George III

George III lost his head less literally than Louis XVI, but it was still enough to trigger a constitutional crisis. A mad monarch, as Shakespeare had realized, would threaten the stability of any realm. But after some weeks of mental derangement, the British king suddenly and unexpectedly returned to sanity in 1789. That transition was marked by a flow of fatherly tears, reported to parliament as evidence of the reappearance of the royal mind. This episode of tearful sanity, in the middle of George III's long reign (1760–1820), illuminates changing ideas about the mind and body, reason and emotion. In medical texts of the period, the relationship between human and animal minds was reassessed. Our modern 'emotions' emerged in this context—a new kind of mental state, discussed by physicians and philosophers alongside older categories of feeling like 'passions', 'affections', or 'sentiments'. In short, science and medicine took on a new-found authority, not only to manage the royal body but also to rename the common mind. This transitional era in the history of British attitudes to weeping—after the reign of sensibility but before that of the stiff upper lip—was an age of pathos, peopled by Romantic poets, earnest intellectuals, devoted parents, and tearful ceremonials. The age of pathos was a time for second thoughts about tears, and—with Ireland becoming part of the United Kingdom, and a German dynasty continuing to occupy the throne—a time in which ideas about nationality played an increasingly important role.

The mind and body of the head of state are symbolic and sensitive things. Medical reports on the British royal family are, to this day, either kept secret or only carefully and very partially published. When Diana, Princess of Wales, seemed repeatedly and publicly to be on the verge of a mental breakdown in the 1980s and 1990s, this was national news, or at least national tabloid gossip.[1] Such matters were even more consequential 200 years earlier, on the eve of the French Revolution. The monarch, that embodiment of the nation and head of the body politic, was expected to govern through the two highest, God-given powers of the human mind: reason and will. The king's actions must be rational and voluntary. The idea of a mad king—a king not in command of his faculties, not in possession of his reason, not in control of his actions— was an unnatural and dangerous thing. Shakespeare had imagined it in *King Lear*. In November 1788, it became an alarming reality in the person of King George.

At the royal palace at Kew, the king was delusional and raving. Queen Charlotte, despairing of the royal physicians, sent for the formidable Dr Francis Willis, keeper of a mad-house in Lincolnshire, said to have a 'peculiar skill and practice in intellectual maladies'. In the first encounter between mad-doctor and monarch, the king seemed to have at least some of his wits about him. Noticing Dr Willis's clerical attire, the king asked whether he was in the employment of the Church. Willis replied that he had been formerly but now 'attended chiefly to physick'. King George responded, with agitation, 'You have quitted a profession I have always loved, & You have Embraced one I most heartily detest.' Not solely on the basis of this put-down, Dr Willis concluded that the king's ideas were deranged and that he would require constant management. Around the same time, the Prince of Wales wrote to his brother that their father had suffered 'a total loss of all rationality' and was now 'a compleat lunatick'.[2] The arrival of Willis, his son, also a physician, and their entourage of assistants in the midst of the royal household at Kew and, especially, the other royal physicians led to weeks of jealousies, conflicts, and contested diagnoses and treatments. Willis insisted on complete authority over who had access to the king, and relied upon methods of physical restraint, sometimes using a restraining-chair, sometimes a strait-waistcoat, combined with a quasi-mesmeric technique of commanding the king's submission with his gaze. This whole astonishing episode has been documented by historians of medicine and brilliantly dramatized in Alan Bennett's 1992 play *The Madness of George III*, and the film based on it.[3]

In January, a period of regency seemed likely to become a necessity, as politicians, including Edmund Burke, Charles James Fox, and William Pitt, debated whether a man who could not govern his own passions was fit to govern the nation.[4] A parliamentary Select Committee interviewed Francis Willis and the other physicians, over a period of six days, to ascertain the prospects of his majesty recovering sufficiently to retake the reins of government. The exchanges were published in full by order of parliament, as well as in various commercial editions, and in the daily press.[5] Almost the entirety of *The Times* for 16 January 1789, for example, was taken up with extended extracts from 'The Examination of the King's Physicians', focusing especially on what Willis had to say. Passions, affections, and emotions were prominent in Willis's medical reports. He justified excluding others from seeing the king on the grounds that the unexpected appearance of physicians or family members might 'excite troublesome emotions' which could 'retard the cure of the patient'. Willis made much of the king's recently recovered ability to read literature and make intelligent comments upon what he had read (although he was taken to task by the committee for having allowed the king, inadvertently it seems, to get his hands on a copy of the uncomfortably apposite *King Lear*).[6] All parties to the discussion agreed that recovery would be indicated by further signs that 'the understanding is strengthened' and that His Majesty's 'frequent gusts of passion', brought on by contradiction or irritation, were becoming less frequent and shorter in duration.

In answer to another question, Willis spoke of the great benefit His Majesty had enjoyed from being allowed to see his wife and children. Even a brief glimpse of his daughters had had the effect of 'softening him into tears'; the king 'shewed the greatest marks of parental affection I ever saw'. The committee asked whether 'observing those emotions, which may naturally take place at the sight of relations or friends' provided the doctor with any basis for judging on the likelihood of a cure in this case. Willis replied that it did indeed: showing 'affection rather than aversion' in such circumstances was a very favourable symptom.[7] The royal tears were signs, for Dr Willis, not of troublesome passions or mental distress, but of the return of reason. Subsequently, the king made a rapid recovery and the need for a regency was, for the moment, forestalled, to the chagrin of the Prince of Wales and Charles James Fox.[8]

The report of that unprecedented Select Committee session offers some intriguing insights into prevailing ideas about weeping. To start with, it is striking that the committee thought tears a normal effect of merely laying eyes on one's friends or relations, especially one's children. This was a widespread belief and arose again in a surprising context when an ex-army officer, James Hadfield, was charged with treason for shooting at the king at Drury Lane Theatre on the evening of 15 May 1800. At his trial, Hadfield's barrister, who happened to be the most famous, and the most famously tearful and theatrical, advocate of the era, Thomas Erskine, successfully mounted an insanity defence.[9] It emerged that Hadfield's state of mind had been deranged since sustaining severe head injuries while fighting for his king against the French in the 1790s. This was a landmark case because Hadfield's insanity was only partial. His delusion—that his own execution for a capital crime would trigger the second coming of Christ—was sometimes manifested in bizarre behaviour, but at other times it was not discernible. As evidence of this, Erskine told the court that Hadfield was the father of an eight-month-old baby, and that if the infant was brought into the court at that moment, Hadfield would 'instantly burst into tears and shew every symptom of parental affection'. In other words, he would react as any sane parent should at such a moment. On the other hand, a couple of days before shooting at the king, Hadfield had attempted to dash the baby's brains out against the wall, believing this to be part of the divine plan he had been called to enact. This latter was, of course, the action of a lunatic, but weeping at the sight of one's child was a characteristic of a sound and balanced mind.[10]

The references to 'emotions' in the reports of the examination of Dr Willis in 1789 are also revealing. The 'emotions' only became established as a mental category analysed by physicians, philosophers, and psychologists in the nineteenth century. This is important, because the language with which we understand our feelings and their expressions (including using terms like 'feeling' and 'expression') is woven into the very fabric of our experiences. To experience one's tears as 'emotional incontinence' or an 'expression of emotion', as some have done since the nineteenth century, is to have a different experience from someone who believed that in weeping they were producing signs of sensibility, marks of parental affection, the fruits of the Holy Spirit, or 'excrementitious humours of the third concoction'.[11] Uses of 'emotion' in the eighteenth century were half way between the earliest English senses of 'emotion' to mean any kind of physical disturbance or agitation and our modern, psychological 'emotions'.[12] Some medical writers used the term, as seems to have been done in the Select Committee report, to refer to physical signs of passion or affection, such as the king's tears.[13] An English physician, and author of a series of medical, philosophical, and theological treatises on the passions, Dr Thomas Cogan, stated that the term 'passion' was properly applied to evil propensities such as pride or avarice, in contrast to virtuous social, friendly, or parental 'affections', and that the 'emotions' were 'the sensible changes and visible effects which particular passions produce upon the frame', such as frowns, sighs, or tears.[14] By no means everyone stuck to these definitions, not even Cogan himself in fact, but they are a useful indicator of how the language of feeling was being renegotiated, and a place being found for 'emotions'.

Dr Thomas Cogan was typical in one other respect, though, in stating that a flow of tears was very often a healthy symptom, offering relief from mental suffering or bodily disease. We have already seen that early modern medical and philosophical texts explained tears as the products of humours and vapours in the body and brain being squeezed out through the eyes.[15] Alongside this view of tears as secretions was the widespread philosophical idea that they were signs—part of a universal language of frowns, sighs, smiles, gasps, and sobs—through which men and women could know the contents of each other's minds. As one philosopher put it, these signs are 'so many openings into the souls of our fellow-men, by which their sentiments become visible to the eye'.[16] The notion of tears as humoral excretions, squeezed out of a fluid and porous human body, was superseded. Now the body was understood as a rationally designed mechanical device, with many well-oiled working parts, and tears were produced to order by the action of the nerves on the lachrymal glands. Despite these changing models of the human body, the interpretations of tears as linguistic signs, and sometimes as medical symptoms too, remained consistent well into the nineteenth century.

The physician, anatomist, and artist whose theories of expression in this period were to be the most influential was Sir Charles Bell. Bell's *Anatomy and Philosophy of Expression*, published in three successive editions between 1806 and 1844, was one of the major reference points for Charles Darwin's research and theorizing into the subject from the late 1830s onwards.[17] Bell was born in Edinburgh in 1774, during the heyday of Henry Mackenzie and his *Man of Feeling*, and educated at the university there by, amongst others, the Professor of Moral Philosophy, Dugald Stewart, who had been present on the occasion that Robert Burns wept over a picture at the house of Adam Ferguson.[18] Bell trained as a physician, treated the wounded of the wars with France and Spain in England in 1809, and in Brussels, in the aftermath of Waterloo, in 1815. He made pioneering discoveries about the nervous system, and was also an accomplished artist, producing arresting images of wounded soldiers as well as many illustrations for his books on anatomy and expression.[19]

Bell, like his fellow physicians, had to live a dual existence: a man of feeling in private, but a resolute and apathetic stoic in his professional activities. Such detachment was especially necessary when those activities included performing amputations (without anaesthetic, of course) on desperate wounded soldiers each begging to be taken next, until the surgeon's arms were weak from exertion and his clothes stiff with blood, as was Bell's experience with the wounded of Waterloo. Several years earlier, treating injured men arriving back in England, Bell had been moved himself to 'bitter curses and lamentations' as well as to 'tears of pity' by the spectacle, but now he had learned not to give the wounded any access to his feelings—to do so would be to 'allow yourself to be unmanned'. Instead Bell was able to keep his mind calm, even with screams of pain and execrations ringing in his ears.[20] The ability of the physician, like the soldier, to remain calm and tearless under extreme stress, and in the face of the gore and carnage of war, was to become, eventually, a much more widely lauded ability, and even a national characteristic.

In private, however, and in his cultural, rather than professional, existence, Bell was attuned to the value of tears in both life and art. In his treatises on expression he treated weeping, along with laughter, as one of 'the most extreme expressions of the passions' but as 'being peculiarly human, arising from sentiments not participated by the brutes'.[21] Having described how the lachrymal glands and the diaphragm acted together in producing tears and sobs, Bell turned to aesthetic matters, offering the view that weeping was an 'expression of emotion' that might be introduced even in the highest forms of art, so long as it was done with 'great taste' and without 'offensive exaggeration'. There is no reason to suppose he was thinking about Hogarth's *Sigismunda* as an example of the latter, although some of his readers might have done.[22] Bell thought the finest example of a portrayal of tears, or of any expression, was to be found in a painting by an Italian master of the seventeenth century, which Bell had himself seen in Milan, Guercino's *Dismissal of Hagar and Ishmael*, depicting the moment in the book of Genesis when Abraham sends away his mistress and son into the wilderness. Bell noted that Hagar's eyes were 'red and swollen', but not in a way that destroyed her beauty, suggesting that the viewer could even 'hear her short convulsive sobs' and perceive her misery, through the painter's rendition of her shoulders, lips, forehead, and eyelids.[23] These bodily signs indeed were openings into the soul.

Bell's assertion that weeping and laughter were uniquely human traits is particularly important, since it would be the point on which Darwin took issue with him. Ancient and medieval sources had all asserted that certain animals could weep. This included not only the infamously false or hypocritical tears of the crocodile, but also the sincere tears that it was believed horses, elephants, and deer could shed. The idea that horses shed tears of grief when their masters died was an ancient one. Homer's *Iliad*, published in popular English translations by George Chapman in the seventeenth and Alexander Pope in the eighteenth century, included not only weeping heroes, but also the weeping horses of Achilles, who shed tears over the death of Patroclus. Pliny and Aristotle also testified to this power of equine expression. Weeping horses appear in medieval bestiaries, and in the thirteenth-century text *De Animalibus*, by Thomas Aquinas' teacher Albertus Magnus, and they continued to figure in travellers' tales and philosophical treatises right up to the eighteenth century (and we have already encountered the tears of St Francis's donkey).[24] Weeping deer were another traditional favourite—there is one in Shakespeare's *As You Like It*—sometimes as part of anti-hunting polemics.[25] In this same tradition, other animals were said to be unable to weep, because of their bad and aggressive natures, especially wolves, tigers, lions, and bears.[26]

From the Renaissance onwards, however, philosophical and medical writers increasingly rejected this tradition, preferring to teach instead that tears and laughter, and the kind of higher sentiments they expressed, were uniquely human traits. As early as 1579, in France, Laurent Joubert claimed that animals had insufficient understanding to engage in weeping proper, even though their eyes could produce tears.[27] René Descartes went even further, in suggesting that all animals were automata, not partaking in any kind of feeling at all.[28] The seventeenth-century English physician and pioneer of neuroanatomy Thomas Willis wrote that 'Man is more fitly made for all Affections, and chiefly for the conceiving of Joy and Sadness, than Brute Animals; and as he is a sociable Creature, he ought to Communicate those sociable things, some signs naturally implanted in him, to wit, Laughing and Weeping.'[29] William Hogarth's friend Dr James Parsons took the same view in his treatise on physiognomy in the 1740s, as did the royal physician to both George II and George III, Dr Peter Shaw, who wrote a paper praising 'moral weeping', which he described as 'peculiar to man' in the 1750s. In the following decade, the Scottish physician and moralist Dr John Gregory wrote in terms very similar to those later adopted by Bell about laughter and tears as 'expressions of certain emotions of the soul unknown to other Animals', including intellectual, moral, and religious pleasures.[30]

Bell's view was the medical and scientific orthodoxy of the day, and remained so until Darwin sought to rediscover animal emotions as a way to bolster the case for evolution in 1872.[31] In the early years of the nineteenth century, people perceived a clear distinction between human beings, made in God's image and set above the animals, with powers of reason and will, and the 'brute creation', driven by passion and sensation. What is crucial to recognize, however, is that tears, later annexed to 'emotion' alone, were at this stage understood in terms of their intellectual and moral basis, at the same time as being expressions of passion and affection. The reason that animals could not weep, even though they possessed lachrymal glands, was that real weeping arose not from brute passion but from refined ideas and moral sentiments unavailable to animals. It is this thought—another version of Blake's idea that 'a tear is an intellectual thing'—which lies behind the observation of a Plymouth surgeon, James Yonge, who encountered enormous turtles on the Atlantic island of Sal during a voyage in the 1660s. Yonge recorded in his journal that when one of these turtles was caught by sailors it would 'sob and sigh, and tears will trickle down his cheek as if he were a rational animal'.[32] And this brings us back to King George and his would-be assassin James Hadfield. The right kind of tears, for them too, could indicate that the one shedding them was a rational animal.

The final two decades of the reign of George III were a transitional period in the history of British tears. Although weeping remained healthy and rational in many contexts, the age of enthusiasm was certainly over. The continuing war against the French, now in the form of Napoleon's empire, cemented anti-French feeling, providing an important context, as we have seen, for an aversion to anything with a whiff of French sensibility. This mixed attitude to tears—as healthy, but a bit foreign—is nicely encapsulated by the fact that the most cited source of medical guidance about tears in British newspapers and periodicals throughout the nineteenth century, starting in 1819 and right up to the 1890s, was a treatise by a French physician on the 'beneficial influence of groaning and crying on the nervous system'. Similarly, as readers of the *British Mothers' Magazine* were informed in 1849, the great French physician Armand

Trousseau held it as an aphorism about sick children that those who shed tears were more likely to recover.[33]

Medical advice about tears of grief remained the same throughout this period. It was to be expected that bereavement might lead to a period of shock and tearlessness, but it was very important that tears should follow soon, to provide relief to the sufferer and to avoid their descent into mental derangement or death. Emma Hamilton's response to the death of her lover, Admiral Lord Nelson, in 1805, was exemplary in this respect. We know from her own account that when she received the news—which she had intuited from the deathly pallor and tearful eyes of the sailor sent by the Admiralty, before he had said anything—she uttered one scream, but then 'for ten hours after I could neither speak nor shed a tear'. Her tears subsequently were ample and, according to a visitor, crying 'seemed to relieve her'. Later she would be bathed in tears as she regaled visitors with tales of Nelson's virtue and heroism, with his bullet-holed and blood-encrusted coat at her bedside. It was appropriate, therefore, that James Gillray chose to model the figure of Britannia, in his representation of the death of Nelson, on a rather theatrically sobbing Emma Hamilton (Figure 11).[34]

Nelson's was one of two tragic deaths in this period to provide moments of national grief that can be compared with the reaction to the death of Diana, Princess of Wales, in 1997.[35] Nelson was killed at the moment of his victory over the French and Spanish fleets at Trafalgar in 1805. He and his naval colleagues were men of feeling. Nelson had written to Emma Hamilton on the eve of the battle about the response he received when he had described his battle plan: 'Some shed tears. All approved.'[36] We know from several first-hand accounts that men of all ranks were reduced to tears by their heroic leader's death, even though some thought such tears womanish. One sailor wrote home, 'all the men in our ship, who have seen him, are such soft toads they have done nothing but blast their eyes and cry ever since he was killed. God bless

Figure 11. James Gillray, *The Death of Admiral Lord Nelson in the Moment of Victory* (1805). © National Maritime Museum, Greenwich, London.

you! chaps that fought like the devil sit down and cry like a wench.' Then, in 1817, the much-loved 21-year-old Charlotte, Princess of Wales, died in childbirth. Both these deaths produced ample tears, both on the cheeks of great crowds of thousands of people, and on the pages of periodicals in endless odes and poems, with titles such as 'Dirge for Lord Nelson', 'Britannia's Tears', and 'The Tears of Albion'.

In Nelson's funeral, however, are some signs of what would later become the internationally recognized tone of pomp and restraint belonging to the British Empire. The procession, including 160 carriages for mourners, was over a mile long, and the route from Whitehall to St Paul's cathedral was lined with troops.[37] It was reported of the sailors who had served under Nelson on HMS Victory that 'the manly tears glistened in their eyes, and stole reluctantly down their weather-beaten cheeks'.[38] Commentary on the funeral of Princess Diana in 1997 tended to take for granted the genius of the British establishment for dignified ceremonial, but to be surprised by the mass expression of grief. Lady Bessborough's account of Nelson's funeral revealed opposite assumptions. 'I do not in general think that grand ceremonies and processions are the genius of the English nation, and therefore they usually fail,' she wrote, 'but in this instance I must say I never saw anything so magnificent or so affecting.' Most touching of all, she thought, was the sight of the 'immense mob', who had previously been very noisy, taking off their hats as one, in a moment of silence, in a 'general impulse of respect' while the funeral march, the cannon, and the 'roll of muffled drums' could be heard. There were tears in eyes, and on cheeks, but this was all quite restrained.[39]

At the same time, the reading public was rapidly tiring of the literature of tears. In 1801, the Morning Post in London carried an advertisement for a new publication: A History of Weeping, From the Creation of Eve to the Present Time. This was a ten-volume compendium covering such topics as 'the state of tears before the flood', 'the origin of whimpering', 'calculation of the depth of tears shed at a tragedy', and 'the use of onions at funerals'. The whole edition was illustrated by engravings of 'all the stages of crying from the *glisten* to the *sob*' and by portraits of 'eminent criers' and 'noted whimperers'. When I first saw this advertisement, my historian's heart leapt with excitement at the thought of getting my hands on such an extraordinary compendium. But of course the whole thing was a joke, an indication of changing literary tastes. The proposed materials for the final volume were:

> On novel-writing; on tears divided into genera and species; salt tears, bitter tears, sweet tears, sweet-bitter tears, salt-delicious tears, tears half-delicious, half-agonizing, and other varieties, manufactured and distilled in the writings of the new philosophers. On sentimental torrents, cataracts of sensibility, and water-falls of fine-feeling.[40]

Another sign of the times came in 1805 when the writer and political philosopher William Godwin, widower of Mary Wollstonecraft, who had died giving birth to their child in 1797, published a novel entitled *Fleetwood: or, The New Man of Feeling*. The novel gently satirizes the excesses of eighteenth-century sensibility, and its failure to address social injustice. Fleetwood himself is an egotist and cynic who has failed to master his feelings. Another character is a countess whose tears break forth almost at will (a little like Sophy Streatfield), as expressions of both suffering and joy, but whose intellect is 'of narrow dimensions', and whose superficial mental life is compared to that of an aquatic insect hovering over the surface of a lake.[41]

By the time of the death of George III in 1820, at the end of a decade in which his madness had returned and deepened, and with the Prince of Wales presiding over a regency, the ethos of tearful sensibility which had been preached to the young king in the 1760s had gone out of fashion. The extremes of that age, in fact, seemed outdated and absurd. Reading from Henry Mackenzie's *The Man of Feeling* to a group of friends in the 1820s, half a century after it first had such a tearful impact on her and her family, Lady Louisa Stuart found that nobody now cried at the passages she used to find the most poignant and exquisite, producing perhaps 'tears half-delicious, half-agonizing', but instead, 'Oh Dear! They laughed.'[42]

10

Strange Blessing on the Nation

At six o'clock in the morning on 20 June 1837, the 18-year-old Princess Alexandrina Victoria was ushered out of her bedroom in her dressing gown, to be informed by the Archbishop of Canterbury and the Lord Chamberlain that her uncle, the king, had died, and as a result she was now Victoria, Queen of Great Britain and Ireland, Defender of the Faith. The next day, at the public proclamation of her accession, at one of the windows of St James's Palace, the young queen stood on the balcony. As soon as she appeared, the crowd responded with 'exclamations of joy and clapping of hands, the ladies waving their handkerchiefs, and the gentlemen their hats in the air'. Victoria, 'completely overcome by the novelty of her situation' and by the events of the last two days, 'burst into tears, which continued, notwithstanding an evident attempt on the part of her Majesty to restrain her feelings, to flow in torrents down her now pallid cheeks, until her Majesty retired from the window'.[1] The new-born Victorian age was thus baptized in tears.

Tears are produced by crises in our individual and collective lives—those moving moments that carry us from one state of existence to another, embodying as they do a potentially overwhelming combination of change, loss, fear, hope, and joy. So, people crying at bar mitzvahs, graduations, or weddings are responding not only to a ceremony that embodies a cherished ideal but also to a momentous existential transition. Such were Victoria's tears of accession, shed in a new era of

Romanticism, intellectualism, and pathos. The Romantics were contemp-
tuous of outmoded tears of sensibility but could still see something
wonderful, if strange, in the right kind of weeping. This included tears
produced by moments of rapturous intellectual rebirth, when a whole
new view of the world suddenly offered itself. One of the era's leading
female intellectuals, originally from a Unitarian family in East Anglia,
shed tears while translating a work of atheistic French philosophy into
English. The eldest son of a dour Scotsman, reared on facts and reasoning
alone, finally discovered his feelings, and with them a whole new philosophy, while reading and weeping over the memoirs of an eighteenth-
century French novelist. A public transition to a momentous new role, or
a private one from Christianity to scientific humanism, or from Utilitar-
ianism to Romanticism, could equally result in tears of idealism and
conversion.

The tears of Victoria on the balcony at St James's were widely and
approvingly reported. The ideal of the godly and virtuous ruler, combined
with the vision of this 'youthful Queen bathed in tears', was, as *The Times*
put it, 'singularly beautiful and affecting'.[2] The woman who would become
the most famous female poet of the age, Elizabeth Barrett, composed two
celebratory poems. Barrett (later Barrett Browning after her marriage to
Robert in 1846) was impressed by Victoria's declaration before the Privy
Council that she would feel herself utterly oppressed by the burden of her
new responsibility were it not for her trust and hope 'that Divine Providence, which has called me to this work, will give me strength for the
performance of it'. In her poem 'The Young Queen', Barrett wrote:

> Yea! Call on God, thou maiden
> Of spirit nobly laden,
> And leave such happy days behind, for happy-making years!
> A nation looks to thee
> For steadfast sympathy;
> Make room within thy bright clear eyes for all its gathered tears.

Barrett wrote to a friend, 'The young Queen is very interesting to me—& those tears, wept not only amidst the multitudes at the proclamation, but in the silence of the dead midnight—(we heard that she cried all night before holding her first privy council, notwithstanding the stateliness & composure with which she received her councillors) are beautiful & touching to think upon.' The same letter went on to refer to lines by Lord Byron about the hardening and chilling effects of power on the human heart. 'But our young Queen', Barrett thought, 'wears still a very tender heart! and long may its natural emotions lie warm within it!' Barrett's feelings of admiration for the tender-hearted monarch caused her a dilemma: 'How can loyalty & republicanism be brought together?'[3] It was loyalty alone, however, which was expressed in her public verses. In the second of these, 'Victoria's Tears', Barrett exclaimed, 'God save thee, weeping Queen! Thou shalt be well beloved! The tyrant's sceptre cannot move, As those pure tears have moved!' The tears were omens of a reign of love and liberty: 'Strange blessing on the nation lies, Whose Sovereign wept—Yea! Wept, to wear its crown!'[4]

Barrett's poetry was both Romantic and religious in its inspiration. Romanticism, the dominant European cultural movement of the early nineteenth century, is often described as giving a special role to 'emotion', but I think that makes it sound too soppy. Indeed, the overemphasis on shared feelings, a hallmark of eighteenth-century sensibility, was one of the tendencies against which Romantics were reacting.[5] Romanticism was more individualistic and less sentimental. While the spirit of sensibility animated Greuze's girl crying over a dead bird in the 1760s, the defining image of Romanticism, produced half a century later, was something altogether more rugged: Caspar David Friedrich's *Wanderer* shows a young man with a walking stick on a rocky outcrop gazing out into a landscape of mountains and forests wreathed in mist. The archetypal Romantic does not gaze down and weep, whether over a dead bird or the plight of beggars or prostitutes, but stands alone, looking upwards, heroically confronting the sublime power of nature, contemplating its primal transcendent forces.[6] Wordsworth, who in 1787 wrote his sonnet about Helen Maria Williams weeping over a tale of distress, and who in 1802 wept with his sister Dorothy as she read Milton aloud, in 1804 composed a poem, later published as *Ode: Intimations of Immortality*, in which the Romantic self, reflecting on nature and eternity, with both melancholy and hope, concluded with the statement that thanks to the enduring tenderness, joys, and fears of the human heart, 'To me the meanest flower that blows can give | Thoughts that do often lie too deep for tears'.[7]

This is not to say that to be a Romantic you had to be always dry-eyed, but rather that your tears had to be sublime rather than sentimental. We have already seen how Coleridge, like Mary Wollstonecraft, scorned the tears of sensibility shed by ladies weeping over sad stories who remained, nonetheless, insensible to the real horror, suffering, and injustices of their world, especially slavery.[8] Byron's early poetry contained plenty of the spirit of the *Man of Feeling* tradition, even composing a poem, 'The Tear', in 1806, at the age of 18, which celebrated the tear as a sign of affection, grief, nostalgia, and sympathy.[9] Such a performance would have embarrassed the more mature Byron, the great figurehead of British Romanticism, who was much more ambivalent about tears.

In the summer of 1819, in Bologna, and now 31, Byron attended a performance of the tragedy *Mirra* by Vittorio Alfieri. He found himself overcome by tears. As we have already seen, there was nothing at all unusual about crying at the theatre, least of all, one might suppose, for a Romantic poet. But the way that Byron wrote about the experience in a letter to a friend is revealing of his discomfort with his own tears. He claimed that it was only the second time in his life that he had been moved to tears by any kind of fiction (the first being a performance in London by the actor Edmund Kean), and explained that his aesthetic convulsions were not at all like 'a lady's hysterics' but were rather 'the agony of reluctant tears', a sort of 'choking shudder'. He was a weeping wanderer not a crying girl. Byron went on to note that the lady in whose box he was watching the play, 'went off in the same way', but that this could be explained by the fact that both she and he had been ill. While a man of feeling, including Byron's younger self, would have revelled in these tears as signs of sympathy and good nature, the Romantic could not: they were either something profound and agonized, to be distinguished from female 'hysterics'; or they were simply a side-effect of illness. The account of the Italian lady whose box Byron shared also survived, shedding doubt on Byron's claim that he had only ever been moved in this way once before. This Italian friend reported that it was not the first time even she had seen Byron convulsed by sobs in the theatre during his time in Italy.[10]

When another great Romantic poet, Percy Shelley, died a perfectly Romantic death in 1822, drowning off the northern Italian coast in a boat called the *Don Juan*, he left his wife Mary a Romantic widow at the age of 24. In Genoa three months later, Mary Shelley started a diary. She called it her 'Journal of Sorrow' and it reveals how she struggled, as her mother Mary Wollstonecraft had done, with the apparently conflicting demands of the intellect and the heart.[11] In the first, desolate entry in the journal, Mary recorded, 'I have now no friend', having spent the previous eight years being guided by a man 'whose genius, far transcending mine, awakened & guided my thoughts' and 'rectified my errors of judgement'. But now, alone—'Oh, how alone!'—Mary depicts herself in communion only with nature and the pages of her journal: 'The stars may behold my tears, & the winds drink my sighs—but my thoughts are a sealed treasure which I can confide to none. White paper—wilt thou be my confident?' Weeping over the instability of her life and relationships, Mary fears that she will be 'dragged back to the same necessity, of seeking for the food of life in my intellect alone'. A later entry reveals the same kind of wrestling—tears and sighs being contrasted with the intellectual powers of the mind. Mary asks herself what power it is that 'wanders up & down my heart chilling its blood & causing the warm tears to gush forth'. She yearns to be 'something greater & better than I am', to be 'full of lofty thought, independent and firm', but her tears reveal that 'the expression "woman's weakness" truly belongs to my nerveless vacillating mind'– 'my reed-like mind shakes beneath each wind'.[12]

The Romantic suspicion of tears comes through in the later poetry of Elizabeth Barrett too, representing her second thoughts about weeping, after the death of her much-loved brother. Two sonnets, entitled 'Tears' and 'Grief', both published in 1844, express the idea, consistent not only with Romanticism but also with ancient and early modern ideas about grief discussed above, that tears are a sign of only moderate grief, and that the most profound sorrow is tearless. As Barrett's poems put it, those whose suffering makes them weep should be grateful–'That is light grieving!'–whereas 'hopeless grief is passionless' and expressed only through deathlike silence. Tears might be appropriate for babies or for women at weddings, but the poet contemplating the sublimity of 'high-faned hills', like Friedrich's *Wanderer*, looking upwards towards the transcendent, forgets such 'moisture on his cheeks', and contemplates the sun and stars without tears. Again, for Barrett, the religious and the Romantic combine. It is depth of thought and feeling, the magnificence of nature, and the hope for God that combine to dry the poet's tears.[13]

The notion that weeping is weak and effeminate is always in the background of discussions of tears in western cultural history. It is against that background that the fluctuating fashions for both male and female lachrymosity have been played out. The British Romantics revived the idea of the effeminacy of tears in their own particular way. Byron tried to portray his own tears as sublime agony rather than feminine hysterics. Mary Shelley contrasted her 'woman's weakness', evident in gushing tears, with the firmness of intellectual thought. Elizabeth Barrett was touched by the tears of an 18-year-old woman but thought, like

Wordsworth, that some thoughts lay too deep for tears. In 1844, the same year that Barrett's sonnets about grief and tears were published, and inspired by Wordsworth's ode on immortality, the artist James Smetham painted a self-portrait entitled *Thoughts Too Deep for Tears*, encapsulating visually this Romantic type: intense, moody, solitary, tearless, and male.[14]

But there was another way to think about the relationship between weeping and thinking, which also had exponents in this period and can be traced back to Romantic writers. I have already referred to the line in William Blake's poem 'The Grey Monk', written around 1803, describing a tear as 'an intellectual thing'. That notion has been one of the key ideas that guided the conceptualization and execution of this book.[15] The statement had a very particular meaning for Blake, as part of his overall vision, part mystical, part philosophical, part Romantic, in which the ultimate reality was the soul, while those things generally thought of as bodily and sensual, including sighs and tears, were merely another aspect of that mental, spiritual reality. The term 'intellectual', for Blake, alluded to this philosophy, and had slightly different resonances from those it has for us today. The contrast was not so much between the rational and the emotional, for Blake, but between the spiritual and the bodily. So to describe a tear as 'intellectual' was less to contrast it with passions and feelings, and more to contrast it with bodily sensations and physical force. In 'The Grey Monk', Blake expresses a view very similar to that suggested by Elizabeth Barrett in 'Victoria's Tears', in fact, by contrasting violent tyranny, conducted in vain through the sword and the bow, with the powers of the mind: 'The Hermits Prayer & the Widows tear | Alone can free the World from fear.' The poem then continues:

> For a Tear is an Intellectual Thing
> And a Sigh is the Sword of an Angel King
> And the bitter groan of the Martyrs woe
> Is an Arrow from the Almighties Bow

On another occasion Blake described his tears as 'aqua fortis', a kind of acid used for making engravings. These tears—intellectual and corrosive— were not the tears of sensibility.[16]

The idea that a tear is an 'intellectual thing' sounds counter-intuitive to us, and would have done to many nineteenth-century readers too, but it is a motto that captures something important about weeping, namely that it is a cognitive activity. This had been recognized by many philosophers and writers since the early modern period, including those who argued that only humans could weep because other animals had insufficient rational understanding. On this view, which has its roots in ancient Stoic ideas about the passions, tears are intellectual in the same sense that the passions and emotions we experience are intellectual, that is to say that they are produced by representations of the world, not by mere sensations or feelings. Stoicism teaches that all passions are forms of judgement. Anger is the judgement that I have been wronged, fear is the judgement that I am in danger, and so on. When we find our bodies convulsed by passion, we are in the grip of a mental judgement about the world. In this sense, tears are intellectual things because they are brought about by cognitive representations of the world as possessing certain qualities.[17] The king's physician Peter Shaw, whose 1755 essay on moral weeping I quoted above, wrote that people cry when their minds 'are filled with dark and confused ideas' or 'representations'. Shaw contrasted those tears, produced by 'real sentiments of the mind' and 'ideas', with merely physical crying.[18]

Tears can be produced not only by changes of social role but also changes of ideology or worldview, and the tears of Victorian intellectuals themselves provide vivid examples of this. Harriet Martineau was born into an affluent Unitarian family in Norwich who were unusual in providing their daughters, as well as their sons, with a thorough academic education. Martineau rose to fame in the early 1830s as a writer of popular, didactic tales designed to illustrate the principles of the kind of political economy on which a modern industrialized society was based.[19] These were not radical tracts—far from it—as witnessed by the fact that their many avid readers included the young Princess Victoria, whose favourite of the tales, 'Ella of Garveloch', was the story of a strong and proud girl, whose efforts to restrain her tears when her father was dying concealed her true depths of feeling.[20] Martineau's mother and aunt were present outside St James's Palace when Victoria's accession was proclaimed and the tears 'ran fast down her cheeks'.[21] Martineau herself was a fierce republican and freethinker, and on her way to becoming a notorious atheist. She attended Victoria's coronation in 1838, observing the assembled dignitaries below, bejewelled with diamonds and occasional tears, while she read her book and ate a sandwich up in the gallery, looking down on them from a great height, disapproving of the 'barbaric' and 'blasphemous' mixing up of God and the queen in a religious service filled with primitive superstitions.[22]

Harriet Martineau's own most remarkable tears came later in her life and were produced by a book that had a crucial role in her intellectual transformation from the earnest and questioning child of a Unitarian family, worrying about the compatibility of divine omniscience and human free will at the age of 7, to a famous Victorian unbeliever.[23] The book was the *Course of Positive Philosophy* by the atheistic French writer, and founding father of the discipline of sociology, Auguste Comte. This multi-volume survey of the history and philosophy of the sciences, tracing them from primitive beliefs, via theology and philosophy, to the rise of modern positive science, was a stodgy, jargon-filled, pedantic, and repetitive piece of work, albeit one with flashes of passion and revolutionary conclusions.[24] It was in the course of translating and condensing Comte's *Course* into a two-volume English version that Harriet Martineau found herself weeping intellectual tears. Moved to moments of rapture by the vast range of knowledge on display and the majesty of the natural world it surveyed, Martineau recalled: 'Many a passage of my version did I write with tears falling into my lap.'[25] One historian has drily commented, with good reason, that this constituted 'a feat of sensibility which only those who have read Comte at length can fully appreciate'.[26]

As with Romantic tears, so too with intellectual tears in this period, they were surrounded by caveats and careful reinterpretations. As a child, Martineau, unlike her creation 'Ella of Garveloch', never succeeded in repressing her tears, despite constant efforts. Martineau recalled that for much of her childhood she wept every day, and blamed herself for it.[27] As an adult, her tears were much less frequent, but still could occasion self-reproach. In 1838 she was visited by the recently orphaned daughters of Lord and Lady Durham, and recalled, 'I behaved (it seemed to me) unpardonably. I could not stop my tears, in the presence of those who had so much more reason and so much more right to be inconsolable.' The only excuse Martineau offered for this apparently blameworthy behaviour was the same as the one used by Lord Byron at the theatre in Italy—she was very ill at the time.[28] Again, the turn away from sensibility could not be clearer. Tears of grief shed in sympathy with orphans for the loss of their parents were among the many kinds shed by Mackenzie's *Man of Feeling*, and were routinely celebrated by preachers, moralists, and charitable fund-raisers of that age.[29] For Martineau they had to be explained away by illness.

The kinds of respectable adult tears that Martineau did allow herself, then, were limited, but included those produced by the grandeur of the scientific and atheistic worldview to which she was converted by Comte and others. These were tears of intellectual 'rapture', Martineau called it, a response to the 'subdued enthusiasm of my author, his philosophical sensibility, and honest earnestness, and evident enjoyment of his own wide range of views and deep human sympathy', which together 'kept the mind of his pupil in a perpetual and delightful glow'.[30] Comte's text itself even contained an assertion of the existence and value of such intellectual tears. He stated that the intellectual and affective powers of the mind were distinct but very closely interconnected. Perhaps it was even when writing the following passage in her translation, about the intellectual faculties, that Martineau's tears fell into her lap: 'their action occasions true emotions or sentiments, more rare, more pure, more sublime than any other, and though less vivid than others, capable of moving to tears; as is testified by so many instances of the rapture excited by the discovery of truth, in the most eminent thinkers that have done honour to their race—as Archimedes, Descartes, Kepler, Newton, etc.'[31] Martineau could signal her affinity with intellectual giants by producing her own tears of rapture. Her conversion to atheism, then, was marked by tears, as had been conversions to Methodist Christianity in the eighteenth century; and her tears were signs of sympathy with humanity, as had been those of the devotees of sensibility. But her choice of words nicely reveals the shifts in values and beliefs through which her tears were now produced and interpreted. The enthusiasm was there, but it was 'subdued', the sensibility was real but it was 'philosophical' and the sympathy was neither superficial nor pious but 'deep' and 'human'.

In the case of John Stuart Mill, the tearful intellectual conversion was from the severe, rationalist creed of his Calvinist-turned-Utilitarian father James, to a philosophy in which feeling and intellect could be more closely allied. Mill's childhood education, conducted at home by his father, was intensive and prodigious. He was schooled in languages, history, and the sciences, but not in religion and the arts. At the age of 7 he was reading Plato's dialogues in the original Greek and at 12 he wrote a book-length history of the government of ancient Rome. Mill's autobiography, published in 1873, contains a vivid pen-portrait of his father, who seems to have embodied much of the spirit of Dickens's Mr Gradgrind:

> For passionate emotions of all sorts, and for everything which has been said or written in exaltation of them, he professed the greatest contempt. He regarded them as a form of madness. 'The intense' was with him a bye-word of scornful disapprobation. He regarded as an aberration of the moral standard of modern times, compared with that of the ancients, the great stress laid upon feeling.

Although his father was a Scotsman, Mill observed of him that he 'resembled most Englishmen in being ashamed of the signs of feeling' and by the absence of outward demonstrations, he starved to death the feelings themselves.[32] In his early twenties, Mill experienced a mental crisis and severe depression, which he later interpreted as the direct result of his father's educational approach. The over-development of his powers of intellectual analysis, Mill believed, had tended to wear away his feelings. The turning point for Mill came through reading the poetry of William Wordsworth, listening to the music of the German composer Carl Maria von Weber, and especially when reading the *Mémoires* of the sentimental French playwright and novelist Jean-François Marmontel.[33]

Mill recalled how he came to the scene in Marmontel's *Mémoires* where the author's father dies, the distressed position of the family is described, and Marmontel recalls his passionate determination, even though still a young boy, to take the place of the father his family had lost. 'A vivid conception of the scene and its feelings came over me', Mill wrote, 'and I was moved to tears.' This was Mill's conversion moment. The death of Marmontel's father, we might surmise, symbolized for Mill the death of his own unfeeling, but still living, Gradgrind of a father. From then on the younger Mill was freed from the thought that 'all feeling was dead within me', and instead sensed that 'I had still, it seemed, some of the material out of which all worth of character, and all capacity for happiness, are made'.[34] 'The cultivation of the feelings,' Mill went on, 'became one of the cardinal points in my ethical and philosophical creed', and he now tried to impress on his English contemporaries something which he thought was widely appreciated in continental Europe: that the 'habitual exercise of the feelings' leads to the 'general culture of the understanding'. An emotional apprehension of an object in the world, Mill argued, was entirely consistent with 'the most accurate knowledge and most perfect practical recognition of all its physical and intellectual laws and relations'. 'The intensest feeling of the beauty of a cloud lighted by the setting sun,' for instance, 'is no hindrance to my knowing that the cloud is vapour of water, subject to all the laws of vapours in a state of suspension.'[35] James Mill would have been appalled; intense feelings of beauty were of no possible relevance.

Byron's early poem 'The Tear' had included among the various causes of tears, along with friendship and love, the moment 'When Truth in a glance should appear'.[36] The moments of insight felt by Harriet Martineau reading Comte and John Stuart Mill reading Marmontel, as well as the experience of the 18-year-old Victoria in the sudden and public realization of her new identity as queen, offer examples of how glimpses of a new truth and a new world could bring intellectual and Romantic tears to British eyes, even after the demise of sensibility. Yet even when they were celebrated, there was something foreign, something strange about these tears. For Martineau and Mill it was French rather than British authors who provoked their most important bouts of tears, and for Mill the expression of feeling in general was something he thought much better understood in Europe than Britain. For Elizabeth Barrett, the sovereign's tears had offered a blessing, but it was a 'Strange blessing on the nation'. Tears were strange to Alfred Tennyson too: 'sad and strange' tokens of melancholy at the passing of time, as he portrayed them in some famous lines from *The Princess*: 'Tears, idle tears, I know not what they mean.'[37] By the time Tennyson died in 1892, his phrase could almost have passed for a British national motto, a statement of a whole people's increasing emotional illiteracy. When it was first published in the 1840s, however, it was a piece of poetical reflection in keeping with the intellectual currents of the times—a philosophical thought written in the midst of a culture in which there was still plenty of room for sentiment and pathos. And it is to the recognized master of that early Victorian pathos that our tale of tears turns next.

11

Little Nell Without Laughing

When Charles Dickens died in 1870, *Reynolds Newspaper* eulogized him as the 'great master of pathos', a writer who 'held the strings of the human heart in his hand'. When he narrated the death of angelic Nell Trent, the heroine of *The Old Curiosity Shop*, the obituary observed, 'the world mourned', including the great Irish nationalist leader Daniel O'Connell. Travelling on a train with a friend, reading the final instalment of the story, as he reached the fatal moment, 'O'Connell's eyes filled with tears—he sobbed as only men of great hearts can do.' He then twice shouted 'He should not have killed her!' before throwing the volume out of the carriage window.[1] This story, like the one about crowds of American readers waiting anxiously on the New York quayside for the final instalment to arrive from England, shouting up to passengers 'Is Little Nell dead?', is probably exaggerated.[2] Another version of the recollection about O'Connell has him expressing not exquisite grief at the pathos of Nell's demise, but annoyance that Dickens lacked the ingenuity to bring the girl's adventures to a happy resolution, and so had killed her off to avoid the difficulty. In this alternative account, O'Connell threw the work aside in disgust, vowing never to read Dickens again.[3] John Ruskin later commented with similar disdain that Nell had been 'killed for the market, as a butcher kills a lamb'.[4]

There are parallels between the saintly figures of Nell Trent and Harley, the title character of Henry Mackenzie's *Man of Feeling*, published seventy years earlier.[5] Unworldly, tender, pitying, and virtuous, both Nell and Harley make their way through a corrupt and fallen world, finally dying with pathetic piety. It is clear from the prefaces to the various editions of *The Old Curiosity Shop* that Dickens was happy for his readers to see him as a successor to Mackenzie, Sterne, and Fielding.[6] Lady Louisa Stuart and her friends may have laughed at the exaggerated lachrymosity of *The Man of Feeling* in the 1820s, but the unprecedented popular success of the writings of Charles Dickens over the decades that followed proved that there was, nonetheless, an enormous market for a Victorian version of the novel of sensibility. Members of the literary, artistic, and political establishments, as well as those who read Dickens's works in popular periodicals or penny-library editions, unashamedly responded with laughter and tears, in all parts of the United Kingdom. Revisiting the social realities, religious ideas, political narratives, and literary performances through which Dickensian pathos was produced, we can put Little Nell back in her proper place: on the Victorian deathbed of sensibility.[7]

Most famous among Dickens sceptics is Oscar Wilde, who reportedly said that one would have to have a heart of stone to read the death of Little Nell without laughing.[8] That quip is often repeated by those wanting to take the side of the clever and unsentimental Victorians against the maudlin and over-emotional ones. Later, in a long letter written from prison, after his conviction for 'gross indecency', Wilde accused his former lover, Alfred 'Bosie' Douglas, of being a 'sentimentalist', defining that term as someone 'who desires to have the luxury of an emotion without paying for it'.[9] Wilde was following earlier generations of writers who had reacted against the literature and political philosophy of the eighteenth century. In an 1821 parody of Sterne's *Sentimental Journey*, Thomas Hood wrote that although some 'sentimentalists' were ready to vent their tears and sighs 'upon the first dead dog or lame chicken they might meet with', he was not such a reader, and hated the 'weeping-willow set, who will cry over their pug dogs and canaries, till they have no tears to spare for the real children of misfortune and misery'.[10] Thomas Carlyle's history of the French Revolution, published in the year of Queen Victoria's accession, cemented the view that the ideology of the revolutionaries had arisen 'out of that putrescent rubbish of Scepticism, Sensualism, Sentimentalism'. Carlyle wrote of the 'rose-pink vapour of Sentimentalism', which could barely hide the stench of the diseased French body politic beneath. 'Is not Sentimentalism,' he asked, 'twin-sister to Cant, if not one and the same with it?'[11]

And yet Carlyle was one of those who wept over Dickens, Thomas Hood was among Dickens's most ardent admirers, and we can hardly categorize Oscar Wilde as an unsentimental writer.[12] It would be hard to think of a more sentimental and tear-jerking Victorian production than Wilde's 1888 book *The Happy Prince and Other Stories*. As with Dickens's tales and some of their precursors, Wilde's stories combine death, childhood innocence, social injustice, and religious imagery to produce, no doubt quite intentionally, a weeping effect. I say this from experience, and especially the experience of reading the stories aloud, which I find makes the tears all the more unavoidable. In the case of 'The Happy Prince', which involves a friendship between a devoted swallow and a self-sacrificing royal statue, I have even found myself in the embarrassing position, thanks to Oscar Wilde, of weeping over a dead bird. At such a moment it is hard to believe in Oscar Wilde the anti-sentimentalist.[13]

Works of Victorian fiction would often have been read aloud, whether in fireside family groups, or at lunches, teas, and other social occasions. Harriet Martineau was moved to tears when her friend Anne Marsh read one of her stories 'The Admiral's Daughter' aloud after dinner one evening. So moved was Martineau by this story of the sufferings and sacrifices of an adulterous heroine that she helped arrange for it to be published. Marsh went on to great success through her moralistic novels, usually celebrating female self-sacrifice, and conforming to all the conventions of didactic and sentimental fiction. After her death, in 1874, the *Athenaeum* reflected that 'No writer had greater power than she of compelling tears. No book of its time produced more irrepressible bursts of tears than "The Deformed," or more solemn silent showers than that heart-rending story of "The Admiral's Daughter".'[14]

The assumption that fictional works would be read aloud to others rather than in silent solitude is also reflected in the Scottish writer Margaret Oliphant's comment in 1855, 'Poor little Nell! who has ever been able to read the last chapter of her history with an even voice or a clear eye?'[15] We know, from their own recollections, that Wilde used to read aloud to his two little boys, and that he had tears in his eyes when he told them the story of 'The Selfish Giant', explaining to them 'that really beautiful things always made him cry'.[16] It is in keeping with his aesthetic persona that Wilde, despite the stiflingly emotional atmosphere of his tales, should cite beauty rather than pathos as the source of his tears. In the story, the little boy's tear-filled eyes prevent him from seeing the giant approaching him; later he dies a Christlike death of love and suffering. Both 'The Happy Prince' and 'The Selfish Giant', like Dickens's child death scenes, conclude with religious references. 'The Happy Prince' ends with God asking one of his angels to bring him the two most precious things in the city. The angel brings God the broken, leaden heart of the statue, and the dead bird. 'You have rightly chosen', said God, 'for in my garden of Paradise this little bird shall sing for evermore, and in my city of gold the Happy Prince shall praise me.'[17]

In short, we should not take Wilde's throwaway comment about Little Nell too seriously. It was made in 1895, over half a century after *The Old Curiosity Shop* was first published, and was delivered by a purveyor of lachrymose stories, involving poverty, angels, dead children, and dead birds. As we have seen, one could, throughout the nineteenth century, be an anti-sentimentalist and yet an admirer, not to mention a producer, of pathetic literature of a Dickensian kind. Victorians were able to distinguish what they thought of as a hollow and ideologically unsound sentimentalism, associated with a discredited revolutionary sensibility, from true pathos, arising from piety and social conscience. Even if some of the individual anecdotes about the power of Dickens's prose to move its readers have become exaggerated to the point of mythology, there is no doubt that, throughout the first three decades of Victoria's reign, Dickens's stories produced pangs of feeling, and bucketsful of tears, especially through the deaths of Nancy Sikes, Paul Dombey, Little Nell, and Sydney Carton. These fatal moments called forth tears of pity, grief, and admiration from Dickens's millions of readers, making their author rich and famous in the process, and giving rise to countless emulations and imitations. Little Nell was immortalized not only in her original Dickensian decease, but also in paintings, sculptures, poems, plays, and songs by others.[18]

Dickens himself cried over his death scenes as he wrote them, as did many in the audiences who heard him perform them in adapted forms at private and public readings.[19] The tale of little Paul Dombey was a particular favourite with audiences, and was thought by many to be his most successful piece of pathos.[20] Paul Dombey is a prematurely wise man-child, philosophical, frail, and out of place among other children—he is repeatedly called an 'old-fashioned' boy by other characters. He slowly fades away, gripped by a vision of a river flowing rapidly out to the sea, carrying him from life to death. With his beloved sister at his bedside, Paul describes the face of their dead mother bathed in a divine light, as the sunlight, reflected from the stream outside his window, creates a golden ripple on the wall: 'The old, old fashion—Death! Oh thank God, all who see it, for that older fashion yet, of Immortality! And look upon us, angels of young children, with regards not quite estranged, when the swift river bears us to the ocean!'[21]

There are several reasons why this kind of writing is more likely to turn the stomachs than dampen the eyes of modern readers. It seems overdone and manipulative to the highest degree. The sentiment is heaped on with a shovel—we are presented with not just an ill child breathing his last, but an innocent boy who has lost his mother in infancy, and suffered throughout his short life, about to be parted from his sister, while adopting an attitude of stoical heroism in the face of his own demise. But even for someone, like me, willing in theory to respond to this kind of writing, the culmination of these death scenes in statements of religious doctrine poses an additional problem. Aside from the question of the existence or otherwise of God, angels, and an afterlife, the assertion of immortality seems to undermine the intended effect, from a literary and emotional point of view. If the departed child has gone to a life of eternal bliss, reunited with his lost mother, what is there to cry about? Dickens sought to inspire agony and reassurance in the same moment. But perhaps it is the conjuring up of just such mixed emotions that especially compels tears. In the case of classical tragedy, the audience's tears came from a combination of terror with pity; for sentimental Victorian novels, the recipe was to mix grief with hope. After all, as Elizabeth Barrett observed, a few years after the world had mourned for Little Nell, 'hopeless grief is passionless'.[22]

And why all these dead children? Setting aside issues of literary genre or affective response, Dickens lived in an era in which infant mortality was at a level that those of us living in the modern West can hardly imagine. Almost everyone would, during their lifetime, lose a baby daughter or son, an infant sister or brother. For most people this was a kind of loss to be endured more than once. Even after the advent of modern medicine and with greatly improved public hygiene, infant mortality remained high. At the end of the nineteenth century a quarter of all deaths were of babies.[23] For the sake of comparison, deaths of infants under a year old in England and Wales in 2012 were fifty times less frequent than that, accounting for about a half of 1 per cent of all registered deaths.[24] For parents in modern Britain, the death of a young child is a rare and terrible ordeal (one, as we shall see, endured by two successive twenty-first-century British prime ministers).[25] For Victorian parents it was just a terrible ordeal.

Infant and childhood deaths afflicted families of all social classes. Infectious diseases such as cholera and scarlet fever, which could spread rapidly in packed urban slums, were among the leading causes. For the labouring classes, whether farmhands or factory workers, the numerous infant deaths survive as little more than statistics.[26] The graves of such children were often unmarked, their final hours unrecorded, the contours of their parents' feelings uncharted. In the cases of the children of the more affluent and educated, records survive of the experience of this kind of bereavement, in the form of private diaries, of pious deathbed memorials shared with family members, and of letters written to and from grieving parents, including novelists, scientists, philosophers, politicians, and churchmen.[27] One of the most extensively documented examples comes from the family of the Reverend Archibald Tait and his wife Catharine. Like James Mill, Tait had a Scottish Presbyterian upbringing, which for both men inculcated a distrust of anything that savoured of emotional indulgence.[28] Tait had a distinguished career, holding posts as the headmaster of Rugby School, then Dean of Carlisle, where he was appointed in 1850, before going on to become Bishop of London and ultimately Archbishop of Canterbury in 1869.[29]

In the early months of 1856, scarlet fever was spreading through Carlisle. Catharine Tait had just given birth to a baby daughter, and the Taits were now a family with seven young children, all aged 10 or under—six girls and a boy—a hectic, lively, noisy household. On 6 March, one of the girls, Chatty, was taken ill and diagnosed with scarlet fever. She died the next day. Her parents immediately took precautions against infection to try to protect their other children. Leeches were applied to young bodies, walls were washed with lime, siblings moved to neighbours' houses, and the girls' long hair cut off and burned, except for a lock of each kept by their mother. None of it worked, and Catharine Tait came to see the cutting of her girls' hair, which she had previously loved to stroke, as a symbolic act, indicating that she had given them up to death. On 6 March Archibald and Catharine Tait had been the parents of seven healthy children, by 8 April only two remained. Five daughters, between 1 and 10 years old—Chatty, Susan, Frances, Catty, and May—died one by one as Easter came and went that year, and the nation celebrated the power of Christ over death. Only the new-born baby girl and her elder brother survived. Their parents poured their thoughts into diaries reflecting on the trial they had endured, which had threatened their health and tested their faith. The house was quieter now.[30]

The Taits' accounts of their bereavements are painful and strangely moving to a modern reader, perhaps not least because of the strength of the hope in God which pervades them. Here was the Dickensian formula in real life. The Taits' children died in agony, suffering in a way that doctors could do virtually nothing to relieve. These girls did not drift off serenely like Paul Dombey, nor did they expire quietly and tactfully away from view in the manner of Little Nell (see Figure 12). They were burned up with fever, twitching with pain, stiff-limbed, in agony, losing consciousness from pain. And yet, for a pious and educated family in the habit of reading aloud together every evening—from the Bible, naturally, and favourite hymns, but also from Shakespeare, Carlyle, and Dickens—these deaths could be fitted into shared narratives.[31] In the case of the older girls, they could themselves understand what was happening and used favourite religious poems to interpret their fate and that of their siblings, looking forward to an eternal reunion in heaven. For the parents, the great struggle was to reconcile their bitter earthly loss with a conviction that the souls of their beloved children were being gathered in by God. When the second-eldest girl, May, asked where her sister Catty was, not yet knowing that she had died, Catharine answered her daughter directly, 'The Lord Jesus Christ has taken your dear Catty to gone. Sorrow was dead indeed in her, but peace and perfect happiness were born; imaged in her tranquil beauty and profound repose.

And still her former self lay there, unaltered in this change. Yes. The old fireside had smiled upon that same sweet face; it had passed like a dream through haunts of misery and care; at the door of the poor schoolmaster on the summer evening, before the furnace fire upon the cold wet night, at the still bedside of the dying boy, there had been the same mild lovely look. So shall we know the angels in their majesty, after death.

The old man held one languid arm in his, and had the small hand tight folded to his breast, for warmth. It was the hand she had stretched out to him with her last smile—the hand that had led him on through all their wanderings. Ever and anon he pressed it to his lips; then hugged it to his breast again, murmuring that it was warmer now; and as he said it he looked, in agony, to those who stood around, as if imploring them to help her.

She was dead, and past all help, or need of it. The ancient rooms she had seemed to fill 'with life, even while her own was waning fast—the garden she had tended—the eyes she had gladdened—the noiseless haunts of many a thoughtful hour—the paths she had trodden as it were but yesterday—could know her no more.

"It is not," said the schoolmaster, as he bent down to kiss her on the

Figure 12. Little Nell 'At Rest', by George Cattermole, in *The Old Curiosity Shop* (1841). The Bodleian Libraries, the University of Oxford: Dunston B 704b, v.2, p. 210.

heaven. He has taken her to Chatty and Frances and Susan; shall you like to go to her?' May became very silent, her mother recorded, 'but her mind seemed satisfied—she never asked again', and soon followed her sisters.[32]

Catharine Tait's account includes moments worthy of Dickens, expressing piety and resignation, combining grief with hope. It was the death of their eldest daughter Catty that the Taits found hardest to endure. Her father declared to her, 'O my Catty, we do so love you, you have been such a treasure to us,' to which the girl responded by looking and pointing up towards heaven. Catharine recorded that at this moment, as Catty caught sight of heaven, a divine light rested on the girl's face and she stretched out her hands towards 'the angels waiting to convey her also to that place'. When Catharine observed to Archibald that Catty wanted to be taken home, to heaven, Archibald Tait 'burst into floods of tears'. Catty stretched forth her hand and wiped her father's cheek.[33]

There was a flowing back and forth between real bereavements and idealized literary representations, with each giving structure and meaning to the other. Dickens relived his grief over the sudden death of his wife's 17-year-old sister Mary in 1837 when writing the death of Little Nell, partly modelled on her.[34] In turn, readers could find, in Dickens's idealized child deaths, stories with which to revisit, but also contain, channel, and learn from their own losses. The actor Charles Macready was one of many who wrote to Dickens to tell him how they had wept over Little Nell or Paul Dombey, and of the moral and emotional benefits they had felt from the experience. Macready wrote to Dickens, of the death of Nell, 'You have crowned all that you have ever done in the power, the truth, the beauty and the deep moral of this exquisite picture.' The actor's own young daughter Joan had died two months previously.[35] Some decades later, George Acorn, who grew up in great poverty in East London, recalled how as a child he read *David Copperfield* together with his parents: 'how we all loved it, and eventually, when we got to "Little Em'ly", how we all cried together at poor old Peggotty's distress. The tears united us, deep in misery as we were ourselves.'[36]

Charles Macready was famed for his own emotional performances on the stage, including his rendering of King Lear, the influence of which can be seen in Dickens's portrayal of the frail, deluded figure of Nell Trent's grandfather.[37] Queen Victoria and Harriet Martineau witnessed Macready's Lear on the same night in February 1839. Victoria arrived late and chatted and laughed inattentively through the opening acts of the play, noting in her journal that Macready's performance was 'too violent and passionate'. Harriet Martineau noticed that Lord Albemarle, by contrast, in attendance with the queen, 'forgot everything but the play', leaning further and further forward in his seat, and weeping 'till his limp handkerchief would hold no more tears'.[38] The behaviour of the tearful Lord, who had been born into an age of sensibility in 1772, was in the style of that earlier generation, whose responses to tragedy had been caricatured by Thomas Rowlandson in 1789 (Figure 13).[39]

At the start of Victoria's reign, despite all the reactions against the world of sensibility that we have already surveyed, which came from rationalists as well as Romantics, from Protestants as well as freethinkers, the age of the man of feeling was not quite over. Prior to her marriage to Albert, by far the most important relationship in Victoria's life with anyone outside her immediate family circle was with her first Prime Minister, Lord Melbourne.[40] Indeed, Victoria and Melbourne seem to have been a little in love with one other. Tears were a prominent feature of their political and personal alliance, almost all of them shed by Lord Melbourne. The queen's journal entries record tears forever welling up and overflowing from the eyes of the beloved 'Lord M.', who seems to have been set off by virtually anything, including the most minor instances of benevolence, consideration, or gratitude exhibited by Victoria to those in her immediate family and social circle.[41] Melbourne also

Figure 13. Thomas Rowlandson, *Tragedy Spectators* (1789). © V&A Images/Alamy.

wept over a speech, written by himself, not only when it was delivered by Victoria at the opening of the first parliament of her reign in November 1837, but also when he read a draft of it out to Victoria a few days earlier, especially when 'reading the concluding part which alludes to my youth and reliance on the Loyalty of my People,—kind, excellent, good man'. Victoria's journal entries referring to the tears of Lord Melbourne often included similar outbursts of admiration. 'How modest he is;' she gushed in February 1838, 'really I must again here repeat how much I admire him, and how very very kind he is to me in every way, in manner, about every trifle, everything. I am truly and really very fond of him. When he speaks of anything which can in any way affect me or the country or even of any subject which affects other people, his eyes fill with tears.'[42]

The image of Queen Victoria as a perpetually dour, dry figure is an untenable caricature; she was passionate and emotional, especially as a young woman. However, she was not a sentimentalist. Her emotional style was markedly different from that of her first Prime Minister, and that of the premier novelist of the first half of her reign. After her first lachrymose appearance as queen on the balcony of St James's, her tears were relatively infrequent, both in public and in private. On her wedding day in February 1840—a day, and night, of unprecedented affection, love, and happiness for Victoria—some newspapers reported that she had cried at the ceremony, an allegation which she indignantly corrected in her journal: 'I did not shed one tear the whole time.'[43]

In conversations with Lord Melbourne, Victoria discussed the tendency of different nations towards emotion and sentimentality. Astonishingly, given Melbourne's own lachrymal promiscuity, the Prime Minister expressed the view that sentimentality was 'the sign of not a good person'. Victoria speculated that her mother's unfortunate sentimentalism was a sign of her German character. Melbourne politely pointed out that there were strong English precedents for such a tendency too, noting the cases of writers 'like Sterne and Mackenzie, "making reflections over donkeys" he said, etc. etc.'.[44] On another occasion Melbourne shared his view of the Irish nation as a 'poor set' who were false and hypocritical, with 'quick feelings' and prone to tears, adding that some of the worst people he had known had such quick feelings. 'All this is very true,' Victoria solemnly affirmed, showing herself quite able to condemn her mother's German sentimentality, and the whole Irish nation's falseness, quick feelings, and too-easy tears, while unreservedly admiring the tears of Melbourne, 'as I know they come from his excellent heart'.[45]

Melbourne's was the standard English view of the Irish. The stereotype of a feckless, drink-soaked, primitive, superstitious, and emotionally excitable people was the product of centuries of religious and political conflict, repression, and rebellion.[46] In the period which saw the political union of Ireland with the rest of the United Kingdom in 1801, the great famine of the 1840s, and the rapid growth of Fenian, Republican, and

Home Rule movements, hatred and violence towards English landowners and politicians gathered pace in Ireland, while existing anti-Irish clichés took on new dimensions in England. Modern scientific ideas about race, as we shall see, were used to assert a biological basis for the supposed moral failings for the Irish nation.[47] But there were still those on both sides who hoped to find a peaceful future through reform and negotiation. In the 1830s, Daniel O'Connell was one of these, and was especially hopeful that the accession of Victoria would signal an era of increased sympathy and reformism on the Irish question.[48] When the tearful young queen's accession was proclaimed on the balcony of St James's, greeted by the waving of hats and handkerchiefs from the people below, newspapers reported that 'Mr O'Connell attracted considerable attention, by waving his hat, and cheering most vehemently.'[49]

O'Connell and his family were rewarded with an audience with their monarch. But this high-society hobnobbing did not bring 'The Liberator' the substantial progress he hoped for.[50] During the general election campaign of 1841, which would see a return to Tory rule, and only modest returns for O'Connell's Irish Repeal group, the *Spectator* complained of O'Connell's campaigning techniques, using his open-air addresses from his carriage to crowds tens of thousands strong to 'stimulate the zeal' of the 'excitable' Irish people. On one such occasion, O'Connell's speech, about the iniquities of landlords who sought to compel tenant farmers to vote as instructed, was interrupted by two women rushing to the front, with their children, 'the whole party bathed in tears', crying out that their husbands had been imprisoned by their landlords for refusing to vote for the Tory faction. One of their children, a little girl about 8 or 9 years old, sobbing inconsolably for her father, was passed up to O'Connell. He kissed her affectionately, exclaiming 'Oh, the cruel monsters, that could rend asunder the dearest ties of the human heart—this is more than I can bear!', before bursting into tears. One observer added, 'there was not a dry eye present. I never witnessed a more affecting sight.'[51] As ever, a child formed the ideal focus for a scene of pathos, in this case attaching feelings like those played upon by Little Nell to political injustice. This little girl was a perfect visual representation of a text from the book of Ecclesiastes: 'So I returned, and considered all the oppressions that are done under the sun: and behold the tears of such as were oppressed, and they had no comforter; and on the side of their oppressors there was power; but they had no comforter.'[52] O'Connell could cast himself as both liberator and comforter.

Charles Dickens harboured some of the standard anti-Irish prejudices of his time, including thinking that the Irish were excitable, and that their quick feelings were more inclined towards humour than to either intellect or pathos. However, his own reading tours of Ireland in the 1850s and 1860s gave him some cause to reconsider. He was surprised to discover that Dublin had fewer spirits shops than comparable English cities, and he found much to admire in the grand architecture and wholesome homes of Dublin, Belfast, Limerick, and Cork. For their own part, the Irish public and press welcomed Dickens as the most loved of English writers and a teacher of 'divine principles of kindness, charity and love'. His sell-out readings were greeted with laughter and tears. In Belfast, *The Christmas Carol* was described as offering 'the pathos of all that is pathetic'. In Dublin, audiences were moved to tears by 'the deep pathos displayed in the delineation of the child cripple, Tiny Tim'. The death of little Paul Dombey brought tears to the eyes of young and old, male and female, in Irish audiences; the crying over Dombey was 'universal'. Dickens had witnessed plenty of such reactions before, in England, and yet even he had never seen men, in particular, 'go in to cry so undisguisedly' as they did at the Belfast reading of Dombey.[53]

The characteristics of Dickensian pathos included the combination of great grief with religious hope. His stories conveyed moral lessons through emotional responses to fictional representations of the poverty, suffering, and death of innocents. In short, Dickens had developed his own Victorian version of the literature of sensibility. It was part of Dickens's genius to be able to sell this stuff to both the paternalistic rich and the suffering poor, to composed English landlords as well as their excitable Irish tenants. The world of Nell Trent and Paul Dombey provided a kind of shared emotional space for a divided nation, into which men and women could pour their tears, while assuring themselves that theirs were the tears of true human sympathy, rather than false sentimentality. As we shall see in Chapter 12, this extended Dickensian sunset of the age of sensibility continued until the 1870s, even including pathetic performances by prisoners, policemen, and judges in criminal trials. But after the setting of that sentimental star, something darker and colder would follow.

12

Damp Justice

If you were asked to name the most emotionally sensitive professions, you might think of artists and musicians, actors, certainly, perhaps writers. Lawyers would probably not be near the top of your list. Yet it was a weeping Victorian judge, to whom we shall return, who first piqued my interest in the whole subject of the history of British tears. It turned out that he belonged to an eminent tradition of sensibility in the legal profession that could be traced back at least to the eighteenth century. Henry Mackenzie, for instance, the creator of the original 'man of feeling', was a Scottish exchequer lawyer as well as a writer.[1] Francis Jeffrey, a struggling young lawyer in 1802, became the founding editor of the hugely successful literary and political periodical the *Edinburgh Review*. By the 1840s, after a career as a reformist politician and a judge, including a stint as Lord Advocate of Scotland, Jeffrey was in his seventies, but still engaged in the world of literature. Having moved in the same circles as Henry Mackenzie in the 1790s, Jeffrey's friendship with Charles Dickens half a century later embodied in a single lifetime the journey from sensibility to pathos.[2] In response to the death of Paul Dombey in 1847, Jeffrey wrote to Dickens, 'I have so cried and sobbed over it last night and again this morning; and felt my heart purified by those tears, and blessed and loved you for making me shed them.' Of a later instalment of the same story, Jeffrey wrote once more, 'I cannot tell you how much I have been charmed with your last number, and what gentle sobs and delightful tears it has cost me.' Jeffrey admired both the 'pleasantry and pathos' of Dickens's writing, and the 'higher and deeper passion' it contained, implying a contrast with the gentler and tender feelings celebrated by the novelists of his youth.[3]

During the Dickensian age, the tears of lawyers and politicians were increasingly expunged from their public appearances, and restricted to their private lives. Today, even though the age of the stiff upper lip, which ensued after Dickens's death, is surely over, public tears of a certain kind are still rare enough to make headlines.[4] In 2009, for example, the parliamentary expenses scandal in Britain exposed in tragi-comic form the stupid greed of prominent politicians. They had filched public money to pay for top-end televisions and dishwashers; nannies, gardeners, and personal assistants; home improvements, and luxury housing for them-selves, their relatives, and, in one case, their ducks.[5] The ensuing pro-secutions gave rise to several courtroom scenes of sobbing politicians: an occasion for general delight. These tears were pathetic, in at least one of the senses of that word. Lord Taylor of Warwick moved himself to tears at the start of his trial, as he recalled his own background and the poverty of his Jamaican father. And then he wept again, removing his glasses to wipe away the tears, after watching a video about himself and his charitable work with young people, offered in evidence of his virtuous character.[6] Those of a comparably charitable disposition might have felt sympathy for Taylor and his foolish submission of fake travel claims, which he said he believed were a legitimate substitute for a salary. However, I imagine many more responded with Wilde-like laughter than with Dickensian tears to the spectacle of self-pitying politicians being offered tissues as they sobbed their way out of the courtroom to start prison sentences for fraud.

The criminal court has long provided a stage for the public perform-ance of inner feelings, including the shedding of tears. Personal tragedies and collective traumas, petty misdemeanours and sensational murders, contrite prisoners and emotional advocates: all have lent the intense emotion of the theatre to British courtrooms. And newspaper reporters have been on hand to record every sigh and sob. As in the West End, as in our own domestic lives, so at the Old Bailey, the response of the audience is all important. The moral context and the physical execution of the courtroom tear must be perfect if it is to be greeted with sympathy rather than derision and, ultimately, with a reprieve rather than imprisonment or even death. We have already seen how tears, or their absence, had real significance in witchcraft trials, and were part of the ritualized behaviour of both criminals and onlookers at public executions, the last of which occurred in England in 1868.[7]

Although witchcraft trials and public hangings are now exotic historical objects, we are familiar enough with tears in the courtroom, shed by the accused, the victim, or by the distraught families of either. The idea that an artfully executed sob might strengthen the case for the defence is not new. A nineteenth-century French cartoon depicted a lawyer instructing his client to try to shed a few tears, at least out of one eye.[8] In England, a sentimental print of the same period by George Cruikshank showed the sister of a convicted thief weeping in court, perhaps hoping that her tears would soften the judge's heart and thus the sentence handed down to her brother (Figure 14).[9] But the worry, of course, about a judge and jury being swayed by penitent tears is that, as in the French cartoon, the tears may be put on. The bizarre and bungled staged kidnap of her own daughter by Karen Matthews in 2008 provides a memorable recent example. Apparently inspired by the massive media coverage of the disappearance of 3-year-old Madeleine McCann the previous year, Matthews arranged for her own daughter to be drugged and hidden under a bed, while she wept copiously on television appealing for information, in the hope of generating a national appeal and a large reward, to be claimed by her co-conspirator. After the plot was uncovered and Matthews brought to trial, the details of her story changed but the

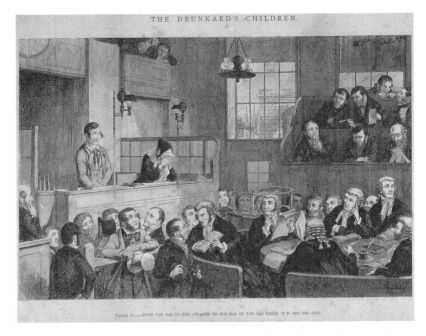

Figure 14. George Cruikshank, *The Drunkard's Children*, plate 5 (1848). Wellcome Library, London.

performance remained the same. Now Matthews, sobbing while giving evidence, denied involvement, and tried to blame it all on her accomplice. The judge and jury at Leeds Crown Court, unmoved, found Matthews guilty of kidnap, false imprisonment, and perverting the course of justice. She was later sentenced to eight years in prison. Her sob-story had backfired.[10]

In the nineteenth century, the stakes could be even higher, with death the penalty for the most serious offences. Court reporters scrutinized the physical demeanour of the accused in minute detail, searching for clues to guilt or innocence. And it was a lack of tears, more often than their excess, which raised suspicions. A prisoner who remained cool, stolid, and dry-eyed when standing trial for their life would be suspected of inhuman indifference, whereas one who wept tears of regret might succeed in making themselves an object of compassion. If found guilty and sentenced to death, the defendant would sometimes remain firm, betraying no emotion, or alternatively collapse in tears, either in the dock, or as they were escorted away. Newspaper reports thus reconstructed courtroom dramas making use of a recognized repertoire of emotional roles: the callous murderer; the innocent victim; the penitent sinner. It was an easy formula for readers to interpret.[11]

Notable among those who remained stolid and self-possessed were two high-profile murderers of the 1860s, Franz Müller and Dr Edward Pritchard. The reporting of both cases was in the spirit of the observation made in the very respectable *Lady's Newspaper* that 'stoical indifference' was 'frequently the accompaniment of great guilt'.[12] Müller was a German tailor accused of murdering a man on the North London railway. *The Times* reported that even after Müller had been sentenced to death, he displayed 'surprising firmness and self-possession', interpreting this as 'an imperturbability which showed him capable of the most desperate deeds'.[13] Dr Edward Pritchard stood trial in Glasgow in 1865 for the premeditated murder of his wife and her mother by a systematic regime of poisoning. Reporters agreed that there was something icy about his demeanour: 'the most cool and unconcerned person in Court', his features 'fixed and immovable by emotion', his eye 'cool, steady, always half-closed, dark-brown or dark yellow', like the 'eye of the cobra or rattlesnake on the other side of a sheet of glass'. Even his production of tears was greeted with cynicism rather than sympathy: 'he almost always wept when, as a fond husband, it was proper that he should be moved—wept, or did something dexterous with his pocket-handkerchief, which might very well pass for weeping.' After he had been convicted and sentenced to death, Pritchard 'laid his face on his handkerchief on the bar for a minute or two, and then walked down the stairs which the trapdoor in front of the dock conceals'.[14] Once the press had formed a view of the guilt of someone like Müller or Pritchard, they could not win. Stoic restraint was interpreted as criminal coldness, expressions of emotion as cynical pieces of fakery.

It is no surprise to find defendants and witnesses in criminal trials weeping in court under the pressure of cross-examination or in response to the intensity of hearing the verdict. What we are much less familiar with today is the spectacle of the presiding judge being reduced to tears too. This was a more common, albeit always remarkable, feature of the performance of justice in earlier periods. One Irish newspaper correspondent writing in 1850 thought it quite usual for a humane judge to 'shed tears of genuine sorrow' in sentencing a murderer to a 'deserved but violent death'.[15] Between the 1750s and 1850s, weeping judges were a regular feature of public justice, and indeed it was the discovery of the tearful performances of one particular judge, Sir James Shaw Willes, that first fired my interest in the whole history of tears. Born in Cork in 1814, the son of a physician, James Shaw Willes was educated in Dublin, and moved to London in 1837, becoming a judge in 1855. Willes was known for his prodigious intellect and for his mercy in criminal cases, as well as his tendency to tears. His appearance and manner were sometimes an occasion for comment, as when he wore white kid gloves while taking down notes of evidence. He was a man of literary sensibilities and said to be 'one of the gentlest of men' and 'no sportsman'. At various stages of his life, Willes suffered from heart disease, gout, and insomnia. He died at his home in Watford in 1872.[16]

Our standard view of the figure of the judge, especially the Victorian judge, would suggest that he should be calm and contained, no matter how dramatic or distressing the case.[17] An 1857 painting by Abraham Solomon, entitled *Waiting for the Verdict*, captures pictorially what I imagine remains our standard view of Victorian justice (Figure 15). The picture is composed of three levels: in the foreground a prisoner's tearful family wait for the verdict; a few steps higher, bewigged barristers mill outside the courtroom; finally, placed far above them all, glimpsed in

Figure 15. Abraham Solomon, *Waiting for the Verdict* (1857). © Tate, London 2014.

his splendid robes, sits the almighty judge. The eye is led on a trajectory of ascending education, affluence, finery, power, and bodily containment. The working-class father has his head in his hands, the mother's eyes brim with tears, the wife's brows are contracted, her eyes swollen, almost bruised. The judge is too distant for his face to be read, but he and the barristers strike bodily attitudes of upright composure which contrast with the dishevelled collapse of the prisoner's family. Solomon's painting suggested a contrast between the suffering and tears of working people, their expressions of grief and despair, and the faceless, indifferent operations of the legal system.[18]

But the discovery of my weeping judge, Justice Willes, changed this picture for me, and further research revealed that, historically, Willes was not alone. He was continuing an august tradition of the dispensing of damp justice. Even 'Hanging Judge' Jeffreys, notorious for his role in the 'Bloody Assizes' of 1685, had been prone to tears, especially of 'rage and vexation' when met with 'bold affronts' by fellow judges.[19] Leading lawyers, including several Lord Chancellors, of the eighteenth and nineteenth centuries, earned reputations either for tearful and histrionic advocacy, or for moments of sentimental weeping from the bench. In 1820 in the House of Lords, during a hearing into alleged adultery by the new Queen Caroline, a former Lord Chancellor (Lord Erskine) was so moved by the speech in defence of the queen by a future Lord Chancellor (Lord Brougham) that he rushed out of the chamber in tears.[20] It is not known whether the sitting Lord Chancellor in 1820, Lord Eldon, wept on that occasion, but his propensity to tears was well known, and featured in satires of the period, including a protest poem by Percy Shelley entitled 'The Masque of Anarchy'. Written in 1819, in response to the government's violent repression of reform protests in Manchester, Shelley's poem personified Eldon as the figure of 'Fraud', weeping deadly tears:

> Next came Fraud, and he had on,
> Like Eldon, an ermined gown;
> His big tears, for he wept well,
> Turned to mill-stones as they fell.
> And the little children, who
> Round his feet played to and fro,
> Thinking every tear a gem,
> Had their brains knocked out by them.[21]

Judicial tears, as Shelley's scathing response to Eldon reveals, were not immune from accusations of insincerity and hypocrisy. In 1855, *Punch* reported on a case of three bankers convicted of fraud. At the conclusion of the trial, the presiding judge and the prosecutor were both reported to have been moved to tears. *Punch* could not 'see the necessity for all this sentimental snivelling' over such a case when 'there is a great deal more to cry about, more matter for sympathy and commiseration in nine cases out of ten at the Old Bailey, than in the case of these dishonest Bankers', declaring they would have 'rejoiced to say that the Prosecutor and the Judge had "done their duty like men," if unfortunately they had not laid themselves open to the charge of having done their duty like women'. One of the judges sitting on that occasion was Sir James Shaw Willes.[22]

In 1859, Willes heard a case involving a ten-month-old baby boy who had died in painful, violent convulsions as a result of a dose of laudanum, administered to him in his bottle, mixed with milk and sugar. The baby's mother confessed that she was the poisoner, and explained her reason: she was convinced she was guilty of some terrible sin for which she would soon be hanged and she 'thought it better that her child should be sent to God, who would take care of it for her'. It was reported that during the trial, and especially while the details of the baby's death were being described, 'the learned Judge became painfully affected, so much so, that at one time he buried his face in his note-book and shed tears and seemed almost unable to proceed with the evidence'.[23] Although this extraordinary image of a Victorian judge sobbing violently into his notebook was certainly considered worth reporting at the time, it was not a source of adverse comment, as it would surely have been in later periods.

In some particularly charged capital trials heard in front of Willes, especially those involving young and sympathetic defendants, almost everyone involved seems to have been in tears, the whole courtroom vibrating with sensation. At the conclusion of such trials, when the sentence was passed, the prisoner, the judge, and the public in the gallery were united by a powerful invisible bond of sympathy, made audible through silence and visible in tears. One such occasion was the trial of Constance Kent in 1865. This trial marked the conclusion of an infamous and mysterious case which had started five years earlier in the village of Road in Wiltshire, with the discovery of a 3-year-old boy's body. The body testified to a brutal attack, with stab wounds to the chest, and the throat cut so violently that the boy had almost been decapitated. The case was made famous again recently by Kate Summerscale's book *The Suspicions of Mr Whicher*.[24] Constance Kent, the boy's half-sister, was standing trial. The proceedings were intense and dramatic but very brief, not lasting more than ten minutes. It was reported, despite the fact that she wore a black veil, that Constance Kent's demeanour showed she 'had been crying very much'. When asked by Justice Willes whether she wished to plead guilty, 'the tremulous vibration of her veil showed that she was deeply agitated'. Eventually she managed to answer in the affirmative. All that remained was for Willes to pass the sentence.

Justice Willes assumed the black cap 'amidst the most profound silence' and passed sentence, commenting on the cruelty displayed by the girl, and on the 'feelings of jealousy and anger' that had motivated her. These passions, Willes told the defendant, had been allowed 'to work in your breast until they at last assumed over you the influence and power of the Evil One'. At this point in his speech—at the mention of the devil— the newspapers reported, Willes 'bent forward and wept for some few seconds'. Having temporarily regained himself, Willes pressed on, commenting that it lay with the queen alone to decide whether clemency should be granted on the grounds of Constance Kent's youth at the time. Reports noted that 'the learned Judge here again wept, and the solemn words of his sentence were almost inaudible'. Seeing Willes's tears, Kent was herself 'forsaken by the extraordinary fortitude which had throughout characterised her demeanour, and she wept audibly'. And it was not just judge and defendant who wept at that trial. According to a later account, the speech delivered by Constance Kent's counsel had been 'punctuated with sobs'. The newspapers agreed that 'the jury were in tears', as was 'the greater part of the public'. One report went further still: 'The jury and everyone in Court were visibly affected.'[25]

But why was everyone crying? This question is all the more troublesome for the historian to answer since no one could reasonably have supposed that the sentence of death by hanging, haltingly delivered through his tears by Justice Willes, would be carried out. The prisoner's voluntary confession, combined with her youth and sex, made it virtually certain that the capital sentence would be commuted, which indeed it was within a few days.[26] So, if not over the imminent doom of this young woman, why was everyone crying? Were they moved by the terribleness of the crime, or by the catharsis of a dramatic confession of guilt? In cases like this one, as with Mary Wollstonecraft's tears over Louis XVI, and Queen Victoria's at her own accession, perhaps it was rather the ritual power of the occasion itself that was at the heart of the phenomenon.[27] In this case, the script played out in the courtroom dramatized a narrative of sinfulness, justice, and death. It was this ritual performance, as much as any psychologically identifiable emotional response, which was product-ive of tears. Some momentous public occasions demand tears, and so tears are produced. They are necessary parts of a communal ritual more than they are expressions of individual emotion.

James Shaw Willes was not the only weeping judge of the nineteenth century, but he was one of the last, and his performances risked appear-ing out of date and over the top. They also reconfirmed the nineteenth-century view that the Irish were especially emotionally excitable and prone to tears, weeping on the Celtic fringe of the nation.[28] With his white kid gloves and his love of poetry, his refinement of manners, his compassion, his sensibility, his tears, Willes was undoubtedly a man of feeling. But, by the 1860s and 1870s, the man of feeling had finally had his day, even in an updated Victorian guise. Judged by the new standards of an imperial nation, Willes's manner seemed 'almost womanly'.[29] An 1873 article in the *Atlantic Monthly* marvelled that Lord Jeffrey had ever sobbed so over little Nell and Paul Dombey, asking, 'Does any peer of the realm now shed tears for their fate?' The author of the same article doubted that Dickens's famous readings of his works would now elicit tears so readily among 'literary company'.[30] In the theatre, too, the tide of tears was turning. An 1882 newspaper article suggested that it was only among the uncultivated that the theatre now provided an occasion for tears. While 'our forefathers delighted in plays that were full of tears', such 'weeping plays' did not appeal to the fashionable members of modern audiences: 'It is not difficult to move pit and gallery to tears; but stall and box occupants are less easily worked upon.'[31] And the taste for weeping judges seemed to be going the same way as the taste for weeping novels and weeping plays. A reporter of the Constance Kent trial in 1865 commented that he had 'rarely, if ever, seen a judge so deeply affected, even on occasions like the present'.[32] By the end of his life, James Shaw Willes was out of step with the times, and his personal life had become increasingly isolated and unhappy. His marriage was joyless and childless, his health was deteriorating, and he lived in emotional isolation, although under the same roof as an extensive domestic staff, in a gloomy Gothic house called Otterspool, in Hertfordshire. There he walked his dogs, read German literature, and fished on a glassy lake, while rooks wheeled and cawed overhead.[33]

After an exhausting period of work on the northern circuit in the summer of 1872, concluding with the Liverpool Assizes, where he heard fifty-seven criminal cases including several of a gruesome and violent nature, Willes returned to Otterspool, exhausted and insomniac, with a 'peculiar glossiness in his eye'. His clerk asked him if he had received bad news, since he looked 'so depressed and miserable, worse than ever I saw you in my life'. The judge said nothing in reply, but walked hurriedly away with a tear in his eye. The following morning at about seven o'clock, the clerk heard a loud bang and a scream coming from the bedroom. Rushing to the scene, he found Sir James Shaw Willes on the sofa, breathing his last, his eyes three-quarters open, a revolver lying by his knee. He was 58 years old. The inquest found that Justice Willes had shot himself in the heart, and concluded that 'suppressed gout' had spread to his brain and driven him mad.[34]

The mournful history of this weeping judge raised again the question of when it was a sign of mental pathology to weep, and when a sign of sanity; when a sign of manliness and when of effeminacy; when of compassionate sensibility and when of frailty. Different periods have come up with different answers, and in the following chapters we will see how modern science and medicine dealt with these issues after the pivotal contributions of Charles Darwin. But thankfully the answers can sometimes be delivered through comedy as well as tragedy.

A satirical piece in the weekly paper *Funny Folks* in December 1888 appeared at the dawn of the age of the stiff upper lip, and reinforces the idea of the courtroom as a stage on which different emotional styles can be performed. The article, headed 'Robert Emotional: A Play of the Period', was inspired by a case heard before a Birmingham magistrate that month, in which a police-sergeant by the name of Holmes (not Sherlock, who had made his first appearance in print a year earlier) was called to give evidence against a police colleague charged with arson. Having been recalled to the stand to give his evidence—namely that he had overheard the prisoner confessing guilt—for a third time, Holmes said he was very sorry to be obliged to give this testimony against a friend and 'broke down and burst into tears'.[35]

In some eras this show of manly sensibility and affectionate loyalty might have been praised, but not in the Britain of the 1880s, with imperialistic jingoism on the rise, the stiff upper lip under construction, and masculinity under threat from aesthetes and decadents. The 'Play of the Period' was introduced with the explanation that 'The brutal bobby has had his day, and now the emotional peeler appears to be coming in.' The action of the very brief and silly 'play' takes place in Bow Street rather than Birmingham and does not follow the actual case of Sergeant Holmes. Instead the policeman in the play sniffs violently, sobs bitterly, and faints away through excessive emotion, all in response to a trivial case involving a beggar with a hard-luck story. After the beggar, despite the emotional bobby's protestations, is sentenced to seven days in jail, the policeman 'goes into screaming hysterics, and kicks the front out of the witness-box'.

The play closes with a commentary delivered by Sir Charles Warren, the perfect antidote to this kind of pathological emotion. Warren was an explorer, an imperial hero, a major-general in the army. He had exactly the military bearing (and military moustache) that one would expect of such a man. Until the previous month, he been commissioner of the Metropolitan Police.[36] The imagined reaction of this embodiment of imperial masculinity to the 'emotional peeler' sets the scene perfectly for the next act in the history of British tears: 'Well I'll be Trafalgar-squared if anybody would have anticipated this sort of thing some twelve months ago. But what can one expect when I'm not at the head of affairs!' The play ends with a terse stage direction: *'Tableau of disgust, and quick curtain.'*[37] The age of pathos was over. Public executions and Dickensian death scenes were a thing of the past and in 1872, shortly after the death of the last of the weeping judges, Sir James Shaw Willes, the leading scientific authority of the age, Charles Darwin, would have his say on the matter too.

IV. RESTRAINT

13

Old Ladies and Other Animals

The Victorian age has a dual inheritance in our collective imagination—an emblem of both pathos and restraint, sentimentality and repression. These two Victorian legacies correspond to two very different images of the woman for whom the age was named: the weeping 18-year-old who was proclaimed Queen of Great Britain and Ireland in 1837, and the forbidding widow who was declared Empress of India, thanks to Benjamin Disraeli, in 1876. The young queen inhabited a world in which sensibility was giving way not to restraint but to Romanticism, pathos, and Dickensian sentiment, while the latter's new status as empress, four decades later, marked a turning point not only in British history but also in emotional style, as the repression of foreign peoples and the repression of foreign feelings progressed together. It was into this world of militarism, empire, and warfare that the British stiff upper lip would be born. The Victorian duality of sentiment and restraint can also be found in the life and writings of that age's most influential scientific figure. There were two Charles Darwins—the doting, weeping, father, friend, and animal-lover who appears in private correspondence and personal reminiscences and the rational observer, staring at emotional expressions with the eyes of science, dry and unblinking.[1] In Darwin's published writings about emotion, and contemporaries' responses to them, we find the powerful Victorian scientific justification for what would become the ideology of the 'stiff upper lip'.[2] In 1872, when he published his book on *The Expression of the Emotions in Man and Animals*, Darwin lent his high scientific authority to the proposition, based on his comparative study of emotions in men, women, children, and animals around the world, that, unlike children, women, 'savages', and the insane, 'Englishmen rarely cry'.[3]

Ever since his beetle-hunting days as a student in Cambridge, Darwin had been an obsessive observer and an imaginative theoretician. He was always looking, always thinking, always feeling. He treated all aspects of his life as opportunities to gather more evidence in support of his theories, including his theories about the expression of the emotions. Even trundling along in a train carriage, when others might have been reading a sentimental novel, Darwin was in observational mode, scientifically scrutinizing the faces of fellow passengers. On one occasion, recalled in the *Expression of the Emotions in Man and Animals*, Darwin was idly observing the old lady sitting opposite him. She had a placid expression, he noted, but as he watched her, the corners of her mouth became slightly turned down, by the action of the muscles known as the *depressores anguli oris* (the depressors of the corner of the mouth). Just as Darwin thought to himself how meaningless such apparent expressions could be, the woman's eyes 'suddenly became suffused with tears almost to overflowing, and her whole countenance fell'. There could be no doubt, Darwin thought, what these tears revealed, namely that 'some painful recollection, perhaps that of a long-lost child, was passing through her mind'.[4]

Even when Emma Darwin gave birth to her first child, William, two days after Christmas in 1839, one of her husband's first thoughts was that this was a great research opportunity. As he recalled, decades later, in his autobiography, 'I at once commenced to make notes on the first dawn of the various expressions which he exhibited, for I felt convinced, even at this early period, that the most complex and fine shades of expression must all have had a gradual and natural origin.' One of the things that

Darwin noticed was that, although his new-born baby made the noise of 'crying or rather of squalling', no tears were shed in the first few weeks. The screams were not accompanied by tears until the baby boy was over four months old (or 139 days, to be precise, as Darwin was).[5] Later, Darwin asked other parents to observe their babies, and was told that tears first rolled down the face (rather than merely welling up in the eyes) during crying fits at ages ranging from 42 to 110 days. He included these observations, along with pioneering photographic illustrations (such as those in Figure 16), in the *Expression*, when it was published. Darwin

Figure 16. Photographs of crying infants, from Charles Darwin's *The Expression of the Emotions in Man and Animals* (1872). Wellcome Library, London.

concluded from this that exciting the lachrymal glands into action, like some other inherited movements and tastes, 'required some practice' before it was perfected, commenting that this was 'all the more likely in a habit like weeping, which must have been acquired since the period when man branched off from the common progenitor of the genus *Homo* and of the non-weeping anthropomorphous apes'.[6] In other words, crying was a learned human habit that could be practised and developed, as had long been recognized by the existence of visual and literary works designed to teach people how and when to weep. As the late medieval poem *De Arte Lacrimandi* had put it, 'Therefor to wepe come lerne att me'.[7]

When I started researching the history of tears and weeping, Darwin's work on the subject was one of the first things I read. My wife and I were expecting our first child at the time and I thought how interesting it would be to replicate Darwin's exercise—keeping an infant diary and making notes of the gradual development of my own son's expressions and behaviours. In the event, once I became a father, I soon abandoned the plan. I now had no idea how Darwin had found the time and energy to keep detailed notes for a psychological sketch of an infant, rather than being, as I was, in a state of near-constant physical and emotional exhaustion. Darwin, I concluded, while undoubtedly a devoted and affectionate father, probably took a somewhat less active role in childcare than I did, as well as enjoying the support of a sizeable domestic staff in his rural home in Kent. Despite my failure to replicate Darwin's scientific study, I did have the experience of becoming a father at the same time as studying the expression of emotions, and so I too have welcomed parenthood as an opportunity for researching, as well as experiencing, tears and weeping. Like Darwin, I noted that my children did not shed tears when they were very young. When, after a few months (sorry, I don't know how many days exactly), their screams were first accompanied by tears rolling down their cheeks, I recognized in myself a new and very strong emotional response. I also observed that in the early months of life, my son was moved to tears generally by what I interpreted as hunger or indigestion, and later by physical pain, and then only from his second year onwards by what I took to be emotional upset and distress, quite often caused by separation from a parent or carer. Like one of the little girls mentioned in Darwin's study, my son was inclined to shed tears profusely when punished—in his case by being put on the 'naughty step', in the case of the Victorian girl, by her chair being turned to face away from the table.[8]

I also noticed that my son's own earliest ideas about tears had something in common with Charles Darwin's theory: they both tended to treat weeping first and foremost from a 'behaviourist' point of view—as an action in itself rather than as an outward sign of inward emotion. When I asked my son, when he was 3, why he sometimes cried, he just said, 'I don't know.' Disappointingly he did not go on, as a Victorian prodigy surely would have done, to quote Tennyson—'Tears, idle tears, I know not what they mean, Papa.'[9] But when I asked him the slightly different question, 'When do you cry?' he replied, 'When I'm at nursery,' in other words, when separated from his parents. When pressed to think of any other examples he couldn't, and he made no reference at all to any feelings. The tears, then, belonged to a situation, not to an emotion. Around the same age there was an occasion when I lost my temper and shouted at my son, and after a shocked pause he started to cry, and then complained, 'But Daddy, now you've made me cry.' Again, he did not complain that I had made him feel sad or feel afraid, but simply that I'd made him cry. His subsequent reports of occasions when he has cried still tend to be couched in purely behavioural terms, and only get connected with feelings and emotions if my wife or I encourage him to interpret them that way. Like my son, and like Charles Darwin, the American psychologist William James, in a famous 1884 article entitled simply 'What is an emotion?', favoured the behavioural approach, prioritizing bodily reaction over any inward feeling. A purely disembodied emotion, William James stated, 'is a nonentity', asking, of grief, 'what would it be without its tears, its sobs, its suffocation of the heart, its pang in the breast-bone?' Crucially, James claimed that it was the bodily reaction that came first, with the emotional interpretation following afterwards. Common sense might say that 'we lose our fortune, are sorry and weep', but James's theory was that in fact we only feel sorrow because we first weep.[10]

The late nineteenth and early twentieth centuries saw the creation of the modern science of psychology. Some saw this discipline as a continuation of ancient philosophical investigations into the nature of mental experience itself, but most put the emphasis, as Darwin and James did, on the bodily and behavioural side of things. Accordingly, when it came to weeping, the questions at issue were not about the subjective meaning and feeling of tears in the present, but their physiological and evolutionary history. One puzzle was how and why the connections between tears, distress, and sympathy got set up in the first place. Why should pain, sorrow, or other strong emotions produce a flow of fluid from the eyes? Why is it not a flow of wax from the ears or of mucus from the nose? Why can we not just rely on vocal cries of distress to communicate our suffering to others? This is a central conundrum in the science of weeping, and it has still not been resolved, despite several attempts, of which Darwin's was one of the earliest.

The details of Darwin's attempts to explain tears and weeping are of importance in the history of science, and are still of interest to contemporary psychologists of weeping (although they almost all think he was wrong).[11] From the point of view of the cultural and emotional history of Britain, his writings, including both published scientific treatises and private correspondence, have further value. They offer evidence of the ideological dimensions of the 'stiff upper lip', and of the tension between manly feeling and rational restraint in the experiences of somebody who happened also to be the author of works of unparalleled scientific importance—works placing human mental lives, including his own, within a systematic evolutionary framework for the first time. It was in the early 1870s, after the public had had a decade to digest the general idea of evolution, that Darwin published his two works applying his theories specifically to human beings. Of course it was the status of humans as the first-cousins of monkeys (not to mention the more distant relatives of mushrooms) that really agitated Darwin's readers. In *The Descent of Man*, in 1871, and then in the following year in *The Expression of the Emotions in Man and Animals*, Darwin explained in detail how the most prized human traits, including the moral conscience, the capacity for sympathy with others, and the expression of emotions of joy, pity, love, and grief, were all shared with other animals, and could be explained by evolution and inheritance.

Darwin's theory of weeping is as interesting for what it does not say as for what it does. Darwin notably takes little interest in the communicative power of weeping. The idea that tears were tokens or signs in a natural language had been central to earlier theories, including those developed in the early nineteenth century by the Scottish physician and nerve specialist Charles Bell.[12] But Darwin wanted to refute Bell's idea that expressions such as weeping and laughter were unique to humans, and that these expressions used special muscles bestowed on humans alone by the Creator. Darwin's aim was to bolster his theory of evolution by showing how many of their mental as well as their physical traits human beings shared with other animals. To do this, he needed to overthrow Bell's theological interpretation of the physiology of expression. This opposition to Charles Bell's theory of expression, and his desire to find as much as possible in common between humans and other animals, also explains why Darwin departed from the view that had prevailed as scientific orthodoxy since the seventeenth century, that animals could not cry.[13]

In amassing the materials that would become *The Expression of the Emotions in Man and Animals*, Darwin collected evidence, anecdotes, and testimony from around the world, through letters and questionnaires to naturalists, clergymen, and colonial officials posted around the empire, as well as through his own observations made at the Gardens of the Zoological Society in London, which had opened to the public in 1847. There, Darwin conducted various tests on animals, including giving snuff to a monkey to make it sneeze, and persuading an elephant to trumpet, in both cases to see if the creatures' eyes would close and secrete tears. Darwin was told by two of the zookeepers that they had seen a macaque from Borneo when 'grieved', or even when 'much pitied', weeping copiously, with tears rolling down its cheeks. Darwin quoted other authorities, including the great Prussian naturalist and explorer Alexander von Humboldt, in support of the statement that monkeys sometimes shed emotional tears, whether from grief, frustration, or fear, but was disappointed not to witness any weeping monkeys for himself on any of his visits to the zoo. The keepers also informed their curious visitor that they had seen tears rolling down the face of an old female Indian elephant when distressed by separation from her offspring. Darwin quoted from a work about Ceylon by the Irish politician Sir James E. Tennent who had been the colonial secretary there, describing a group of bound and captured elephants who 'lay motionless on the ground with no other indication of suffering than the tears which suffused their eyes and flowed incessantly'. On another occasion, Tennent wrote of a male elephant, overpowered and tied up, whose 'grief was most affecting; his violence sank into utter prostration, and he lay on the ground, uttering choking cries, with tears trickling down his cheeks'.[14]

Charles Darwin's endorsement of these sentimental tales of animal tears make him something of an embarrassment to hard-headed modern scientists, most of whom are sure that emotional tears are shed only by human beings. Even Darwin himself seems to have been uneasy about the reports. He thought there was 'something strange' about the case of the weepy macaque from Borneo at London Zoo, since other monkeys of the same species could not be induced to replicate the behaviour. And when reading Darwin's remark, referring to the example cited by the great Alexander von Humboldt, 'I do not, however, wish to throw the least doubt on the accuracy of Humboldt's statement', one cannot help suspecting that this is a very British way of throwing substantial doubt on the accuracy of Humboldt's statement.[15] Nonetheless, these examples of weeping monkeys and elephants supported Darwin's overriding aim of breaking down the barrier between human and animal emotion, and so were included in his book.

When it came to explaining the origin of the mysterious connection between tears and emotions, Darwin relied on a series of speculations, linking the tight closing of the eyes with various behaviours and states of mind. In our evolutionary past, he supposed, infants screamed very loudly, because they were hungry or in pain and needed to attract attention. When doing this, they would close their eyes very tightly to protect them from damage, and this closing of the eyes squeezed the lachrymal glands sufficiently to bring out the tears. Then by a process of association thereafter, any kind of pain or suffering could become connected with tears. It is worth noting, incidentally, that this explanation did not appeal to natural selection (Darwin proposed no evolutionary advantage to shedding tears when in distress), but rather to the inheritance of an habitual or acquired characteristic (a mechanism frequently invoked by Darwin, but subsequently rejected by neo-Darwinians). After the habit of weeping had been inherited, the primal connection with infant pain was eventually lost and, as Darwin rightly observed, tears could now be produced 'under the most opposite emotions, and under no emotion at all'.[16] Darwinian tears were the involuntary relics of a complex inherited habit, once useful to our ancestors, when screaming in their infancy, but now incidental and purposeless—truly these were 'idle tears'.[17]

Having shown how weeping could be explained away as a by-product of our evolutionary past, Darwin turned back to tears in the modern world. In this period of empire-building, and emergent nationalism, acts of European domination were explained and legitimized by racial stereotypes, which in turn were endorsed by science. The passionately anti-slavery Darwin was one of the most liberal on such questions, yet even he took for granted the existence of a racial hierarchy underlying the variety of human types.[18] Darwin reported that 'savages weep copiously from very slight causes', giving the example of a New Zealand chief who had 'cried like a child because the sailors spoilt his favourite cloak by powdering it with flour'. Darwin added an example from his own experience: 'I saw in Tierra del Fuego a native who had lately lost a brother, and who alternately cried with hysterical violence, and laughed heartily at anything which amused him.' This kind of emotional instability was just one example of what seemed to the young European traveller like shockingly barbarous behaviours among the Fuegians.[19]

The question of race had particular relevance in the United States, where slavery was only ended in 1865, after the devastation of the Civil War. Thomas Wentworth Higginson was a Unitarian clergyman and abolitionist who had commanded a regiment of black soldiers in the Union army. Higginson had visited the Darwins at their home in Kent in 1872 and, back in Newport, Rhode Island, he read the *Expression of the Emotions* with great interest. Higginson wrote to Darwin, rejoicing at the Englishman's 'kindly feeling toward the colored race', and enclosing some notes about the expression of emotions. One of these included a comment in response to Darwin's statement that 'Savages weep copiously from very slight causes.' Higginson confirmed that this was true of 'Americanized negroes', noting, 'I often noticed it among my black soldiers who wept easily from anger, shame, or disappointment,' and mentioning in particular a soldier who returns from a military skirmish in which he has behaved well and then weeps because 'his comrade has stolen a piece of sugar cane'.[20] Even among abolitionists like Darwin and Higginson, there was an unquestioned attitude of racial superiority, evident in their condescending descriptions of the supposedly childlike emotional reactions of 'savages' and 'negroes'.

Racial comparisons could also be made between the different 'civilized nations of Europe', as Darwin termed them. There were lively debates at this time about the relative emotional temperaments of Angles, Celts, Saxons, and others.[21] One medical expert asserted that cases of 'excited melancholia' were more common in 'the Celtic race' and in women, giving as the most characteristic example the 'wailing and weeping, the gesticulations and motor grief of an Irish woman'.[22] Darwin particularly commented on the difference between the English and their continental neighbours. 'Englishmen rarely cry,' he wrote, 'except under the pressure of the acutest grief; whereas in some parts of the Continent the men shed tears much more readily and freely.'[23] One reviewer of Darwin's book mentioned that public expressions of violent grief of the kind witnessed in 'savage nations' were 'not altogether extinct in Ireland', although, by implication, they were not witnessed in England.[24] The kind of extreme Catholic mourning rituals condemned by Protestant reformers in the sixteenth century were still being observed, and condemned, by English observers of Catholic Ireland three centuries later.[25]

In general, outward weeping seemed to Darwin to be more common among those thought to have diminished powers of will and reason, among whom he included women, children, and the so-called 'lower races', as well as the insane who, as he put it, 'notoriously give way to all their emotions with little or no restraint'.[26] In this respect, the mental patients observed in Victorian asylums resembled the 'savages' encountered on foreign shores. Both groups were notable for their excessive tearfulness. Even in the fifteenth century, some had considered the prolific weeping of Margery Kempe a sign of madness rather than of spiritual insight.[27] In the Darwinian age, Margery would almost certainly have been locked up in an asylum. Darwin quoted from Dr James Crichton-Browne, Medical Superintendent of the West Riding Lunatic Asylum in Yorkshire, who had informed him that 'nothing is more characteristic of simple melancholia, even in the male sex, than a tendency to weep on the slightest occasions, or from no cause', as well as weeping disproportionately over real causes of grief.[28] Some of Crichton-Browne's other patients could, like Margery Kempe, sometimes weep prolifically for hours at a time, even a whole day, while others would sit rocking themselves backwards and forwards in silence, bursting into tears if spoken to.

One widely used *Manual of Psychological Medicine* noted that a healthy flow of tears could be a sign of relief and recovery, but added that in other cases weeping indicated a 'deep-seated disease of the nerve centres'. These two kinds of tears, the manual went on, were 'as distinct as the rush of the mountain torrent after the removal of some obstruction, and the stream caused by the bursting of a water pipe'. The Victorian physician tried to distinguish the mountain torrent from the broken pipe.[29] In the attempt to do this, some medical writers in the final decades of the century started to refer to the 'emotional incontinence' of those who were unable to restrain their feelings.[30] That phrase would become a standard term among those opposed to public displays of emotion in the century that followed. The conservative newspaper columnist Richard Littlejohn, opposing a proposal in 1998 for a two-minute silence to mark the first anniversary of the death of Princess Diana, described the previous year's public mourning as 'menacing mass hysteria' and 'a revolting orgy of emotional incontinence'. In 2012, *Spectator* columnist Toby Young declared himself disappointed by Andy Murray's 'emotional incontinence', after the tennis player's tearful speech thanking his supporters at Wimbledon.[31] The theories and attitudes of Victorian doctors live on in such statements, which offer modern versions of the idea held by Darwin and his contemporaries that there was a scale of tearfulness and restraint, ranging from the animal weeping of savages and lunatics at the bottom, via the tearfulness of women, children, and European men, up to the lachrymally continent English gentleman at the top. Victorian men of science constructed a comparative anthropology of weeping suited to an imperial power, and to an age of reason. The publication of Darwin's book on the expression of the emotions indicated a new stage not only in the scientific study of weeping, but also in British culture more broadly, with tears, especially male tears, gradually being pushed further and further from public sight.

The best-known cause of grief in Darwin's own life was the death of his 10-year-old daughter Annie in 1851. It has been discussed by historians of science as a turning point in Darwin's intellectual life—an agonizing personal realization of the ruthlessness of nature. It was a milestone in the history of his emotions too. Darwin wrote in 1872 that Englishmen rarely cried 'except under the pressure of the acutest grief', and there can be no doubt that the death of Annie occasioned such grief. Darwin wept bitterly, both with his wife Emma, and on his own, but rarely mentioned Annie afterwards, even among his family. The feelings were acute but private.[32] Adrian Desmond and James Moore, in their emotionally charged biography of Darwin, mention a letter that Emma Darwin had written to her husband during the early months of their marriage. The letter expressed her fears that Charles's religious doubts meant that he and she would be separated in the afterlife. Darwin returned to the letter decades later, as he wrote his autobiography, and reflected on thoughts of their parting, as well as on the heart-breaking loss of Annie. Reading again the old letter from Emma, Darwin wrote at the bottom of it, 'When I am dead, know that many times, I have kissed and cryed over this.'[33]

When Darwin sat observing that tearful old lady in his railway carriage, calculating the meaning of her expression, he was engaged in a bit of scientific, but also highly personal, and characteristically Victorian, mind-reading. His immediate thought was that the painful recollection of a long-lost child was passing though the woman's mind.[34] But was it through her mind, through Darwin's mind, or through the collective Victorian mind, that this thought of a dead child was passing? All those Little Nells, all those Paul Dombeys—the figure of the dead child was still at the centre of both domestic pain and literary pathos.[35] 'I have myself felt', Darwin confessed elsewhere in the *Expression of the Emotions*, 'and have observed in other grown-up persons, that when tears are restrained with difficulty, as in reading a pathetic story, it is almost impossible to prevent the various muscles, which with young children are brought into strong action during their screaming-fits, from slightly twitching and trembling.'[36] The image of Charles Darwin, that great Victorian Socrates, struggling against his tears while reading a sentimental novel, his sagelike face twitching and trembling with the effort, encapsulates perfectly the late Victorian campaign to counter animal emotion, wherever it was met, with civilization, and restraint.

14

The 'If' Upper Lip

On 26 May 1895, Oscar Wilde was found guilty of committing acts of 'gross indecency' and sentenced to two years' imprisonment with hard labour. As he left the dock, Wilde's eyes filled with tears.[1] Later in the year, during his transfer from London to Reading, Wilde was, for a time, standing on a platform at Clapham Junction railway station, hand-cuffed and in his prison clothes. People started to recognize the disgraced author, and to laugh at him. 'For half an hour I stood there in the grey November rain surrounded by a jeering mob,' Wilde wrote in the long prison letter that would later be partially published as *De Profundis*. 'For a year after that was done to me I wept every day at the same hour and for the same space of time.'[2] Wilde had devised his own personal ritual of tearful remembrance. Something similar was also done by the patient in a case study of Sigmund Freud's in the 1890s.[3] 'A day in prison on which one does not weep,' Wilde wrote, 'is a day on which one's heart is hard, not a day on which one's heart is happy.'[4] In prison and in pain, Wilde continued to draw on Christian ideas about weeping, as he had in his sentimental children's stories. In *The Ballad of Reading Gaol*, the tears of the 'man who had to swing'—an inmate facing the hangman for killing his sweetheart—have a redemptive Christian power:

> For only blood can wipe out blood,
> And only tears can heal:

And the crimson stain that was of Cain
Became Christ's snow-white seal.

The other prisoners enact their compassion and lamentation in tears:

And as molten lead were the tears we shed
For the blood we had not spilt.[5]

Irish, effeminate, decadent, and with more than a hint of Roman Catholicism about him too: Oscar Wilde and his tears stood at one end of the
spectrum of models of masculinity and emotion available at the end of
the nineteenth century.[6] His religious and literary sensibilities contrasted
with the stoicism and militarism of the new imperial man.

At the end of December 1895, Scottish colonial administrator Leander
Starr Jameson led a military raid from Britain's Cape Colony into the
Transvaal, trying and failing to trigger an uprising of British settlers
against their Boer rulers. Jameson was reprimanded and briefly
imprisoned for the manner in which he led the raid, but he still became
an imperialist hero, and a model of British endeavour, stoicism, and
derring-do. He was the inspiration for a poem by Rudyard Kipling, first
published in 1910, which distils more effectively than any other piece of
writing the spirit of the British stiff upper lip, and which is entitled simply
'If—'. In 1995, a full century after the Jameson raid, and decades after the
apparent demise of the stiff upper lip as a national characteristic, a BBC
poll found that Kipling's 'If—' was the nation's favourite poem.[7]

In his posthumous autobiography, Kipling wrote of the poem that it
was 'drawn from Jameson's character, and contained counsels of perfection most easy to give'.[8] Written in the form of advice from a father to his
son, the poem is a litany of conditionals, starting:

If you can keep your head when all about you
Are losing theirs and blaming it on you,
If you can trust yourself when all men doubt you,
But make allowance for their doubting too

The speaker proposes various further tests of endurance and self-control:

> If you can dream—and not make dreams your master;
> If you can think—and not make thoughts your aim;
> If you can meet with Triumph and Disaster
> And treat those two impostors just the same

That last couplet was engraved above the players' entrance to Centre Court at Wimbledon in 1923, and is still there to this day.[9] The addressee of 'If—' is required to have a pretty detached attitude not only to external events, but to other human beings too:

> If neither foes nor loving friends can hurt you,
> If all men count with you, but none too much;

The multiple conditionals delay the reader's gratification to the end. What is to be the reward of this remarkable individual, this human rock, who can achieve such a level of ice-cool indifference? The answer, more or less, is that he will have proved his masculinity and so inherit the British Empire:

> Yours is the Earth and everything that's in it,
> And—which is more—you'll be a Man, my son.[10]

Kipling was a friend and admirer not only of Jameson but also of other leading figures in the Boer War of 1899–1902, including Cecil Rhodes and Sir Alfred Milner. British victory in that war laid the groundwork for the creation of the Union of South Africa as part of the British Empire in 1910, the year that 'If—' was published.[11] Kipling's own only son, John, was then 13. Four years later, when the whole imperial project seemed under threat at the outbreak of the First World War, John Kipling would finally have a chance to prove his mettle. Oscar Wilde's son Cyril, nearing his thirtieth birthday, and already a military man, would also see active service. The tears, ideas, and experiences of the Irish-born Wilde, the Indian-born Kipling, and their sons, help us understand how the 'stiff upper lip' mentality was created, resisted, and tested, in an era of increasing imperialism and patriotism, from the 1870s to the time of the Great War.[12]

The 'stiff upper lip' as a phrase was originally an Americanism. In 1871, the year after the death of its founding editor Charles Dickens, the magazine *All the Year Round* carried an article introducing 'Popular American Phrases' in which to 'keep a stiff upper lip' was explained: 'to remain firm to a purpose, to keep up one's courage'.[13] That was not the phrase's only meaning: it could also mean the possession of high self-esteem, independence, and self-sufficiency. Even by the end of the nineteenth century its meaning was not certain for British readers. It often appeared in quotation marks, and was sometimes still treated as an Americanism.[14] From the period of the Boer War onwards, however, it occurred more frequently, especially in discussions of international relations and warfare, and its meaning gradually settled on one central quality, namely the ability to put on a display of bravery and to hide one's true feelings in times of trial and suffering.[15] Within the wider culture there had been a turning away from sentimentalism and towards stoicism and emotional restraint from the 1870s onwards, at the same time that imperialism and jingoism were on the rise.[16] The idea of the value of a 'stiff upper lip' was popularized in this context.

Even before the rise of the 'stiff upper lip' as an ideal, self-control and emotional restraint had long been inculcated in boys and men by the nation's educational institutions. The general approach was not confined to the public schools. For some it began at birth. Late Victorian and Edwardian parenting manuals warned that infants were tearful tyrants. Instead of relenting to children's manipulative tears, the wise parent would teach them, by example, how to 'suffer in silence, to control one's self, and to be master or mistress' of their emotions.[17] Boys who were later sent away to boarding schools of various kinds had to learn how to deal with the feelings caused by separation. Often the answer was not to talk about them and, perhaps, not even to feel them. A similar ethos prevailed in day schools run by the Church of England for less well-off children. One pupil at such a school in the English midlands in the 1870s recalled that the children were beaten with a cane by the teachers for all sorts of minor misdemeanours, and that it was 'a point of honour not to cry', although 'if a boy could not help a tear, he could hide his face in his arms without exciting derision'.[18] As we shall see, this same attitude—expecting emotional and physical pain both to be met without tears—persisted in many schools at least until the 1960s, and in some respects still survives today.[19]

Harriet Martineau's 1841 novel *The Crofton Boys* was an early example of the genre of school fiction later made famous by books from Thomas Hughes's *Tom Brown's Schooldays* in 1857 to Rudyard Kipling's *Stalky & Co.* in 1899.[20] On one occasion before being sent to Crofton school, Harriet Martineau's young protagonist Hugh, having struggled with his lessons at home, cries himself to sleep, wishing he could be a Crofton boy: 'He supposed the Crofton boys all got their lessons done somehow, as a matter of course; and then they could go to sleep without any uncomfortable feelings or any tears.' On arriving at the school, young Hugh is given advice by another boy, who tells him, 'You will find in every school in England that it is not the way of boys to talk about feelings—about anybody's feelings. That is the reason why they do not mention their sisters or their mothers—except when two confidential friends are together, in a tree, or by themselves in the meadows.' Instead, Hugh is advised to hold his tongue, to be 'full of action', and to show 'manly spirit' but without being proud of it, if he wants to become a true Crofton boy.[21]

Children's literature of the mid-Victorian period introduced a new term for the shedding of tears—'blubbing'—first used in the 1860s, and another indicator of the rise of the stiff upper lip. One such use, characteristic of many others, came in a story published in *Beeton's Boy's*

Annual: A Volume of Fact, Fiction, History, and Adventure, in 1868, in which a boy, embarrassed by the tears of another, tries to buck him up: 'Well, don't blub, there's a good fellow.' When the sobbing continues, the other boy can hardly stand it, and 'chokily' reassures him that although it's 'awfully queer always the first night away from one's own people', the holidays are not too far off, and the two of them can be friends.[22] 'Don't blub' was no doubt an exhortation uttered by countless boys in fact and fiction in this period, as public school education became both more widespread and more stiff upper lipped.[23] It was possibly said by the chums and teachers of a 10-year-old pupil at Charterhouse boarding school in Surrey in May 1915, Geoffrey Gorer, when he learned over breakfast that his father had drowned in the sinking of the *Lusitania* by a German U-boat. As usual, the master at the head of the table read out the war news from the morning paper, apparently unaware of the relevance of this particular story to young Gorer, who recalled the 'almost physical shock' with which he heard the news, before bursting into 'uncontrolled sobbing'. He remembered that he was treated with kindness, but like an invalid, and that conversation was hushed in his presence and no direct reference ever made to the death thereafter.[24]

Elite British educational institutions aimed to inculcate self-control, good manners, and patriotism, through a combination of classical education and team sports. A newspaper report of the annual Oxford and Cambridge rugby match in 1925 admired the good manners of the crowds of spectators: 'everywhere there is repression of the passion which such a game between sides must create'—this, the report concluded, was a grand 'parade of the stiff upper lip'.[25] An article in *The Times* in 1936, about Chinese 'weeping parties', contrasted eastern emotions with the 'English tradition' of repressing tears: 'When young children cry they are told to stop. At public schools and even earlier to blub is to disgrace oneself.' By the end of university, the article suggested, a young man might look at his disastrous examination results on a notice board, and wait for his eyes to fill up, but find he had entirely lost the power of tears. That was when he knew that his education as an English gentleman was complete.[26] There was a note of regret in this *Times* article, and E. M. Forster had earlier lamented that the English public school produced young men 'with well-developed bodies, fairly developed minds, and undeveloped hearts'.[27] It would not be until after the Second World War, however, that a substantial number of influential voices would join the call for boys to receive a less emotionally repressed education. One of those voices, as we shall see, belonged to Geoffrey Gorer, who grew up to be an anthropologist with a special interest in the English national character and the repression of emotion.[28]

During and after the Second World War it would be the British as a whole who gained a reputation for their 'stiff upper lip'. But in the earlier decades of the century, it was largely to Englishmen—frequently men with fighting connections—that an unsentimental stiff upper lip was ascribed. The moment that cemented the notion came in 1937. The Hollywood musical comedy *Damsel in Distress*, starring Fred Astaire, Joan Fontaine, George Burns, and Gracie Allen, included a song by George and Ira Gershwin entitled 'Stiff Upper Lip', affectionately caricaturing the English spirit. Gracie Allen sang:

> What made good Queen Bess
> Such a great success?
> What made Wellington do
> What he did at Waterloo?
>
> What makes every Englishman
> A fighter through and through?
> It isn't roast beef or ale or home or mother,
> It's just a little thing they sing to one another:
>
> Stiff upper lip, stout fella,
> Carry on, old bean.
> Chin up, keep muddling through!

And so on. Needless to say, it was not a serious piece of cultural analysis, but this trifling song, accompanying an elaborate, and Oscar-winning, dance routine, distilled into a memorable form, and for a large international audience, an idea that had been circulating in various forms for some decades.[29] And it completed the circle by which an Americanism unknown to a British audience became a phrase by which the British were explained to an American audience.

For the inhabitants of the British Isles themselves, there was a keen sense of the differences of emotional style among different nations, and even different regions. Revivalist religion in the eighteenth century, and its bodily expressions of spiritual awakening, was strong in both industrial and rural areas, including the working communities of south-west and north-east England, and especially of Wales. There Methodist preachers including George Whitefield and Daniel Rowland had 'kindled the fervid Welsh with enthusiasm'.[30] In the early twentieth century, the Welsh still had a reputation for emotional excitability, partly thanks to the Liberal politician David Lloyd George. In 1909, Lloyd George was Chancellor of the Exchequer and struggling against opponents in both houses of parliament to introduce his 'People's Budget', raising taxes and introducing new elements of social welfare. At a meeting in a schoolroom in his own constituency of Carnarvon Boroughs in December 1909, Lloyd George was greeted with cheers as he formally declared his desire to be readopted by the constituency to stand in the following year's general election. He spoke passionately of his fight against his opponents in the House of Lords, of his desire to instil more of the 'spirit of Cromwell' into the people of Britain, and of his identity as a Welshman and a 'man of the mountain'. As the audience rose and cheered, Lloyd George broke down in tears, hardly able to complete his speech, and choking on his words as he expressed his thanks to the assembled people. He may or may not have been aware that in this public display of tears he was himself channelling something of the political style of Oliver Cromwell.[31]

The event was widely reported, and with different emphases in different parts of the regional press. In Scotland, the Dundee *Evening Telegraph* was relatively restrained but certainly saw the episode as reflecting the Chancellor's nationality: 'The meeting began with an outburst of Welsh enthusiasm. It ended with an audience overwhelmed by an access of fervid Welsh emotionality.'[32] The *Hull Daily Mail* was openly hostile to this 'display of fulsome feeling' before a crowd of 'frenzied Welshmen', suggesting that in 'hard-headed and self-possessed Yorkshire, such an exhibition would have been enough to empty the hall!' The paper's editorial line was strongly against Lloyd George's budget, and it used its disgust at his Welsh tears, Welsh 'revivalism', and the whole 'flowery and fervid national character' of his homeland, as one more set of reasons to oppose him.[33] Similar views were in Lord Kitchener's mind five years later, when he expressed reservations about the idea, championed by Lloyd George, of recruiting an exclusively Welsh Corps to join with other regional battalions in his recruiting drive at the start of the war, telling the Liberal Prime Minister H. H. Asquith that the Welsh were 'always wild and insubordinate and ought to be stiffened by a strong infusion of English and Scotch'. Kitchener's doubts were overruled and a Welsh regiment was indeed raised, but it is interesting to know that the man whose massively moustached upper lip adorned the famous recruiting posters announcing 'Your Country Needs You' thought that the stiffness of men from some parts of the nation made them even more needed than others.[34]

As the conflict wore on, both domestic and foreign writers promoted the idea that British soldiers—or 'Tommies'—were marked by a special kind of stoical unconcern. Countess Marie van den Steen was an aristocrat, nurse, and educator who was one of the founders of a Catholic school of nursing in Brussels in 1907. The director of a rival, liberal nursing school in Brussels, which opened in the same year, was the stoical Englishwoman Edith Cavell.[35] The Belgian Countess van den Steen wrote

an article for the French press, after the outbreak of war, about the
character of English soldiers. It was republished in translation in the
Liverpool Echo, under the proud headline 'Not Emotional: A Character
Sketch of our Tommies'. The article centred on the 'impassiveness' of the
English, which van den Steen explained by way both of ancestral attitudes
and a relative lack of imagination. Englishmen, she believed, possessed
'only the merest trace of responsiveness to emotions', sincere and genuine though such hints of emotion were. These 'Anglo-Saxon' qualities of
silence and reserve combined with self-sacrifice and sportsmanship in the
English Tommy, and were best symbolized by his unconcerned puffing
on his pipe while bombs dropped around him: 'The pipe, a moral
thermometer, a symbol of self-control! The white cloud from his pipe is
the crest of the Anglo-Saxon. It attests a normal pulse, regular breathing,
and a clear brain.'[36]

Of course this was all propaganda, designed to boost morale and
national resilience during a time of war; it was partly from such propaganda, frequently repeated during both the First and Second World
Wars, that people came to believe in the British stiff upper lip. The reality
of the emotional life of military men on active service was more turbulent
than that image of the slow-pulsed, unimaginative, nonchalantly puffing
Tommy would suggest. The poet and novelist Frederic Manning experienced action on the Somme in 1916, and later wrote an autobiographical
novel about the war called *The Middle Parts of Fortune*, in which men
reacted to witnessing the dismemberment and death of their comrades
with tears as well as shock, disbelief, and bitterness. One description of
a soldier named Pritchard, recounting to others the final moments of a
severely wounded colleague, captures the attempt simultaneously to
express and contain a raw and painful experience: 'Tears were running
down Pritchard's inflexible face, like raindrops down a window pane; but
there was not a quaver in his voice, only that high unnatural note which a
boy's has when it is breaking.'[37] The tears of soldiers occasionally even

made it into newspaper reports, although these were more likely to be tears of relief than of agony. In June 1916, for instance, the *Daily Mirror* reported that a train full of wounded British prisoners of war had been handed over in Berne, and was welcomed by thousands of Swiss well-wishers, who showered the men with cheers and flowers, while a local band played 'God Save the King'. The British diplomat who reported the scene said of the wounded soldiers, 'Many of them were crying like children; a few fainted from emotion. As one private said to me, "God bless you sir! It's like dropping right into 'eaven from 'ell." '[38]

The imperial and military man was not always emotionally restrained.[39] Indeed it may have been that the exaggerated stoicism required in the course of duty, and reinforced through jingoistic mythology and propaganda, created an even greater need for sentimental outpourings, which now had to be executed as a kind of covert operation. In the semi-privacy of a darkened theatre or the secrecy of a private encounter, the tears of the military man could be spilled. The playwright Walford Graham Robertson, for instance, had a huge success with a Christmas play, first performed at His Majesty's Theatre in London in 1908 by a cast led by the celebrated Ellen Terry, entitled *Pinkie and the Fairies*. He had intended to capture the hearts of children, which he undoubtedly did, but he also inadvertently won a military following—'Night after night the stalls at His Majesty's looked like a parade at Aldershot.' Enquiring with a soldier friend about the appeal of the play to these men, he was told they came in order to cry, and that what they found 'most devastating' was a scene in which the child's vision of Fairyland slowly faded away. Night after night, in the darkness of His Majesty's, the soldiers wept over Pinkie, the fairies, and their own lost fairylands, 'and the lights went up upon rows of bedewed shirt-fronts'.[40] The production possibly appealed to sailors as well as soldiers: it later transferred to both Portsmouth and Woolwich (see Figure 17).[41]

Royal Artillery Theatre, Woolwich
Monday, December 26th ∅ ∅ One Week only
Twice Daily, at 2.30 and 8.

PINKIE *AND* THE FAIRIES
THE ENTIRE AND ACTUAL PRODUCTION
FROM HIS MAJESTY'S THEATRE, LONDON

Figure 17. Poster advertising a staging of W. G. Robertson's Christmas play *Pinkie and the Fairies* at the Royal Artillery Theatre, Woolwich, in 1910. University of Bristol/ArenaPAL/Topfoto.

This kind of sentimental behaviour was replicated in the highest echelons of the British establishment. Mrs Elinor Glyn was the author of racy romantic novels and included among her male admirers Sir Alfred Milner, the British high commissioner in South Africa at the time of the Boer War. In 1903 they spent time together in the Bohemian spa town of Carlsbad. In the evenings one of Milner's great pleasures, although one senses not necessarily Mrs Glyn's, was to read aloud from the dialogues of Plato, especially the *Phaedo*, 'the final pages of which never failed to move him to tears'.[42] Those final pages chronicled the death of Socrates as he took his leave from his friends and family, before calmly drinking the cup of poison which the jailer had given him in fulfilment of his sentence. As with the soldiers weeping over *Pinkie and the Fairies*, it is a vivid image, and a telling reminder of the incompleteness of our ideas of the repressed British male in this period. It is also a nice example of the phenomenon of people weeping over others not weeping, a characteristic product of the era of the stiff upper lip, later exploited in the films of the 1940s and, as we shall see, with considerable resonance to this day.[43] In the final pages of the *Phaedo*, Socrates chides his friends for behaving like women in sobbing and weeping over him, and insists instead on philosophical calm and resignation as he faces the end.

At the start of this chapter I drew a contrast between Oscar Wilde and Rudyard Kipling as emblems of contrasting versions of late Victorian masculinity—Wilde the sensual aesthete versus Kipling the stoical imperialist. Things are always more complicated than such contrasts allow, however. Wilde and Kipling lived and moved in the same cultural world. Oscar Wilde was an admirer of Kipling's stories; the last gift he gave his younger son before he was separated from him—permanently as it turned out—by his criminal trial in 1895 was a copy of *The Jungle Book*.[44] And Kipling's literature and attitude was by no means always unemotional. One of his early stories, 'Thrown Away', written and published in India in 1888, is about a pampered young Englishman who falls apart and commits suicide when faced with the trials and temptations of military life in India. The story includes a scene in which a major, reading the young soldier's final letter back to his sweetheart, rocks back and forth weeping. The narrator–a junior soldier and the only other person present at the discovery of the suicide–respects the senior officer for not trying to cover up his emotions, noting that the major 'simply cried like a woman without caring to hide it'.[45] In private, highly emotional moments, man to man, even a major might cry. Nonetheless, to do so was to behave 'like a woman', and indeed the whole moral of Kipling's tale of the suicidal soldier was that if he had been toughened up early in life rather than being cosseted by his parents, he would have been more prepared to cope with life in India–in short, he would have been better able to be a man.

There was, then, a movement of prevailing emotional style from the sentimental towards the disciplined and restrained in the run up to the First World War–a movement which had many different sources. It was not so much a question of eliminating all feeling, as of restricting the domains and the ways in which feelings might be expressed, including their expression through public tears. In 1895, the year of Wilde's imprisonment and of the Jameson raid which inspired 'If–', a book by an eccentric Austro-Hungarian physician and social critic, Max Nordau, appeared in English translation. It was entitled *Degeneration*, was recommended by *The Times*, and provoked extensive debate in the periodical press.[46] Nordau argued that there were many influential artists and authors who were suffering from a kind of pathology and should be treated with the same suspicion as degenerate criminals and lunatics. Nordau identified 'emotionalism' as a central characteristic of the artistic degenerate–a man who will laugh until he cries or who 'weeps copiously without adequate occasion'. Indifferent poetry or paintings will send the degenerate into raptures and 'music especially, even the most insipid and least commendable, arouses in him the most vehement emotions'.[47]

Nordau's description was supposed to sum up all sorts of figures in contemporary culture, including Richard Wagner, Henrik Ibsen, and Oscar Wilde. But his description would also seem to apply to the behaviour, on at least one occasion, of that poster boy of the stiff upper lip, Lord Kitchener. The world-famous soprano Nellie Melba and Lord Kitchener were both staying at Government House in Melbourne in 1909. According to Melba's version of the encounter, Kitchener, who had recently left India after serving since 1902 as commander-in-chief of the British army there, fell on his knees in front of her and begged, 'Madame Melba, I've been an exile for eight years. Won't you—won't you sing me just one verse of "Home Sweet Home"?' As she sat at the piano and sang her signature song for this exile, which she had sung to thousands before, Kitchener said nothing, 'but there were two big tears on his cheeks' and he came over and kissed Melba's hand.[48] Weeping over the death of Socrates, or the suicide of a young comrade, is one thing, but over *Pinkie and the Fairies*, or 'Home Sweet Home'? Surely Dr Nordau would have diagnosed degenerate emotionalism.

We know that this kind of attitude was in the mind of Oscar Wilde's elder son Cyril too. When Wilde was imprisoned in 1895, Cyril was 10, and soon after that was taken abroad to live with an uncle, and had his name changed from 'Wilde' to 'Holland'. Holland was subsequently educated at Radley College, where he became an outstanding athlete, the best oarsman and swimmer of his year, a prefect, and the head of his house. One day in 1900, at the breakfast table, he read in the newspaper of the death of his father, and overheard other boys, quite unaware of the true parentage of their schoolmate 'Holland', discussing it. Unlike Geoffrey Gorer, who would sob over the breakfast table on learning of his father's death, Cyril Holland had to keep his sorrow to himself. Cyril later trained at the Royal Military College in Woolwich and was commissioned as a second lieutenant in the Royal Field Artillery in 1905. By 1914 he had, after three years in India, risen to the rank of captain.[49] In June of that year, and on the eve of war, he wrote to his brother Vyvyan about the determination he had felt ever since childhood to live down the reputation of their father: 'first and foremost, I must be a *man*. There was to be no cry of decadent artist, of effeminate aesthete, of weak-kneed degenerate.' 'I am no wild, passionate, irresponsible hero,' Cyril continued, 'I live by thought, not by emotion.'[50] In reality, it was not so much a question of replacing emotion with thought, but of replacing a decadent kind of sentiment with another, more patriotic kind. 'I ask nothing better', he wrote, 'than to end in honourable battle for my King and Country.' In this world, as a character in one of his father's plays observed, there are only two tragedies: 'One is not getting what one wants, and the other is getting it.'[51] On 9 May 1915, near Neuville-Saint-Vaast, in northern France, Cyril Holland was shot dead by a German sniper.[52]

Rudyard Kipling's only son Jack, meanwhile, despite his very poor eyesight, had been commissioned as a second lieutenant in the Irish Guards thanks to his famous father's contacts. In August 1915, the month of his eighteenth birthday, Jack was dispatched to take part in active service in France. The following month he fought in the Battle of Loos, which was the first major test of Lord Kitchener's new armies. Twenty thousand British troops were killed by shells and machine guns. Second Lieutenant Kipling was reported missing presumed killed. His parents and their friends contacted and interviewed men who had served alongside him to try to discover what happened, but they never received a definite answer.[53] The writer Henry Rider Haggard was one of those who conducted interviews, including one with a man who was sure he had seen Kipling, 'trying to fasten a field dressing round his mouth which was badly shattered by a piece of shell'. This soldier said he would have helped but that 'the officer was crying' from pain and he had not wished to 'humiliate him by offering assistance'.[54] The teenaged second lieutenant had broken the code of the stiff upper lip, and his tears cost him the aid of one of his regiment. You'll be a Man, my son.

15

Patriotism is not Enough

On 17 March 1920, in St Martin's Place in London, under the granite gaze of Admiral Nelson on his nearby column, Queen Alexandra unveiled a new statue. Its subject had, like Nelson, died in a patriotic cause. In other respects, however, the two individuals differed dramatically. The great Horatio had been the ultimate military man of feeling: a romantic warrior-hero, a creature of tears and kisses.[1] The subject of this new memorial, by contrast, was restrained and unassuming, a figure of self-discipline and restraint—and a woman. The queen mother, speaking at the unveiling, recalled how the monument's subject had 'met a martyr's fate with calm courage and resignation'. She predicted that future generations throughout the British Empire would think 'with affection' of this 'unselfish and womanly character'.[2] In 1928, the dashing American aviator Amelia Earhart visited the statue during a visit to London, leaving a bouquet of roses as a mark of her respect for the martyred Englishwoman.[3] In 1932, Madame Tussaud's asked their younger visitors to choose amongst the waxworks the character they most wished to be like when they grew up. Daring explorers including Captain Scott and Sir Ernest Shackleton were popular choices, but the first three places in the poll were taken by women. In third place was Joan of Arc, second was Amy Johnson (Britain's answer to Amelia Earhart, and the first woman to fly solo from England to Australia), and the winner was the same woman whose statue had been unveiled twelve years

earlier.[4] So, who was this hugely admired Englishwoman? She was a middle-aged nurse from Norfolk called Edith Cavell, and one of the first British women to be celebrated for her 'stiff upper lip'. Cavell's life, death, and posthumous celebrity are emblematic of one dimension of the changing female roles and emotional demeanours available in the first half of the twentieth century. This was a time when modern women struggled to escape from the age-old idea that theirs was the lachrymose sex—soft, caring, soppy, sobbing, hysterical, and manipulative.

Edith Cavell was the pious, reserved daughter of a Church of England clergyman. She trained as a nurse and proved herself an effective educator and organizer. In 1907 she was appointed the director of a new nurses' training school in Brussels. After war broke out and Belgium was occupied by the German army, Cavell's educational work was disrupted, and she now devoted herself to caring for injured soldiers. She also became involved in an undercover resistance network, disguising allied soldiers as patients, providing them with false papers and hiding places, and assisting their escape into allied territory. In August 1915, as the Germans' suspicions about the network increased, Cavell was arrested and, after a period of imprisonment during which she confessed to her activities and named her co-conspirators, she was court-martialled by the German military, found guilty of treason, and sentenced to death. Five days later, on 12 October 1915, she was shot at dawn. The military chaplain who visited Edith Cavell on the last night of her life found her 'perfectly calm and resigned', expressing herself unafraid of death. She prayed and took communion with the clergyman, and joined him in saying the words 'Abide with me'. He reported that she said to him, 'standing as I do in view of God and eternity, I realise that patriotism is not enough. I must have no hatred or bitterness towards anyone.' The German military chaplain who attended her in the moments before her death confirmed that she was 'brave and bright to the last', professing her

Christian faith and her willingness to die for her country. 'She died like a heroine,' the German chaplain said—a heroine whose stoical indifference allowed her to face even the loss of her own life with equanimity.[5]

The shooting of Cavell—a woman, a nurse, an icon of feminine care-giving, an angel—became an international scandal. Cavell was depicted as a martyr. Her shooting by a barbaric enemy was a powerful image to aid allied recruitment. Later, the American artist George Wesley Bellows, in his *The Murder of Edith Cavell* (1918), depicted the English nurse as something between the Virgin Mary and the Angel Gabriel, almost hovering at the top of a staircase, dressed in white, above a dark scene of the brutality and chaos of war.[6] The immediate public reaction to the killing of Cavell back in Britain was one of outrage and grief, but this was soon followed by calls in the press for resolve and stoicism. One period-ical article complained about the 'hysterical outburst' which had followed the execution, interpreting it as 'one among many signs of the flabbiness of certain people's minds'. It may have been a brutal sentence, brutally carried out, but 'that England should be kept rocking on its base, as it were, for a whole fortnight over such a tragedy is, in our opinion, to be deplored'. For the author of that particular article, a fortnight of public emotion was too much—probably fourteen days too much. The piece concluded with the observation that 'nobody would have been more startled or distressed by the public attitude in the matter than Miss Cavell herself, who, when all is said, died not in the spirit of sentimental patriotism but because she was a firm woman and insisted on the stiff upper lip'.[7]

A few weeks later, a poem entitled 'Edith Cavell', written by a female contributor called Helen Key, was published in *The Cornishman and Cornish Telegraph*. It struck the same tearless and defiant note, and placed the death, as Cavell had done herself, within a Christian frame-work. The poem starts, 'Weep for her, sigh for her, cry for her? No!', going on to celebrate Cavell's exemplary life and death as evidence of how proudly a woman may die, and how close a woman may come to the example of Christ. It continued:

> To think on her name is to thrill and to glow—
> But weep for her, sigh for her, cry for her? No!
> Fight for her, ache for her, wake for her? Yes!
> Brothers! This murder is yours to redress!

'Our Empire of ages, our lordship of seas' were in the balance and 'vengeance' was required. The unjust death of this woman was to be greeted not with tears but with male violence. The message here was the opposite of a sentimental novel such as Henry Mackenzie's *The Man of Feeling* (1771) in which the protagonist Harley, as we saw above, reacted to suffering and injustice not with a sword but with a tear.[8]

When I first noticed the 1920 memorial to Cavell on St Martin's Place— the one unveiled by Queen Alexandra and made by the sculptor Sir George Frampton (see Figure 18)—I did not know anything about Cavell or her story. I was immediately struck by the large word 'Humanity' directly above Cavell's head. My first thought was that this was some sort of humanist icon.[9] On closer inspection, however, the construction seems to bear mixed messages. At the top, perched on a squat granite cross, are the figures of a woman and an infant, perhaps symbolizing humanity, but also suggestive of the Christian image of the Virgin and child. At the foot of the cross are the words 'For King and Country'. Beneath the figure of Cavell in her nurse's uniform, about to face her firing squad, are engraved her famous words, 'Patriotism is not enough. I must have no hatred or bitterness for anyone.' These words, shorn of Cavell's theological interpretation of them, and only added in 1924, somewhat contradict the 'King and Country' message of Frampton's 1920 statue.[10] Cavell's statement was an expression of an exacting kind of Christian love, going beyond loyalties of class or nationality. This memorial, in its confusions between love of country, love of God, and love of humanity, between

Figure 18. The London monument to nurse Edith Cavell, first unveiled in 1920.
© David Rowland/Alamy.

secular stoicism and Christian devotion, fixed in stone some of the conflicting ideological forces that were shaping ideas about emotion, gender, and national character in the inter-war years. A woman seen by herself and some contemporaries as a kind of female Christ now became, in the minds of others, a much more secular and athletic type of modern girl—like Amelia Earhart or Amy Johnson, flying solo into the 1930s. The poignant phrase 'Patriotism is not enough' can be taken as a warning to the historian. Whether we are seeking to explain Cavell's own actions and beliefs, or the much broader desire among women in this period not to be seen as emotional and tearful, patriotism is only one part of the story.

The admiration of Cavell as an exemplar of a newly firm femininity was just one part of a multifarious process through which the 'stiff upper lip' mentality was extended beyond a cadre of elite men, to include all classes and both sexes. In one way, the stiff upper lipped modern woman was a successor to the selfless and suffering female of the previous century. Virginia Woolf looked back with disdain to that idealized figure of Victorian femininity, the altruistic *materfamilias*, part saint, part slave, known as the 'Angel in the House'. In a lecture on the subject of 'Professions for Women' in 1931, Woolf spoke about her need to overcome this idealized phantom before she could embark on her career as a writer. 'You who come of a younger and happier generation may not have heard of her,' Woolf said. 'The Angel in the House', she explained, was 'immensely sympathetic. She was immensely charming. She was utterly unselfish. She excelled in the difficult arts of family life. She sacrificed herself daily. If there was chicken, she took the leg; if there was a draught she sat in it—in short she was so constituted that she never had a mind or a wish of her own, but preferred to sympathize always with the minds and wishes of others.'[11] First and foremost among those others was her husband, followed by her sons and daughters. In a time of war, the Angel in the House became the military wife and mother, facing the threat of bereavement with selfless fortitude and a stiff upper lip.[12] There was nothing especially modern about this version of restrained and resilient womanhood.

Back in 1915, as events such as the sinking of the *Lusitania* and the shooting of Cavell made apparent the extent and brutality of the war, the propaganda of the stiff upper lip was on the increase. The *Pall Mall Magazine* announced its pride in being permitted to publish a series of letters from 'a splendid type of British soldier' sent home to 'his best pal—his mother'. Published under the title 'Billet Notes: Being Casual Pencillings from a Fighting Man to his Mother', these letters were in fact the work of a 29-year-old female author named Marguerite Barclay.[13] They were homely fictions designed to reassure womenfolk that their boys were doing them proud, enduring the pains of war manfully. The author writes to his mother of the callousness to blood, pain, and suffering that a fighting man must cultivate, and recalls how much harder it was in childhood, and how he had tried even then to 'keep a stiff upper lip', when he had 'caught my eye on the key of the nursery door and fainted on the mat'—it was now the mother as well as the son who had to remember that lesson.[14] In June 1915, one evening paper carried a poem entitled 'The Soldier's Wife' by Edith Talbot, again seeking to stiffen the resolve and stem the tears of the women left behind. Written in an attempted cockney voice, the poem starts:

> I didn't cry w'en 'e went
> To join 'is companee—
> A woman must keep a stiff upper lip
> When she's got a family!

As the poem progresses, the imagined wife restrains her tears as she looks after the children alone, and then again when they receive the news that all families dreaded:

> I'm not a-cryin' now,
> Though you think I'd ought, maybe,

To 'ear that 'e's wounded and dead out there
And won't never come back to me?
No, the children and I, we'll smile that proud.
And I'll learn 'em that though they've 'ad
An ord'nary sort of mother like me
They's a 'ero for their Dad![15]

Keep smiling through—that was the message for the widows and orphans of the Great War, as it would be for their children and grandchildren twenty-five years later, even if they would never see their dead, heroic husband or father again.

Newspaper advice columns from the 1890s to the 1940s, in times of both war and peace, advised female readers not to weep, for many reasons: it would spoil their make-up, it would harm their complexion, it would make them age, it would annoy their husbands, it would alienate their friends.[16] A *Daily Mirror* editorial in 1908, yet again using the device, by now a century old, of a supposedly recent report from a 'French doctor' about the health benefits of crying, expressed its disapproval of tears—especially those used by women 'as a means of threatening their husbands and of keeping them in order'.[17] If we must weep, the article concluded, 'let us at least close our doors, lock them, and weep in private'.[18] The paper repeated the advice to women the following year, in a column on 'Weeping Wives', warning new brides not to accept the proverbial notion that a woman's strength was in her tears: 'it is astonishing how callous a husband will soon become to a wife who is always ready to cry.'[19] In 1911 the *Mirror* announced that 'The woman who indulges in the luxury of "a good cry" no longer exists.' This was on the strength of a couple of interviews prompted by a recent novel in which the heroine declared that she cried about once every two years. A Harley Street doctor was quoted to the effect that boarding-school education and organized games were making girls 'more self-reliant and more capable of taking care of themselves', while the actress Lena Ashwell commented that while people might like to cry for a minute at the theatre, in real life there was no good in crying: 'You must be up and doing these days.' The publisher Eveleigh Nash agreed that the tearful, Victorian heroine, prone to sobs and faints, was a thing of the past: 'writers who set out to portray an up-to-date heroine know that a weeping woman would now be an anachronism.'[20] The message for *Mirror* readers remained the same in the 1920s, as the popular actress Dorothy Brunton argued that, unlike 'Victorian maidens' who were always dissolving into tears, 'Modern girls don't cry, even if they feel like it.' Medical science, psychoanalysis, and common sense dictated that weeping was bad for one's eyes, health, self-esteem, appearance, and romantic prospects.[21]

So, conventional female concerns of appearance, romance, and friendship were enlisted in the campaign against womanly tears. But there were new and more modern reasons for women to hide their emotions too. One of the arguments most frequently used against full female participation in professional and political life was that they were too emotional: the feminine mind lacked the requisite powers of reason and resolve. In 1884, for instance, the Liberal MP Edward Leatham, rejecting the latest attempt to give votes to women, had asked colleagues in the House of Commons why they thought that democracy had succeeded in Britain better than in other places such as Spain and France. Leatham had the answer: the democratic system required calm, rational minds, and 'the Anglo-Saxon race is less impulsive, less emotional, less capricious and crotchety—I had almost said less feminine—than the Latin races'. Allowing women themselves a place in the body politic, Leatham said, would have similar results: 'feminine alloy will penetrate into your policy', producing 'feminine inconsequence at the very moment when you desire to be most calmly logical, and a feminine flutter in your courage at the moment when you require to be the most manly and robust'.[22] This fear continued to dominate in Britain for some decades. How could a mere woman—an emotional creature by nature—have the strength of nerve for surgery, the intellectual capacity for law, the objective detachment for diplomacy, or the cool decisiveness for politics?[23]

In politics as in aviation, it was American women who led the way. Jeannette Rankin was the first woman to be elected to the US Congress. Her first attendance at the House of Representatives, as its solitary female member, coincided with President Woodrow Wilson seeking support for American entry into the Great War, in April 1917. Rankin was a pacifist, and when called to express her view, stated that although she wished to stand by her country she could not vote for war. She was one of a substantial minority of fifty representatives who voted against joining the war. As Rankin spoke, she was reported to have shed tears. Some of the male representatives wept too, as they agonized over this momentous question of war and peace, but the American press focused on the actions and tears of Rankin. Some alleged that she had thrown her head back, covered her face, sobbed, or even fainted, in line with the prevailing stereotype of the emotional female. The *New York Times* commented that this display was more evidence of the 'feminine incapacity for straight reasoning'.[24] In Britain the story became distorted still further as one commentator, even while trying to defend the entry of women into the British parliament, wrote with disapproval about the 'lady member of Congress who, asked to decide between war and peace at the great session, could only burst into tears and say nothing'.[25] A principled pacifist stand, albeit a tearful one, had been recast as feminine flutter and inconsequence.

No wonder the modern girl felt, as one newspaper put it, 'a little bit ashamed' of revealing her womanly character by having a 'good cry'.[26] Whether seeking to please her husband, or to display sufficient calm and logic for politics and the professions, the modern girl had plenty of reasons not to cry. Women who still found themselves prone to tears must sometimes have wondered if there was something wrong with them. The same newspapers that carried editorials and advice columns about the pathology of female tears also advertised potential remedies, often including testimonials about their power to restore women's nerves. A typical example, headed 'Tears of Pain', boasted, 'This Southampton Woman cried with Weakness resulting from Anaemia until Dr Williams' Pink Pills made her well.'[27] Another, in the *Manchester Evening News* in 1914, announced, 'Despondent Women Find Relief in Lydia E. Pinkham's Vegetable Compound', and included a testimonial from a woman who had suffered from backache, weakness, insomnia, and nervousness. 'I would weep at the least noise', the patient reported, but after taking Lydia E. Pinkham's compound, 'my nerves are in better condition', and the emotional attacks had passed.[28]

Strained and undernourished nerves were widely blamed for emotional outbursts and unwanted tears. Remedies were also sold on the basis of their ability to solve the marital problems associated with nervous debility. 'They Get on Each Other's Nerves!' was the headline of an advertisement for a restorative powder in the 1920s: 'He "goes in off the deep end" over trifles; she bursts into tears at the slightest hint of criticism.' The diagnosis was clear: 'Nerves—all nerves! Theirs is a case where a course of Virol and Milk will do more good than volumes of advice.'[29] In the 1930s, Fry's '4 in 1 Food Drink' was promoted to women in the same way: 'When a thoughtless word brings tears to your eyes—and you find yourself brooding hours later over a slight that was probably never intended: that's the danger signal! You're living on your nerves— and you've got to stop.'[30] These advertisements were satirized by Dorothy L. Sayers in one of her Lord Peter Wimsey mysteries, *Murder Must Advertise* in 1933. An advertising firm is promoting a new nerve tonic called 'Nutrax'. One of their advertisements is headed 'And Kissed Again with Tears', continuing: 'But Tears, and Fallings-Out, however poetical, are nearly always a sign of Nerve-Strain.'[31]

Female tears had been praised, admired, and inculcated in earlier periods, albeit not uniformly. In 1789, Mary Wollstonecraft, as we have seen, edited an anthology of extracts for female readers which was, amongst other things, a literary and religious handbook of appropriate weeping.[32] A century and a half later, in a quite different emotional climate, Virginia Woolf, writing a short essay about Wollstonecraft, looked back at the revolutionary feminist pioneer's tears over Louis XVI with curiosity. For Woolf, as also for Wollstonecraft and for her daughter Mary Shelley, there was no easy way to connect emotions with reasons, whether of a personal or a political nature.[33] The fact that tears came to Wollstonecraft's eyes on beholding the accomplishment of one of her most cherished convictions demonstrated that she had been a woman of contradictions and 'no cold-blooded theorist'.[34] If Woolf remembered Wollstonecraft's tears with mild discomfort, other women of the period recalled the lachrymosity of earlier periods with utter disbelief. The journalist Mary Howarth, editor of the women's column in the *Daily Mail*, contributed an essay about Henry Mackenzie's 1771 novel of sensibility, *The Man of Feeling*, to the *Gentleman's Magazine* in 1907.[35] Howarth was scathing about the book, deeming it a second-rate imitation of the higher-grade sentimentalism of Laurence Sterne, and mocking Mackenzie's penchants for odes to dead rabbits, dying bunches of flowers, and endless tears. In the novel's protagonist Harley, Howarth wrote, Mackenzie had 'created a human watering-pot of tears', an 'emotionalist of the most extravagant type', who probably had no equal in the whole of English literature. Harley's tears, which had moved men of feeling like Robert Burns, and amused indulgent nineteenth-century readers, provoked incomprehension and mild disgust in Mary Howarth, who summarized Mackenzie's hero as 'a being in whom hysterics were a glory, and "nerves" a possession of which he might be quite properly proud'.[36]

Howarth's remarks reinforce something especially important about what changed in the first half of the twentieth century. Not only had the prevailing attitude to tears shifted, and become broadly more negative, since the eighteenth century, but so had the register in which that attitude was articulated—from the moral to the medical, from the spiritual to the psychiatric. The terms that Howarth used to describe Harley—'nerves' and 'hysterics'—were increasingly attached to tears, and especially feminine tears, during the age of the stiff upper lip. It is no surprise, then, to find that the first publication, in 1936, of the newly discovered and translated *Book of Margery Kempe* was met with both amused astonishment and retrospective psychiatric diagnoses. Margery had wept so spectacularly, of course, that some even in her own day thought she was mad. One reviewer of the 1936 edition commented that if Margery were still alive she would either have been institutionalized 'or at least sent to a psycho-analyst', who would have much to say about her fear of rape, her desire to kiss lepers, and her incessant crying.[37] The English Jesuit scholar Father Herbert Thurston described Margery's behaviour as a kind of 'terrible hysteria', but warned it would be rash to dismiss her as 'no more than a neurotic and self-deluded visionary', since she also showed signs of having courage and a genuine love of God.[38] Even the American scholar who first discovered Kempe's extraordinary book, Hope Emily Allen, adopted the psychiatric approach. Citing the authority of the same Father Thurston, Allen agreed that Margery had suffered from 'Pithiatism' or 'Hysteria', and noted that she could be described, among her other more positive characteristics, as 'petty, neurotic, vain, illiterate and nervously over-strained'.[39] She perhaps would have benefited from a course of 'Virol and Milk'.

Charles Kingsley's Victorian poem 'The Three Fishers' had included the line 'For men must work and women must weep'. If women in Britain in the twentieth century wanted to start working—and voting—on equal terms with men, they were going to have to stop weeping. A statement by the National Union of Women's Suffrage Societies in 1914 alluded to Kingsley's lines, urging that suffragists should strive to understand and heal the madness of war, thinking rather than just feeling their way: 'The modern woman must drive back her tears; she has work to do.'[40] In 1918 women over 30 who satisfied certain economic and educational criteria won the right to vote. Then, finally, in 1928, the Representation of the People Act extended the vote to women on an equal footing with men. The following year, when women voted on equal terms with men in a general election for the first time, *The Times* reported that they did so in a confident and assured way, displaying 'the coolness attributed to the modern generation'.[41] Feminist campaigners had other successes in this era too, and the two world wars provided unprecedented opportunities for women to enter into new kinds of work and to achieve much greater independence.[42] The creation of a new style of rational and self-controlled femininity was both a cause and an effect of these social changes and, as we have seen, this meant trying to break the link between women and tears. But this attempt was only very partially successful. It often rested on an unchallenged and continued misogyny, directed either towards emotional women who did not live up to the new standards or even towards the dry-eyed 'modern girl' herself. It also left unresolved the Catch-22 of femininity and tears, discussed above as 'the witch's dilemma'—that is the fact that women are condemned as weak and manipulative if they weep, but hard-hearted and unfeminine, even a witch, if they do not.[43]

A column by the journalist John McCaffrey in 1926 announced approvingly that 'the modern girl has no time for tears'. The 'tall, lithe, lissom lass' of the moment—'Miss 1926', McCaffrey called her—'believes in keeping a stiff upper lip', seeing weeping as a sign of both childish weakness and lack of self-control. When they first entered the workplace, McCaffrey claimed, women had been all too prone to tears under pressure, but the modern girl had learned that all forms of success, whether in business, sport, or love, were best achieved without tears.[44] Modern women did not shed tears when criticized, did not cry after quarrels, and did not even weep at weddings: 'Men, of course, admire this new type of woman.'[45] A decade later, an advice column in the *Daily Mirror* by the no-nonsense American journalist with the pen name 'Dorothy Dix' reinforced the romantic implications of this, under the headline 'If she keeps on saying "Boo-hoo," he'll reply—"I'm through!"'. In response to a letter from a woman signing herself 'Cry-Baby', confessing to being 'very sensitive' and feeling much better after a 'good cry', despite the disgust of her fiancé, Dorothy Dix sided violently with the fiancé, describing the 'millions of women' who weep as 'weak and contemptible' creatures, using their tears to avoid their responsibilities and tyrannize their husbands.[46] Similarly, a rhyme written from a male point of view in the *Daily Mail* declared: 'Women weep, and with their tears | They've ruled us now for countless years!'[47]

These claims about women, emotion, tears, and manipulation had been made for countless years too. A newspaper feature in 1936, headed 'Are You One of the Hard-Faced Hussies? An Exasperated Man Holds an Inquest', showed how even in the twentieth century women could not escape the witch's dilemma. The 'exasperated man' railed against 'beauty experts' who had instructed women not to spoil their make-up and false eyelashes by crying, stating that while he admired modern women who suppressed their emotions he did not like or respect them.[48] So, apparently, if women wept they were hysterical, weak, neurotic, and manipulative, and men did not like them. If women refrained from tears, they were hard-faced, pitiless, false, and unfeeling, and men did not like them. The modern girl could fly an aeroplane, vote, stand for parliament, enter previously all-male professions, and even risk her life for her country like Edith Cavell, but when it came to tears she still couldn't win.

16

Thank You for Coming
Back to Me

T he refreshment room at Milford Junction, a fictional railway station
somewhere in England, provides the backdrop to one of the most
passionate, and most restrained, of love stories.[1] Laura and Alec, the
protagonists who meet there in David Lean's 1945 film *Brief Encounter*,
are both married to other people. Laura has some grit in her eye, thrown
up by a passing, symbolic express train. Alec gallantly insists on helping—
'Please let me look, I happen to be a doctor'—removing the offending
particle with his neatly folded handkerchief. The experience leaves a
grateful Laura dabbing her watering eye with her own hanky, a premon-
ition of more tears to come, both for her and for generations of cinema
audiences. This impromptu ophthalmological examination is about as
physically intimate as it gets for the would-be lovers, who meet again, by
chance, then design, alternately fighting against and surrendering to their
burgeoning romantic attraction. Aside from a couple of hurried kisses,
their affair remains unconsummated. Alec takes a job pursuing his
professional passion, preventive medicine, in South Africa, while Laura
returns loyally to her dependable and unemotional husband, Fred, his
Times crossword puzzle, and their two children.

Brief Encounter was not a film to everyone's taste. The French new-wave
film director François Truffaut described it as 'the least sensual and most

sentimental film ever wept over', expressing disdain for the 'inexhaustible tears from English crocodiles' that David Lean's creation had provoked.[2] Even for those who admire *Brief Encounter* as a classic of British cinema, it seems trapped in the 1940s, bearing witness to an era of emotional repression, with its uptight protagonists, imprisoned by convention, clipping their vowels and denying their feelings.[3] The task of the historian is to try to get beyond these impressions to understand how and why the film connected with middle-class audiences as it did, moving them to tears perhaps more than any other in the years after the Second World War. Thanks to records preserved in the Mass Observation Archive, we can look back at Laura and Alec through the eyes of some of *Brief Encounter*'s first viewers, and consider the film alongside others of the period that made audiences cry.[4]

In August 1950, Mass Observation sent its panel of volunteers their monthly questionnaire, known as their 'directive'. It asked for their feelings about other nationalities (including the Japanese, who attracted some vitriolic comments), for their thoughts on the relative merits of margarine and butter, and for information about which bits of music they found especially moving. Then finally, the questionnaire asked: 'Do you ever cry in the pictures? Which films, if any, have made you cry, how much, and—if you remember—which part of the film?' There was one further supplementary question, itself revealing contemporary assumptions about public displays of emotion: 'How far, if at all, do you feel ashamed on such occasions?' The responses to these questions, some handwritten, others typed, preserve in the form of paper and ink the tears and feelings of a sample of British men and women of all ages and classes in 1950. These first-person documents can offer insights into prevailing emotional attitudes and also help us reconstruct fragments of particular emotional lives. The film that was named more than any other as one that had made respondents cry was *Brief Encounter*.[5]

Over 300 responses were received to this particular directive, ranging in tone from the eloquent and effusive to the terse and dismissive. On the question about crying in the pictures, 40 per cent of men and 72 per cent of women replied that they had done so.[6] Given our image of the restrained Briton of this period, especially the repressed and unemotional male, these figures may seem high. There is also evidence suggesting there has been much less change in this kind of lachrymosity since 1950 than one might suppose. A survey undertaken for Kleenex tissues in 2004 found that 44 per cent of men and 80 per cent of women said that they cried at films or television programmes.[7] Admittedly, as the connection with Kleenex emphasizes, there has been a marked decline in handkerchief use since 1950, whether for removing things from strange women's eyes, or for soaking up tears produced at 'the pictures'. People working at cinemas no longer probably have the experience reported in 1938 by the staff of the Gaiety in Hastings, Sussex, of finding large numbers of abandoned handkerchiefs in the auditorium after an especially sentimental picture had been showing.[8]

If the 1950 Mass Observation responses are a reliable guide, then about 40 per cent of the owners of those wet hankies, whether male or female, would have felt ashamed of their cinematic tears.[9] One 37-year-old female teacher wrote, 'I always feel ashamed on these occasions and hope that no one is noticing, and I cannot understand the people who say that they enjoy a good cry.' Another woman wrote, 'I try so hard not to cry. I'm furious with myself for crying & yet the tears do come.' A 30-year-old secretary who reported that she never cried at the pictures said that she disliked 'giving way to emotion in public'. She added that she would feel extremely embarrassed and so 'whilst I feel like crying on occasions always restrain myself'.[10] These were modern girls, struggling against their tears, and worrying how weeping would make them look. Even among the majority of weepy men and women who declared themselves unashamed of their tears many said that they felt self-conscious, embarrassed, or foolish, and that they tried to conceal their tears.

The Mass Observation responses suggested that men and women tended to be moved by different things, with men somewhat more likely to mention war films and documentaries, and women more often picking out stories involving romance, children, or animals.[11] Two particular respondents, with extremely specific ideas about what could reduce them to tears, capture something of this contrast between a male preference for heroic self-sacrifice, and a female taste for stories of touching vulnerability. A 53-year-old salesman, mentioning his 'Celtic', Irish origins by way of explanation, stated that he was often moved to tears in the cinema, usually when 'the hero after a trying experience at the hands of the villain has come out "good", triumphant and when he has, say, the villain's son or daughter in his mercy, say risks his life to save them from an awkward position'.[12] An unmarried woman in her forties, an artist and teacher, had a quite different but no less specific list, writing that it was '(a) Animals in dire trouble (b) Old people in dire trouble (c) Children in dire trouble, in that order, that make me cry in the cinema'. The same lady offered the tip that gently wiping rather than blowing the nose was a good way to avoid the embarrassment of drawing attention to the fact that one had been crying over animals, or old people, or children in dire trouble.[13]

Some men expressed their disdain for 'weepies', describing tears explicitly as 'effeminate' or 'unmanly', or saying that it was a 'sign of weakness' to cry. A 22-year-old male bank clerk stated that he never cried at the pictures, adding, 'it's only the Welsh that do that—and a lot of silly women'.[14] But there was something of a mismatch between these expressions of tearless male bravado—trotting out the expected orthodoxy—and the substantial male emotionality revealed in other answers, even answers by the same men. Several denied crying in the pictures before going on to talk about being 'very nearly' moved to tears, or having a lump in their throat, or 'watery eyes'.[15] A warehouseman in his forties boasted, 'I do not cry in the pictures except for sheer boredom,' and yet stated that he had 'felt strong emotion enough to have damp eyes', and whilst not feeling ashamed of it, had made an effort to 'conceal my emotion from my companion'.[16] If this was a description of a man not crying in the cinema, then that figure of 40 per cent of men who shed tears over movies from the 1950 sample was perhaps an underestimate. Men and women did not always respond strictly according to gender stereotypes. More women than men reported weeping over *Scott of the Antarctic*, a story of heroic self-sacrifice, and the film most often mentioned by men as moving them to tears was the 1942 war film *Mrs Miniver*, which might have been considered a 'weepie' aimed more at a female audience.[17] The fact that *Brief Encounter*, a film about the emotional life of a frustrated housewife, could move men as well as women to tears further reinforces the point that men did not always conform to the level of stiffness to which they gave lip-service, especially not under the cover of a darkened cinema.

One 28-year-old married man who wept over *Brief Encounter* was a publisher. He would have been in his early twenties when the film came out. His answers to the whole directive give us a flavour of the kind of person with whom the film could connect. To start with, this respondent commented, 'I loathe these questions,' having to 'work out, as it were, what my "feelings" are'. 'But,' he added gnomically, 'am I sure I have any?' His views about foreign nationals were various but generally restrained. About the Japanese he responded: 'No feelings, I think, except slight revulsion,' Australians, he found good-hearted individually but 'collectively rather unpleasant'. The French were charming, inefficient, hardworking, and 'mixed up'. To the Russians, he applied a simple political logic: 'I hate Communists and therefore I hate Russians.' Finally it came to Americans: 'Like many Englishmen I regard them with amused tolerant superiority.' To the question of emotional responses to music, this respondent mentioned pieces that moved him to tears, including 'God Save the King', 'Land of Hope and Glory', and the

THANK YOU FOR COMING BACK TO ME

theme to the popular 1945 war film *The Way to the Stars*. Finally this patriotic publisher confessed that he frequently cried in the pictures: 'I'm a real sucker and almost any picture will make me cry', especially one with a happy ending, 'however corny and however stupid'; this happened so much, he wrote, that he no longer felt ashamed of it.[18] An 'emotionally supercharged film, such as *Brief Encounter*', he recorded, 'made me cry most of the way through, but most of all at the end. So did *Mrs Miniver* although I didn't even think it was well done.'[19] What is striking about this example is how a conventional set of male, British attitudes and preferences—an aversion to 'feelings' in general, predictable views about foreigners, and a patriotic taste in music—could be combined with a great susceptibility to crying in the pictures.

Tearful responses to films were nothing new. The impact of Hollywood movies, especially melodramatic and romantic pictures aimed at women, was such that new phrases had arrived in the English language in the 1920s to describe them—'tear-jerkers' and 'weepies'.[20] The taste for weepies spread right across the country, even to hard-headed and self-possessed Yorkshire, where the *Evening Post* reported in 1930 that the reason for the great popularity of the cinema among both men and women was that 'folk can have a nice quiet cry there without being seen', and this accounted for 'the success of the "weepies", mammy films, sonny films, and the latest all-talking and nearly-all-crying pictures. Tears in the pictures, tears in the voices, tears in the audience, and a 95 per cent humidity in the atmosphere.'[21] 'Who says the English are an unemotional race?' asked Dorothy Drew in the *Hastings and St Leonards Observer* in 1938. 'Cinemagoers know better,' she wrote, noting that both men and women had needed their hankies at the ready recently for *Captains Courageous*, released the previous year, starring Spencer Tracy, and based on the novel of the same name by Rudyard Kipling. Dorothy Drew signalled her own suspicion of such tears: 'we are not so unemotional as we like to make ourselves out to be, though heaven knows it would have to be a real "weepy" to make me feel for my handkerchief.'[22]

Another great tear-jerker screened across Britain in 1938 was *Stella Dallas*, starring Barbara Stanwyck as a woman of humble origins who sacrifices her own happiness to allow her beloved daughter to marry a well-to-do suitor.[23] The *Aberdeen Journal* noted that the 'novelettish stories of the servants hall' were increasingly popular for film plots and that no doubt *Stella Dallas* was 'swimming round the country in a flood of tears', although it was a cut above the average 'weepie', thanks to the 'wonderfully true performance by Miss Stanwyck'.[24] At the other end of the land, on the south coast, the *Portsmouth Evening News* advised its readers 'to take an outsize in handkerchiefs' to see this 'evergreen epic of mother love'.[25] The film was also screened in the Midlands, at the State cinema in Grantham, where a young Margaret Roberts—later Margaret Thatcher—regularly found herself 'entranced' by the romantic world of Hollywood—with its 'dramatic form, human emotion, sex appeal, spectacle and style'. She remembered seeing films 'from imperialistic adventures like *The Four Feathers* and *Drum*, to sophisticated comedies like *The Women* (with every female star in the business), to the four-handkerchief weepies like Barbara Stanwyck in *Stella Dallas* or Ingrid Bergman in anything'.[26] Over half a century later, as we shall see, Margaret Thatcher would star in her own weepie when departing Downing Street for the last time in November 1990. According to one recollection, however, it was a box of Kleenex, rather than any number of handkerchiefs, that helped her through her final cabinet meeting.[27]

In recent years both Mrs Thatcher, the Iron Lady, and her great wartime predecessor Winston Churchill, the legendary embodiment of the Blitz spirit, have been recalled as dry-eyed and defiant, by way of contrast with the soft and weepy politicians of our own era. In both cases the contrast is misplaced. A commentary piece by Barbara Gunnell in 1999 wrote of Churchill's 'obdurate endurance' during wartime bombing raids. With reference to public and tabloid demands for the queen to show her grief after the death of Princess Diana, Gunnell wrote that 'nobody leapt out of the blitz rubble and shouted at him "Show us you care, Winnie" as "Ma'am" was instructed to do during the National Outpouring'.[28] That may have been true, but only because Churchill needed no prompting, as an incident in September 1940 revealed, when he visited a bomb site in Peckham, South London. At least twenty small houses had been destroyed in a very poor neighbourhood. 'Already little pathetic Union Jacks had been stuck up amid the ruins,' Churchill wrote in his history of the war, and when his car was recognized a huge crowd started to gather—up to a thousand people, in 'a high state of enthusiasm', and 'manifesting every sign of lively affection, wanting to touch and stroke my clothes'. Churchill wrote that he was 'completely undermined, and wept'. One of those who was with Churchill heard an old woman saying, 'You see, he really cares. He's crying.' On Churchill's own account, his were 'tears not of sorrow but of wonder and admiration' for the resilience and patriotism of the people.[29] Churchill wept in the House of Commons too. In a particularly important speech in July 1940, Churchill told the House of his decision to destroy the French fleet in North Africa rather than let it fall into German hands. 'No-one who heard his speech will ever forget it,' the *Spectator*'s correspondent reported. 'The tears that reluctantly rolled down his cheeks, as he sat down and everyone else stood up to cheer, were a measure of the deep emotion that stirs this great and gallant man.'[30] Finally, the great wartime Prime Minister, like so many of his fellow Britons, shed tears in response to movies. Churchill was a film-lover who projected the latest releases for his colleagues and confidants during the war, both at his official residence in Chequers and while on board ship in the Atlantic. His favourite was *Lady Hamilton* (1941)—Alexander Korda's romantic study of Lord Nelson's mistress, depicting her descent into alcoholism and poverty after the great admiral's death. At the end of what was probably his fifth viewing of the film, in which Laurence Olivier played Nelson to Vivien Leigh's Lady Hamilton, Churchill was seen wiping the tears away from his eyes.[31]

In his first speech as Prime Minister, in May 1940, Churchill had, after all, said he could offer the nation nothing but 'blood, toil, tears, and sweat'. The war, especially the bombing of British cities from 1940 onwards, provided the British people with many opportunities for tears of grief. In the summer of 1941 a pioneering magazine of 'people's writings' called *Seven* carried a section with short autobiographical articles describing different jobs in wartime. A London clergyman reflected that, in his profession, a funeral was not usually an occasion for emotion, but after a big air raid, with the ensuing train of coffins carrying civil defence workers, Home Guards, airmen, women, and children, every moment was 'heavy with emotion'. The funeral processions wound through the streets, with weeping families following them. These were tough, working people: 'They do not cry easily, these people. Sorrow and grief and suffering are nothing new to them. They are hard people, more accustomed to curse than to cry.' But at times like these, the 'terror of death is over them all and there is nothing left but tears'.[32]

People still wept in wartime, even tough working people, but, for the most part, the prevailing attitude was that the blood, toil, and sweat should be endured without tears. It was considered selfish to wallow in one's own feelings, let alone to display them through hysterical weeping, when the whole nation was suffering together.[33] This ideal was captured in C. R. W. Nevinson's 1940 painting of a resolute London child 'Cockney Stoic; or Camden Town Kids Don't Cry'. The Britishness of this attitude was reinforced by way of contrast with the behaviour of the nation's enemies. Tears, previously associated with the French, the Irish, and 'savages', were now additionally linked with German and Italian fascists. In March 1938, the *Daily Express* published an article by the Australian historian Stephen H. Roberts, author of a book published the previous year entitled *The House that Hitler Built*, warning about the Nazi persecution of Jews and the risk of war. In his *Express* article, Roberts described Hitler's populist oratorical techniques. 'No display of emotionalism is too crude for him,' Roberts observed, noting several examples of the Führer's own propensity to tears. 'We can always get Adolf to weep,' Goering is supposed to have said.[34]

An American journalist writing about allied forces in 1940 entitled his book *The Wounded Don't Cry*.[35] With the conflict drawing towards its end four years later, the *Yorkshire Post*'s war correspondent Joe Illingworth met a group of Yorkshire lads on the road to Nijmegen in the Netherlands. One of them, Lance-Corporal Herbert O'Neill, from Edlington, commented on the behaviour of the wounded from each side of the conflict: 'Some of the German wounded weep and cry, but all a wounded Tommy asks for is a cigarette and a cup of tea, and he stays quiet.'[36] Then there was Captain William Martin, whose defiant response to Japanese captors in 1945 opened this book: 'No Britisher ever weeps!'[37] This British resilience was contrasted with the pathetic spectacle, reported by war correspondents, of German and Japanese commanders breaking down in tears as they surrendered to their allied conquerors.[38]

Victory in Europe, and then in Japan, during 1945, brought tears of joy and relief, as people who had been imprisoned, physically or emotionally, found release.[39] It was a year of reunions and happy endings. In September a group of thin and sunburnt men, among the first to arrive back from a Japanese prisoner of war camp, walked up a wooden gangplank to the quay at Poole, Dorset, after landing in a flying boat. They were welcomed by local dignitaries and an impromptu crowd of well-wishers: 'The men cheered—most of the women wept. Many of them had sons in Japanese prisons.' One of the men, a Colonel Giblin, believed that his wife and sons were still in Australia, where he had sent them from Singapore early in 1942, but while speaking to his mother in London on the telephone, for the first time since the start of the war, he discovered that his wife was there too with their sons Dennis and Ivor. Tears ensued. Colonel Giblin's mother wept, and as the colonel himself looked around at the reporters watching his telephonic reunion he apologized to his wife—'I can't just burst into tears myself. It is rather trying, darling, this room is full of people'—before walking away, wiping his eyes, embarrassed if not ashamed.[40] Mothers and wives were reunited with sons and husbands. Married couples, separated for years, were re-joined. Wartime romances were curtailed. Women who had found unprecedented independence through war work returned to more conventional domestic roles.

It was into this world of returns and endings that *Brief Encounter* was released. Remember the patriotic publisher who responded to the Mass Observation questionnaire in 1950. He cried over any happy ending, as well as most of the way through *Brief Encounter*, 'but most of all at the end'. Ronald Neame worked as a writer and producer on *Brief Encounter*. He was 34 when the film came out in 1945. He later explained that whenever he was going to watch the film he would have stern words with himself—we might almost imagine a 1940s father or schoolteacher speaking them—'Now, Ronnie, don't be stupid, this is a film, it's just a film and you really must not get into a state about it because that's stupid.' Neame still found the ending of the film unbearably moving. Laura is broken and despairing, and her stolid husband Fred, for all his lack of emotional depth, senses that something has happened. He says, 'Whatever your dream was, it wasn't a very happy one, was it?' and asks if there is anything he can do to help. Laura replies that he always helps. Fred says, 'You've been a long way away,' and when Laura says 'Yes,' he replies, 'Thank you for coming back to me' (the moment is captured in Figure 19). With a single stifled sob, Laura clings to Fred; Sergei Rachmaninoff's second piano concerto surges towards its climax; and Laura and Fred are replaced on the screen by two large and final words—'The End'. For Ronald Neame, the result was always the same: 'there are tears

Figure 19. A publicity shot reproducing the closing scene of David Lean's restrained weepie *Brief Encounter* (1945). Laura's dependable husband Fred says, 'Thank you for coming back to me'. © Pictorial Press Ltd/Alamy.

streaming down my face and great embarrassment when the lights go on in the theatre.'[41] For others, from the 1960s onwards, however, the film produced derision and laughter rather than tears and sympathy.[42] The prevailing emotional style of the nation was to change, just as it had between Louisa Stuart's first, tearful reading of *The Man of Feeling* in 1771, and her friends' laughter at the book in the 1820s.[43]

The ending of *Brief Encounter*, to modern eyes, is perhaps not a happy one. Laura's whirlwind romance is over, her emotional excitement squashed by dull domesticity. But for viewers in 1945, as for Ronald Neame, there was something admirable and moving about the emotional sacrifices made by both Laura and Fred for the sake of their marriage and their family, symbolizing the stability and happiness of post-war Britain. Selfish feelings—in Laura's case the desire for romance, in Fred's case jealousy or anger over a half-perceived infidelity—are put aside. For men and women trained in the philosophy of the stiff upper lip, this ending was good, if not exactly happy. The would-be adulterers manage, in Laura's words, to 'control ourselves' and 'behave like sensible human beings'—a triumph for 'decency' and 'self-respect' over the selfish hysteria of romance. Like the injured Tommies on the road to Nijmegen in 1944, Laura and Alec, in one key scene in the film, need nothing more than a cup of tea and a cigarette to help them curb their powerful emotions.[44] The *Derby Daily Telegraph*'s review of the film, headed 'It Could Happen to Anybody', praised the sincerity and intensity of this 'mild domestic drama'. It also expressed approval that the relationship ended 'as such things should end, one supposes'.[45] It was a film that could connect with the countless men and women who, after six years of sacrifices, separations, and real or imagined infidelities, had their own reasons for saying, 'Thank you for coming back to me' in 1945. That poignant closing line spoke to the hearts of *Brief Encounter*'s first audiences, expressing on the screen their often secret feelings of guilt, loss, gratitude, relief, or disappointment.[46]

Other films of the period shared *Brief Encounter*'s ability to tap into a wartime ethic of containment, stoicism, and self-sacrifice. In 1942, *Mrs Miniver* offered a Hollywood version of British grit, and ended with a rousing rendition of 'Onward Christian Soldiers' sung in a bombed-out church in a grief-stricken but determined English village community. In case all that was not enough to bring on the waterworks, this was followed, as the credits rolled, by Elgar's *Pomp and Circumstance March No. 1*, the tune of 'Land of Hope and Glory'. No wonder our patriotic publisher was moved to tears. The *Documentary News Letter* film critic complained bitterly of the way this Hollywood fiction was greeted: 'You can sit at the Empire and hear practically the whole house weeping— a British audience with 3 years of war behind it crying at one of the phoniest war films that has ever been made.'[47] But such literal-mindedness missed the point. It was the lack of opportunity for tears in everyday life that made the ability to weep in the pictures such a welcome release. The Second World War marked the apotheosis of the stiff upper lip mentality. The more that British tears were repressed in public, the more they leaked out elsewhere, as the psychoanalytic theories in vogue at the time suggested they should, especially in the semi-privacy of that great lacrimatorium, the movie theatre.[48] Several men responding to the 1950 Mass Observation directive noted that they had become more emotional in their responses to films since their experiences during the war.[49] Nothing was more likely to bring on such a response than an on-screen display of emotional control.

In 1945 *The Way to the Stars*, which started as a Ministry of Information production, provided a British take on the heroism and self-sacrifice of allied airmen.[50] During the film, a poem, 'For Johnny', about the ultimate sacrifice of one heroic flyer, is repeatedly read by various characters. The poem is a paean to stoicism and resolve, exhorting Johnny's nearest and dearest to keep their heads, and to focus on feeding the hero's children, rather than indulging in acts of mourning: 'And keep your tears | For him in after years.'[51] *The Way to the Stars* was voted the best film of the whole war by *Daily Mail* readers. The *Observer* praised the restrained realism of the characters, noting that 'like real people they do not make much of their private emotions'. The *Daily Telegraph* contrasted this 'essentially English' movie with the 'maudlin sentiment' and 'hysteria' of Hollywood weepies, while the *Daily Sketch* commented, 'In all its admirable emotional restraint it is far more moving than any picture deliberately designed as a tearjerker.'[52] Many of the 1950 Mass Observation respondents made the same point, that realistic and restrained films were more moving than out-and-out weepies. As one man put it, he would be deeply moved by 'any event which could really happen and is not merely Hollywood sob-stuff'.[53] Another man reflected, 'One cries at the tragic parts, but more at the parts where the hero or heroine is putting up a brave show and is obviously bracing against emotion.'[54]

All those comments applied equally when transferred into a domestic peacetime setting in *Brief Encounter*, which was much praised at the time for both its realism and its restraint, despite its highly emotional nature.[55] David Lean's film restated for a post-war audience a lesson frequently taught during the preceding six years of war, and before: your own emotions, whether terror, grief, desire, or despair, are of secondary concern, should be kept out of sight, and should be overcome by devotion to others.[56] *Brief Encounter* has become a classic example of a very modern and very British phenomenon—weeping over the stiff upper lip, crying at people not crying. The audiences for these wartime weepies could, through their own tears, provide something that was lacking in their own lives as well as those of the on-screen stoics they admired. In earlier eras, sentimental ladies had wept over dead birds, men of feeling over penitent prostitutes, and Victorian families over Dickensian death-beds. British men and women now wept over acts of self-sacrifice and renunciation, whether undertaken for king and country, husband and children, or even for a fictional eighteenth-century French aristocrat, as in *A Tale of Two Cities*.

Dickens's novel set during the French Revolution, first published in 1859, became a favourite of film-makers. It was adapted for the big screen on seven separate occasions during the twentieth century.[57] A 1940 survey of film-goers' favourite endings resulted in a clear preference for death, but also a taste for resurrection. The fifth most popular 'fade-out' was the ending of the 1935 version of *A Tale of Two Cities*, starring Ronald Colman as Sydney Carton. Carton prepares to face the guillotine in the place of Charles Darnay, with whom he has exchanged places for the sake of the woman he loves, unrequitedly, Darnay's wife. Before the blade falls, the audience hears Colman saying the final lines Dickens famously gave to Carton: 'It is a far, far better thing that I do, than I have ever done; it is a far, far better rest that I go to than I have ever known.' As the blade of the guillotine falls, the camera pans upwards to a heavenly sky where, as the tune of 'O Come All Ye Faithful' plays, a text from St John's Gospel appears: 'I am the Resurrection and the Life: he that believeth in me, though he were dead, yet shall he live.'[58] As with the self-sacrifice of Edith Cavell twenty years before, and in keeping with Dickens's own religious sentiments, the death is presented as an echo of Christ's and as the gateway from an earthly city to a heavenly one.[59]

The 1958 film version of *A Tale of Two Cities*, starring Dirk Bogarde, takes a different approach.[60] The tale is now more love story than sermon, and the ending is rewritten to appeal to a post-war audience. The final line remains the same, but Bogarde, as Carton, is given a whole new speech, delivered immediately before 'it is a far, far better thing', replacing a longer section in Dickens's original which has Carton looking prophetically into the future lives of other characters. The new speech is based on the image, in Dickens's novel, of Darnay's wife Lucie, weeping for Carton many years later. This thought is elaborated and tailored to an audience wanting to cry over people not crying. Carton now says: 'Suddenly I want to weep. But I must hold my tears in check lest they think it is myself that I weep for, and who would weep for Sydney Carton? A little time ago, none in all the world, but somebody will weep for me now. And that knowledge redeems a worthless life—worthless but from this final moment which makes it all worthwhile.' The love and sentimental tears of Lucie, rather than Christ and the world to come, are now the agents of redemption, and the audience is presented with a self-sacrificing hero nobly holding his tears in check. Who would weep for this stiff upper lipped Sydney Carton? A 1950s cinema audience would. The English journalist Roger Alton was only 10 years old when his father took him to see the film in Oxford. He recalls the effect of this final speech: 'I was aware of this huge snuffling going on all around me as rugged Fifties-style men who'd probably fought in World War Two started furtively wiping their eyes. And then I realised I was too.'[61] Dickens, suitably modified for the 1950s, still had the nation in tears.

V. FEELINGS

17

Grief Observed

In July 1958, the BBC Home Service broadcast a radio talk by a celebrated cancer-survivor, Reverend Brian Hession, on the subject of 'Healing Tears'. He told his listeners about a woman he had visited in Bournemouth whose husband, dying of cancer, lay in a coma in the next room. As was common practice at the time, the woman had been advised not to tell her husband the truth about his condition. Hession explained: 'She had to invent all sorts of falsehoods and I was the first person she had ever told.' As she did so, the woman burst into tears. 'I put my arms round her,' Hession said, 'and told her not to mind her tears—it was time she had a good cry, and we knelt together and prayed.'[1] Denial and repression were the normal accompaniments of terminal illness and death at the time. People sometimes refer to the taboo on speaking of death as a 'Victorian' one. In fact, the Victorians mourned openly and elaborately. It was the collective trauma of two world wars, along with the medicalization of death, and the decline in religious observance, during the first half of the twentieth century, that conspired to detach death from traditional communal acts of mourning and to leave the bereaved suffering in silence while their friends and acquaintances shuffled around them, with a mixture of awkward sympathy and revulsion, as though they were dealing with lepers. Death was denied, cancer not spoken of, bereavement solitary, tears repressed. Brian Hession's was a rare voice, crying out against these silences and denials in post-war Britain.[2]

Millions of people found themselves in the same situation as the woman in Bournemouth who wept in Brian Hession's arms: entrusted with the knowledge of the terminal diagnosis of a spouse, having to decide whether or not to follow the advice to keep the truth from the sufferer and any children involved, and then, after the death, having to face yet more silence, embarrassment, and denial in a culture that had forgotten how to mourn. In such a situation some remained resolutely dry-eyed, others wept alone, and a few found an understanding friend or counsellor with whom to share their suppressed words and tears, whether in person or on paper. Pioneers of a tentative return to public expressions of grief in the 1950s and 1960s—or even just a public acknowledgement of grief's existence—were able to draw on established religious ideas as well as new psychological ones to try to get the nation talking, and weeping, about disease, death, and loss again. At the same time, new genres of television programme, including soap operas and what would become 'reality' shows, provided national audiences of millions with examples of both stoicism and sentiment designed to provoke a tearful response. Nationwide radio and television broadcasts provided, for the first time, an opportunity for millions of Britons to weep in unison, to a fixed schedule, whether over the coronation in 1953 or *Coronation Street* from 1960 onwards.[3]

Brian Hession, whose books and radio talks gained him a national audience in the mid-1950s, was a rather dashing Anglican clergyman, a former RAF chaplain, and a maker of religious movies in both Britain and Hollywood. He came to wider attention through his 1956 book *Determined to Live*, which documented his survival of stomach cancer two years earlier, after being given only days to live when the condition was first diagnosed.[4] It was one of the earliest such cancer memoirs. Hession's confessional and emotional approach to the subjects of cancer and death was in defiance of the prevailing cultures of silence and denial. When he spoke of tears, in his 1958 talk on the subject, he invoked both

psychological and spiritual ideas, describing weeping as a valuable way 'to
relieve the tension' that built up inside, and as a 'medium of emotional
release', whether expressing joy, sorrow, pain, or sympathy. Hession
recalled the tears of Mary Magdalene at the empty tomb, and quoted
from Jesus' beatitudes: 'Blessed are they that mourn for they shall be
comforted.'[5] 'True tears,' Hession said, 'are for cleansing and healing.'[6]
A devotional column in the *Church Times* the previous year had endorsed
a similar view, this time with reference to the moment at the grave of
Lazarus when 'Jesus wept': 'the words have a verse all to themselves, as if
to remind us that a constantly stiff upper lip in adversity is not a Christian
but a Stoic quality. The physical act of shedding tears has a cleansing,
chastening effect.'[7] After decades of secularization and stoicism, a return
to the Christian tradition was one way to try to remember the value of
tears.[8]

A few days after the broadcast of Brian Hession's talk on 'Healing
Tears', another woman learned that her husband had terminal cancer,
which was attacking his stomach and liver. She wrote about it, under her
pen name 'Glen Heather', to fellow members of the 'Co-operative
Correspondence Club' (C.C.C.), which had been formed in 1935 by a
lonely mother in Ireland seeking friendship and support. The hospital
doctor had spoken to Glen Heather's adult son Ralph about the progno-
sis, suggesting they keep it from her husband, Don, while he recovered
from the post-operative shock. Glen Heather wrote, 'I knew very well
I could never keep up a pretence of lies etc. for a fortnight. Besides it is
not our way of meeting catastrophe. I decided to tell him. The children
agreed. It was hard, but I managed to do it and he was absolutely
wonderful.' A couple of weeks later it was the couple's wedding anniversary. Don had arranged for a parcel for his wife with 'little roses and lace
handkerchiefs and perfume'. The unexpected gift reduced her to tears
and, for the first time since his operation, 'Don covered his face and
wept.' The tender, romantic moment provided a permissible outlet for

tears for both husband and wife, which were otherwise denied: 'I wish I could come and cry in each of your arms! Here I have to be constantly dry-eyed and brave for the sake of Ralph and Don and to repay the kindness of my friends, but dear C.C.C. doesn't call for such control.' The letters from her correspondents acted as a 'safety valve' for her grief.[9] Talking to BBC Radio 4's *Woman's Hour* fifty years later, one of the other women in the club said, 'There was so much of the stiff upper lip business around. We couldn't really express to our family and friends real grief, you know, but we could put it out on paper.'[10]

The scholar, Christian apologist, and children's writer C. S. Lewis was similarly able to express his grief better on paper than in person, after the death of his wife Joy from cancer in 1960. They had married only a few years earlier. For Lewis it was not in letters to friends, but in a series of notebooks, that he tried to verbalize and understand his feelings of desolation and despair. The analysis is unsparing and the text testifies to Lewis's intense pain and theological doubts, as well as a gradual recovery from grief, partly achieved after a vivid experience of the presence of his dead wife Joy—an intimation of her mind which he describes as being brisk, business-like, and bracing—entirely unemotional, in fact. Lewis published the book the following year, anonymously, as *A Grief Observed*. After Lewis's own death in 1963, when its true authorship was revealed, the work became a widely read contribution to the literature of consolation, and it is still a bestseller of the genre. It remains also a fascinating document of its time, offering an insight into the thoughts and feelings of an extraordinarily cultured, articulate, and conflicted middle-aged man dealing with cancer, death, and grief in 1960, at the passing of an age of emotional restraint and the birth of one of psychological introspection and therapeutic self-involvement.

Lewis was born in Belfast to Protestant parents. When he was only 9 years old, his mother died from cancer. His father, whose volatile emotions had always seemed alarming, showed his grief in tears and fits of rage. Only a fortnight later, the young Lewis was sent away to join his elder brother at a particularly brutal little English boarding school—an experience he later likened to confinement in a concentration camp.[11] Lewis's father also died of cancer, so that, in *A Grief Observed*, Lewis lamented a triple loss to the disease, 'Cancer, and cancer, and cancer. My mother, my father, my wife. I wonder who is next in the queue.' Despite his immersion in Christianity, Lewis's version of the religion was too rational and too severe to allow for a belief in 'healing tears'. He wrote scathingly of the phase, early in his grief, of 'tears and pathos'. The anti-Catholic element of his upbringing was evident in his use of the phrase 'Maudlin tears', first used by seventeenth-century Protestants, to denounce his own weeping.[12] Lewis wrote that he almost preferred the moments of 'clean and honest' agony to the tearful 'bath of self-pity, the wallow, the loathsome sticky-sweet pleasure of indulging it—that disgusts me'. He also thought that tears obscured reality, making him for the moment replace the real woman he had lost, Joy, with a 'mere doll to be blubbered over'. Writing and rewriting his grief, Lewis found himself fascinated but frustrated by his own emotions and determined to escape them through the power of thought: 'Feelings, and feelings, and feelings. Let me try thinking instead.'[13]

Lewis encountered and tried to analyse an array of different feelings in his bereavement, including that powerful strain of disgust at his own tears. In the responses of others to his situation, he noted one emotion primarily in evidence: embarrassment. He dreaded encounters with others who knew of his loss, hating it if they mentioned it, and hating it if they did not. The response he found least painful was that of the 'well brought-up young men' who 'walk up to me as if I were a dentist, turn very red, get it over, and then edge away to the bar as quickly as they decently can. Perhaps the bereaved ought to be isolated in special settlements like lepers.' Lewis also discerned in Joy's children something he interpreted as a great embarrassment. Whenever he tried to talk about her, 'there appears on their faces neither grief, nor love, nor fear, nor pity, but the most fatal of all non-conductors, embarrassment. They look as if I were committing an indecency. They are longing for me to stop. I felt just the same after my own mother's death when my father mentioned her.'[14] One of the boys in question, however, later said that Lewis had been quite mistaken about the emotion behind that outward awkwardness. Douglas Gresham recalled that, after seven years of 'British Preparatory School indoctrination', the lesson he had learned above all others was that 'the most shameful thing that could happen to me would be to be reduced to tears in public. British boys don't cry.'[15] Young Douglas knew that if Lewis spoke to him of his mother, 'I would weep uncontrollably and, worse still, so would he. This was the source of my embarrassment.'[16] In fact, Gresham recalled that the brittle shell of British reserve was broken, on just one occasion, the first time he saw Lewis after Joy's death. The boy and the man clung on to each other in inarticulate tears: 'That was the only occasion upon which any physical demonstration of our love for each other ever occurred.'[17]

Here were the fruits of the good old British stiff upper lip: a bereaved man disgusted by his own tears, treated like a leper by others, misreading the grief of his stepchildren, who dare not speak of their dead mother for fear of weeping. 'It took me almost thirty years', Douglas Gresham wrote in 1994, in an introduction to *A Grief Observed*, 'to learn how to cry without feeling ashamed.'[18] Lewis, at least, had his notebooks to help him. He had set out to create a literary 'map of sorrow'. In that endeavour, he concluded, he had failed, because sorrow was, after all, 'not a state but a process. It needs not a map but a history.' Nonetheless, the writing had been therapeutic: as a 'defence against total collapse, a safety valve, it has done some good'.[19] Lewis certainly had a stiff upper lip, but it was also a painstakingly examined upper lip. *A Grief Observed*, with its interest in the unconscious, in depth psychology, in the personal history of an emotion, and in the need for a 'safety valve', showed that even

C. S. Lewis had been influenced by the Freudian and therapeutic models of the mind which were becoming increasingly popular and influential when he wrote. Later versions of Freudianism would create the kind of 'therapy culture' which has been associated with a rather self-indulgent kind of emotional navel-gazing combined with an expressive free-for-all.[20] In the middle decades of the twentieth century, however, psychoanalytic thinkers were more ambivalent about the public expression of feelings.

There were two ideas at the heart of the psychoanalytic approach to tears that entered into psychological orthodoxy among professionals and the lay public alike: repression and regression. The first implied that tears were a kind of overflow or discharge of previously repressed emotion, while the second presented the phenomenon of adult weeping as some sort of return to infantile, even prenatal, experiences and emotions. In their 'Preliminary Communication' on the 'Psychical Mechanism of Hysterical Phenomena' of 1893, Josef Breuer and Sigmund Freud had explained how repressed memories of traumatic events could, for years afterwards, give rise to hysterical symptoms. They believed that hypnosis could access these traumatic memories, which they thought of as 'foreign bodies' that needed to be flushed out of the psyche. Freud and Breuer reported that once a patient had put the memory into words, given it utterance, the hysterical symptoms would disappear. Tears featured in this model of the psyche in various ways, both pathological and healthy. Weeping itself could be a hysterical activity, revealing the remaining presence of repressed trauma. On the other hand, tears could function healthily, along with other voluntary and involuntary reactions to traumatic events, as a channel for the discharge of affect. Affect here was conceived as a psychic fluid that needed to be drained out of the system; weeping was one way to achieve that. As an example of another such expedient, Breuer and Freud had suggested acts of revenge. Tears, then, alongside words and deeds, were affect-discharge mechanisms, overflow channels, safety valves.[21]

For psychoanalysts and other psychological theorists, weeping was treated as an essentially excretory function. Tears could be associated symbolically with other bodily fluids, such as blood and sweat, as they had been in Churchill's first speech as Prime Minister.[22] In a couple of articles in the 1940s, the influential American Freudian Phyllis Greenacre put forward the view that weeping was to be understood as a displacement of urination. There were two elements to this view. First, urination and weeping were interchangeable activities, both functioning as hydraulic release mechanisms for tension and affect. Secondly, Greenacre developed a more complex theory about how suppressed infantile penis envy in women could result, years later, in fits of weeping which were symbolic attempts to achieve the longed-for accomplishment of male urination. In support of the first view—the equivalence of weeping and urinating as outlets of anxious tension—Greenacre cited increased rates of bedwetting among evacuated children in wartime England, and in army camps.[23] Some of the records of Mass Observation supported this association. One observer in 1940 described a middle-class woman, aged about 40, who lived in a street where three houses had recently been destroyed by a bomb, and who would grow increasingly nervous and agitated as it grew dark each day, trembling and repeatedly running upstairs to the lavatory. Finally, when the air-raid warning sounded, 'she urinated on the spot and burst into tears'.[24] An abrasive male respondent to the directive asking about tears in 1950 wrote, 'I have never cried "in the pictures"—I've sometimes urinated. "Ashamed"—yes— that I've chucked my money away.'[25]

We might call this the incontinence theory of weeping—the idea that the shedding of tears was directly parallel to the leaking out of other bodily fluids. Psychoanalysis, for all its interest in the healthy outflowing of suppressed affect, could also bolster the belief, itself the product of a range of religious, political, and social attitudes, that there was something excessive and slightly disgusting about the public shedding of tears. The public shedding of tears on television for an audience of millions was, of course, more disgusting still. In 1955, commercial television stations started to broadcast in the UK for the first time, and to compete with the BBC who had previously held a monopoly on the medium. From the earliest days there were fears, substantially justified as it turned out, that this development would lead to a race by broadcasters to secure the highest audiences by airing the most sensationalist programmes, often modelled on American formats.

Even in the 1950s, long before the age of Oprah Winfrey, American culture had a reputation for greater emotionality, which was reflected in its television programmes. The *Daily Mirror* reported that American medical men had 'gone on record as saying a sob is essential to our mental well-being! They say we men should weep at least once every three weeks—and if we do not exercise our tear ducts we'll upset our glands!'[26] In 1953, in the *Daily Express*, Eve Perrick wrote about the most popular programme on American television at the time, a new 'weepie' format called *This is your Life*. Perrick explained that the formula involved a notable person being surprised by the host, who then took his 'victim' to a studio where assorted friends and family, an aged mother, or an estranged daughter were sprung on him to review his life. The result: '*He* weeps, *she* weeps, *we* weep, they *all* weep. And the show is a riotous success.'[27] *This is your Life* was imported and broadcast on British television by the BBC from 1955. The first episode featured the host of the American version of the show, Ralph Edwards, surprising the Irish broadcaster Eamonn Andrews, who then became the regular host of the programme, which proved a great ratings hit for the BBC.

One of Andrews's victims in the second series of *This is your Life* was the Reverend Brian Hession, who was furious to have been tricked into participating, believing that he was being invited to give a radio talk raising public awareness about cancer. Hession sent round a public letter denouncing the BBC for their subterfuge. He was later offered a platform on the 'Flashback' programme at the end of the series, to get across the messages he had hoped to include in his radio broadcast. He told Eamonn Andrews that people needed to realize that cancer was not infectious in any way, and that it could be cured, or endured, by a combination of medical skill, human endeavour, and faith in God. Hession's initial anger was applauded in the press. One article wrote that he had been right to hit back against this 'deplorable' programme, while admitting that 'many of those who suddenly find themselves confronted by their past enjoy it a good deal, and that such tears as are shed are usually tears of sentiment'.[28]

Tears of sentiment aplenty were provided by the film star Anna Neagle when she was surprised by Eamonn Andrews in 1958.[29] 'Anna Neagle Weeps Before TV Millions' was the *Daily Express* headline, noting that the main cause of her tears had been a clip showing her friend and colleague Jack Buchanan singing to her in one of their early films.[30] When Neagle's husband, the film director Herbert Wilcox, came in, she hung on to him and sobbed, and then struggled to speak about Buchanan, who had died of cancer a few months before. One of Neagle's many starring roles had been as *Nurse Edith Cavell*, in a Hollywood dramatization of the heroic nurse's life and death, directed by Herbert Wilcox in 1939.[31] The reading of an admiring telegram from the nurses at the Brussels nursing home named after Cavell again reduced Neagle to tears. Edith Cavell, about to be shot by a firing squad, had remained firm. Anna Neagle, looking down the barrel of a TV camera, dissolved in tears. Press coverage tended to sympathize with Neagle, but to denounce the programme for its unforgivable intrusion into her private emotions. The *Express* thought the broadcast was 'the most embarrassing' yet of all the episodes of this 'American-invented' programme. The *Daily Sketch* agreed: the show had reached its 'high-water mark, measured in the sobs and tears which reduced this lovely and well-liked actress to humiliation'. The *Daily Mail* called it 'maudlin mush'. Another critic blamed the BBC's determination to beat commercial TV for the unforgivable intrusion of this 'weekly peepshow' of shock, embarrassment, and sentiment.[32] To see someone's emotions leaking out through tears was, it seemed, not only embarrassing, but more or less obscene.

Anna Neagle and her husband, however, defended the BBC against the charge of intrusion. They did not mind her grief being observed by millions. Neagle was quoted as saying that she had reacted with 'genuine emotion' of nostalgia and gratitude, and that she had not thought 'that millions of people were watching my tears'. Now the thought had occurred to her, she was not worried: 'I know the public is not adversely affected by genuine emotion—it's only false emotion which makes them shy away.' Wilcox agreed that the show revealed nothing more than the 'ordinary emotions' of an 'ordinary woman'.[33] Critics, if not viewers, remained unpersuaded of the virtues of *This is your Life*. William Connor's *Cassandra* column in the *Daily Mirror* conducted a concerted campaign against the programme, calling it 'icky-icky', 'saccharine-encrusted', a 'phoney, cloying, repulsive stunt', and a 'preposterous, snivelling charade'.[34] Connor expressed his delight, in an article entitled 'Unshed Tears', when the footballer Danny Blanchflower, Belfast born and bred, like C. S. Lewis, became the first person to refuse to take part. When surprised by Eamonn Andrews, live on air, Blanchflower literally ran away from the cameras, and the friends and relatives assembled from around the world for the occasion, later saying that he considered the programme an invasion of privacy.[35]

In 1960, on an interview programme called *Face to Face*, the broadcaster Gilbert Harding welled up with tears when he was asked by the journalist John Freeman, the programme's presenter, if he had ever been with someone when they died.[36] Freeman did not know that Harding's mother had recently died. This incident is sometimes described as the first instance of someone crying on British television. In fact, *This is your Life* was already noted for the tears of participants in 1957, before either

Anna Neagle or Gilbert Harding had cried on screen.[37] Broadcasters and their audience had now tasted tears, and despite divided opinions about early experiments in emotional 'reality' television, the flow could not be stemmed. Indeed, some critics started to find fault in television programmes that failed to include enough weeping. In 1961, the *Mirror*'s TV critic Sheila Duncan reviewed a new nightly drama serial, *Home Tonight*, under the headline 'Crying Might Help'. The opening episode had showed the funeral of a woman, Mrs Sutton, whose husband and children reacted with a stiff upper lipped restraint that Duncan found laughable and reminiscent of the cinematic style of a bygone age. In 1961, 'even middle-class families like the Suttons burst into tears', Duncan wrote, wishing that the daughter of the piece would 'blow up about it, or at least sob over her chores, in her stream-lined twentieth-century kitchen'. The Suttons would have to 'behave more like real people', if Sheila Duncan was to take an interest in them.[38] The mixed responses to tears and their absence on television reflected, of course, divergent attitudes to death, loss, and emotion in real life. There was no single agreed answer to basic questions about feeling and expression, especially in relation to grief. What was real emotion and what was fake? What was ordinary behaviour and what abnormal? What could be shown and what kept hidden?

A key figure in the effort to shift public opinion away from denial and towards expression of grief was the social investigator Geoffrey Gorer, whom we last encountered in 1915, as he sobbed over his boarding-school breakfast table on learning of the death of his father in the sinking of the *Lusitania*.[39] In 1961, Gorer's brother Peter was diagnosed with lung cancer. The doctors decided, as was usual, that the truth of his imminent death should be best kept from the patient. The silence and denial continued after Peter's death as his wife behaved as if nothing had happened, protecting her children, as she thought, by keeping them away from their father's funeral, taking them for a picnic instead, and completely hiding her own feelings. But of course bereavement was no picnic, as Geoffrey Gorer discovered, once more, as he sobbed himself to sleep, lost weight, and was treated with 'shocked embarrassment' if he told people that he was mourning his brother. Peter's widow Elizabeth also felt she was treated like a leper. It was this experience that inspired Gorer to undertake a detailed survey of social attitudes, which resulted in 1965 in his book *Death, Grief and Mourning in Contemporary Britain*. Gorer discovered that about half of deaths now occurred in hospital and that, although well over 70 per cent of those he studied were nominally Christian, fewer than 20 per cent were regular churchgoers. Belief in an afterlife was patchy: a quarter had no such belief, another quarter were uncertain, and even among the rest, orthodox Christian teaching was a minority view. All of this had resulted in a national detachment from older traditions of grief and mourning, and a widespread denial of death, combined with the acceptance of the view that 'giving way to grief' was 'morbid, unhealthy, demoralising'. The true pathology, for Gorer, how-ever, was the refusal to acknowledge death in public or to express appropriate emotions.[40]

Gorer's book was an important milestone in the history of British attitudes to grief. He was not yet in a majority in 1965, but his use of anthropological, sociological, and psychoanalytic ideas to argue for a radical rethink of emotions and their expression in relation to death signalled an influential new approach. In February 1965 the *Daily Mirror*'s agony aunt Sara Robson wrote about children and grief in response to a letter from a young wife whose husband was dying. The woman wanted advice about what to tell their 4-year-old daughter. The man's mother had said it was better not to tell her, but his wife thought it seemed wrong to 'exclude her from our grief'. Sara Robson's response was unequivocal. To hide the facts from the child out of a supposed kindness would be a grave error: mourning must be lived through completely, without shortcuts. To repress a child's grief at this early stage, or even to pretend that a parent had 'gone to America', could lead to feelings of guilt and desertion, and to depressive illness in later life. For adults too, grief and dejection had to be faced up to and experienced. To do otherwise was to store up physical and emotional illness for the future. If the woman had religious beliefs about an afterlife, she was advised to share those with the child, if not she would simply have to say, 'Daddy has died and we shall never see him again. It is absolutely horrible for us both, but we just have to accept it.' When the sad time comes, the advice concluded, the little girl should be allowed to 'cry as much as she wants', to see her mother express her grief and loss too, and to find comfort in talking about her father. 'The British stiff upper-lip beliefs may be wonderful in battle,' Sara Robson mused, 'but they are disastrous for those left bereaved.'[41]

18

Ha'way the Lads!

On or about April 1973 British masculinity changed.[1] It was 101 years since Charles Darwin had asserted that 'Englishmen rarely cry' and now, under the influence of second-wave feminism, pop music, American psychiatry, and the British tabloid press, male feelings were finally back in fashion. Men in the 1970s were moved to tears by all sorts of things, from listening to Joan Baez sing 'Kumbaya', or contemplating monochrome paintings by Mark Rothko, to accidentally killing a hedgehog with their lawnmower.[2] The latter happened to the poet Philip Larkin in 1979. The mangled hedgehog caused him desolation and private tears, and inspired him to compose an elegy—'The Mower'—a simple and, by Larkin's standards, sentimental poem, sounding a postmodern echo of the dead birds and dead dogs of the age of sensibility.[3] More popular by far, however, than folk music, abstract expressionism, or the postmodern poetry of discontent, as a vehicle for male emotion, was association football, and especially the romance and passion of the FA Cup. According to the conventional wisdom bequeathed by the age of the stiff upper lip, tears were signs of sorrow, ideally shed in private, and normally the preserve of weak women or flamboyant foreigners. The tears of joy shed in public by a sturdy British man on a Sheffield football pitch in April 1973, therefore, need some explaining and provide a revealing case study at this turning point in the history of male weeping.

Bob Stokoe, a rugged Northumbrian son of a miner, was born in 1930 and won the FA Cup as a player for Newcastle United in 1955. By 1973 he had made the transition to management and, after spells at Charlton, Carlisle, and Blackpool, was back in the north-east of England, now leading Newcastle's arch-rivals, Sunderland AFC. Stokoe took over at Roker Park in November 1972, when the team was struggling near the bottom of the second division. His management style reflected his own personality: a mixture of old-school toughness, a homespun psychology of expressiveness, and strong personal emotion. He aimed to inspire brutal physicality in his players, saying jokingly of the opposition, 'They can't run without their legs.' On the other hand he was described as emotional and sensitive: he took care of his appearance, sported a trilby in emulation of Frank Sinatra, enjoyed quiet evenings at home, and was so devoted to the family pet that on one occasion he even missed a game when he was manager of Charlton Athletic because his dog had just died.[4] On being appointed Sunderland manager, Stokoe said he wanted to allow the players 'greater freedom of expression both on and off the pitch'.[5] Rated by bookmakers as 250–1 outsiders at the start of the FA Cup that season, a series of wins earned Stokoe's team a semi-final game against first-division Arsenal. It was played at the neutral venue of the Hillsborough ground in Sheffield, on Saturday 7 April 1973, in front of a crowd of 55,000 people. Sunderland won the match 2–1, securing a place in the final at Wembley. The occasion is still remembered by fans as one of the most emotional in their club's history. One recalls that when the final whistle sounded, an elderly man 'threw his arms around me and then broke down in tears on my shoulder', saying 'We're gannin' to Wembley yer bugga, we're gannin' to Wembley!'[6] The Sunderland fans refused to leave until the 'miracle man', their 'messiah', Bob Stokoe, returned to the pitch to receive their acclaim. He did so, blowing kisses towards the terraces. He used both hands to wipe away the tears from his cheeks, 'mopping his face with the dignity of one man who has wept, and now has finished weeping', to borrow a phrase from a poem published a few years earlier.[7]

The triumph, and the tears, continued the following month at Wembley, when Sunderland again defied predictions to beat a Leeds United team packed with international stars and managed by the legendary Don Revie.[8] In the run up to the final, Stokoe continued to think about his players' emotions. He told the press that he would be keeping his squad relaxed, adding: 'I don't want to bring them to the boil too early and run the risk of them draining themselves emotionally.'[9] At the same time the Chairman of the Professional Footballers' Association commented on the fact that several of the Sunderland players had come down with flu, wondering whether this was a sign of 'nervous disorder' brought on during the 'emotional countdown to kick-off'.[10] When Stokoe, in his bright red tracksuit, led his team out at Wembley, alongside the more conventionally suited Don Revie, he looked relaxed. As they came out of the tunnel, the teams were hit by the deafening cheering, whistling, and singing of tens of thousands of fans, who then joined in the national anthem. It was an atmosphere of hectic quasi-religious enthusiasm, combining national patriotism with fierce local devotions. Around the country the event was watched on television by an estimated twenty-nine million people. During the first half-hour, the Sunderland faithful sang their loyal chants: 'Ha'way the lads'—not, I have now learned, to be confused with the rival Newcastle song 'Ho'way the lads'—and 'You'll never walk alone'. Both managers looked tense as they sat in the rain on the bench. They also appeared much less conventionally image-conscious than their twenty-first-century counterparts. Stokoe wore a mac and trilby over his club tracksuit and, over his knees, a blanket, which he shared with the player next to him. Revie had put a turquoise towel on his head.[11]

Even when Sunderland's Scottish striker Ian Porterfield scored, Stokoe remained impassive, biting his nails. The commentator for the broadcast on ITV observed, 'Bob Stokoe, showing very little emotion, knows that there may be even more to lose now.' Stokoe himself later said of that moment, 'Inside I was bursting with emotion but the last thing I wanted to do was to physically release that feeling. I wanted to keep it under control, harnessed to use to motivate my players through the remainder of the game.'[12] Only towards the very end of the match, with Sunderland still leading 1–0, did their manager start to get agitated, taking the blanket repeatedly on and off his knees—'Bob Stokoe doesn't know how to contain himself on the bench.' When the final whistle sounded, Stokoe famously sprinted across the pitch to hug and congratulate the goalkeeper Jim Montgomery who had made a remarkable save (Figure 20). As Stokoe and his players celebrated, the commentator rehearsed the familiar underdog narrative, reminding viewers how the 'miracle man' had steered a struggling second-division team to this

Figure 20. An emotional Bob Stokoe embraces the Sunderland goalkeeper Jim Montgomery after their side's historic victory over Leeds in the FA Cup final of 1973. Mirrorpix.

moment of glory—'Bob Stokoe smiling away, but crying as well I'm sure.'[13] In an interview after the game Ian Porterfield was asked how it felt to score the winning goal. He replied that it was 'the first time I've ever felt emotion in my life. I'm not an emotional fella. But I could feel, you know, the tears sort of coming to my eyes.'[14] Few have scored the winning goal in an FA Cup final, but many who would perhaps describe themselves, like Porterfield, as 'not an emotional fella' have had the experience of tears breaking through their normally resolute defences thanks to the collective drama of a football match.

Since Paul Gascoigne's famous sobs in the semi-final of the Italia '90 World Cup, the spectacle of the weeping sportsman has become very familiar.[15] The tears of Bob Stokoe and Ian Porterfield during the romantic Sunderland cup run of 1973 marked the start of an era of greater male emotionality—the tentative forerunner of more recent developments. During the 1970s and 1980s men were increasingly, and repeatedly, encouraged to get in touch with their feelings, and Stokoe's tears were admired in both broadsheet and tabloid newspapers. A *Times* profile of Stokoe approved of the fact that he had developed emotional relationships with his players and added that 'The tears he brushed away after the semi-final victory over Arsenal were endearingly genuine.'[16] Stokoe was held up as a poster boy for male expressiveness by the nation's favourite agony aunt, Marje Proops. 'I admire a man who can burst into tears,' Proops wrote in her 'Dear Marje' column, 'who clobbers the stiff upper lip image of the British male at a stroke by letting the tears flow, unashamedly unchecked. And remains undeniably manly.' Footballers could joyfully 'kiss and embrace each other', without impugning their masculinity, and so when Stokoe wept for joy, Proops concluded, 'I weep for joy with him.'[17]

Proops's campaign for male emotional liberation sat alongside her support for female social and sexual freedom. On the same page as her eulogy of Stokoe's manly tears, in May 1973, were items by Proops praising Australian feminist Germaine Greer for her battle for sexual liberty and Labour MP Barbara Castle for steering the Equal Pay Bill through parliament. Proops wrote that perhaps the best thing Germaine Greer had done for women was to make it 'respectably sexy' for them to be intellectual. The need for men to express their feelings through tears rather than bottling them up was a recurring theme in Proops's answers to letters in the 1970s and 1980s. One male correspondent worried that not only sad music, movies, or novels, but even 'sentimental reunions on *This Is Your Life*' could move him to tears. Marje reassured him: 'strong men do weep.'[18] The *Daily Mirror* had a circulation of over 4 million readers at this time. Marje Proops's attempts to promote a more emotional masculinity, and a more intellectual femininity, were reaching a mass audience.[19]

Proops was not a lone campaigner on the issue of masculinity and emotion. Later in the decade, Bel Mooney had a woman's page, also in the *Mirror*, which she used to defend and promote male tearfulness. In a column in April 1979 headlined 'Sit right down and CRY', Mooney wrote that the American actor Jon Voight had recently cried when accepting an Oscar for his portrayal of a paralysed Vietnam veteran in the film *Coming Home*. Voight was not the first man to shed tears when accepting the best actor Oscar—John Wayne had been the first to do so, at the 1970 ceremony, and Gene Hackman had followed suit the next year. These men were pioneers. The real heyday for weepy acceptance speeches was still two decades away.[20] Bel Mooney, in the same 1979 article, reported that the British boxer Joe Bugner had wept with joy on his wedding day, and that 'it was SWEET'. She added that she had recently seen a mother berating a 10-year-old boy who was crying at a school football match, admonishing him with the phrase 'big boys don't cry'. Mooney was outraged and wanted to shout back, 'THEY DO!' Like Proops, Mooney linked the topics of male emotion and female intellect: 'Bringing boys up to believe there is something wrong with showing emotion is as bad as telling girls that education is a waste of time.' She hoped that other famous men would follow Voight and Bugner in setting a public example and striking a blow for 'men's liberation'.[21]

Proops and Mooney, like Porterfield and Stokoe, Voight and Bugner, were pioneers of a new mode of masculinity that was very unwelcome in some quarters. Even while Marje Proops was eulogizing tearful men in her advice column, her *Daily Mirror* colleague Frank Taylor took a different line on the sports pages. Ten days after Sunderland's triumph at Wembley in May 1973, under the headline 'Where Have All the He-Men Gone?', Taylor awarded his £10 prize for the best letter of the week to a Mrs McDonald of Gravesend in Kent who lamented the loss of the 'tough, strong, he-man image of the footballer'. Players these days, Mrs McDonald wrote, aside from the new habit of 'protecting themselves with their hands' when facing free kicks, seemed to be always 'either kissing one another or shedding tears'. Even big Jack Charlton had wept when playing his last match for Leeds: 'An emotional occasion? Yes. But was this necessary?'[22] Mrs McDonald could have added Jack's brother Bobby to her list. Bobby Charlton cried when Manchester United won the European Cup in 1968. In April 1973, ten days after Bob Stokoe's tearful performance at Hillsborough, when Bobby announced his retirement as a player at a press conference, his manager Sir Matt Busby had tears streaming down his cheeks.[23] Another correspondent struck the same tone as Mrs McDonald three years later when the Newcastle striker Malcolm Macdonald cried after his team's defeat by Manchester City in the League Cup final: 'It was pathetic to say the least,' wrote E. Limb of Grantham.[24]

For some, the new proneness to tears among footballers and other men was a sign not of admirable emotional openness but rather of weakness, effeminacy, abnormality, or homosexuality. Sex between men had remained a criminal offence until 1967, and remained so for anyone under 21. The age of consent for heterosexual and homosexual sex was equalized for the first time only in 2001. The first British Gay

Pride march took place in London in July 1972. This was not a time when homosexuality had yet achieved any kind of wide acceptance.[25] Marje Proops received a letter from a young wife in 1971, worried about the fact that her husband had cried after their first big row: 'Do you think it indicates that he could be effeminate?' Proops reassured her correspondent that 'strong men shed tears', perhaps when watching a film, or when getting 'maudlin' after a few beers, and that the blame for the myth about male tearlessness lay with 'those silly mothers who tell their little sons it's unmanly to cry'.[26] A few years later one such silly mother wrote to 'Dear Marje', describing her 'cry-baby' 10-year-old son, and the attempts of herself and her husband to toughen him up with a mixture of play-boxing and advice: 'We've told him over and over again that only cissies blubber.' Marje was, of course, unimpressed. She thought it was meaningless to tell a boy that only cissies cried. 'What makes a cissy anyway?', she asked, 'I suppose you mean they're men who are weak-kneed or homosexual.' Proops quickly dismissed that idea, stating that homosexual men had to have a pretty tough exterior to survive 'in this prejudiced world', and sternly telling the woman to take a more supportive attitude to her 'timid and ultra-sensitive' son.[27] Supporters of the new, more tearful kind of manhood were aware of what their critics might think. When interviewed for an article suggesting that men who showed their emotions by crying had more successful marriages, the actors Oliver Reed and Edward Woodward added their voices to the cause. Reed said: 'All tough men weep at some times in their lives. It doesn't mean they are raving fruits. A man should be able to blub without it casting aspersions on his masculinity.'[28]

The new expressive masculinity, exemplified by weeping sportsmen and movie stars, and advocated by women writing for the tabloid press, received further support from British pop music and American psychiatry. The phrase 'boys don't cry' made the transition from received wisdom to knowing irony thanks to its uses in popular culture. In 1975, the 10cc song 'I'm Not in Love' featured a woman's voice repeatedly speaking the words 'Big boys don't cry', and four years later the second single released by The Cure was called 'Boys Don't Cry'. The song was re-released in 1986, when The Cure, with their famous Goth-dandy frontman Robert Smith, had achieved greater fame.[29] The song expressed the heartbreak of a rejected lover trying, but failing, to repress his feelings: 'I try to laugh about it | Hiding the tears in my eyes.'[30] The idea that boys don't cry was now an object for poignant pop parody.

I sang along to this and similar songs myself as an adolescent boy in South London in the 1980s, getting in touch with my feelings, in a newly masculine way. One of my favourite bands was Tears for Fears. I remember my excitement buying their 1985 album *Songs from the Big Chair* (1985) on cassette tape from the Our Price record shop in Hammersmith shopping mall (see Figure 21). That album included the song 'I Believe', which opens with the lines:

> I believe that when the hurting and the pain has gone
> We will be strong. Oh yes, we will be strong.
> And I believe that if I'm crying while I write these words,
> Is it absurd? Or am I being real?
> I believe that if you knew just what these tears were for
> They would just pour like every drop of rain.

The song concludes:

> I believe, no I can't believe that every time you hear a new born scream,
> You just can't see the shaping of a life.

Another track on the same album begins, 'Shout, shout, let it all out, these are the things I can do without.'[31] I couldn't have told you exactly what I thought any of these lyrics meant at the time—nor could I now—but they were part of a sentimental education in keeping with the psychological theories of the time, through which the propensity for tears was gradually spread by osmosis from the more to the less emotionally expressive parts of British society.

Figure 21. New men Roland Orzabal
and Curt Smith of Tears for Fears,
pictured on the cover of their
second album *Songs from the Big
Chair* (1985). © Mercury
Records Limited.

The name of the band, 'Tears for Fears', was taken from a 1980 book
by the American psychiatrist Arthur Janov, called *Prisoners of Pain*, and it
encapsulated Janov's central idea that suppressed or 'blocked' emotions
of fear and anxiety could be released through the shedding of tears.[32]
Janov's theory of repressed affect being released through tears was shared
with many psychological and psychoanalytic approaches to emotion,
going right back to the earliest writings of Sigmund Freud and Josef
Breuer.[33] Janov's original contribution was to pioneer a form of therapy
in which patients were encouraged to regress to early infancy and let out
primal screams and tears, to let out all the emotions that had subsequently been blocked through socialization and adult repression.[34] 'Tears
for Fears' were not the only pop musicians inspired by Janov's idea.
A Glaswegian alternative rock group formed around the same time
gave themselves the name 'Primal Scream'. But Janov's most famous
patient was the former Beatle John Lennon, who experimented with
Janov's therapy for several months in California in 1970, with his wife
Yoko Ono, and brought the therapeutic value of primal crying to the
attention of the British public. John Lennon had plenty of experience of
the hysterical screaming and weeping of teenage girls afflicted with

Beatlemania in the 1960s. Indeed, pop concerts, along with large sporting events, had taken over many of the communal emotional functions previously performed by open-air religious revivals or public executions. The weeping prophet in his surplice was replaced by a tearful trainer in his tracksuit or a gyrating guitarist in his blue jeans. The Beatles' own performances, however, unlike those of some American singers, were not themselves lachrymose.[35] It was in his private, therapeutic journey after the band split up in April 1970 that Lennon discovered his tearful side. In a nutshell, Lennon said, primal therapy was valuable because it 'allowed us to feel feelings continually, and those feelings usually make you cry. That's all. Because before, I wasn't feeling things, that's all. I was having blocks to feelings, and when the feelings come through, you cry.' He denounced the common practice of telling boys, from the age of about 12, to stop crying: 'You know, "Be a man", what the hell's that? Men hurt.'[36]

Arthur Janov was one of several American psychiatrists invoked by British journalists seeking some basis for the new masculinity. Ivor Davies, in his 'This Is America' column for the *Daily Express*, reported his attendance at Janov's Primal Institute's unusual Christmas party in 1970, with adults role-playing as children, receiving from Santa Claus gifts they were denied in their childhood, and 'rolling around on the carpet sobbing'.[37] 'The British are so repressed', Janov said in a later interview for the British press, describing the stiff upper lip mentality as 'a total disaster if you are trying to come to terms with the problems in your own life', adding that the British 'are unquestionably the least advanced psychiatrically of the developed nations'.[38] The article in which Oliver Reed was quoted on the subject of weeping and masculinity was based on the research of another American psychiatrist, Dr Jack Balswick, the co-author of a study entitled 'The Inexpressive Male: A Tragedy of American Society'.[39] Later it was Dr William Frey of Minnesota, yet another American psychiatrist, whose new research was reported under the headline 'Stiff Upper Lips Can Harm your Health'. It drew on Frey's ideas about the chemical composition of tears and their role in eliminating stress chemicals, and connected the advice to men to let their feelings out through tears with the bigger 'changing pattern in sexual relationships'.[40] Frey's approach offered a biochemical version of the already dominant incontinence theory of weeping and his research was to make many more appearances in the British media over the following decades. Ever since the 1950s, the British had been looking to America to learn about the cultural production and psychological explanation of tears.[41] The figure of the American psychiatrist had now taken over from the French physician, often cited in the previous century, as the most frequently invoked authority figure among advocates of the health benefits of tears.[42] It is a role that William Frey has very much made his own, gently coaxing the unemotional Brits into a closer relationship with their feelings for more than thirty years now, including an appearance in a television documentary about tears presented by the comedian Jo Brand in 2011.[43]

One puzzle remains about Bob Stokoe's tears at Hillsborough in April 1973: why did his positive, joyful emotion give rise to tears, which are normally considered expressions of grief? The fact that happiness as well as sadness could move people to tears was not news, of course. Medieval mystics had wept when experiencing ecstasy as well as compunction, and men and women who listened to Methodist preachers were moved to tears through sorrow over sin but also with a sense of joy.[44] In the twentieth century, happy endings as well as sad ones could be effective techniques for cinematic tear-jerkers. It was nothing new, but it proved a puzzle of particular interest to psychoanalysts and psychologists in the post-war decades. There were essentially two theories that could account for tears of joy. Either they were really tears of sorrow, or they were tears of relief from some prior affective tension. The former theory received its classic expression in a paper entitled 'Crying at the Happy Ending' by the

American analyst Sandor Feldman, published in 1956. Contrary to appearances, Feldman said, there was no such thing as weeping for joy. Those who cry at the happy ending of a film or at a moment of pride or joy in their own lives—at the birth of a child, or when reunited with a loved one who had been away or in danger, or, we might add, when winning a football match—may think they shed tears of joy.[45] In fact, these are all merely cases of a delayed or displaced discharge of negative affect. Perhaps the tears express sadness about the fleetingness of the moment, a realization that this happiness cannot last. In short, it's all downhill from here. Or such tears could be interpreted as a postponed expression of the fear and grief that were repressed prior to the happy outcome. In the case of triumphant sportsmen and women, Feldman's theory might be extended to suggest that tears at the moment of triumph express sorrow over the sacrifices and hardships which were endured to achieve it.[46] An alternative theory, put forward in the 1970s, was that all weeping was a kind of relief—or even, as the authors of one research article put it, an expression of 'joy', marking the moment when an individual made the transition from a state of arousal and distress to one of bodily and mental recovery.[47]

Which explanation can account for the tears of joy shed by Bob Stokoe in April 1973? Stokoe recalled the overwhelming effect of the Sunderland fans' reaction to him after the semi-final victory over Arsenal: 'People, grown men, were crying and bowing to me as though I was some kind of god they were worshipping. It was then that I heard thousands of them calling me the "Messiah".' As we know, tears rolled down Stokoe's own cheeks. 'I walked off the pitch', he said, 'as I could feel myself breaking down with emotional joy.' The imagery here resonates with Janov's idea of a barrier being removed. Did the response of the Sunderland fans finally break down the blockages to primal feeling that had built up in Stokoe's psyche since infancy? On the other hand, Stokoe made comments in interviews after the semi-final victory that are consistent with

Feldman's theory that apparent tears of joy are really tears of sorrow. Stokoe said of the moment at Hillsborough in front of the fans: 'In a way, I wish I could have retired right then, because nothing can ever top the feelings I experienced in that moment.'[48] Did the secret fear that this moment, soon to pass, would never be matched, cause him to weep? In an interview for the *Radio Times* in the run up to the final Stokoe spoke explicitly of other negative emotions. 'It's sad really,' he reflected, 'I know I'm a poor husband and an inadequate father. I provide for my family to the very best of my ability but I know that I am remote from them. I just can't help it. My whole life is football. We've lived in twelve different houses and my daughter has been to five different schools.'[49] Perhaps those thoughts about the cost to him and his family incurred by his triumph at Hillsborough were the real cause of the display of manly feeling admired by so many.

Emotional regimes—the rules and values governing the experience and interpretation of feelings—change only slowly, gradually, and partially. Grandparents and parents pass on to the next generations the attitudes to emotion and expression ingrained in them as children, even as they attempt to correct what they see as the failings of their own upbringing. No culture has a unanimous attitude to emotions or a single emotional regime. The new idea about male tears in the 1970s was that they should be met with understanding rather than derision, sympathy rather than punishment, love and support rather than insults and boxing lessons.[50] Veronica Papworth told her *Sunday Express* readers in 1980 that stiff upper lips would harm their health, Marje Proops claimed in the *Mirror* in 1983 that the 'stiff upper-lipped Englishman went out of style several decades ago', and that the 'salty flow' of tears was a 'harmless release' which was infinitely preferable to the harmful bottling up of feelings.[51] An editorial in the *Daily Express*, responding to the fears expressed by an educational psychologist that British boys were still receiving an emotionally repressive education thanks to outdated teaching materials, asked, 'Do not the kissing and cuddling footballers set a psychologically splendid example to British youth? Cheer up, professor. Not everybody reads schoolbooks!'[52] And yet this transformation of the emotional regime, in reality, had only just started, and many men were left behind under the old dispensation, including one of the stars of Stokoe's Sunderland team.

As the Sunderland team prepared for their big semi-final clash with Arsenal, their stolid centre-back Dave Watson had a feeling of destiny and was determined to keep his head. In a later interview he said, 'Rudyard Kipling: triumph and disaster: you should treat those both the same; I firmly believe that and I always tried to do that. It is sometimes difficult but it helped me to have a calm approach to matches'—it was the philosophy of the 'If—' upper lip. Watson's wife used to make sure he was in the right frame of mind before big matches: 'She would go through a little routine to make sure I was sharp before a game, maybe even slapping me across the face to make me angry. She did this in the Cup run and it helped me a lot.' Given his preference for restrained anger over gushing emotion, it is not surprising that Watson was not a fan of big goal celebrations, saying 'I never did that, running forty yards to congratulate somebody. I thought it was a waste of time, I really did. I always wanted to get back into my position on the pitch. I was never one for kissing and stuff like that.' Getting back to his position on the pitch rather than kissing and hugging—one could not want a better image of a dutiful and deferential man—a man with a stiff upper lip, getting on with things rather than wallowing in his feelings. This was what the pop culture of the 1960s and 1970s had been rebelling against. Watson paid a psychological price for his restrained and dutiful approach. After the win against Arsenal at Hillsborough, Watson ran straight back down the tunnel as usual, rather than staying on the pitch with the other players and Stokoe as they received the acclaim of the crowd. 'I must have been in the dressing room on my own for at least five minutes,' Watson remembered, 'It was strange, I never let myself enjoy that game or that win. I didn't let myself enjoy the feeling or the moment.' He sat 'completely on my own' in the bath, thinking to himself 'Where are all the boys?' They were hugging and weeping on the pitch. Eventually they came into the dressing room carrying champagne, 'and it dawned on me what I'd missed'. He'd missed the birth of the new man of the 1970s. 'I left the pitch too quickly and I regret that now,' Watson said. 'I have actually regretted it ever since.'[53]

19

The Thatcher Tears

Victorian and Edwardian opponents of female suffrage argued that women were too emotional to hold their own in the political realm.[1] Fifty-one years after the passing of the Equal Franchise Act of 1928, Britain chose a woman as its Prime Minister for the first time. If any feared that Margaret Thatcher would prove too feminine, too fluttering, or too soft-hearted for the job, they soon learned their mistake. Over a period of eleven-and-a-half years she pursued her chosen course resolutely and bloody-mindedly, waging war against Argentina in the Falklands, against trade unions, Irish nationalists, and the improvident poor at home, and ruling over her party and country as ruthlessly as any man. The satirical television puppet show *Spitting Image* portrayed Thatcher as a power-mad man, wearing a suit and tie, smoking a Churchillian cigar, eating her steak raw, and terrorizing her feeble cabinet colleagues, alongside whom she stood to urinate in the gents' toilet. In one sketch, the Michael Heseltine puppet confesses, 'I can never go when she's standing next to me.'[2] This apparent ultra-masculinity led the Labour backbencher Leo Abse, in his extraordinary Freudian psycho-biography of Thatcher, to describe her as a 'phallic woman'.[3] Such accusations of gender reassignment persist to this day. In 2014, Hilary Mantel published a short story entitled 'The Assassination of Margaret Thatcher', in which the narrator describes Thatcher as a pitiless vampire who 'lives on the fumes of whisky and the iron in the blood of her prey'. 'I thought there's not a tear in her,' the narrator reflects. 'Not for the mother in the rain at the bus stop, or the sailor burning in the sea.' In Mantel's story the Prime Minister is having an eye operation: 'Is it because she can't cry?' In an interview about her story, Hilary Mantel said that Thatcher embodied the anti-feminist belief that women 'must imitate men to succeed'. 'She was not of woman born. She was a psychological transvestite.'[4]

It is true that Margaret Thatcher's persona became increasingly macho during the 1980s—commander in chief, scourge of the miners, nemesis of terrorists. It is not true, however, that Thatcher was unable to cry. Throughout her career, Thatcher's public persona incorporated traditionally feminine traits, including the expression of emotion, alongside supposedly masculine qualities of leadership and aggression. The image offered to the public by the Conservative leader and her aides was female without being feminist: the loyal daughter, the thrifty housewife, the doting mother.[5] In all of these roles, the display of appropriate feelings was important. From her election as leader in 1975 onwards, Mrs Thatcher took the politics of personality and emotion to a new level. In 1982, in the aftermath of the Falklands conflict, Thatcher became the first Prime Minister to appear on the cover of a glossy women's magazine, *Woman's Own*. Inside, an interview explored Mrs Thatcher's feelings during the recent war. The interviewer noted that, 'For long periods of our conversation her eyes were misted over.'[6] In 1984, during the miners' strike, Thatcher was the first serving Prime Minister to appear on a television chat show, sitting next to the singer Barry Manilow on ITV's *Aspel and Company*, chatting about her hobbies, her family, and her feelings.[7] The next year she became the first Prime Minister, and perhaps the first British politician, to weep on television, during an interview with Dr Miriam Stoppard for an ITV programme called *Woman to Woman*.[8] Thatcher's performance of traditional female roles was embellished with the woman's gift of tears, although, as we shall see, they by no means always succeeded in securing her either a softer public image or a more favourable press.

Mrs Thatcher's premiership changed the political weather, and it has been mistier ever since, although politicians on both sides of the Atlantic, from the American presidential hopeful Ed Muskie in 1972 to London mayoral challenger Ken Livingstone in 2012, have learned that weeping is a risky political strategy. Muskie shed angry tears in public while defending his wife from press attacks. He was speaking outdoors during a snowstorm and afterwards claimed, rather poetically, that it was melted snowflakes rather than tears that the press could see on his cheeks. Muskie's campaign for the Democratic nomination was badly damaged.[9] In 2012, Ken Livingstone sobbed and rubbed his eyes as he watched his own campaign video, in which Londoners spoke of their hardships and urged Livingstone to defeat the Conservative incumbent Boris Johnson for their sake. In a *Channel 4 News* feature, political analyst Peter Kellner said that voters were impressed by tears that seemed genuine rather than fake, but genuineness was not enough. People also preferred tears that implied humanity rather than weakness.[10] Livingstone's tears, like Muskie's before him, looked uncontrolled, undignified, and weak. It was also unfortunate timing for Livingstone that a couple of days later, the far-right Norwegian mass-murderer Anders Breivik seemed to behave similarly, when he sobbed in court during a screening of his own propaganda film.[11]

Despite these dangers, politicians in recent years have tended to calculate that the potential image benefits of some carefully produced televisual tears outweigh the possible risks. In the run up to the 2010 general election, two leading politicians used tears to help deal with their contrasting image problems. The serving Labour Prime Minister Gordon Brown was thought to be intellectually impressive but psychologically brooding and obsessive. He welled up on camera when speaking about his baby daughter Jennifer, who had been born prematurely and died after only ten days in 2002.[12] David Cameron's eyes welled with tears and his voice cracked with emotion in two separate pre-election television interviews, when speaking about his 6-year-old son Ivan, who had died a year earlier, having suffered all his life from cerebral palsy and epilepsy.[13] Cameron had almost the opposite image problem to Brown. Voters feared not that Cameron had a dark or troubled personality, but that he had no personality at all. A poll found that 56 per cent of voters agreed with the idea that Cameron, who had a professional background working as a public relations manager for a television company, was a 'slick salesman'.[14] The production of tears on camera could itself be an effective exercise in public relations, deploying a different, apparently more genuine or revealing, media image to challenge the media image of a politician too obsessed with media image. Later in 2010, by now Prime Minister and the leader of a coalition government, Cameron was photographed shedding tears during a visit to his son's old school.[15] In 2014, in his final party-conference speech before the 2015 general election, Cameron again had himself and his wife Samantha on the point of tears, when connecting the illness and death of their son with Conservative attitudes to the National Health Service.[16] Cameron's team clearly believed that such displays of sentiment were vote-winners. What would once have been purely private emotions were now displayed for viewers and voters in their millions.

Commentators unimpressed by the current weepiness of politicians often invoke the supposedly dry-eyed restraint of bygone leaders, especially Winston Churchill and Margaret Thatcher. In 2011, Cristina Odone, writing in her *Telegraph* blog, contrasted the self-pitying tears of the Deputy Prime Minister Nick Clegg, shed while listening to music in the evenings—to which he had confessed in a recent interview—with the 'Churchillian' ideal of an 'unyielding statesman' leading troops into battle with 'a brandy bottle rather than a hanky at the ready'. As we have seen, Churchill himself would in fact have signally failed any test of leadership that required him to be hankyless and tearless.[17] Odone added that 'it was, I think, only after she was leaving Downing Street after 11 years that Mrs Thatcher gave way to tears'.[18] In fact Thatcher wept several times in public during her premiership and talked about her tears in interviews too. In the *Independent*, the political journalist Andy McSmith, despite acknowledging two occasions when Mrs Thatcher was known to have wept in public, offered a similar view to Odone's on the subject of politicians confessing to private tears. 'There was a time,' McSmith wrote, 'when it would have been career-destroying for a politician to admit to shedding a tear. Margaret Thatcher would never have risked her prized reputation as the Iron Lady with such an admission of weakness.'[19] But in fact Thatcher made exactly such an admission on more than one occasion, including in a magazine interview in 1978, becoming Prime Minister the following year.

We may now think of Tony Blair as the author of the new touchy-feely style which has become so familiar in the political culture of the twenty-first century. However, it was Margaret Thatcher, two decades earlier, who was the true pioneer of the politics of emotion. Blair did his emoting through his labile face and halting voice rather than his lachrymal glands. Margaret Thatcher's fifteen years as leader of the Conservative Party both began and ended in tears. When compared with leaders of much earlier historical periods, Thatcher was emotionally restrained. By post-war twentieth-century standards, her weeping was a minor public deluge. It also differed in two crucial respects from the political tears of earlier ages. As we have seen, figures from Oliver Cromwell to Winston Churchill, via Charles James Fox, Edmund Burke, and David Lloyd George, not to mention several monarchs, all shed tears while fulfilling their public roles. What changed from the Thatcher years onwards was the acceptance of the idea that emotional tears shed for personal reasons were also of relevance when considering an individual's suitability for office.[20] The second major change was the rise of television as a medium through which a politician's emotional tears could be brought into the living rooms of millions of voters, in colour and in close-up. Mrs Thatcher was the first British Prime Minister to realize television's potential as a technology of feeling.

On 11 February 1975, the day that she was elected leader of the Conservative Party, Thatcher was interviewed for the BBC by Michael Cockerell, who later recalled her cutting a feminine and fragile figure that day. 'When I think of my predecessors, Edward Heath, Alec Douglas-Home, Harold Macmillan, Anthony Eden and of course the great Winston,' the new Conservative leader said, 'it is like a dream. Wouldn't you think so?'[21] Then in this, her first on-camera interview as leader, she confessed, 'I almost wept when they told me I'd won,' adding, after a crucial split-second, perhaps a moment of unconscious political calculation, 'I did weep.' Cockerell recalled that as she said these words, 'she bit her lip, as her eyes glistened with tears—she looked anything but an iron lady'.[22] Cockerell was not alone among men at the time in being struck, and being moved, by the fragility and femininity of Thatcher in her early days as leader. Geoffrey Howe, who would later play a role in her downfall, remembered Mrs Thatcher's first appearance as leader in front of the 1922 Committee of Conservative MPs: 'Suddenly she looked very beautiful—and very frail, as the half-dozen knights of the shires towered over her. It was a moving, almost feudal, occasion. Tears came to my eyes.'[23]

Some of Thatcher's most notable uses of her own tears came in interviews aimed specifically at women. A 1978 interview for *Woman's World* magazine with the woman who had already been dubbed the 'Iron Lady' was widely reported in the press. The interview had covered a range of issues thought to be of relevance to women, including romance, marriage, and childcare. Thatcher described herself as 'a romantic' in matters of the heart, believing in true love and its potential to last between two people for a lifetime. She expressed guarded support for the idea that women should be able to work, so long as it was not at the expense of family life. Like a latter-day Mrs Beeton, Thatcher declared that 'Any woman who understands the problems of running a home will be nearer to understanding the problems of running a country.' In comments which would be echoed by Nick Clegg over thirty years later, Mrs Thatcher spoke about the pressures of her job: 'There are times when I get home at night and everything has got on top of me, when I shed a few tears silently alone. I am a very emotional person. I've never known a person to be insensitive about things which are wounding and hurtful and I'm no exception.'[24]

The *Daily Express* pounced on the 'very emotional person' part of the *Woman's World* interview, in an article headed 'Why I Cry by Maggie', which began by announcing, with a hint of cynicism, the discovery that, 'Deep down the Iron Lady is a softie' (see Figure 22). The *Express* solicited the responses of other female politicians and printed almost exclusively critical comments made by Labour women.[25] The Minister for Overseas Development, Judith Hart, said that she never shed tears when things got her down, although she might get irritable, and would distract herself from her emotions by working or listening to the radio. Renée Short, the Labour MP for Wolverhampton North-East, professed herself appalled: 'Good grief, for someone who wants to be Prime Minister it is quite a confession. I can't imagine a Prime Minister having a cry when things go wrong. I don't cry myself. When things get on top of me I try and keep my mind off it by taking my two poodles out for a walk. Tears don't help. They don't get the work done.' Finally, Dr Shirley Summerskill, a Home Office Junior Minister, said: 'I like to listen to music when things are getting me down. Mrs Thatcher should divert her attention to other things. I'm speaking now as a doctor!'[26] Dr Summerskill's medical advice, favouring distraction and denial over expression, was out of step with the latest scientific guidance which, as we have seen, was that weeping was beneficial to both physical and mental health.

Figure 22. Tabloid coverage of a 1978 magazine interview in which Mrs Thatcher, then leader of the opposition, spoke about her emotional side. Express Newspapers.

Margaret Thatcher's public tears in the 1980s paint a miniature portrait of her political and personal values. Newspaper reports recorded her tears on seeing the Berlin Wall at first hand in October 1982, and on visiting the Yad Vashem holocaust museum in Jerusalem in 1986, while Thatcher's adviser Charles Powell recalled her being moved to tears when listening to the singing of the Polish Solidarity anthem in a church in Gdańsk in 1988.[27] The wall, the museum, and the anthem were all emblems of the human suffering caused by ideologies against which she, and her father, had struggled since her childhood. Two events conspired in 1982 to create the most tearful year of Thatcher's premiership—the temporary disappearance of her son Mark during a car rally in the Sahara in January, and the Falklands war, which was waged from April to June. In both cases, Thatcher wept maternal tears. During the period when her son was missing, Thatcher broke down during an official engagement. One tabloid reported that this was not a mere dab at the eyes: 'She was sobbing hysterically' and the tears 'cascaded down her cheeks on to her blue suit'. 'The Prime Minister with the iron reputation', the sympathetic article stated, had become 'just a desperately worried mother'.[28] A few months later, reunited with her son, her maternal emotions were now extended to the young British servicemen whose lives were at risk in her military campaign in the South Atlantic. She was reduced to tears in private several times by her anxiety and grief for these, her surrogate sons. On one occasion, reported by the Conservative MP Gillian Shepherd, Thatcher cried continuously for forty minutes. Around the same time, a picture of Mrs Thatcher with her face awash with tears was taken by a tabloid photographer, but not published.[29] During her *Woman's Own* interview later in the year, Mrs Thatcher welled up as she spoke of the pain of keeping her feelings private. Asked whether the events in the Falklands had ever moved her to shed tears, she replied, 'Oh yes, you can't help it. They just come. But you pull yourself together very quickly.'[30] The following year Thatcher was filmed and photographed in tears when honouring fallen soldiers in the Falklands, and when receiving the freedom of the islands.[31]

The weeping of 'Mama Thatcher'—as she proudly reported once being called in Italy—was consistent with the new biochemistry of tears popularized by Dr William Frey.[32] In his 1985 book *Crying: The Mystery of Tears*, Frey described crying as an excretory process expelling stress hormones from the body. It also noted the much greater frequency and duration of women's bouts of tears, compared with men's, speculating that this was caused by higher levels of prolactin, the hormone which stimulates the development of breast tissue and milk production.[33] To cry was motherly. As the education secretary responsible for ending free school milk, Mrs Thatcher had earned the sobriquet 'milk snatcher', and with it an image that was anything but maternal. Perhaps tears could help to create a more caring and more motherly persona. When interviewed by health and maternity expert Dr Miriam Stoppard for an ITV programme called *Woman to Woman* in November 1985, Thatcher's instinct again was to head into the female domains of feeling and family, speaking both about herself as her father's daughter, as a housewife like her mother, and as a woman who had experienced the 'miracle of birth'.[34]

The interview with Stoppard, produced by Yorkshire Television, was trailed in advance as 'one of the most candid, revealing, human and relaxed' that the Prime Minister had ever given.[35] In the broadcast, Thatcher spoke of her own maternal pain during the disappearance of her son in 1982 and her fear that it might be a permanent separation, comparing her feelings with those of the mothers of servicemen killed in the Falklands conflict: 'I was lucky. They were not.' The Prime Minister also outlined her theory of gender difference. While her own career proved that there was no limit to what a woman might achieve in public life, she insisted that there was a 'fundamental difference' between men and women, which was both a 'biological difference' and an 'emotional difference'. Thatcher offered two reasons for this emotional difference. The first was the experience of motherhood, after which a 'great physical and mental and emotional change' comes over a woman. Dr William Frey would have endorsed this idea. Secondly, Thatcher spoke of the fact that women as housewives are left to cope in difficult circumstances, holding the family together in times of hardship and crisis, looking after the children, and drying their tears. The woman, then, as both emotional mother and stoical housewife, experienced the world differently from the man who, on this analysis, would experience a narrower range of emotions.

Miriam Stoppard wanted to ask Thatcher especially about her mother, Beatrice Roberts. Thatcher painted a picture of a submissive and silent housewife, cleaning the house and preparing the meals while Alfred Roberts, a Grantham councillor and alderman, and his clever younger daughter had animated political arguments. Indeed, it was in response to questions about her mother that Thatcher gave her most emotional answer, visibly shedding tears, while speaking about her father. I am not aware of any earlier example of a British politician crying on television, and it is quite extraordinary to watch the interview now. Thatcher tells the story of the day that her father, the alderman, was turned out of office by his Labour opponents in Grantham. One senses this is a tale she has told before. 'It was such a tragedy,' she says, getting into the flow of her sentimental narrative. But Miriam Stoppard interrupts to ask again about Thatcher's mother. The Prime Minster is not to be deflected and tailors her answer so that she can press on with the story: 'I remember when my father was turned off that council, making a speech for the last time, very emotional.' Then, taking on the role of her father, Thatcher repeats his words, accompanied by theatrical gestures, 'In honour, I took up this gown; in honour, I lay it down!' 'That is how he felt,' the daughter explains, by now having moved herself to tears, her eyes filling, her lip wobbling, before putting on a brave and childlike smile. A modern interviewer would surely have paused to allow the camera to zoom in, before asking, 'Why does that memory make you so emotional, Prime Minister? Did you cry for your father at the time? Why do you think that story makes you weep? Does it make you foresee your own inevitable political demise?' But in 1985 a weeping Prime Minister was an unexpected thing and such emotional inquisitorial conventions had not been established. Miriam Stoppard, brisk and embarrassed, moved on to ask a prepared set of questions about the Roberts family's Methodism and ideas of social duty, while her interviewee slowly wiped the tears from both her eyes with a hanky and continued to give her answers.

Daughter Thatcher's weeping for her absent parent chimed with a major strand of psychotherapeutic thought of the 1970s and 1980s. 'Attachment theory' was pioneered by the British psychiatrist John Bowlby and was an offshoot of traditional Freudian psychoanalysis. It emphasized the bond between mother and infant as the key to a child's emotional development. It was full of anti-feminist possibilities, blaming cold and unresponsive mothers for their offspring's subsequent insecurities. Leo Abse's psychobiography of Thatcher, although based more on Freud than on Bowlby, foregrounded the theory that Thatcher's bond with her mother was insufficiently strong, and that this lack of mother–daughter bonding was to blame for many of the evils of Thatcherism. Without the experience of a nurturing mother in her own childhood, Thatcher would not or could not nurture the nation.[36] During the 1970s, under the influence of 'attachment' thinking, standard childcare advice gradually shifted so that mothers were now encouraged to pick up and comfort crying babies. It was previously assumed that responding to a crying child would teach them to become manipulative and demanding. The new attachment-centred approach reversed this advice, and told parents that a child whose cries were heeded early in life would ultimately cry less than one who was ignored. Unattached infants would grow up insecure and needy. According to attachment theory, crying is always an interpersonal behaviour, a call for care and nurture from an absent carer, in the primal case an absent mother.[37] Perhaps, then, an attachment theorist would say, when Margaret wept ostensibly for the downfall of her father, the real pain was the permanent absence of a caring mother. The Barbara Stanwyck film that she remembered weeping buckets over as a girl in the Grantham cinema, *Stella Dallas*, was about a mother who sacrificed her own relationship with her daughter, so that the daughter could go on to achieve great success and leave her humble parentage behind her.[38]

The press response to the prime ministerial tears on display in the Miriam Stoppard interview was almost entirely unfavourable. Nicholas Shakespeare wrote in his television review in *The Times* that 'A handkerchief materialized from nowhere to dry a red eye and before you could say "onions" we had rattled on to religion.' He found the whole interview 'frequently hilarious', mocking Thatcher's regal use of 'one' instead of 'I', and regretting her 'dry sob of a voice, a voice that came from the heart but got unfortunately stage-managed on the way'.[39] In *The Listener*, the interview was dissected by the psychiatrist Anthony Clare, who doubted the authenticity and spontaneity of the 'tiny tear' wept by the Iron Lady, since the average television interview was 'about as spontaneous as the Trooping of the Colour'. Thatcher's tears in this interview, in fact, provide an interesting example of the difficulty of separating the authentic from the artificial. As Nancy Banks-Smith noted in the *Guardian*, it was most likely that Thatcher was genuinely devoted to her self-made and self-educated father, and that his life-story really moved her. 'On the other hand,' Banks-Smith rightly observed of the resulting tears, 'she brought that emotional moment on herself.' She had made a calculated display of authentic feelings.[40] Whatever the fairest interpretation of Thatcher's performance, the rarity of weeping interviewees in 1985 was confirmed by the fact that Clare and Shakespeare, when reaching for points of comparison, both harked back a full quarter of a century to the tears of Gilbert Harding in his interview on *Face to Face* in 1960.[41]

The satirical magazine *Private Eye* honoured the Stoppard interview with two separate items. A spoof tabloid article headed 'Maggie in TV Tears Shocker' started, 'Millions of viewers gasped last night as they saw Mrs Margaret Thatcher on television visibly struggling to force out the tears as she spoke of her early life in Grantham,' going on to refer to the Prime Minister 'visibly struggling to extract a small onion from her handbag'. In the same issue's 'Dear Bill' column—a long-running series of buffoonish letters purportedly sent by Denis Thatcher to an old chum—the tears shed in the Stoppard interview were described as the latest wheeze to promote a 'Softer than Soft' version of his wife, devised by the advertising agency Saatchi and Saatchi, portraying her as 'the velvet-voiced Carer, a far cry from the Grantham Mauler with her thumbs locked around the Kinnock throat'. The hope, the letter suggested, was that such a performance would boost her flagging poll ratings.[42] If that was the intention, it did not work in the short term, although eighteen months later, in June 1987, the Conservatives easily won their third successive general election victory under Thatcher's leadership, winning 42 per cent of the vote, compared to the 31 per cent polled by Neil Kinnock's Labour Party.[43]

Among the new intake of Labour politicians elected to parliament in 1987 were Britain's three first black MPs: Bernie Grant, Diane Abbot, and Paul Boateng. A few months after the election, Boateng featured as one of the contributors to a series of television programmes about human emotions by the film-maker Sally Potter, entitled *Tears, Laughter, Fears and Rage*.[44] These were broadcast on Channel 4 in September and October 1987, delivering a highbrow and politicized version of the message that Marjorie Proops and others had been promoting in the tabloid press for over a decade—that it was natural and healthy to express one's emotions, including through tears. One positive review of the programme admired Potter's interesting use of film clips, many from the 1940s, and interviews to illustrate the 'un-Englishness of weeping', complaining nonetheless that 'in its dullest aspect, the series is yet another instalment of the great campaign (centrally co-ordinated by the *Woman's Hour* unit) to get Anglo-Saxon males to express their Feelings'.[45] Among the films Potter used were the two most cited by the Mass Observation respondents who were asked in 1950 about films that made them cry: *Brief Encounter* and *Bicycle Thieves*. Potter's agenda was revealed in her questions to the veteran film director Michael Powell, asking him whether he thought 'the inability to laugh, the inability to cry, are intrinsically linked with oppressive people and structures'. Powell paused for a long time, before replying simply 'Yes,' pausing again and then apologetically asking, 'More?'

In the programme on tears, Potter's interviewees were almost all drawn from those groups traditionally considered to be more tearful, because mentally weaker, than the Anglo-Saxon male: children, women, and non-Europeans. This was the return of the repressed. The underlying argument was that shedding tears was something 'natural'; that in non-western cultures there were fewer restraints; and that the English should now follow this example by throwing off the cultural impediments which currently interfered with the natural expression of their feelings. A rabbi, Dr Rabinowicz, stated that Jewish people, being from the East, had 'an Oriental mentality' that encouraged people to allow their feelings to pour out rather than suppressing them—that tears thus offered a 'release from the poisonous streams' of the human mind. For Rabinowicz, the Bible too supported the idea of tears as a 'natural phenomenon'. The novelist Hanif Kureishi described men in Pakistan and other Muslim societies of the world as being much more 'demonstrative' creatures than the hostile but repressed denizens of English suburbs. Pakistani men 'cry at all times', he said, referring to a scene of men weeping and embracing each other in *My Beautiful Launderette*, which reflected the behaviour of his own relatives. Kureishi's English schooling, however, had led him to be afraid of his feelings, and embarrassed by them, learning instead to be ironic and detached. Seeing someone else crying, he said, evoked a powerful emotion in himself: 'I have a strong urge to hit them.'

Paul Boateng, born in 1951 to a Ghanaian father and a Scottish mother, told Potter that he had often felt like crying in the course of his work as a solicitor, especially when feeling the impotence and injustice of a client's situation. He had indeed sometimes wept with his client. Even though 'the stereotype of a lawyer is not somebody who cries', Boateng said, he hoped that in addition to being calm and confident when required, his tears showed that he could 'empathise with the client'. Boateng did not mention his experience as a Methodist lay preacher. While Margaret Thatcher grew up in a dry and austere strand of English Methodism—more Wesley than Whitefield—before conforming to Anglicanism in adulthood, Boateng's Methodism was of a more enthusiastic kind.[46] His tears had some continuity with those of British preachers and lawyers of earlier ages.[47] They could serve to reinforce, however, the long-established idea, rehearsed again as immigration from former British colonies in Africa, South Asia, and the West Indies increased in the 1950s and 1960s, that black people were childlike, excitable, and unrestrained in their emotional reactions.[48] Anglican observers in the 1980s envied the lively, emotional style of worship in evidence in inner-city black Pentecostal churches. Even if the mourners at Pentecostal funerals were perhaps 'naive' and 'too emotional', as one contributor to the *Church Times* put it, this was better than the cold restraint of the Church of England, where people still apologized for funeral tears.[49] In this same spirit, Sally Potter's 1987 series sought to lay out a new emotional template for a post-colonial and multi-cultural Britain, in which uptight white men would learn to emulate those from more expressive cultures. Michael Powell, blaming the two world wars for the creation of the unnatural stiff upper lip mentality, suggested that 'a whole generation or two has to die out before an Englishman behaves naturally'.[50] It is striking that in Potter's programmes, the imperialist comparative anthropology popularized by Darwin and others, with civilized Englishmen contrasted with less restrained, more 'natural', and thus more tearful non-western peoples, was reproduced.[51] The difference was that Englishmen were now to be condemned rather than admired for their restraint. The inability to cry was a hallmark of a psychological repression conjoined with political oppression. In a post-imperial Britain, it was time to give expression both to repressed feelings and to oppressed peoples. The task of dispensing entirely with these kinds of racist anthropological stereotypes was not yet even attempted.

Margaret Thatcher and Sally Potter used tears in pursuit of quite different political visions. While Potter celebrated the prospect of a more emotional, post-colonial Britain, Mrs Thatcher shed tears over the loss of the colonies. Watching in private on television, as the Union Jack was lowered during Zimbabwe's ceremony of independence, Thatcher was moved to tears and commented to her parliamentary aide Ian Gow, 'The poor Queen. Do you realise the number of colonies that have been handed over from the British Empire since she came to the throne?'[52] While Potter was interested in retrieving the tears of the oppressed and using emotions to break down divisions of class, race, and sex, Thatcher was happy to deploy her tears in a way that reinforced conservative ideas about gender, family, and motherhood. Thatcher famously declared that there was no such thing as 'society', which she considered merely an abstract concept: it was individuals and families who really comprised the nation.[53] Her tears, similarly, had often flowed along familial rather than social channels of affection. This contrasted with seventeenth- and eighteenth-century theories of weeping as a fundamentally sociable activity, capable of creating liquid bonds of affection across the whole of society. Both Potter and Thatcher nonetheless appealed to the idea that emotions were natural, biological phenomena, and that they were experienced differently and more powerfully by women.

Figure 23. A tearful Margaret Thatcher, leaving Downing Street for the last time, in 1990, with her resolutely grinning husband, Denis, next to her. Mirrorpix.

Margaret Thatcher died in April 2013 at the age of 87. The public response revealed the enduring potency of the witch as an emblem of hard-hearted womanhood. Opponents of Thatcher started a campaign to get the song 'Ding Dong the Witch is Dead', originally from the film *The Wizard of Oz*, to the number one spot in the music download charts. Although over 50,000 copies were sold, the song just missed out on the top spot.[54] Supporters and former colleagues sought to defend Margaret Thatcher's reputation by appealing to her softer side, recalling private instances of her tearfulness, including the most famous and most remembered of her tears—those visible in her eyes as she left Downing Street for the last time in 1990 (Figure 23). Again an old argument was, in effect, being rehearsed: if this woman was capable of weeping, then she cannot have been a witch. In a television interview, Cecil Parkinson, who had attended Thatcher's final cabinet meeting that morning, described arriving to find the Prime Minister sitting with a box of Kleenex. She became tearful and choked up more than once as she tried to read her prepared statement to her colleagues. Several members of the cabinet were in tears, Parkinson told *Newsnight*, welling up again himself as he recalled the moment.[55]

At Thatcher's funeral, the Conservative Chancellor of the Exchequer, George Osborne, was pictured with tears running down his cheeks as he listened to the eulogy. Comments in the press and online met these tears with derision, although Osborne's coalition colleague Nick Clegg came to his defence. Osborne was even grilled on the nation's leading morning news broadcast, BBC Radio 4's *The Today Programme*, about his funeral tears. Presenter John Humphrys wanted to know whether Osborne was generally the 'sort of person' who wept, rather than being too 'macho' to show his feelings. The Chancellor replied, guiltily and defensively, that he was caught on camera so there was no point denying it, but that the occasion was a 'powerful', 'emotional', and 'moving' one and that the combined effects of the sermon, the music, and the ritual of a state occasion did make him 'well up a bit', although he thought 'weeping' was a bit strong.[56]

When I heard John Humphrys's interrogation of George Osborne about his tears at Margaret Thatcher's funeral, putting aside my professional and historical interest in the subject, I felt I was witnessing something surreal. Was this man really being cross-questioned about a few mild and restrained tears at a funeral? Crying at funerals is a more or less universal human behaviour. Osborne was showing grief for a woman he had admired and who had led the party of which he was a member, and who had died after a considerable period of mental deterioration. And this was 2013. It was not the 1590s, the 1790s, or the 1950s. This was not a Britain that needed to resist the threat of lachrymose Catholicism, sentimental revolutionary fervour, or embarrassing and unwanted emotions. This was a post-Oprah, post-Diana Britain, not the stiff upper lipped Britain in which a silent denial of death and a ban on public tears were still enforced. Or was it? John Humphrys was one of many who felt that the public grief over Princess Diana's death in 1997, real though it may have been for some, was reported by the media in an overblown, one-sided, and sentimental way, creating an intolerant, even totalitarian emotional atmosphere.[57] The mourning for Diana, and its representation on television, divided opinion and created a backlash against the new emotionalism. The stiff upper lip, which since the 1960s had seemed quaint and embarrassing, was set to make a comeback, this time as an object of sentimental nostalgia.

20

Sensibility Regained

'Od save thee, weeping Queen!', Elizabeth Barrett exclaimed in 1837, responding to the tearful accession of the 18-year-old Victoria on the balcony at St James's Palace.[1] As Victoria's lengthy reign wore on, her tears, and those of her subjects, became less frequent, and the empire of the stiff upper lip was born. In 1952, another young woman acceded to the British throne. Born in 1926, Princess Elizabeth was 25 when her father, George VI, died. Her childhood and adolescence coincided with the peak of British public restraint in the years before, during, and after the Second World War. The princess shed no public tears at her accession, nor at her coronation as Queen Elizabeth II in June 1953. The new monarch remained dry-eyed, but the same cannot be said of her subjects, as they huddled round flickering black-and-white television sets to watch the coronation ceremony, the first live broadcast of its kind. An estimated twenty million people witnessed the event in this way. A 13-year-old schoolgirl, Anne Watts, watched with her family and their neighbours at home in rural North Wales, eating piles of sandwiches and cakes, a Union Jack flying outside, and her patriotic merchant-seaman father failing to hide his tears.[2] In the new shared space created by television-viewing, national events could be experienced by millions simultaneously, in an intimate and emotional way. In the BBC's *Listener* magazine immediately afterwards, Christopher Salmon wrote, 'Something extraordinary, which may perhaps even have been unique, happened in England last week.' What Salmon thought so remarkable was the emotional involvement of the people in a national event: 'Through their television sets they found means, on that day, themselves to participate in the service and commonly, very commonly I am told, those who were watching were moved to tears.' For Salmon these tears had unified the nation: 'We were all one.'[3]

A nation glued to their television sets, unified in their tears in response to a royal event: to read this account at any time after 6 September 1997, is to be reminded immediately of the funeral of Diana, Princess of Wales. During the time that I have been researching the history of British tears, I have given public talks to many audiences, followed by questions and discussion. In these conversations, two questions, in one form or another, recur more frequently than any other: What was the true impact of the death of Diana? And whatever happened to the British stiff upper lip? Diana and the stiff upper lip: these two ghosts have haunted not just my own research, but public discourse about emotions and Britishness since 1997. The enduring impact of Diana's death and funeral on most people's everyday lives was minimal. The mourning for Diana was an extraordinary event, nonetheless, and it gave added momentum to a turn to tears that had been under way throughout the 1990s. Diana's primary importance was more as representation than reality. She was the symbol and harbinger of a new emotional era—a televised, postmodern re-run of the eighteenth-century age of sensibility.[4]

Diana's emotional style contrasted with that of her buttoned-up mother-in-law. Elizabeth II ruled over an increasingly expressive nation, but was not once publicly moved to tears during the first forty-five years of her reign. She cried for the first time in public in 1997, at the age of 71. But it was not over the death of Diana that the monarch shed these tears, but for the loss of a luxury boat (Figure 24).[5] The royal yacht *Britannia*, launched in Elizabeth's coronation year, had been a favoured vehicle for overseas visits and receptions throughout her reign. A new Labour—and

Figure 24. Queen Elizabeth II shedding tears at the decommissioning of the royal yacht *Britannia* in 1997. © Rex.

'New Labour'—administration headed by Tony Blair came to power in May 1997. The royal family's popularity was at a low ebb, and Blair's government decided that it could not justify the refurbishment or replacement of her majesty's yacht at public expense: *Britannia* was to be taken out of service and turned into a tourist attraction. On 1 July 1997, *Britannia*'s final mission was to transport the last British governor of Hong Kong, Chris Patten, away from the territory after its handover to China. The ceremony marking this transition included music designed to stimulate any patriotic British lachrymal gland: Elgar's 'Nimrod' variation, 'God Save the Queen', and the Last Post, which played as the Union Jack came down. A British colonial past was giving way to an uncertain Chinese future. Chris Patten wept, alongside a dry-eyed Tony Blair, before leaving the territory for the last time, in the pouring rain, carried on his way by the condemned royal yacht *Britannia*, and accompanied by the Prince of Wales, whose marriage to Diana had ended in divorce a year earlier, marking a new low point for an already unpopular royal family.[6] The whole episode was a big, wet, floating metaphor for the decline of the British ruling class.

At the end of the following month, on 31 August 1997, Princess Diana was killed in a car crash in Paris, in the early hours of the morning, at the age of 36. As Britain woke to the news on that Sunday morning, Tony Blair gave one of his most remembered speeches, in the drizzle outside the church in his Sedgefield constituency in the north-east of England. He did not weep, but employed the uneven staccato delivery and earnest facial expressions that would soon become hallmarks of Blair in emotional mode. The BBC reported that the Prime Minister's voice was 'breaking with emotion' as he spoke of the shock, pain, and grief caused by the sudden loss of the 'people's princess', paying tribute to her humanitarian work, and saying the nation's thoughts would be with her two sons, William and Harry, then aged 15 and 12.[7] The ensuing mass expressions of grief and mourning were on an unprecedented scale. More than a million bouquets were left outside Kensington and Buckingham palaces in London, and television and newspaper reports overflowed with flowers and tears.

In the days after the death of Diana, the queen was with her grandsons, William and Harry, and their father, in the royal residence at Balmoral in Scotland. During that week, as they attended to their grief in private, the royal family's behaviour was portrayed as out of tune with the emotional tone of the country. The tabloid press led calls for the queen to return to London, to demonstrate that she felt the pain of her people. A leading article in the *Daily Express* contrasted the 'old school' reserve of an out-of-touch royal family with the new spirit embodied by Diana and embraced by the nation, which it summarized as 'love, openness, compassion'. In an accompanying column, the veteran journalist Ludovic Kennedy expressed his doubts about whether the royal family were even able to weep: 'They have been taught from birth not to show emotion, to keep a stiff upper lip at all times. Yet to weep can be wonderfully therapeutic, as well as a sign of being human.' The *Express* warned that if the queen continued to fail to emote, in response to Diana's death, the end of the monarchy and the creation of a British republic would come 'a giant step closer'.[8]

The queen's indirect response to such criticisms came in the form of a live televised tribute to Diana, broadcast on the eve of the funeral. Speaking from Buckingham Palace, against a backdrop of crowds of mourners, the monarch pointedly remarked that 'we have all been trying in our different ways to cope'. 'It is not easy to express a sense of loss,' she explained, going on to speak of the emotions of disbelief, anger, and concern for others, which a death can trigger, and assuring her people that she was speaking 'from the heart', as a grandmother as well as a queen.[9] The text, couched in the language of pop psychology and emotional literacy, was in stark contrast with the monarch's clipped tone and impassive physiognomy. While the words were in the spirit of *Oprah*, the body language and delivery owed more to *Brief Encounter*. When the queen did finally shed the first public tears of her reign, weeping over *Britannia*, it was three months too late to satisfy her critics, but it was seen nonetheless as a belated updating of the royal emotional style, a post-Diana side-effect.[10]

Much of the media coverage of the response to Diana's death suggested that the whole nation had been unified in its grief. Just as the *Listener* magazine had claimed of those who watched and wept over the coronation in 1953, it was made to seem as if 'We were all one.' That was not true. A poll taken after the funeral found that about two-thirds of the British population declared themselves to have been 'upset' or 'very upset' by Diana's death, with the remaining third either 'not very upset' or 'not upset at all'. Over a quarter stated that they had signed a book of condolence, with a further fifth intending to do so. On the other hand, half the population had not and did not intend to sign a book of condolence, and 70 per cent had felt no inclination to join in the mass flower-laying outside the London palaces and the princess's final resting place at the Althorp estate in Northamptonshire.[11] Many who did not join in with the tear-shedding and flower-laying felt alienated by the television and newspaper coverage. Television coverage tended to zoom in on tear-streaked faces and then juxtapose these individual images with pictures of huge crowds. Such coverage conveyed the false impression of a collective response of mass weeping. The social anthropologist Kate Fox has pointed out that the supposed 'unprecedented outpouring of national grief' was largely expressed through the very English activity of orderly and patient queueing, whether to buy and lay flowers, sign a book of condolence, or catch a glimpse of the coffin.[12]

Whether it was primarily the people or the press who were responsible for creating an atmosphere of fervid emotion at the start of September 1997, there were plenty who found it suffocating. Older respondents to surveys were the most likely to express their discomfort, likening the Diana event to scenes of excessive mourning in foreign countries, or to the dangerous group emotions inspired by fascist leaders in German and Italy decades earlier.[13] These responses dredged up old ideas of tears as the prerogative of those of other nationalities, other races, and other religions. The Conservative politician and journalist Boris Johnson was initially of this school of thought. In 1995 Johnson spoke about the emotional adulation received by Tony Blair at the Labour Party conference that year, observing that 'Hard-eyed feminists in burgundy suits were weeping like an Alabama congregation hearing of O. J. Simpson's acquittal.'[14] In 1997 Johnson conjured up images not of Pentecostal African-Americans but of Catholic South Americans in expressing once more his distaste for public emotion, comparing the response to Diana's death to a 'Latin American carnival of grief', in a column in the *Daily Telegraph* headed 'Where is this, Argentina?'[15]

Long before national debates about Diana and her death, football had led the way in providing men in particular with new models of emotional expression, with players and managers becoming more prone to tears from the 1970s onwards.[16] In 1990, continuing the north-east of England's tradition of producing weepy footballers (including Bobby Charlton and Bob Stokoe), Gateshead-born Paul Gascoigne famously sobbed in disappointment during England's World Cup semi-final in Turin. The reason for Gascoigne's tears was that his second yellow card meant that if England made the final he would not be allowed to play. As it turned out, England lost the match. Another Geordie, the England manager Bobby Robson, told the press that he was not ashamed to admit that tears had been flowing in the dressing room after the game, adding 'I've tried to hide mine and put on a brave face. But it's hard.'[17] Gascoigne's tears became an abiding image of that 1990 defeat (Figure 25), and were immortalized by *Spitting Image*'s creation of a puppet with spurting eyes, and a song to mark the occasion—'Cry, Gazza, Cry!'[18]

Gazza's tears came near the start of the new age of sensibility, and were followed later in 1990 by another iconic moment when Mrs Thatcher left Downing Street in tears.[19] By 2012 the culture of tears had spread beyond football and politics into other sports, including athletics and tennis, and into the newly dominant genre of 'reality' television. When London hosted the Olympic games in 2012, the combination of patriotic pride and sporting success created an irresistible opportunity for weeping—one that was taken not only by medal-winning British athletes themselves, but also by the broadcasters interviewing them on television.[20] Tears shed by athletes were not a novelty. The earliest examples I have found of Olympic medal-winners shedding tears date back to 1956 and 1964, and were in both cases shed by swimmers.[21] In 1996, the number of athletes weeping in Atlanta, Georgia, earned that summer Olympics the title of 'The Crying Games'.[22] In 2004, in Athens, the British rower Matthew Pinsent shed tears the 'size of gobstoppers', according to the *Daily Telegraph*, as he stood on the gold-medal podium, revealing the strength of emotion beating through his 'great heart of oak'.[23] Rod Liddle, in *The*

Figure 25. Paul Gascoigne's tears at the 1990 World Cup became an emblem of the new sensibility. Billy Stickland/Allsport/Getty Images.

Spectator, was appalled. 'Eton apparently taught Matthew Pinsent very little,' Liddle wrote. 'It is all well and good to be able to row a small boat very quickly, but nothing excuses blubbing like a baby—or, worse, a foreigner—up on the medal podium in Athens.'[24]

By the time of London 2012, Boris Johnson, who had expressed views similar to Rod Liddle's in the 1990s, had embraced the new sensibility. In May of that year, he secured a second term as Mayor of London, once more defeating his Labour challenger Ken Livingstone (whose sobs over his own campaign video failed to win over the electorate).[25] The opening ceremony of the London Olympic and Paralympic games was a triumph for Danny Boyle, its left-leaning creator, who used the occasion to celebrate Britain's National Health Service and modern multiculturalism, but also for the royal family. One sequence featured the queen and James Bond (played by the actor Daniel Craig) apparently parachuting into the

Olympic Park together. Boris Johnson commented, 'People say it was all leftie stuff. That is nonsense. I'm a Conservative and I had hot tears of patriotic pride from the beginning. I was blubbing like Andy Murray.' A couple of weeks later, the mayor proclaimed the end of the games a 'tear-sodden juddering climax'.[26] Johnson's choice of words on both occasions was double-edged. He was apparently joining in with the lachrymosity of participants and public, while also maintaining a dry-eyed and somewhat ironic distance. He was talking about tears rather than publicly shedding them, after all, and his use of the suggestive imagery of 'hot tears' and a 'juddering climax' could be read either as patriotism of such fervour as to border on the sexual, or as a neo-Freudian take on weeping as a kind of ocular ejaculation really best done in private.

The Scottish tennis player Andy Murray, to whom Boris Johnson referred in his comments about crying, had recently inherited the mantle of Paul Gascoigne as the nation's most notable weeping sportsman. Given the prominent role played by Scottish philosophers and writers, from David Hume and Adam Smith to Henry Mackenzie and Robert Burns, in creating and theorizing the original eighteenth-century version of the man of feeling, it is appropriate that one of its most prominent modern reincarnations should be a Scot.[27] Prior to 2012, Murray was known for his taciturn and bad-tempered demeanour. The emotion he was most likely to show during a match was petulant anger. In July 2012, Murray became the first British man to reach the men's singles final at Wimbledon since 1938. He was defeated by Roger Federer, and in his post-match interview, he struggled to speak through his tears. He broke down repeatedly as he tried to thank all those who had helped him, and the more he wept, the more the crowd cheered. Many newspapers afterwards proclaimed that he had won the hearts of the nation with this show of feeling.[28] Others, including some of the callers to a BBC Radio phone-in on the subject, and *Spectator* columnist Toby Young, were disgusted by the 'emotional incontinence' of what Young called Murray's 'big girl's blouse routine'.[29] The rhetoric on both sides was familiar, with support for male expressiveness generally winning the day. The following year, Murray reached the final at Wimbledon again, this time emerging as champion, and again breaking down in tears, thus giving a new interpretation to those lines of Rudyard Kipling's lines above the entrance to Centre Court about treating triumph and disaster just the same.[30]

Murray's tears after his performances at Wimbledon in 2012 and 2013 were partially explained in the press with reference to a tragic episode in his early life, namely his witnessing of the Dunblane school massacre. Thomas Hamilton, a former youth leader, known to Murray and his family, shot dead sixteen children and a teacher at Dunblane Primary School in 1996, before killing himself. Andy Murray and his elder brother hid under a desk in the headmaster's office. A documentary about Murray's life, aired by the BBC in advance of the 2013 Wimbledon championship, featured an interview by Sue Barker (also Murray's on-court interviewer after both finals). When she asked Murray about the school massacre, he broke down in tears before managing to start his answer. In 2014, at a meeting in Dunblane High School, Murray was awarded the freedom of Stirling in recognition of his sporting achievements. Yet again, his crying made it almost impossible for him to speak. After a few words of thanks, Murray started to puff his cheeks and touch at his nose repeatedly, struggling to get his words out through his tears. He finally managed, after long pauses, to say, 'Everyone knows how proud I am of where I come from,' breaking down again with a high-pitched whimper, composing himself, smiling, and sitting down, saying, 'I apologize for this behaviour.'[31]

In these public performances, Murray's tears displaced his words. It was the attempt to put thoughts into speech that brought tears, uninvited and unwanted, choking him up, and drowning his voice.

These non-verbal signifiers conveyed a strength of feeling which was, literally, applauded. At Stirling Council, as at Wimbledon, Murray's pauses as he struggled to choke back tears were greeted with as much applause as his words. This is just one example of the way that the recent rediscovery of the emotional economy of tears has unconsciously reproduced aspects of the eighteenth-century culture of sensibility. Writing in the *Gentleman's Magazine* in 1907, as we have already seen, Mary Howarth wrote with bafflement of the extravagant tearfulness of Henry Mackenzie's character Harley—the original *Man of Feeling*, created in 1771. Howarth picked out several descriptions which she thought incomprehensible to a modern age, including the phenomenon of 'voices lost in tears' and the shedding of one single tear. This 'gymnastics of the emotions' was an entirely forgotten art.[32] Mary Howarth would have been astonished to see the emotional behaviour of the contestants and judges on British 'reality' talent shows such as *The X Factor* and *Britain's Got Talent*, which were launched on ITV in 2004 and 2007 respectively. Here the form and feeling of the eighteenth-century novel of sensibility are rediscovered. Fragments of narratives of personal tragedies, poverty, illness, and bereavement are the backdrop to performances by ordinary people. These performers are the descendants of the beggars and madmen, injured soldiers and fallen women, who populated the cultural productions of the first age of sensibility. When successful, now as then, these narratives and performances are rewarded with both tears and money. The successful performance is greeted by rapturous standing ovations, flowing tears, and hopefully a lucrative recording deal. Tears are offered as tributes by the judges, especially the female judges, and these in turn produce more tears, in the eyes of performers and audience alike, sometimes followed with hugs between weeping contestants and weeping judges. All aqueous emotion is here—'from the glisten to the sob', as that 1801 spoof book prospectus for a history of weeping put it.[33]

Figure 26. Cheryl Fernandez-Versini (formerly Cheryl Cole) crying while judging on *The X Factor*. © Syco/Thames/Corbis.

The Newcastle-born singer Cheryl Fernandez-Versini (formerly Cheryl Cole), whose career was launched by the ITV reality show *Popstars: The Rivals* in 2002, has become the quintessential weeping judge on *The X Factor*. While judges like Sir James Shaw Willes and jurors shed tears in earlier periods as they decided on matters of life and death in the criminal courts for defendants who sometimes wept in the dock, Cheryl's tears trickle down her cheeks as she and her fellow judges decide between fame and obscurity for those supplicants who appear before them, begging for celebrity, and recounting their hard-luck stories (Figure 26).[34] In a documentary about the recent flood of televisual tears in 2011, the comedian Jo Brand perhaps had Cheryl Cole (as she then was) in mind when she complained, 'I think there's too much pretty crying on television, where one tear comes down. There's no snot, is there? No red face.'[35] About half a century earlier, in a talk broadcast on BBC radio's *Woman's Hour*, the journalist Kay Withers had similarly noted that some women were 'able to cry prettily', with a slight wobble of the chin and a tremble of the lip, before 'finally great crystal tears well up and spill over, rolling slowly down their cheeks in a gentle, melancholy way. It's all very touching and feminine.' Withers contrasted such pretty crying, as Jo Brand would too, with her own experience of crying: 'A hideous picture of blood-shot eyes, swollen eye-lids and upper lip, a blotchy face and a runny, snuffly red nose.'[36] Going back to the eighteenth century again reveals a precedent. As we saw in an earlier chapter, Fanny Burney's acquaintance Sophy Streatfield was 'very pretty, very gentle, soft & insinuating', and able to cry at will, with her 'sweet eyes full of tears'. In 1779, Burney was shocked by this ability of Streatfield's, and noted that the latter's pretty face was not contorted or 'blubbered' but remained 'smooth and elegant' as she wept.[37] In Cheryl Fernandez-Versini, the new age of sensibility has perhaps found its Sophy Streatfield.

The emotional hyperinflation that has hit Saturday-night television has led to understandable tear-weariness. The claim that these sentimental shows are 'reality' television has proved hard to stomach. The television critic Charlie Brooker, writing about *The X Factor* in 2007, noted the extent of artful selection and manipulation needed to create the desired emotional effect. 'Currently only the good singers are allowed to have tragic back stories,' Brooker observed. 'The show must have amassed a staggering archive', he reasoned, 'containing hour upon hour of boss-eyed fatsos with voices like harpooned gnus blubbering into camera about how they're entering *The X Factor* in honour of a dead relative— none of which makes it into the edit because it doesn't suit the "story".'[38] In 2013 the online satirical website *The Daily Mash* carried a story headlined 'Crying now meaningless', which began, 'The act of shedding tears has been made emotionally meaningless by *The X Factor*. The show's over-exploitation of visible despair has disabled the sympathetic response formerly evoked by seeing a crying person.' The article then quoted an imaginary 'plasterer Bill McKay' who said, 'The wife was sobbing because her nan died. All I felt was mild annoyance and the urge to make withering comments from the sofa while eating crisps.'[39] As had also occurred after the first age of sensibility, a surfeit of tears is met with satire and cynicism.

In these most recent developments, the figure of Diana has generally been left behind. Journalists no longer feel obliged to refer to public displays of emotion as signs of living in a 'post-Diana' world. Another cliché, however, has proved more resilient, namely the question, 'Whatever happened to the stiff upper lip?' The idea that a 'stiff upper lip' was a British national characteristic had become fully established only in the 1930s, but as early as 1953, the year of the queen's coronation, some were already starting to doubt its value. In the women's pages of the *Daily Express*, Anne Edwards wrote about the heartbreak of mothers who wondered if it was worth the pain as they dispatched their young sons to boarding school, before receiving tear-stained letters home, showing 'what a tough process it is all round inheriting the British tradition of keeping a Stiff Upper Lip'.[40] As the nation gradually emerged from the collective trauma of two world wars, more voices joined the calls to overthrow the stiff upper lip attitude, especially in connection with death and bereavement, and with the tears and emotions of men and children. From Geoffrey Gorer's book about death and mourning in 1965, via Marje Proops's advice columns in the 1970s, to Sally Potter's Channel 4 television series in 1987, there was a lengthy and apparently successful rebellion against emotional repression.[41] By the time of the death of Diana in 1997, it was very old news when newspapers noted that the stiff upper lip was no longer in fashion.

In November 1997, the *Sunday Times* carried a commentary piece entitled 'Goodbye Stiff Upper Lip'.[42] But it was—and still is—proving to be a very long goodbye, as the period of rebellion against the stiff upper lip has been succeeded by a mixture of cultural stagnation and nostalgia. Poll after poll, article after article, has announced in almost identical terms that the British stiff upper lip is a thing of the past. In 2004 Kleenex tissues commissioned a detailed study of crying behaviour, which was reported widely.[43] 'The great British stiff upper lip is a thing of the past,' the *Daily Express* announced, 'with three-quarters of grown men saying it's all right to cry.'[44] Six years later Warburtons the bakers (whose products' links with tears are less obvious) used a similar survey to generate publicity. The *Daily Express* duly reported the news that the British stiff upper lip was now a thing of the past and more people were prepared to weep in public.[45] In 2011 it was the turn of Clinton's gift cards to cash in on the fashion for feeling, with a survey timed to coincide with Valentine's day, showing that, yes, British men who adopted the 'stiff upper lip' approach to life were 'becoming a thing of the past'. This new research had found that 'men are happy to show their emotions— and even cry in front of others'. In the Clinton's survey, men from the north of England were found to be the most comfortable expressing their feelings, with Newcastle topping the list of the most emotional cities. About half of those who took part put their emotional openness down to the rise of the 'metrosexual' man, who was comfortable exploring his feminine side. Later in 2011, two newspapers with conservative tendencies both ran features asking whatever had happened to our stiff upper lip.[46] During the emotional displays of the London 2012 Olympic and Paralympic games, the same old story was wheeled out again, and in October of that year YouGov commissioned a poll which found that 57 per cent of Britons (not an enormous majority) thought that British people no longer had a stiff upper lip, and 62 per cent agreed that the nation had become more emotional in recent decades.[47] But why was the question even being asked, seventy years after the Second World War, and half a century after the concerted campaign against emotional restraint began? Virginia Woolf once said, of her attempt to kill off that idealized Victorian figure of soft and altruistic femininity, the 'Angel in the House', that 'It is far harder to kill a phantom than a reality.' We could say the same of this other phantom, which haunted British self-perceptions in the twentieth century and beyond, the 'stiff upper lip'.[48]

Reading beyond the headlines and clichés in the surveys and commentaries listed in the previous paragraph, however, we find something of a mismatch between the rhetoric and the reality. The psychological orthodoxy that crying is good for you, that modern men should express their feelings, and that the stiff upper lip is a thing of the past commands broad assent superficially, but it seems that underlying behaviours and attitudes have not changed as much as all that. I noted above that there seems to have been little change in the propensity to cry over films, for instance, with 40 per cent of men and 72 per cent of women confessing to this in 1950, and these figures rising only slightly to 44 per cent and 80 per cent respectively in 2004.[49] The figure of the weeping man has become almost a fetish object within the new cult of sensibility. In 2004 the photographer Sam Taylor-Wood produced an exhibition and book of *Crying Men*, and in 2014 an anthology was published of *Poems That Make Grown Men Cry*, each accompanied by brief tearful testimonial by a notable male writer or artist.[50] And yet studies throughout the western world, including Britain, continue to find that men cry substantially less often and less intensely than women, perhaps because of biological and hormonal differences between the sexes.[51] Pioneers in the 1960s and 1970s had hoped that new norms of emotional and sexual expression would help to bring about a gender revolution.[52] Yet it was already clear during the Thatcher era that this was not happening. Eileen Fairweather, writing in 1985, refused to endorse Margaret Thatcher's view that the battle for women's rights had been largely won, or to join in with the tide of articles writing about 'how wonderful life is now that men know how to cry, women to come, and for the first time the all-England champion rabbit breeder is female'. Fairweather saw how emotional styles could change without social or economic equality being achieved.[53] More recently, the writer Mark Mason has suggested that 'New Man lachrymosity' can often be a cover for some pretty unreconstructed attitudes: 'Once we've earned our relationship brownie points with a little light weeping, we happily ignore the pile of washing-up that's been sitting there since dinner.'[54]

There is also evidence that the belief that crying is a sign of weakness, effeminacy, or even homosexuality in men has not gone away.[55] One member of the public, a man interviewed for a BBC *Woman's Hour* feature on male tears in 2004, commented, 'It's like the whole modern thing now—men can be gay, men can cry, men can wear make-up. It's just like that.'[56] The unexpected death—apparently a suicide—of the Welsh football manager Gary Speed in late 2011 led to a spate of discussions about male depression and the inability of boys to express their feelings. The journalist Ally Fogg wrote of being told repeatedly by family and teachers that 'boys don't cry'—a lesson which was brutally reinforced in the playground. 'Like pretty much all boys,' Fogg wrote, 'I learned that tears and sobs were markers of failure. Whether facing up to playground beatings, bullies or teachers, the rules of the game were simple: if you cry, you lose. As little boys begin to construct the identities of grown men, the toughest lesson to learn is toughness itself. Never show weakness, never show fragility and above all, never let them see your tears.'[57] It was the message that had been taught in schools at least since the nineteenth century, and which had been learned by Joy Gresham's son Douglas in the 1950s and by Hanif Kureishi in the 1960s too.[58]

So the stiff upper lip survives as a cliché, a phantom, a recalcitrant ideology, and finally also as an object of sentiment and nostalgia. In 2012 Ian Hislop, the editor of the satirical magazine *Private Eye*, and a long-standing critic of public displays of emotion, from the time of Diana's death onwards, presented a series on BBC television entitled *Ian Hislop's Stiff Upper Lip: An Emotional History of Britain*.[59] Hislop's survey of changing emotional attitudes included his own experience of being sent to boarding school. Revisiting his old school, he read out some stoical letters sent home by a boy during a nineteenth-century outbreak of scarlet fever, during which more than one of his classmates died. Hislop's own lip seemed to wobble in this sequence, as he was moved by the image of this brave Victorian lad learning not to show his emotions, in the most frightening and upsetting of situations. With reference to the funeral of Diana, Hislop said that he was moved not by Elton John's song 'Candle in the Wind', nor by Diana's brother's eulogy, but by the sight of Diana's two young sons, walking behind their mother's coffin, retaining their composure, not crying.

Crying over others not crying, weeping over the British stiff upper lip, from *Mrs Miniver* and *Brief Encounter* to the twenty-first century, remains a most British form of sentimentality.[60] It was also a factor in the success of a Hungarian shadow-theatre troupe called 'Attraction' who performed in the final of *Britain's Got Talent* in 2013, watched on ITV by a peak audience of 13 million viewers. Their highly sentimental mini-dramas throughout the series had won audience ovations and tears from the judges. In the final, their piece was a tribute to the British bulldog spirit, accompanied by Elgar's 'Land of Hope and Glory', and featuring scenes of British resolve, stoicism, and triumph, from Churchill's wartime speeches to the recent 2012 Olympics. The performance ended with the death of George VI and the 1953 coronation of the young princess, becoming Queen Elizabeth, whose silhouette was formed by the dancers' bodies as the music came to its climax. The tears flowed, the phone-lines were jammed with votes, and the Hungarian dancers were crowned champions, becoming the first foreign performers to win the show. One of the judges, Amanda Holden, had a pretty, multicultural tear in her eye as she told the group, 'You've embraced Britain and we embrace you back!'[61]

I Am the Sea

William Blake once wrote that a tear was an intellectual thing, and David Hume before him that reason is and ought only to be the slave of the passions.[1] Writing of the fate of the aristocracy in the French Revolution, Edmund Burke suggested that 'in events like these our passions instruct our reason', we are 'alarmed into reflexion', and our minds 'are purified by terror and pity'.[2] History, like tragedy, taught its lessons through human passions. Burke's political adversary Thomas Paine thought that 'the enormous expense of governments has provoked people to think, by making them feel'.[3] In recent years, lessons about the intimate relationship between thinking and feeling, commonplaces in the age of sensibility, have been relearned. History in both its academic and its popular forms has been touched by the return to feeling, moved by the thought that if we can think again the thoughts of the dead, then perhaps we can feel their feelings too. The history of emotions has emerged as a sub-discipline in its own right, producing works ranging from the dry and intellectual to the more dramatic and sentimental.[4] The historian can set out to describe the social rules, moral attitudes, scientific ideas, and bodily gestures through which emotions were once produced and inter-preted without necessarily aiming to conjure up, respond to, or elicit in others any kind of feeling, past or present. For those who do wish to use history itself, however, as an imaginative route into the feelings of the past, it can provoke people to feel by making them think and to think by making them feel.

Some histories made for television make a very direct appeal to the feelings both of their historical subjects and their audience. One of the most successful of the numerous celebrity and reality shows of recent years—one of the televisual grandchildren of *This is your Life*—is a BBC history programme called *Who Do You Think You Are?* A different celebrity each week is guided through a carefully orchestrated set of encounters with long-dead ancestors, accompanied by academic historians and genealogical researchers. And, as with participants on *This is your Life* from the 1950s onwards, the chosen celebrity is often reduced to tears by the experience. The programme has produced some unlikely weepers, including the abrasive political interviewer Jeremy Paxman, who was moved to anger and tears by the poverty, disease, and early deaths met by his Victorian great-grandparents.[5] He may have been among those whom the comedian Jo Brand had in mind in 2011 when she complained about having to watch not only wannabe celebrities shedding tears on talent shows, but also established public figures 'crying on *Who Do You Think You Are?* because they've just discovered their great-great-great-great-grandma worked in a factory'.[6] This is social history as tear-jerker—using the genealogical connection of a weeping celebrity with their ancestor to inject a new shot of emotion into familiar historical stories about the injustices and deprivations of the past.

In August 2014, the Yorkshire-born actor and adventurer Brian Blessed—famed for his distinctive booming voice and huge beard—appeared on *Who Do You Think You Are?*, entering into the hunt for his ancestors with gusto, imagining the feelings of his orphaned great-grandfather Jabez Blessed who was apprenticed, at the age of 12, to a master mariner transporting coal by boat from Newcastle to London. Blessed quotes from the poem 'Sea Fever' by John Masefield—'I must go down to the seas again, to the lonely sea and the sky'—and imagines the impact on the young lad of the starlit nights at sea: 'it would have opened his heart up.' In later life, Jabez Blessed became a successful hawker in Lincolnshire, raising thirteen healthy children with his first wife, marrying again, and dying in 1890 at the age of 73. At the end of the programme, Brian Blessed visits Jabez's grave. As he stands in front of the gravestone he addresses his ancestor directly, reciting the opening lines from Emily Brontë's final, stoical composition:

> No coward soul is mine
> No trembler in the world's storm-troubled sphere
> I see Heaven's glories shine
> And Faith shines equal arming me from Fear[7]

As Blessed speaks these words, he gets choked up, contorts his mouth and cheeks to resist the emotion, then covers his face, in tears, uttering a muffled 'Damn!' Perplexed, shaking his head, Blessed says, 'I don't think I've ever cried in my life. I've never cried in my life. Never cried. Not even as a baby.' In interviews about the programme Blessed repeated this statement that throughout his life, and even when acting in Shakespearian tragedies, he had never been able to cry. Blessed performed stoical sensibility to perfection. What moved him was not a sentimental scene of childhood poverty and death but the stoical resolution he imputed to his great-grandfather, sailing calm and untrembling across life's stormy seas.[8] It was yet another example of the British tradition of crying over others not crying—being moved exactly by their determination not to give in to their feelings. And thanks to Blessed's own manful struggle against the ocean of feeling within, viewers in their living rooms had an opportunity to cry over Brian Blessed almost not crying over his ancestor not crying.

Brian Blessed told the *Hull Daily Mail* that his appearance on *Who Do You Think You Are?* had been an extraordinary and 'mystical' voyage for him: 'everything melted away, the cameras melted away and I suddenly became one with myself.'[9] For Blessed, this was inner-reality television. But, for the rest of us, was this not all very artificial? Here was an actor, giving a rehearsed performance of lines of poetry, for a television camera, exploring an imaginary emotional relationship with a long-dead ancestor. To some this kind of thing seems the very antithesis of emotional reality. As one critic of the genre of ancestor-hunting television put it, participants who deliver tearfully 'extravagant obsequies' for 'very distant relatives' are 'weeping over the deaths of strangers'.[10] The lack of a personal relationship with the deceased was also a complaint about the response to the death of Diana in 1997.[11] Why is everyone crying over Diana, people asked, when they didn't even know her? The implication in both cases is that tears for strangers are either deranged or deceitful: these celebrities and members of the public are being self-indulgent, inauthentic, or both. From any perspective other than dry-eyed twentieth-century cynicism, such objections are absurdly literal-minded, not to mention anti-social and inhumane. Who, these cynics ask, would weep for a stranger? Who, we might ask in reply, on behalf of the tradition of sensibility, would reserve their tears only for themselves and their loved ones?

At the start of the age of the stiff upper lip, in 1871, the Prince of Wales, Queen Victoria's eldest son and the heir to the throne, was gravely ill with typhoid fever. In the midst of a bout of national anxiety, expressed and sustained by the newspapers, an article in the *Spectator* magazine complained about the exaggeration and sentimentalism of press reports, but asserted that 'The feeling of the English people about the Prince's illness has been as sincere and real as possible.' This article commented on the emotional relationship of the British public to its royal family, in terms which could also be applied to more recent events such as the death of Diana, suggesting that the feelings evoked fell somewhere between the acute pain of a personal bereavement and the milder sadness evoked by a death in popular fiction such as that of Dickens's Little Nell. 'The sufferings and griefs of the Royal Family', the article observed, 'constitute to Englishmen at large a sort of vivid parable of human calamity, into which we all enter the more deeply because we know it fascinates all alike,—a lesson in sympathy, not in fortitude, in geniality and breadth of feeling, not in patience or courage.'[12] In our own age, thanks to television, the internet, and social media, parables of human calamity, to which we respond with real feeling, can be entered into by an ever-widening community of feeling. Reality television, as much as classical tragedy or soap operas (including the soap opera of the Windsor family), can purify our minds through pity and fear.

In fact, the most truly detached and stoical attitude may be to weep equally for all, whether fictional characters, strangers, friends, loved ones, or ourselves, getting our own lives and losses into more objective proportions in comparison with those of others, while not departing completely from the domain of human feeling. It was René Descartes who once wrote that the greatest souls responded to tragedies in their own lives as they would to events in a play—that is to say with a combination of real feeling and philosophical detachment.[13] David Hume, in his essay on 'The Stoic' a century later, imagined the philosophical sage seated on a rock observing the thunder and fury of human life below. Hume's Stoic was a product of the age of sensibility, however, and tempered his indifference with social affections and compassion. Bathed in tears, lamenting the miseries not only of his own friends, but of his country and the whole human race, Hume's Stoic took pleasure in the qualities of pity, compassion, and humanity—moral sentiments whose operation 'brighten up the very face of sorrow, and operate like the sun, which, shining on a dusky cloud or falling rain, paints on them the most glorious colours which are to be found in the whole circle of nature'.[14]

Works by moral philosophers, whether ancient or modern, do not have wide readerships today, but there is still plenty of appetite for that equally ancient vehicle of emotional education—the stage tragedy. Shakespeare's first tragedy, *Titus Andronicus*, was excluded from the canon on the grounds of taste and decency for much of the last three centuries.[15] It was first performed again in an unexpurgated version in 1955, and since the 1990s has enjoyed a real revival. In 1995 Anthony Sher starred in a National Theatre production which was later also staged at the Market Theatre in Johannesburg, and Anthony Hopkins took on the title role in the 1999 film *Titus*, directed by Julie Taymor. With its representations of revenge, beheadings, mutilations, sexual violence, and honour-killing, as well as its litres of blood, sweat, and tears, *Titus Andronicus* has plenty of contemporary resonance. In 2013 I saw a Royal Shakespeare Company production of the play, directed by Michael Fenti-man, performed at the Swan Theatre in Stratford-upon-Avon. The com-bination of horror with humour—encapsulated in Titus' own laughter on beholding the heads of his sons—was the key to Fentiman's production. In the final scene, Stephen Boxer, playing Titus, cross-dressing as a jaunty French maid, oversees a bloodbath of a dinner party worthy of *The Godfather* or *Reservoir Dogs*. Having killed Lavinia with violent tender-ness—'her for whom my tears have made me blind'—Titus meets his own end with an added laugh, not in the original script, echoing his earlier 'Ha, ha, ha!' The audience is thrown into alternate convulsions of laughter and horror. I looked around me in the Swan Theatre. There was some shock, a few sniffs, and some dabbing of eyes. I removed my spectacles and wiped the snot, sweat, and tears from my face.

In the interval at the Stratford *Titus*, the couple next to me came back to their seats with an ice cream. I had entered fully into the woes of the Andronicus family and actually caught myself thinking of my neighbours, 'How can they eat an ice cream at a time like this?' We can choose how far we let our imaginations take us into the reality of a story, and ever since Plato worried about the harmful effects of stage tragedies on the weak-minded, there have been those, like me, who have been inclined to get very involved.[16] The part of the performance at Stratford that affected me most was the scene in which Titus' brother Marcus finds Lavinia—her mouth opening and spilling blood down her front to gasps from the audience—and presents her, in her mutilated state, to her father. Titus asks 'What fool hath added water to the sea?' The sea imagery continues throughout the scene. To begin with Titus, like Hume's later Stoic sage perched upon his rock, declares,

> For now I stand as one upon a rock,
> Environed with a wilderness of sea,
> Who marks the waxing tide grow wave by wave,
> Expecting ever when some envious surge
> Will in his brinish bowels swallow him.

Later, as the ocean of passion engulfs Titus on his rock, he delivers the speech I quoted above in which he declares, 'I am the sea.'[17] It is the central moment of the play. Playing the role of Titus in South Africa in 1995, Anthony Sher wondered at how other tragedians, especially Fiona Shaw, whom he had seen in both *Electra* and *Hedda Gabler* a few years earlier, could produce the emotion required for such scenes, night after night. In her performances, Sher wrote, Shaw inhabited her roles and produced the required emotions without cheating—without even acting—this was 'The real thing'.[18] Shaw's performance in Sophocles' *Electra* in Derry in Northern Ireland in 1992, during a week in the troubles marked by a spate of revenge killings, and not long after the death of her own brother in a road accident, has become a legendary instance of the power of classical tragedy to channel raw—and real—contemporary emotions.[19] In his memoir about the production of *Titus* in Johannesburg, Anthony Sher writes of his own struggle to produce 'real emotion' in the key scenes, including the 'I am the sea' speech, and expresses his disappointment about those occasions when 'real emotion' was not forthcoming.[20] For actors on stage, as in our own lives, there is no clear line between performed emotion and real emotion. Weeping is a performance, no doubt, even when we are our own audience, but to think the emotion is not therefore real is to set up a false dichotomy.

Emotional performances, like sexual ones, do not always go to plan. 'Tears are like sperm,' Anthony Sher writes in his memoir. 'If you think about it too much, it doesn't flow.'[21] As we have seen throughout this book tears have long been understood as secretions as well as signs—as 'excrementitious humours of the third concoction', to use Robert Burton's evocative phrase.[22] That is part of their power. They are bodily fluids, like and yet unlike blood, mucus, sweat, urine, and sperm, oozing meaningfully out of us into the public world, part performance, part leakage. Unlike our feelings, tears can be seen and touched and tasted by others. The incontinence theory of weeping, however, which we have encountered in several forms, from Burton and Descartes to Freud and Frey, is not currently in scientific vogue. William Frey's experiments, purporting to demonstrate that emotional tears serve as vehicles for the excretion of stress hormones, have not been successfully replicated by others. Freudian concepts of repression and regression no longer reign supreme. The idea that when women weep they are seeking to replicate the act of male urination, longed for since infancy, is a doctrine as quaint and incredible as anything produced by ancient physicians or medieval theologians.[23] And the most recent research on the science of crying— surveyed in a comprehensive book on the subject by the Dutch psychologist Ad Vingerhoets—does not support the idea that crying is an overflow of affect, an excretion, or a kind of catharsis. It is impossible to pin tears down. Darwin observed in 1872 that they could be produced by the most opposite of emotions, or by none. A pioneering American psychological study of crying in 1906 found that respondents named 307 different occasions for tears. The author of the study grouped these into forty-seven kinds, including every human emotion recognized by psychological science, and assigned them to three broader domains: grief and sadness; anger, fear, and pain; and finally joy, gratitude, tenderness, and the sublime.[24] In his recent survey, Vingerhoets similarly points out that the antecedents of tears are multifarious and involve a whole series of apparent contraries—states of conflict, loneliness, and defeat, but also of reconciliation, social bonding, and triumph—suffering and pain, but also comfort and sympathy, and ecstatic, even orgasmic pleasure. When we cry, it seems, we express both sides of some basic human paradoxes of feeling. And perhaps what is welling up from within is something more basic and less differentiated than our modern psychological categories.[25]

Sandor Feldman's theory was that all tears, whatever their apparent cause, and whether seemingly happy or sad, were ultimately tears of mourning over the fact of death—our own death and the deaths of all we love. The theory had a certain bleak simplicity to it. Feldman pointed out that children do not cry over happy endings, suggesting that this is because they do not yet accept the fact of death. That acceptance, once it occurs, turns every happy ending into an occasion to experience suppressed, or postponed, or pre-emptive grief for the unhappy ending which comes to everyone.[26] The histories of British attitudes to tears and to death are, as we have seen, closely connected. One of the deepest roots of our suspicion of public tears is the Protestant reaction against Catholic forms of mourning perceived as sensual, blasphemous, uncontrolled, and ineffective in the sixteenth century. For the Victorians, the peaks of Dickensian pathos were narrations of childhood deaths, offering imaginative conduits for a widely experienced parental grief—stories later condemned as the height of sentimentality. In the twentieth century, the silences and denials around death formed an important strand of the 'stiff upper lip' tradition which reformers tried to pull apart from the 1950s onwards—this time in the name of psychology rather than spirituality. And today it is over dead relatives, dead celebrities, or celebrities' dead relatives that viewers of reality television are likely to shed their tears.

In exploring the history of British tears, and the ideas and attitudes they revealed and contained, I have been struck by the collective amnesia that is one of the lasting legacies of the era of the stiff upper lip. Those decades of wartime and restraint broke many of the threads that had connected British people with a body of imaginative and religious literature which once constituted the primary resources of an emotional education. And even in the last fifty years, each new generation of social commentators seems to have been ignorant not only of the history of British sensibility before the anomalously dry-eyed twentieth century, but also of the repeated rediscovery of feeling since the 1950s. Endless death notices for the British stiff upper lip, announcing the birth of a new era of expressiveness, have been written and printed, alongside articles about the psychological harm that same 'stiff upper lip' mentality apparently continues to perpetrate nonetheless. Since we are now in the midst of a new era of weepiness, we can turn to cultural and intellectual history to discover how and why tears have been valued at earlier times in our national history, and to understand the largely submerged fears and convictions that inform our residual distaste for public displays of emotion. History can lead as back through a vast and rich museum of cultural artefacts—emotional texts, objects, and beliefs—and help to bring them back to life.

That museum, as I have suggested, must have a large section devoted to the culture of death—not just rituals of mourning and remembrance surrounding the deaths of individuals, but also the very fact of death itself, as a defining parameter of human existence. Psychoanalysis inherited from ancient Jewish and Christian traditions a sense of the inherent brokenness of the world, and of the human mind. This had once been expressed in terms of the fall of man and the reign of sin and death, but the rediscovery of public tears was not generally accompanied with a recollection of those earlier traditions. So, while Sandor Feldman cited the biblical story of the tearful reunion of Jacob and Esau as a prime example of the phenomenon he wished to analyse, namely crying at a happy ending, his conclusions were, of course, couched in the language of psychoanalysis. 'As children we do not know that the time will come when death will put an end to our happy object relationships,' he wrote. Later we cry because 'the happy childhood with its illusions is gone and we cry for the sad end which is sure to come: the separation from the beloved ones.'[27] A haunting passage from Anna Laetitia Barbauld's eighteenth-century 'Hymn on Death' suggests a similar idea, but in a different idiom. Barbauld juxtaposes the vigorous man with glowing cheeks in the prime of his life, with the stiff, cold, corpse he will become: 'therefore do I weep, because death is in the world; the spoiler is among the works of God: all that is made must be destroyed; all that is born must die: let me alone, for I will weep yet longer.'[28]

The spoiler is among the works of God. British writers steeped in Christian cultures expressed in various ways the idea of weeping as a response to the fallen state of the world itself, and to a life lived under the shadow of death. Over several centuries the idea recurred that to bring someone back to life would be to give them cause to weep, lamenting over the necessity of living another human life, and of dying another death. C. S. Lewis wrote, in *A Grief Observed*, of his desire that his wife Joy might come back to him from beyond the grave, but noted that such a return would hardly be for her benefit. 'Could I have wished her anything worse', he asked, than to call her back to life so she would 'have all her dying to do over again?' 'They call Stephen the first martyr. Hadn't Lazarus the rawer deal?'[29] Oscar Wilde used to tell a story with a similar message, about a series of imagined encounters between Christ and those he had healed, including a former leper now devoted to a life of hedonism, and a man using his miraculously restored sight to gaze lustfully at women. Finally the Christ figure meets a young man weeping at the roadside and asks him the reason for his tears. 'But I was dead once and you raised me from the dead,' the young man replies. 'What else should I do but weep?'[30] John Donne, in his sermon on the subject in the 1620s, suggested several reasons for Christ's tears over the grave of Lazarus. One was that although Lazarus' family would be happy, and Jesus' disciples would have their faith strengthened by the miracle, 'yet *Lazarus* himselfe lost by it, by being re-imprisoned, re-committed, re-submitted to the manifold incommodities of this world'. Jesus wept for what he was bringing Lazarus back to.[31]

British attitudes to tears, in forms inspired by both classical and Christian culture, have perhaps also been shaped by the nation's topography. British islanders have learned to resist the sea as something primal, chaotic, and dangerous—a body of salt-water threatening to erode, dissolve, or drown them. The ocean symbolized both tears and death. The dry-eyed Britisher of the mid-twentieth century appeared like a latter-day Titus Andronicus, like a mad stoic, like an emotional Cnut, perched on a rock, environed by a churning, heaving, roaring sea of tears, commanding the waves to recede.[32] A tear is an intellectual thing, but it is also something elemental, watery, meteorological, oceanic. British writers across the ages understood tears as part of a system of humours and fluids, precipitations of the mind, incorporating human beings into their environment. Such writers have made the link between literal and emotional seas, describing tears in terms of springs, waterways, and oceans. One of these was the Hungarian-born intellectual Arthur Koestler, who became a British citizen in 1948.

Koestler was a prolific and an incontinent man—intellectually, politically, and sexually uncontained. A 1998 biography revealed him to have been a brutal sexual predator. It contained an interview with the writer and film-maker Jill Craigie who stated that Koestler had raped her in 1951.[33] Koestler was also one of the very few thinkers in Britain to pay sustained psychological attention to tears and weeping during the twentieth century. He was dismissive of many kinds of crying as soft-hearted and feminine, but he wrote that more attention should be given to 'self-transcending' emotions, which gave rise to tears of 'raptness'. Koestler listed the possible occasions for such tears: 'Listening to the organ in a cathedral, looking at a majestic landscape from the top of a mountain, observing an infant hesitantly returning a smile, being in love'—and described these as instances of the 'oceanic feeling', a concept introduced to Freud by the French writer and scholar of eastern religions, Romain Rolland. In such moments the self 'seems no longer to exist, to dissolve in the experience, like a grain of salt in water' and awareness expands into 'the oceanic feeling of limitless extension and oneness with the universe'. Brian Blessed's account of his experience on *Who Do You Think You Are?* perhaps describes such a moment: 'everything melted away, the cameras melted away and I suddenly became one with myself.' For Koestler, tears at such moments pointed both backwards and forwards: back towards the womb, and to a state of pre-differentiated consciousness, and forwards towards the possibility of an impersonal afterlife in which the self would be dissolved in an eternal oneness. Koestler wrote that these experiences can evoke 'Faust's prayer: *O Augenblick verweile*—let this moment last for eternity, let me die.'[34]

The submission to tears in an oceanic moment can signal an acceptance of both emotion and death. By the same token, during the decades of restraint in twentieth-century British history, the struggle against tears was a struggle against both emotion and death—against the sea of time that laps at our shores. 'How fast the river runs,' little Paul Dombey exclaims as he approaches death. 'But it's very near the sea. I hear the waves!'[35] Percy Shelley drowned in the Mediterranean in 1822. The previous year he had written a poem describing time as an unfathomable sea whose 'waters of deep woe' were 'brackish with the salt of human tears!'[36] And for John Donne two centuries earlier, in his 'Elegie on the Lady Markham', 'Man is the World, and death th'Ocean', while in his sermon on the text 'Jesus wept', Donne described Jesus's tears of sacrifice on the cross as a sea—'*Mare liberum*, a Sea free and open to all; Every man may saile home, home to himselfe, and lament his own sins there.' The sea contains the possibility of both death and new life. Donne's sermon is one of the texts to which I have returned with most interest and pleasure in my attempts to understand the cultural history of British tears. Donne envisaged humanity itself as a porous creature of the deep— 'Every man is but a spunge, and a spunge filled with teares: and whether you lay your right hand or your left upon a full spunge, it will weep.'

A sponge without tears, burned up by worldly lusts, would become a dry pumice stone. 'And when God shall come to that last Act in the glorifying of Man, when he promises *to wipe all teares from his eyes*', Donne asked his congregation, 'what shall God have to doe with that eye that never wept?'[37]

NOTES

Introduction

1. 'Prolonged Brutality To Prisoner: "No Britisher Ever Weeps"', *The Times*, 20 Dec. 1945, p. 3; 'Pigs Before Men: Sadism at the Kuching Camp', *West Australian*, 20 Dec. 1945, p. 7; 'Revolting Details of Japanese Atrocities', *The Advocate* (Tasmania), 20 Dec. 1945, p. 5.
2. On movie-going and tears in the mid-twentieth century, including the 1950 Mass Observation question about weeping at the pictures, see Ch. 16.
3. H. E. Marshall, *Our Island Story: A History of England for Boys and Girls* (London: T. C. and E. C. Jack, n.d. [1905]); available online at The Internet Archive, <https://archive.org/details/ourislandstoryhioomarsuoft>.
4. On these recent developments, see Chs 19 and 20.
5. *Educating Yorkshire*, Series 1, Episode 8, Channel 4, first broadcast 24 Oct. 2013, <http://www.channel4.com/programmes/educating-yorkshire>; on the new emotional communities and norms created by television and social media since the 1990s, see Ch. 20.
6. On early modern precursors to the concept of 'emotional incontinence', see Chs 3 and 9, and on later uses, Chs 13 and 20.
7. Joan Bakewell, 'What the Crying Game Says About Us', BBC News Magazine, 17 Dec. 2010, <http://www.bbc.co.uk/news/magazine-12021519>.
8. Jo Brand, 'For Crying Out Loud', What Larks Productions for BBC Four, first broadcast 14 Feb. 2011, <http://www.bbc.co.uk/programmes/booymhqz>.
9. The comment was posted in response to: 'The Myth of Britain's Stiff Upper Lip', BBC News Magazine, 16 Feb. 2011, <http://www.bbc.co.uk/news/magazine-12447950>.
10. [Alexander Pope], 'On a Lady who P—st at the Tragedy of Cato: Occasion'd by an Epigram on a Lady Who Wept at It' (1713), in Norman Ault, *New Light on Pope: With Some Additions to his Poetry Hitherto Unknown* (London: Methuen, 1949), p. 132; the poem was often ascribed to Jonathan Swift in the eighteenth century.
11. Paul Simon, 'I Am a Rock' (CBS, 1965).
12. Geoffrey Gorer, *Death, Grief, and Mourning in Contemporary Britain* (London: The Cresset Press, 1965). On changing attitudes to death and grief in the 1960s, see Ch. 17, and Pat Jalland, *Death in War and Peace: Loss and Grief in England, 1914–1970* (Oxford: Oxford University Press, 2010), ch. 11.

13. On the cognitive view of emotions implied here, see Ch. 10 and Conclusion, and also Jerome Neu, *A Tear is an Intellectual Thing: The Meanings of Emotion* (Oxford: Oxford University Press, 2000); Martha C. Nussbaum, *Upheavals of Thought: The Intelligence of Emotions* (Cambridge: Cambridge University Press, 2001); Robert C. Solomon, *Not Passion's Slave: Emotions and Choice* (Oxford: Oxford University Press, 2003).

14. Charles Darwin, *The Expression of the Emotions in Man and Animals* (London: John Murray, 1872), p. 163. For more on Darwin's theory of weeping in its Victorian context, see Ch. 13.

15. Thomas Dixon, 'The Waterworks', Aeon Magazine, 22 Feb. 2013, <http://aeon.co/magazine/psychology/thomas-dixon-tears>.

16. Keith Thomas, 'Bodily Control and Social Unease: The Fart in Seventeenth-Century England', in Garthine Walker and Angela McShane (eds), *The Extraordinary and the Everyday in Early Modern England: Essays in Celebration of the Work of Bernard Capp* (Basingstoke: Palgrave Macmillan, 2010), pp. 9–30.

17. On the connection of weeping with the sorrow and compassion of the Virgin Mary, see Ch. 1.

18. 'The Grey Monk' (*c.*1803), in *The Complete Prose and Poetry of William Blake*, newly revised edn, ed. David V. Erdman, with commentary by Harold Bloom (Berkeley and Los Angeles: University of California Press, 2008), pp. 489–90; for further discussion, see Ch. 10 and Conclusion.

19. Neu, *A Tear is an Intellectual Thing*, ch. 2, p. 14.

20. Judith Kay Nelson, *Seeing Through Tears: Crying and Attachment* (New York: Routledge, 2005).

Chapter 1. Looking for Margery

1. On Margery's life, her *Book*, and her tears, see Karma Lochrie, *Margery Kempe and Translations of the Flesh* (Philadelphia: University of Pennsylvania Press, 1991); Sandra J. McEntire (ed.), *Margery Kempe: A Book of Essays* (New York: Garland Publishing, 1992); Charity Scott Stokes, 'Margery Kempe: Her Life and the Early History of her Book', *Mystics Quarterly* 25 (1999): 9–68; John H. Arnold and Katherine J. Lewis (eds), *A Companion to the Book of Margery Kempe* (Cambridge: D. S. Brewer, 2004); Barry Windeatt, 'Introduction' to *The Book of Margery Kempe*, trans. with an introduction by Barry Windeatt (London: Penguin, 2004), pp. 9–30; Santha Bhattarcharji, 'Tears and Screaming: Weeping in the Spirituality of Margery Kempe', in Kimberley Christine Patton and John Stratton Hawley (eds), *Holy Tears: Weeping in the Religious Imagination* (Princeton: Princeton University Press, 2005), pp. 229–41; Felicity Riddy, 'Kempe, Margery (b. *c.*1373, d. in or after 1438)', *Oxford Dictionary of National Biography* (Oxford University Press, 2004; online edn, May 2009), doi:10.1093/ref:odnb/15337.

2. Margery's *Book* recounts a period of particularly strong temptation, including meeting her would-be seducer, after evensong. The *Book* describes lechery as a

'sin' and a 'snare' and notes that it continued to be a temptation despite Margery's wearing a hair-shirt, doing bodily penance, and weeping many bitter tears; *The Book of Margery Kempe*, trans. with an introduction by Barry Windeatt (London: Penguin, 2004), ch. 4, pp. 49–50, hereafter cited as *Book*.

3. *Book*, ch. 67, pp. 202–5. On the place of this incident in the context of other figurative connections between meteorological phenomena and Margery's spiritual journey, see Jeffrey J. Cohen, *Medieval Identity Machines* (Minneapolis: University of Minnesota Press, 2003), ch. 5 (p. 180).

4. Windeatt, 'Introduction', pp. 15–18; authors included Walter Hilton and Richard Rolle. For an example of the kind of devotional advice, including advice about tears and weeping, that such texts included, see Walter Hilton, *The Ladder of Perfection*, trans. Leo Sherley-Price, with an introduction by Clifton Wolters (London: Penguin Books, 1988), pp. 37–41.

5. On pricking and compunction, see Sandra McEntire, *The Doctrine of Compunction in Medieval England: Holy Tears* (Lewiston, NY: Edwin Mellen Press, 1990); and, especially, Piroska Nagy, *Le Don des larmes au Moyen Âge: un instrument spirituel en quête d'institution, V^e–XIIIe siècle* (Paris: Albin Michel, 2000), pp. 425–30.

6. Ad Vingerhoets, *Why Only Humans Weep: Unravelling the Mysteries of Tears* (Oxford: Oxford University Press, 2013), p. 226.

7. Miri Rubin, *Mother of God: A History of the Virgin Mary* (London: Allen Lane, 2009), ch. 15; Miri Rubin, *Emotion and Devotion: The Meaning of Mary in Medieval Religious Cultures* (Budapest: Central European University Press, 2009).

8. Elizabeth Psakis Armstrong has written, comparing Margery's *Book* with other mystical memoirs, 'No matter how much other mystics are sincerely conscious of their humility, none of them, as far as I know report experiences that arise as these do out of the smallest domestic details of life, utterly devoid of dignity'; '"Understanding by Feeling" in Margery Kempe's *Book*', in Sandra J. McEntire (ed.), *Margery Kempe: A Book of Essays* (New York: Garland Publishing, 1992), pp. 17–35 (p. 20). Stokes ('Margery Kempe', p. 31) points out that Chaucer's Wife of Bath, like Margery, undertook a pilgrimage to the Holy Land. On tears in Chaucer, see Mary Carruthers, 'On Affliction and Reading, Weeping and Argument: Chaucer's Lachrymose Troilus in Context', *Representations* 93 (2006): 1–21; and for an explicit comparison between the tears of Margery Kempe and the Wife of Bath, see Katherine K. O'Sullivan, 'Tears and Trial: Weeping as Forensic Evidence in *Piers Plowman*', in Elina Gertsman (ed.), *Crying in the Middle Ages: Tears of History* (New York: Routledge, 2012), pp. 193–207 (pp. 198–9).

9. *Book*, ch. 28, p. 103.

10. Ibid., ch. 9, pp. 56–7.

11. Ibid., ch. 11, pp. 58–60.

12. Stokes, 'Margery Kempe', p. 19.

13. *Book*, ch. 61, p. 188.

14. Ibid., ch. 46, p. 149; Clarissa W. Atkinson, *Mystic and Pilgrim: The Book and World of Margery Kempe* (Ithaca, NY: Cornell University Press, 1983), p. 107; Stokes, 'Margery Kempe'; Windeatt, 'Introduction', pp. 11–14; Riddy, 'Kempe'.
15. Stokes, 'Margery Kempe', p. 17.
16. *Book*, chs 26–30 (p. 97).
17. Stokes, 'Margery Kempe', pp. 30–4.
18. *Book*, ch. 28, p. 104.
19. Ibid., ch. 28, pp. 104–6. For additional references to handsome young men, and to changing colour, see also ibid., ch. 35, p. 123, and ch. 44, p. 143, respectively. On the varieties, extremity, and meanings of some of these episodes of 'roaring', see also Bhattarcharji, 'Tears and Screaming'.
20. For one summary, see *Book*, ch. 7, p. 54.
21. Ibid., ch. 3, p. 46.
22. Ibid., ch. 52, p. 163.
23. Ibid., ch. 60, pp. 186–7.
24. Psalm 6: 6. On clerical tears and masculinity, see Katherine Harvey, 'Episcopal Emotions: Tears in the Life of the Medieval Bishop', *Historical Research* 87 (2014): 591–610. On male lust and religious life, see J. Murray, 'Masculinizing Religious Life: Sexual Prowess, the Battle for Chastity and Monastic Identity', in P. H. Cullum and Katherine J. Lewis (eds), *Holiness and Masculinity in the Middle Ages* (Chicago: University of Chicago Press, 2005), pp. 24–37. On depictions of manly tears in late medieval writings, see Tracey-Anne Cooper, 'The Shedding of Tears in Late Anglo-Saxon England', in Gertsman (ed.), *Crying in the Middle Ages*, pp. 175–92; Stephanie Trigg, 'Langland's Tears: Poetry, Emotion, and Mouvance', *Yearbook of Langland Studies* 26 (2012): 27–48; Stephanie Trigg, 'Weeping like a Beaten Child: Figurative Language and the Emotions in Chaucer and Malory', in Holly Crocker and Glenn Burger (eds), *Affect, Feeling, Emotion: The Medieval Turn* (forthcoming).
25. Margery visited both Hailes and Walsingham, the latter being the closest site of pilgrimage to her home in Lynn; Stokes, 'Margery Kempe', pp. 16–17, 35.
26. Kimberley-Joy Knight, '*Si puose calcina a' propi occhi*: The Importance of the Gift of Tears for Thirteenth-Century Religious Women and their Hagiographers', in Gertsman (ed.), *Crying in the Middle Ages*, pp. 136–55 (p. 150n.), citing René Crozet, 'Le Monument de la Sainte Larme à la Trinité de Vendôme', *Bulletin Monumental* 121 (1963): 171–80; and Katja Boertjes, 'Pilgrim Ampullae from Vendôme: Souvenirs from a Pilgrimage to the Holy Tear of Christ', in Sarah Blick and Rita Tekippe (eds), *Art and Architecture of Late Medieval Pilgrimage in Northern Europe and the British Isles* (Leiden: Brill, 2005), pp. 443–72.
27. Sarah McNamer, *Affective Meditation and the Invention of Medieval Compassion* (Philadelphia: University of Pennsylvania Press, 2010), pp. 84–5. On the central role of the Virgin Mary in medieval devotional practices, see Rubin, *Emotion and Devotion*.

28. Robert Max Garrett, 'De Arte Lacrimandi', *Anglia: Zeitschrift für englische Philologie* 32 (1909): 269–94; McNamer, *Affective Meditation*, pp. 126–7.
29. Thomas of Celano, *The Second Life of St Francis*, bk 1, ch. 6, no. 10, in Marion A. Habig (ed.), *St Francis of Assisi: Writings and Early Biographies* (Chicago: Franciscan Herald Press 1973), p. 370. See also Scott Wells, 'The Exemplary Blindness of Francis of Assisi', in Joshua R. Eyler (ed.), *Disability in the Middle Ages: Reconsiderations and Reverberations* (Farnham: Ashgate, 2010), pp. 67–80.
30. Moshe Barasch, 'The Crying Face', *Artibus et Historiae* 8 (1987): 21–36; Diane Apostolos-Cappadona, ' "Pray With Tears and your Request Will Find a Hearing": On the Iconology of the Magdalene's Tears', in Kimberley Christine Patton and John Stratton Hawley (eds), *Holy Tears: Weeping in the Religious Imagination* (Princeton: Princeton University Press, 2005), pp. 201–28.
31. On Kempe's arrival in Bologna in 1414, see *Book*, p. 101; Stokes, 'Margery Kempe', pp. 31–2. On the dating of the dell'Arca *Lamentation* to the 1480s, see James H. Beck, 'Niccolò dell'Arca: A Reexamination', *Art Bulletin* 47 (1965): 335–44.
32. Garrett, 'De Arte Lacrimandi', p. 270. On the rediscovery of this insight, in an evolutionary context, by Charles Darwin, see Ch. 13.
33. McNamer, *Affective Meditation*, especially ch. 3.
34. Jill Bough, *Donkey* (London: Reaktion Books, 2011), pp. 153–5.
35. On other weeping animals, see Chs 9 and 13.
36. Thomas of Celano, *First Life of St Francis*, trans. A. G. Ferrers Howell, part III, para. 125; online edn, Indiana University, <http://www.indiana.edu/~dmdhist/francis.htm>, ed. Leah Shopkow.
37. Stokes, 'Margery Kempe', p. 33.
38. *Book*, ch. 18, pp. 77–8; Atkinson, *Mystic and Pilgrim*, p. 64. On the similarities between the devotional and emotional styles of Margery and other female medieval mystics, including Bridget of Sweden, Mary of Oignies, and Angela of Foligno, see Windeatt, 'Introduction', pp. 17–22.
39. *Book*, ch. 16, p. 72. On Arundel, see Jonathan Hughes, 'Arundel, Thomas (1353–1414)', *Oxford Dictionary of National Biography* (Oxford University Press, 2004; online edn, May 2007), doi:10.1093/ref:odnb/713.
40. Harvey, 'Episcopal Emotions', p. 598, citing *The Chronica Maiora of Thomas Walsingham (1376–1422)*, trans. David Preest, ed. James G. Clark (Woodbridge: Boydell, 2005), p. 393. On Oldcastle, see John A. F. Thomson, 'Oldcastle, John, Baron Cobham (d. 1417)', *Oxford Dictionary of National Biography* (Oxford University Press, 2004; online edn, May 2008), doi:10.1093/ref:odnb/20674.

Chapter 2. *Marie Magdalen's Funeral Teares*

1. See Chs 19 and 20 on Thatcher and Diana, respectively.
2. [Robert Southwell], *Marie Magdalens Funeral Teares* (London: Printed by J.W. for G.C., 1591), pp. 8–10 (p. 8ʳ).

3. Richard Challoner, *Modern British Martyrology: Commencing with the Reformation* (London: Keating, Brown and Co., 1836), pp. 167–72; Scott R. Pilarz, *Robert Southwell and the Mission of Literature 1561–1595: Writing Reconciliation* (Aldershot: Ashgate, 2004), pp. 278–9; Nancy Pollard Brown, 'Southwell, Robert [St Robert Southwell] (1561–1595)', *Oxford Dictionary of National Biography* (Oxford University Press, 2004; online edn, Jan. 2008), doi:10.1093/ref:odnb/26064.

4. Richard Strier, 'Herbert and Tears', *ELH* 46 (1979): 221–47 (pp. 221–2); Götz Schmitz, *The Fall of Women in Early English Narrative Verse* (Cambridge: Cambridge University Press, 1990), pp. 181–98; Alison Shell, *Catholicism, Controversy and the English Literary Imagination, 1558–1660* (Cambridge: Cambridge University Press, 1999), ch. 2; Gary Kuchar, *The Poetry of Religious Sorrow in Early Modern England* (Cambridge: Cambridge University Press, 2008), ch. 1.

5. The story of the sinful woman who anointed the feet of Jesus with tears and ointment is at Luke 7: 38, and the tears of Mary Magdalene weeping at the empty tomb at John 20: 11–18. On the creation of the traditional composite figure of the Magdalene, see Diane Apostolos-Cappadona, ' "Pray With Tears and your Request Will Find a Hearing": On the Iconology of the Magdalene's Tears', in Kimberley Christine Patton and John Stratton Hawley (eds), *Holy Tears: Weeping in the Religious Imagination* (Princeton: Princeton University Press, 2005), pp. 201–28 (p. 207).

6. [Southwell], *Funeral Teares*, p. 2^r.

7. Apostolos-Cappadona, 'Pray With Tears'; Patricia Phillippy, *Women, Death and Literature in Post-Reformation England* (Cambridge: Cambridge University Press, 2002); Katharine Goodland, *Female Mourning in Medieval and Renaissance English Drama: From the Raising of Lazarus to King Lear* (Aldershot: Ashgate, 2005); Vibeke Olsen, ' "Woman why weepest thou?" Mary Magdalene, the Virgin Mary and the Transformative Power of Holy Tears in Late Medieval Devotional Painting', in Michelle Erhardt and Amy Morris (eds), *Mary Magdalene, Iconographic Studies from the Middle Ages to the Baroque* (Brill: Leiden, 2012), pp. 361–82.

8. Jenny Wormald, 'James VI and I (1566–1625)', *Oxford Dictionary of National Biography* (Oxford University Press, 2004; online edn, Sept. 2014), doi:10.1093/ref:odnb/14592; Eamon Duffy, *The Stripping of the Altars: Traditional Religion in England, c.1400–c.1580* (New Haven and London: Yale University Press, 1992); Peter Marshall, *The Reformation: A Very Short Introduction* (Oxford: Oxford University Press, 2009).

9. The passages in question are 2 Samuel 18: 33–19: 4; John 11: 35; John 20: 11–18. On the King James Bible, see Gordon Campbell, *Bible: The Story of the King James Version, 1611–2011* (Oxford: Oxford University Press, 2010); Hannibal Hamlin and Norman W. Jones (eds), *The King James Bible after 400 Years: Literary, Linguistic, and Cultural Influences* (Cambridge: Cambridge University Press, 2010); Adam Nicolson, *When God Spoke English: The Making of the King*

James Bible (London: HarperPress, 2011); Wormald, 'James VI and I'. On David and Absalom as exemplars, see Goodland, *Female Mourning*, pp. 5, 209; on interpretations of the tears shed by Jesus over the grave of Lazarus, see Ch. 7.

10. G. W. Pigman III, *Grief and English Renaissance Elegy* (Cambridge: Cambridge University Press, 1985); Duffy, *Stripping of the Altars*, pp. 360–1; Goodland, *Female Mourning*; Alison Shell, *Catholicism, Controversy and the English Literary Imagination, 1558–1660* (Cambridge: Cambridge University Press, 1999); Phillippy, *Women, Death and Literature*.

11. Andrea Brady, 'To Weep Irish: Keening and the Law', in Austin Sarat and Martha Umphrey (eds), *Mourning and the Law* (Stanford, Calif.: Stanford University Press, forthcoming).

12. [Southwell], *Funeral Teares*, p. 1ᵛ.

13. *The Book of Margery Kempe*, trans. with an introduction by Barry Windeatt (London: Penguin, 2004), ch. 57, pp. 178–9; see also ch. 7, p. 54 on weeping for souls in purgatory. For imagery of tears washing away the stain of sin in Southwell, see 'St Peter's Complaint', in Robert Southwell, *St Peter's Complaint and Other Poems, Reprinted from the Edition of 1595*, ed. W. Joseph Walter (London: Longman, Hurst, Ress, and Orme, 1817), pp. 4–5; on the use of similar imagery by George Herbert, see Strier, 'Herbert and Tears', pp. 230–3.

14. Edmund Campion, *Two Histories of Ireland* (Dublin: Society of Stationers, 1633), p. 14; quoted in Brady, 'Weep Irish'; Campion visited Ireland in 1571.

15. Barnabe Rich, *A New Description of Ireland* (London: Thomas Adams, 1610), pp. 12–13; Brady 'Weep Irish'.

16. Edmund Spenser made these comparisons in his *View of the Present State of Ireland*, written in 1596 and published in 1633; Sujata Iyengar, *Shades of Difference: Mythologies of Skin Color in Early Modern England* (Philadelphia: University of Pennsylvania Press, 2005), pp. 90–2; see also Brady, 'Weep Irish'.

17. Thomas Crofton Croker, *The Keen of the South of Ireland: As Illustrative of Irish Political and Domestic History, Manners, Music, and Superstitions* (London: T. Richards, 1844), p. xlviii.

18. 'The Day of Anger and Sorrow', *Daily Mirror*, 3 Feb. 1972, pp. 14–15.

19. Goodland, *Female Mourning*, p. 135.

20. Diarmaid MacCulloch, *Thomas Cranmer: A Life* (New Haven: Yale University Press, 1996).

21. Clarissa W. Atkinson, *Mystic and Pilgrim: The Book and World of Margery Kempe* (Ithaca, NY: Cornell University Press, 1983), pp. 58–9; Santha Bhattarcharji, 'Tears and Screaming: Weeping in the Spirituality of Margery Kempe', in Kimberley Christine Patton and John Stratton Hawley (eds), *Holy Tears: Weeping in the Religious Imagination* (Princeton: Princeton University Press, 2005), pp. 229–41 (p. 234). The texts of the Book of Common Prayer and the Sarum Missal can be searched and compared online at 'The Book of Common Prayer: Church of England', Anglican Resources, Society of Archbishop Justus, updated 14 Aug. 2014, <http://justus.anglican.org/resources/bcp/england.htm>.

22. Keith Thomas, *The Ends of Life: Roads to Fulfilment in Early Modern England* (Oxford: Oxford University Press, 2009), p. 188; also quoted in Bernard Capp, '"Jesus Wept" But Did the Englishman? Masculinity and Emotion in Early Modern England', *Past and Present* 224 (2014): 75–108 (p. 84), which surveys philosophical and political as well as religious attitudes to tears in this period.
23. Michael Neill, *Issues of Death: Mortality and Identity in English Renaissance Tragedy* (Oxford: Clarendon Press, 1997), p. 180; Goodland, *Female Mourning*, ch. 5.
24. Goodland, *Female Mourning*, pp. 102–3, 139.
25. Ibid. 108; citing Clare Gittings, *Death, Burial and the Individual in Early Modern England* (London: Routledge, 1984), p. 137.
26. See Ch. 19.
27. John Calvin, *Institutes of the Christian Religion*, quoted in Strier, 'Herbert and Tears', p. 224. For a discussion of Calvin's views on tears and godly sorrow, see Kuchar, *Poetry of Religious Sorrow*, p. 18. For a detailed study of the Protestant theology and piety involved in the production and interpretation of one Protestant noblewoman's plentiful tears in the seventeenth century, see Raymond A. Anselment, 'Mary Rich, Countess of Warwick, and the Gift of Tears', *Seventeenth Century* 22 (2007): 336–57.
28. John Knox, *The History of the Reformation of Religion within the Realm of Scotland, Together with the Life of the Author* (Glasgow: J. Galbraith and Company, 1761), p. 286; Jane E. A. Dawson, 'Knox, John (c.1514–1572)', *Oxford Dictionary of National Biography* (Oxford University Press, 2004; online edn, Jan. 2008), doi:10.1093/ref:odnb/15781.
29. This comes out in the private diaries of Mary Rich in the seventeenth century; see Anselment, 'Mary Rich'.
30. Luke 23: 28.
31. Nicholas Breton, *A Divine Poeme Divided into Two Partes: The Ravisht Soule and the Blessed Weeper* (London: John Browne and John Deane, 1601), E2ᵛ.
32. George Herbert, *A Priest to the Temple, or The Country Parson, his Character, and Rule of Holy Life* (London: T. Garthwait, 1652), p. 145. This passage is also quoted in Strier, 'Herbert and Tears', p. 224, and in Marjory E. Lange, *Telling Tears in the English Renaissance* (Leiden: E. J. Brill, 1996), p. 210.
33. John Donne, 'John 11.35. Jesus Wept' (1622/3), in *The Sermons of John Donne*, ed. with introductions and critical apparatus by George R. Potter and Evelyn M. Simpson, 10 vols (Berkeley and Los Angeles: University of California Press, 1959), iv. 324–44 (pp. 340, 341). On this sermon, see the Conclusion, and also Jeanne Shami, *John Donne and Conformity in Crisis in the Late Jacobean Pulpit* (Cambridge: D. S. Brewer, 2003), ch. 6.
34. [Thomas Playfere], *A Most Excellent and Heavenly Sermon upon the 23rd Chapter of the Gospell by Saint Luke* (London: Andrew Wise, 1595).
35. *A Legacy for Saints; Being Several Experiences of the Dealings of God with Anna Trapnel* (London: T. Brewster, 1654), p. 2; see also Arnold Hunt, *The Art of*

Hearing: English Preachers and their Audiences, 1590–1640 (Cambridge: Cambridge University Press, 2010), pp. 91–4.

36. [Playfere], *Sermon*, B3ᵛ.
37. Kuchar, *Poetry of Religious Sorrow*, ch. 4; Femke Molekamp, 'Reading Christ the Book in Aemilia Lanyer's *Salve Deus Rex Judaeorum* (1611): Iconography and the Cultures of Reading', *Studies in Philology* 109 (2012): 311–32.
38. Donne, 'Jesus Wept', p. 330.
39. 'maudlin, adj.', *Oxford English Dictionary* (Oxford University Press, online edn, Sept. 2014).
40. On allegations about drunken and licentious wakes, see Brady, 'Weep Irish'. For examples of the maudlin drunkard as a stock seventeenth-century character, see Robert Basset, *Curiosities: Or the Cabinet of Nature* (London: N. and I. Okes, 1637), pp. 58–9; Thomas Jordan, *Pictures of Passions, Fancies, and Affections Poetically Deciphered, in Variety of Characters* (London: R. Wood, 1641), B4ʳ-B5ᵛ.
41. On the importance to reformed Protestants of devotional tears, especially during prayer, see Alec Ryrie, *Being Protestant in Reformation Britain* (Oxford: Oxford University Press, 2013), pp. 187–95.

Chapter 3. Titus Andronicus: Ha, Ha, Ha!

1. Diana Poulton, *John Dowland*, new and revised edn (Berkeley and Los Angeles: University of California Press, 1982); Peter Holman, *Dowland, Lachrimae (1604)* (Cambridge: Cambridge University Press, 1999); David Greer, 'Dowland, John (1563?–1626)', *Oxford Dictionary of National Biography* (Oxford University Press, online edn, 2004), doi:10.1093/ref:odnb/7962.
2. For an introduction to Shakespeare's tragedies in this context, see Martin Coyle, 'The Tragedies of Shakespeare's Contemporaries', in Richard Dutton and Jean E. Howard (eds), *A Companion to Shakespeare's Works*, i: *The Tragedies* (Oxford: Blackwell, 2003), pp. 23–46.
3. I refer to *Titus*, throughout this chapter, as a work by Shakespeare. Several scholars believe that the first act may have been written by George Peele, and categorize the play as a collaborative work. See Brian Vickers, *Shakespeare, Co-Author: A Historical Study of Five Collaborative Plays* (Oxford: Oxford University Press, 2002), ch. 3.
4. The text of the play that I have consulted, including a very full introduction by Jonathan Bate, and hereafter cited simply as *Titus*, is William Shakespeare, *Titus Andronicus*, ed. Jonathan Bate (London: Arden Shakespeare, 1995); on early stagings, see Bate, 'Introduction', pp. 37–48. See also Ian Smith, '*Titus Andronicus*: A Time for Race and Revenge', in Richard Dutton and Jean E. Howard (eds), *A Companion to Shakespeare's Works*, i: *The Tragedies* (Oxford: Blackwell, 2003), pp. 284–302.

5. For a rich contextual study of the medical, theological, and poetic meanings of tears in the English Renaissance, see Marjory E. Lange, *Telling Tears in the English Renaissance* (Leiden: E. J. Brill, 1996).
6. See Ch. 4.
7. Levinus Lemnius, *The Touchstone of Complexions Generallye Appliable, Expedient and Profitable for all Such as be Desirous and Carefull of their Bodylye Health* (London: Thomas Marsh, 1576), pp. 17^v-18^r (back of page 17, erroneously numbered 18 in 1576 edition, and front of page 18).
8. Thomas Wright, *The Passions of the Minde* (London: Printed by V.S. for W.B, 1601), 'Preface unto the Reader' (unpaginated). On the political and religious context of Wright's work, see also John Staines, 'Compassion in the Public Sphere of Milton and King Charles', in Gail Kern Paster, Katherine Rowe, and Mary Floyd-Wilson (eds), *Reading the Early Modern Passions: Essays in the Cultural History of Emotion* (Philadelphia: University of Pennsylvania Press, 2004), pp. 89–110 (pp. 93–6).
9. Lemnius, *Touchstone of Complexions*, pp. 102^v-103^r, 149^r; the description of drunken men is not specifically attached by Lemnius to English drunks. See also John L. Flood, ' "Safer on the battlefield than in the city": England, the "Sweating Sickness", and the Continent', *Renaissance Studies* 17 (2003): 147–76.
10. George Cheyne, *The English Malady: or, A Treatise of Nervous Diseases of All Kinds* (London: G. Strahan, 1733). See also Paul Langford, *Englishness Identified: Manners and Character 1650–1850* (Oxford: Oxford University Press, 2000), pp. 52–3; Mary Floyd-Wilson, *English Ethnicity and Race in Early Modern Drama* (Cambridge: Cambridge University Press, 2003), ch. 3; Jeremy Schmidt, *Melancholy and the Care of the Soul: Religion, Moral Philosophy and Madness in Early Modern England* (Aldershot: Ashgate, 2007), pp. 176–84.
11. Diana Poulton, *John Dowland*, new and revised edn (Berkeley and Los Angeles: University of California Press, 1982), pp. 119–20; David Greer, 'Dowland, John (1563?–1626)', *Oxford Dictionary of National Biography* (Oxford University Press, online edn, 2004), doi:10.1093/ref:odnb/7962.
12. See, for instance, Walter Charleton, *Natural History of the Passions* (London, James Magnes, 1674), p. 157, describing how, in weeping, the lachrymal glands were 'squeezed by certain nerves' with the effect that tears were 'squeezed forth' or 'expressed out of them'.
13. On Victorian and more recent uses of the phrase 'emotional incontinence', see Chs 13 and 20.
14. Timothie Bright, *A Treatise of Melancholie* (London: Thomas Vautrollier, 1586), pp. 135–48 (p. 145); for more on Bright's place in Renaissance medical theories of weeping, see Lange, *Telling Tears*, ch. 1.
15. [Robert Burton], *The Anatomy of Melancholy, What it is: With all the Kindes, Causes, Symptomes, Prognostickes, and Severall Cures of It, by Democritus Junior* (Oxford: Henry Cripps, 1621), p. 21. On Burton's theory of tears and the four humours, see Lange, *Telling Tears*, pp. 22–6. On Burton's famous text and its

broader intellectual, cultural, and medical context, see Angus Gowland, *The Worlds of Renaissance Melancholy: Robert Burton in Context* (Cambridge: Cambridge University Press, 2006); Erin Sullivan, 'A Disease Unto Death: Sadness in the Time of Shakespeare', in Elena Carrera (ed.), *Emotions and Health, 1200–1700* (Leiden: Brill, 2013), pp. 159–81.

16. Quentin Skinner, 'Hobbes and the Classical Theory of Laugher', in Tom Sorell and Luc Foisneau (eds), *Leviathan After 350 Years* (Oxford: Oxford University Press, 2004), pp. 139–66; Matthew Steggle, *Laughing and Weeping in Early Modern Theatres* (Aldershot: Ashgate, 2007); Indira Ghose, *Shakespeare and Laughter: A Cultural History* (Manchester: Manchester University Press, 2008); Beatrice Groves, 'Laughter in the Time of Plague: A Context for the Unstable Style of Nashe's *Christ's Tears over Jerusalem*', *Studies in Philology* 108 (2011): 238–60; Bridget Escolme, *Emotional Excess on the Shakespearean Stage: Passion's Slaves* (London: Bloomsbury Arden Shakespeare, 2013), ch. 2.

17. Ghose, *Shakespeare and Laughter*, ch. 4; see also section on William Prynne in Ch. 4 of this volume.

18. Steggle, *Laughing and Weeping*, ch. 1; Skinner, 'Classical Theory of Laughter', p. 143.

19. *Titus*, 3.1.265, p. 204.

20. I was inspired to make a further study of tears in *Titus Andronicus* having read the analyses offered in Steggle, *Laughing and Weeping*, pp. 128–31; and Cora Fox, *Ovid and the Politics of Emotion in Elizabethan England* (New York: Palgrave Macmillan, 2009), ch. 3. See also Mary Laughlin Fawcett, 'Arms/ Words/Tears: Language and the Body in Titus Andronicus', *ELH* 50 (1983): 261–77; Robert Cohen, 'Tears (and Acting) in Shakespeare', *Journal of Dramatic Theory and Criticism* 10 (1995): 21–30.

21. Fox, *Ovid and the Politics of Emotion*, introduction and ch. 3.

22. *Titus*, 3.1.256, p. 203.

23. Ibid. 3.1.59–61, p. 193.

24. Bright, *Treatise of Melancholie*, pp. 193–5; Lange, *Telling Tears*, ch. 1.

25. [Robert Southwell], *Marie Magdalens Funeral Teares* (London: Printed by J.W. for G.C., 1591), p. 55ᵛ.

26. *Titus*, 3.1.26, 114–16, 137–50, 3.2.36, pp. 192, 196–7, 208. On Southwell, see Ch. 2.

27. *Titus*, 3.1.209–32, pp. 200–2.

28. Ibid. 1.1.162, 3.1.270, pp. 138, 204.

29. Ibid. 3.2.50, 5.2.169, pp. 208, 262; the line 'Shed yet some small drops from thy tender spring' is spoken to the boy by his father, Lucius, in a textual variation to the final scene; see *Titus*, p. 275.

30. Bright, *Treatise of Melancholie*, pp. 143–4, 175; René Descartes, *The Passions of the Soul*, trans. Stephen Voss (Indianapolis: Hackett, 1989), Article 133, p. 89 (original publication 1649); Lange, *Telling Tears*, p. 29; Margo Swiss, 'Repairing Androgyny: Eve's Tears in *Paradise Lost*', in Margo Swiss and David A. Kent (eds), *Speaking Grief in English Literary Culture: Shakespeare to Milton* (Pittsburgh: Duquesne University Press, 2002), pp. 261–83 (p. 274).

31. Gail Kern Paster, *The Body Embarrassed: Drama and the Disciplines of Shame in Early Modern England* (Ithaca, NY: Cornell University Press, 1993), p. 25; Andrea Brady, 'The Physics of Melting in Early Modern Love Poetry', *Ceræ: An Australasian Journal of Medieval and Early Modern Studies* 1 (2014): 22–52 (p. 37).
32. [Burton], *Anatomy of Melancholy*, p. 20.
33. George Herbert, 'Grief', in *The Temple: Sacred Poems and Private Ejaculations* (Cambridge: Thomas Buck and Roger Daniel, 1633), p. 158; see also Richard Strier, 'Herbert and Tears', *ELH* 46 (1979): 221–47; Lange, *Telling Tears*, pp. 204–22.
34. Descartes, *Passions of the Soul*, Articles 128–34, pp. 86–90; *Titus*, 5.1.117, p. 250.
35. *Titus*, 3.1.234, 260–7, pp. 202, 203–4.
36. Ibid. 5.3.48, p. 267.
37. Ibid. 4.3.31, p. 231; William Matthews, 'Peter Bales, Timothy Bright and William Shakespeare', *Journal of English and Germanic Philology* 34 (1935): 483–510; Page Life, 'Bright, Timothy (1549/50–1615)', *Oxford Dictionary of National Biography* (Oxford University Press, 2004; online edn, Jan. 2008), doi:10.1093/ref:odnb/3424.
38. Bright, *Treatise of Melancholie*, pp. 138–9; Descartes, *Passions of the Soul*, Article 128, pp. 86–7; Lange, *Telling Tears*, pp. 38–45.
39. Bright, *Treatise of Melancholie*, pp. 138–9.
40. On weeping in classical literature, see Thorsten Fögen (ed.), *Tears in the Graeco-Roman World* (Berlin: Walter de Gruyter, 2009). See also Timothy Webb, 'Tears: An Introduction', Timothy Webb, 'Tears: An Anthology', and Henry Power, 'Homeric Tears and Eighteenth-Century Weepers', all in *Litteraria Pragensia: Studies in Literature and Culture* 22 (2012): 1–25, 26–45, and 46–58, respectively.
41. Both quoted in Bernard Capp, ' "Jesus Wept" But Did the Englishman? Masculinity and Emotion in Early Modern England', *Past and Present* 224 (2014): 75–108 (pp. 76, 88); see also Audrey Chew, *Stoicism in Renaissance Literature: An Introduction* (New York: Peter Lang, 1988).
42. *Titus*, 5.3.87–94, 173–4, pp. 270–1, 276.
43. Wright, *The Passions*, p. 86.
44. *Titus*, 1.1.107–23, 2.2.139–41, 288–91, pp. 134–5, 176, 185.
45. Ibid. 5.3.198–9, p. 277.
46. All derive from the Latin term *pietās*; see 'pity, n.', *Oxford English Dictionary* (Oxford University Press, online edn, Sept. 2014). On the tears of the Virgin Mary, see Chs 1 and 2.
47. *Titus*, 5.3.145–99, pp. 274–7.
48. On Catholic and Protestant perspectives on tears of mourning, see Ch. 2. For an introduction to scholarly discussions of Shakespeare and Catholicism, see Alison Shell, *Shakespeare and Religion* (London: Arden Shakespeare, 2010). On the relationships between Renaissance tragedies by Shakespeare, Kyd, and Webster and the trauma of the Reformation, see Katharine Goodland, *Female Mourning*

in Medieval and Renaissance English Drama: From the Raising of Lazarus to King Lear (Aldershot: Ashgate, 2005).

49. *Titus*, 5.3.159–60, p. 275.
50. Ibid. 3.1.149, p. 197.
51. Ibid. 5.3.173–4.
52. Steggle, *Laughing and Weeping*, p. 83, includes the observation that many Renaissance theorists believed the tears shed by audiences over tragedies were beneficial and cathartic; in the words of the 1576 translation of Della Casa's *Galateo*, audiences 'were by their weeping, healed of their infirmitie'.
53. Abbé le Blanc, *Letters on the English and French Nations*, 2 vols (London: J. Brindley, 1747), ii. 205, 259.
54. Edward Capell, *Notes and Variant Readings to Shakespeare*, 3 vols (1783); quoted in Bate, 'Introduction' to *Titus*, pp. 67–8, 80.

Chapter 4. The Actor, the Witch, and the Puritan

1. John Morrill, 'Cromwell, Oliver (1599–1658)', *Oxford Dictionary of National Biography* (Oxford University Press, 2004; online edn, May 2008), doi:10.1093/ref:odnb/6765; Ian Gentles, *Oliver Cromwell: God's Warrior and the English Revolution* (Basingstoke: Palgrave Macmillan, 2011).
2. For a rich and pioneering study of English male tears in this period, see Bernard Capp, '"Jesus Wept" But Did the Englishman? Masculinity and Emotion in Early Modern England', *Past and Present* 224 (2014): 75–108 (Cromwell anecdote, p. 108).
3. In the eighteenth and nineteenth centuries, the debate about actors, tears, and emotions often referred to Diderot's essay on the subject, *Paradoxe sur le comédien* (1773). See William Archer, *Masks or Faces: A Study in the Psychology of Acting* (London: Longmans, Green, and Co., 1888); Joseph R. Roach, *The Player's Passion: Studies in the Science of Acting* (Newark: University of Delaware Press, 1985).
4. On Mary Wollstonecraft's attitudes to female tears of sensibility, see Ch. 8, and on the persistence of the witch's dilemma into the twentieth century, see Chs 15 and 19.
5. William Shakespeare, *Hamlet*, ed. Ann Thompson and Neil Taylor (London: Arden Shakespare, 2006), 2.2.486–97, pp. 274–5. For further discussion, see Matthew Steggle, *Laughing and Weeping in Early Modern Theatres* (Aldershot: Ashgate, 2007), pp. 52–3; Cora Fox, *Ovid and the Politics of Emotion in Elizabethan England* (New York: Palgrave Macmillan, 2009), pp. 105–7.
6. The Wachowski Brothers (dir.), *The Matrix* (Warner Bros, 1999).
7. John Donne, 'Elegie on the Lady Marckham' (1609), quoted and discussed in Marjory E. Lange, *Telling Tears in the English Renaissance* (Leiden: E. J. Brill, 1996), p. 196.
8. Steggle, *Laughing and Weeping*, p. 88.

9. Thomas Browne, *Religio Medici* (1642), quoted in Steggle, *Laughing and Weeping*, p. 89.

10. Matthew Parker, funeral sermon for Martin Bucer (1551), quoted in Katharine Goodland, *Female Mourning in Medieval and Renaissance English Drama: From the Raising of Lazarus to King Lear* (Aldershot: Ashgate, 2005), pp. 102–3; see also Ch. 2 in this volume.

11. Arthur F. Kinney, 'Gosson, Stephen (bap. 1554, d. 1625)', *Oxford Dictionary of National Biography* (Oxford University Press, 2004; online edn, May 2007), doi:10.1093/ref:odnb/11120; on Southwell, see Ch. 2.

12. Deuteronomy 22: 5 (King James Version).

13. Stephen Gosson, *Playes Confuted in Five Actions* (1582), quoted in Steggle, *Laughing and Weeping*, pp. 17, 85.

14. William Prynne, *Histrio-mastix, The Players Scourge, or Actors Tragaedie* (London: Michael Sparke, 1633); William Lamont, 'Prynne, William (1600–1669)', *Oxford Dictionary of National Biography* (Oxford University Press, 2004; online edn, May 2011), doi:10.1093/ref:odnb/22854.

15. Prynne, *Histrio-mastix* (1633), quoted in Steggle, *Laughing and Weeping*, p. 18.

16. Lamont, 'Prynne'.

17. Prynne, *Histrio-mastix*, pp. 6, 212–15.

18. Prynne, ibid. 624, gives the year of the relevant council erroneously as 1560 instead of the correct date of 1565; 'Concilium Provinciale Mediolanense Primum' (1565), in Severinus Binius (ed.), *Concilia Generalia et Provincalia*, 4 vols (Coloniæ Agrippinæ: Ioannis Gymnici, 1618), vol. iv, part II, pp. 359–98 (p. 363).

19. Lamont, 'Prynne'.

20. William Shakespeare, *The Taming of the Shrew*, ed. Barbara Hodgdon (London: Arden Shakespeare, 2010), Induction 1.123–7, p. 148; Barbara Hodgdon, 'Introduction', in *Taming of the Shrew*, pp. 1–131 (p. 16 for 1633 performance); Robert Cohen, 'Tears (and Acting) in Shakespeare', *Journal of Dramatic Theory and Criticism* 10 (1995): 21–30 (p. 24); Goodland, *Female Mourning*, p. 112; Steggle, *Laughing and Weeping*, p. 54; Lamont, 'Prynne'.

21. Lamont, 'Prynne'.

22. Austin Woolrych, *Britain in Revolution, 1625–1660* (Oxford: Oxford University Press, 2002); Ian Gentles, *The English Revolution and the Wars in the Three Kingdoms, 1638–1652* (Harlow: Pearson, 2007).

23. H. R. Trevor Roper, *The European Witch-Craze of the Sixteenth and Seventeenth Centuries* (Harmondsworth: Penguin Books, 1967); Malcolm Gaskill, *Witchfinders: A Seventeenth-Century English Tragedy* (London: John Murray, 2005).

24. Patricia Crawford, *Women and Religion in England, 1500–1720* (London: Routledge, 1993), pp. 107–9; Ann Hughes, *Gender and the English Revolution* (London: Routledge, 2012), pp. 78–81; on Trapnel's earlier life see also Ch. 2 of this volume.

25. Alan C. Kors and Edward Peters (eds), *Witchcraft in Europe: A Documentary History* (Philadelphia: University of Pennsylvania Press, 1972), pp. 183, 215;

Richard E. Spear, *The 'Divine' Guido: Religion, Sex, Money and Art in the World of Guido Reni* (New Haven and London: Yale University Press, 1997), p. 172; Ulinka Rublack, *The Crimes of Women in Early Modern Germany* (Oxford: Clarendon Press, 1999), ch. 3; Ulinka Rublack (trans. Pamela Selwyn), 'Fluxes: The Early Modern Body and the Emotions', *History Workshop Journal* 53 (2002): 1–16.

26. On bears, tigers, and wolves, see Alexandre de Pontaymeri, *A Woman's Worth, Defended Against All the Men in the* World (London: John Wolfe, 1599), p. 41; Edward Topsell, *The History of Four-Footed Beasts and Serpents* (London: E. Cotes, 1658), p. 578. On witches, wolves, and werewolves, see Gary L. Ebersole, 'The Function of Ritual Weeping Revisited: Affective Expression and Moral Discourse', *History of Religions* 39 (2000): 211–46 (pp. 222–4). On the Swiss as 'a cold, an insensible, a phlegmatic people' who 'never weep, and are never affected', see *A Picturesque Description of Switzerland; Translated from the French of the Marquis de Langle* (London: David Fowler, 1791), p. 19. On the Vikings' abomination for tears and mourning, even for deceased relatives, see 'Turner's *History of the Anglo Saxons*, Vols 2 and 3', *Monthly Epitome and Catalogue of New Publications* 5 (1801): 158–65 (p. 162).

27. On the Magdalene, see Ch. 2.

28. Edmond Bower, *Doctor Lamb Revived, Or Witchcraft Condemn'd in Anne Bodenham* (London: R. Best and J. Place, 1653), pp. 1, 35, 42. The Bodenham case is discussed in detail in Malcolm Gaskill, 'Witchcraft, Politics, and Memory in Seventeenth-Century England', *Historical Journal* 50 (2007): 289–308.

29. The character Pandulpho in John Marston's *Antonio's Revenge* (1602) dismisses the idea of weeping in mourning, saying, 'Away tis apish action, player-like'; Steggle, *Laughing and Weeping*, p. 49.

30. Nathaniel Bernard, *Esoptron Tes Antimachias, or A Looking-Glasse for Rebellion, Being a Sermon Preached upon Sunday 16 June 1644* (Oxford: Leonard Lichfield, 1644), pp. 14–15.

31. Lorraine M. Roberts and John R. Roberts, 'Crashavian Criticism: A Brief Interpretative History', in John R. Roberts (ed.), *New Perspectives on the Life and Art of Richard Crashaw* (Columbia: University of Missouri Press, 1990), pp. 1–29 (p. 13); Richard Rambuss, 'Crashaw and the Metaphysical Shudder; Or, How to Do Things with Tears', in Susan McClary (ed.), *Structures of Feeling in Seventeenth-Century Cultural Expression* (Toronto: University of Toronto Press, 2013), pp. 253–71. On Crashaw's place in the poetry of tears in this period see Richard Strier, 'Herbert and Tears', *ELH* 46 (1979): 221–47; Lange, *Telling Tears*, pp. 222–44; Paul Parrish, 'Moderate Sorrow and Immoderate Tears: Mourning in Crashaw', in Margo Swiss and David A. Kent (eds), *Speaking Grief in English Literary Culture: Shakespeare to Milton* (Pittsburgh: Duquesne University Press, 2002), pp. 217–41. For a study of the place of tears in French literature in this period, see Sheila Page Bayne, *Tears and Weeping: An Aspect of Emotional Climate Reflected in Seventeenth-Century French Literature* (Tübingen:

Narr, 1981). On the literature of tears of the sixteenth and early seventeenth centuries, see also the discussion of Robert Southwell in Ch. 2.

32. John Featley, *A Fountaine of Teares, Emptying It Selfe into Three Rivelets, viz. of 1. Compunction, 2. Compassion, 3. Devotion, or: Sobs of Nature Sanctified by Grace* (Amsterdam: John Crosse, 1646). On Featley's career, see Stephen Wright, 'Featley [Fairclough], John (1604/5–1667)', *Oxford Dictionary of National Biography* (Oxford University Press, 2004; online edn, Jan. 2008), doi:10.1093/ref:odnb/9243.

33. *Loyalties Tears* was published anonymously in 1649 and later attributed to Sir John Birkenhead; *Mercurius Heraclitus* was a short-lived weekly periodical published in June and July 1652; both can be consulted at the British Library.

34. Gentles, *The English Revolution*, p. 460.

35. John Staines, 'Compassion in the Public Sphere of Milton and King Charles', in Gail Kern Paster, Katherine Rowe, and Mary Floyd-Wilson (eds), *Reading the Early Modern Passions: Essays in the Cultural History of Emotion* (Philadelphia: University of Pennsylvania Press, 2004), pp. 89–110.

36. Don M. Wolfe (ed.), *Leveller Manifestoes of the Puritan Revolution* (London: Thomas Nelson, 1944), p. 370; Gentles, *The English Revolution*, pp. 459–61.

37. William Allen, *Killing, No Murder: With Some Additions, Briefly Discourst in Three Questions* (London: 1659), pp. 5–6; for more on Cromwell's tears and their significance, with reference to religion, politics, class, and gender, see Capp, 'Jesus Wept'.

38. Abraham Cowley, *The Guardian: A Comedie* (London: John Holden, 1650), Act 3, Scene 3; on Cowley, see Alexander Lindsay, 'Cowley, Abraham (1618–1667)', *Oxford Dictionary of National Biography* (Oxford University Press, online edn, 2004), doi:10.1093/ref:odnb/6499.

39. Abraham Cowley, *A Vision, Concerning His Late Pretended Highnesse, Cromwell, the Wicked* (London: Henry Herringman, 1661), pp. 52–3.

Chapter 5. Stop, Gabriel!

1. See Chs 14–17.

2. A classic study of the eighteenth-century culture of sensibility is G. J. Barker-Benfield, *The Culture of Sensibility: Sex and Society in Eighteenth-Century Britain* (Chicago: University of Chicago Press, 1992); for more on this see Chs 6–8, and the 'Further Reading' section.

3. On the many meanings of 'enthusiasm', especially in the eighteenth century, see Susie I. Tucker, *Enthusiasm: A Study in Semantic Change* (Cambridge: Cambridge University Press, 1972); Jon Mee, *Dangerous Enthusiasm: William Blake and the Culture of Radicalism in the 1790s* (Oxford: Clarendon Press, 1994); Jon Mee, *Romanticism, Enthusiasm, and Regulation: Poetics and the Policing of Culture in the Romantic Period* (Oxford: Oxford University Press, 2003); Thomas Dixon, 'Enthusiasm Delineated: Weeping as a Religious Activity in Eighteenth-Century Britain', *Litteraria Pragensia* 22 (2012): 59–81.

4. R. S. Crane, 'Suggestions Toward a Genealogy of the "Man of Feeling"', *ELH* 1 (1934): 205–30; Donald Greene, 'Latitudinarianism and Sensibility: The Genealogy of the "Man of Feeling" Reconsidered', *Modern Philology* 75 (1977): 159–83; Frans De Bruyn, 'Latitudinarianism and its Importance as a Precursor to Sensibility', *Journal of English and Germanic Philology* 80 (1981): 349–68; Barker-Benfield, *Culture of Sensibility*, pp. 65–77; Jeremy Gregory, '*Homo Religiosus*: Masculinity and Religion in the Long Eighteenth Century', in Tim Hitchcock and Michèle Cohen (eds), *English Masculinities 1660–1800* (London: Longman, 1999), pp. 85–110; Paul Goring, *The Rhetoric of Sensibility in Eighteenth-Century Culture* (Cambridge: Cambridge University Press, 2005), pp. 70–90; William Van Reyk, 'Christian Ideals of Manliness in the Eighteenth and Early Nineteenth Centuries', *Historical Journal* 52 (2009): 1053–73; Herman Roodenburg, '*Si vis me flere*...: On Preachers, Passions and Pathos in Eighteenth-Century Europe', in Jitse Dijkstra, Justin Kroesen, and Yme Kuiper (eds), *Myths, Martyrs and Modernity: Studies in the History of Religions in Honour of Jan N. Bremmer* (Leiden: Brill, 2010), pp. 609–28.

5. 'Craig Bellamy Sheds Tears of Joy after Cardiff Clinch Promotion', BBC Sport, 17 Apr. 2013, <http://www.bbc.co.uk/sport/0/football/22178092>.

6. For more on the tears of footballers and others sportspeople and fans, see Chs 18 and 20.

7. David Hempton, *The Religion of the People: Methodism and Popular Religion c.1750–1900* (London: Routledge, 1996); Henry D. Rack, *Reasonable Enthusiast: John Wesley and the Rise of Methodism*, 3rd edn (London: Epworth Press, 2002); Phyllis Mack, *Heart Religion in the British Enlightenment: Gender and Emotion in Early Methodism* (Cambridge: Cambridge University Press, 2008); Emma Major, *Madam Britannia: Women, Church, and Nation 1712–1812* (Oxford: Oxford University Press, 2011), ch. 4; Misty G. Anderson, *Imagining Methodism in Eighteenth-Century Britain: Enthusiasm, Belief and the Borders of the Self* (Baltimore: Johns Hopkins University Press, 2012).

8. For historical examinations and reappraisals of the Enlightenment and its advocates, especially in relation to religion, see Peter Harrison, *'Religion' and the Religions in the English Enlightenment* (Cambridge: Cambridge University Press, 1990); Peter Lineham, 'Methodism and Popular Science in the Enlightenment', *Enlightenment and Dissent* 17 (1998): 104–25; S. J. Barnett, *The Enlightenment and Religion: The Myths of Modernity* (Manchester: Manchester University Press, 2003); Jane Shaw, *Miracles in Enlightenment England* (New Haven: Yale University Press, 2006); Mack, *Heart Religion*; Thomas Dixon, *Science and Religion: A Very Short Introduction* (Oxford: Oxford University Press, 2008).

9. David Hume, *A Treatise of Human Nature*, ed. L. Selby-Bigge and P. Nidditch (Oxford: Clarendon Press, 1978), p. 415; first published 1739–40. See also Thomas Dixon, *From Passions to Emotions: The Creation of a Secular Psychological Category* (Cambridge: Cambridge University Press, 2003), pp. 104–9.

10. Dixon, *Passions to Emotions*, ch. 3; Adam Phillips and Barbara Taylor, *On Kindness* (London: Hamish Hamilton, 2009); Michael L. Frazer, *The Enlightenment of Sympathy: Justice and the Moral Sentiments in the Eighteenth Century and Today* (Oxford: Oxford University Press, 2010).

11. Stuart Andrews, *Methodism and Society* (London: Longman, 1970), p. 41; Anderson, *Imagining Methodism*, pp. 136, 249n.; Barker-Benfield, *Culture of Sensibility*, pp. 267-71.

12. John Gillies (ed.), *Memoirs of the Late Reverend George Whitefield* (London: T. Williams, 1812), appendix, p. xxxvi.

13. See Ch. 1.

14. William Jay, *Memoirs of the Life and Character of the Late Rev. Cornelius Winter*, 2nd edn (London: Williams and Smith, 1809), pp. 27-8; quoted in Boyd Stanley Schlenther, 'Whitefield, George (1714-1770)', *Oxford Dictionary of National Biography* (Oxford University Press, 2004; online edn, May 2010), doi:10.1093/ref:odnb/29281. See also Revd J. B. Wakeley, *Anecdotes of the Rev. George Whitefield* (London: Hodder and Stoughton, 1872), pp. 23-4.

15. George Whitefield, *The Works of the Reverend George Whitefield*, 6 vols (London: Edward and Charles Dilly, 1771-2), v. 47, 371.

16. *George Whitefield's Journals: A New Edition Containing Fuller Material than Any Hitherto Published* (London: The Banner of Truth Trust, 1960), 17 Feb. 1739, p. 216.

17. Sydney G. Dimond, *The Psychology of the Methodist Revival: An Empirical and Descriptive Study* (London: Oxford University Press, 1926), p. 108; Schlenther, 'Whitefield'.

18. Gillies, *Memoirs*, pp. 41-2; Whitefield, *Journals*, pp. 216-27.

19. Jay, *Memoirs*, p. 26; Schlenther, 'Whitefield'.

20. Whitefield, *Journals*, 17 Feb. 1739, p. 216; Andrews, *Methodism and Society*, pp. 35-42; Rack, *Reasonable Enthusiast*; Schlenther, 'Whitefield'.

21. Barker-Benfield, *Culture of Sensibility*, pp. 73-4; Mack, *Heart Religion*, pp. 41-54.

22. The line is spoken by an artist character, Frederick, played by Max von Sydow in Woody Allen (dir.), *Hannah and her Sisters* (Orion Pictures, 1986).

23. 'The Scheming Triumvirate' (London: G. Gibbs and William Tringham, 1760), The British Museum, Registration No. 1868,0808.4125; Major, *Madam Britannia*, p. 141; Anderson, *Imagining Methodism*, pp. 146-7.

24. George Whitefield to Lady Huntingdon, 27 May 1755, in John R. Tyson with Boyd S. Schlenther (eds), *In the Midst of Early Methodism: Lady Huntingdon and her Correspondence* (Lanham, Md: Scarecrow Press, 2006), p. 88; also quoted in Schlenther, 'Whitefield'.

25. Travis Glasson, *Mastering Christianity: Missionary Anglicanism and Slavery in the Atlantic World* (Oxford: Oxford University Press, 2012), ch. 4; Schlenther, 'Whitefield'.

26. J. A. Leo Lemay, *The Life of Benjamin Franklin*, ii: *Printer and Publisher, 1730-1747* (Philadelphia: University of Pennsylvania Press, 2006), ch. 17.

27. Quoted in D. Bruce Hindmarsh, '"My Chains Fell Off, My Heart Was Free": Early Methodist Conversion Narrative in England', *Church History* 68 (1999): 910–29 (p. 910).
28. 'The Life of Mr John Haime', in Thomas Jackson (ed.), *The Lives of Early Methodist Preachers, Chiefly Written by Themselves*, 3rd edn, 6 vols (London: Wesleyan Conference Office, 1865), i. 269–311.
29. 'The Life of Mr Thomas Mitchell', in Jackson (ed.), *The Lives of Early Methodist Preachers*, i. 252.
30. On the Teares, and Whitefield's visit to them, see C. H. Crookshank, *Memorable Women of Irish Methodism in the Last Century* (London: Wesleyan-Methodist Book-Room, 1882), pp. 6–13; on women within Methodism, see Hempton, *Religion of the People*, ch. 10; Mack, *Heart Religion*, pp. 19–21, 26–8; Anderson, *Imagining Methodism*.
31. [Mary Saxby], *Memoirs of a Female Vagrant, Written by Herself* (Dunstable: J. W. Morris, 1806); Jane Rendall, '"A Short Account of my Unprofitable Life": Autobiographies of Working-Class Women in Britain *c*.1775–1845', in Trev Lynn Broughton and Linda Anderson (eds), *Women's Lives/Women's Times: New Essays on Auto/Biography* (Albany: State University of New York Press, 1997), pp. 31–50; Philip Carter, 'Saxby, Mary (1738–1801)', *Oxford Dictionary of National Biography* (Oxford University Press, online edn, 2004), doi:10.1093/ref:odnb/66786.
32. Alleine's book was first published, posthumously, in 1671, and was reprinted numerous times throughout the eighteenth century, becoming a classic of puritan and evangelical devotion; Joseph Alleine, *An Alarm to Unconverted Sinners* (London: Tho. Parkhurst, 1703), pp. 141, 153.
33. Saxby, *Memoirs*, pp. 27–8, 31–2, 35; I am grateful to Tim Hitchcock and Stuart Hogarth for giving me access to their electronic transcription of the Saxby memoirs, which I consulted alongside the original published version, held in the British Library.
34. 'The Life of Mr John Haime', in Jackson (ed.), *The Lives of Early Methodist Preachers*, i. 275–8, 293–4.
35. Thomas Pennant, *Tours in Wales*, ed. John Rhys, 3 vols (Caernarvon: H. Humphreys, 1883), ii. 320–1; Ceridwen Lloyd-Morgan, 'Marged ferch Ifan (bap. 1696, d. 1793)', *Oxford Dictionary of National Biography* (Oxford University Press, online edn, 2004), doi:10.1093/ref:odnb/62908.
36. Hempton, *Religion of the People*, ch. 3; Nigel Yates, *Eighteenth-Century Britain: Religion and Politics 1714–1815* (Harlow: Pearson, 2008), pp. 88–95. On Anna Trapnel and some of the earlier religious contexts, see Chs 2 and 4. James Nalton, in the seventeenth century, like George Whitefield in the eighteenth, was known as 'the weeping prophet'; William Lamont, 'Richard Baxter, the Apocalypse and the Mad Major', in Charles Webster (ed.), *The Intellectual Revolution of the Seventeenth Century* (London: Routledge and Kegan Paul, 1974), pp. 399–426 (p. 410).

37. Abel Stevens, *The History of the Religious Movement of the Eighteenth Century Called Methodism*, 2 vols (London: Alexander Heylin, 1858–9), ii. 88–92.
38. Adrian Harvey, *Football: The First Hundred Years; The Untold Story* (Abingdon: Routledge, 2005), p. 5.
39. On Paul Gascoigne and more recent sporting tears, see Ch. 20.

Chapter 6. Four Hundred Pounds to Cry

1. James Elkins, *Pictures and Tears: A History of People Who Have Cried in Front of Paintings* (London: Routledge, 2001), pp. x–xi, 97.
2. Ibid. 12.
3. See Chs 7 and 8 for fuller discussions of the cultural and political dimensions of the cult of sensibility. A classic study is G. J. Barker-Benfield, *The Culture of Sensibility: Sex and Society in Eighteenth-Century Britain* (Chicago: University of Chicago Press, 1992).
4. Kevin Chua, 'Dead Birds, or the Miseducation of the Greuze Girl', in Alden Cavanaugh (ed.), *Performing the 'Everyday': The Culture of Genre in the Eighteenth Century* (Newark: University of Delaware Press, 2007), pp. 75–91; Emma Barker, 'Reading the Greuze Girl: The Daughter's Seduction', *Representations* 117 (2012): 86–119.
5. Elkins, *Pictures and Tears*, p. 109.
6. Ronald Paulson, *Hogarth*, iii: *Art and Politics, 1750–1764* (Cambridge: Lutterworth Press, 1993); David Bindman, 'Hogarth, William (1697–1764)', *Oxford Dictionary of National Biography* (Oxford University Press, 2004; online edn, May 2009), doi:10.1093/ref:odnb/13464.
7. Charles H. Hinnant, 'Dryden and Hogarth's *Sigismunda*', *Eighteenth-Century Studies* 6 (1973): 462–74; Marcia Pointon, 'A Woman Weeps: Hogarth's *Sigismunda* (1759) and the Aesthetics of Excess', in Penelope Gouk and Helen Hills (eds), *Representing Emotions: New Connections in the Histories of Art, Music and Medicine* (Aldershot: Ashgate, 2005), pp. 155–72.
8. William Hogarth, *The Analysis of Beauty, with the Rejected Passages from the Manuscript Drafts and Autobiographical Notes*, edited with an introduction by Joseph Burke (Oxford: Clarendon Press, 1955), p. 220; John Ireland, *A Supplement to Hogarth Illustrated, Compiled From the Original Manuscripts*, 2nd edn (London: Messrs Boydell, 1804), pp. 195–6.
9. Charles Lamotte, *An Essay Upon Poetry and Painting, With Relation to the Sacred and Profane History* (London: F. Fayram, 1730), pp. 30–1.
10. Lord Kames, *Elements of Criticism*, 3 vols (Edinburgh: A. Kincaid and J. Bell, 1762), i. 117.
11. On tears in these versions of the tale, see Stephanie Trigg, 'Weeping like a Beaten Child: Figurative Language and the Emotions in Chaucer and Malory', in Holly Crocker and Glenn Burger (eds), *Affect, Feeling, Emotion: The Medieval Turn* (forthcoming).

12. John Dryden, *Fables Ancient and Modern; Translated into Verse from Homer, Ovid, Boccace, & Chaucer* (London: Jacob Tonson, 1700), p. 148; Ireland, *Supplement to Hogarth Illustrated*, pp. 189-208; Hinnant, 'Dryden and Hogarth's *Sigismunda*'.

13. John Nichols, *Biographical Anecdotes of William Hogarth*, 2nd edn, enlarged and corrected (London: J. Nichols, 1782), pp. 62-5; Paulson, *Hogarth*, pp. 226-8.

14. Nichols, *Biographical Anecdotes*, p. 68.

15. Ibid. 60-8; Ireland, *Supplement to Hogarth Illustrated*, p. 202; Paulson, *Hogarth*, pp. 226-33, 324; Pointon, 'A Woman Weeps'.

16. Ireland, *Supplement to Hogarth Illustrated*, p. 196; Hinnant, 'Dryden and Hogarth's *Sigismunda*', p. 471.

17. Nichols, *Biographical Anecdotes*, pp. 61-2; Pointon, 'A Woman Weeps', p. 165.

18. Hinnant, 'Dryden and Hogarth's *Sigismunda*', p. 460; Pointon, 'A Woman Weeps'.

19. See Ch. 2.

20. *The North Briton*, No. 17, 21 May 1762, p. 155; Paulson, *Hogarth*, p. 228.

21. Charles Churchill, *An Epistle to William Hogarth* (London: Printed for the Author, 1763), pp. 23-4.

22. *The Bruiser Triumphant* (London: *c*.1763), The British Museum, registration no. 1868,0808.4342, <http://www.britishmuseum.org>.

23. Ireland, *Supplement to Hogarth Illustrated*, p. 205.

24. Ibid. 209-19; Hogarth, *Autobiographical Notes*, in *The Analysis of Beauty*, p. 221.

25. For examples of this suspicion in relation to recent reality television and other cultural productions, see Ch. 20.

26. Marcia Pointon, for instance, writes, of Hogarth's *Sigismunda*, 'Pearls—in fluid and serpentine manner—seep out of the jewel-box, rhetorically instantiating tears and semen, the expenditure of precious bodily fluids in extremes of emotion'; Pointon, 'A Woman Weeps', p. 155. On Diderot's sexual interpretation of Greuze, see Emma Barker, 'Reading the Greuze Girl'.

27. Ireland, *Supplement to Hogarth Illustrated*, p. 206; Pointon, 'A Woman Weeps', p. 166.

28. Ireland, *Supplement to Hogarth Illustrated*, pp. 226-42; Bernd Krysmanski, 'We see a Ghost: Hogarth's Satire on Methodists and Connoisseurs', *Art Bulletin* 80 (1998): 292-310; Emma Major, *Madam Britannia: Women, Church, and Nation, 1712-1812* (Oxford: Oxford University Press, 2011), pp. 137-9; Misty G. Anderson, *Imagining Methodism in Eighteenth-Century Britain: Enthusiasm, Belief and the Borders of the Self* (Baltimore: Johns Hopkins University Press, 2012), pp. 150-70.

29. Psalm 56: 8 (King James Version). Krysmanski, 'We See a Ghost' (p. 300), speculates that this figure is a representation of the Swiss artist and enameller Theodore Gardelle, who brutally murdered his landlady and was executed in 1761.

30. Anderson, *Imagining Methodism*, p. 167.

31. Lavington quoted in Ireland, *Supplement to Hogarth Illustrated*, p. 231; see also: John Scott, *A Fine Picture of Enthusiasm, Chiefly Drawn by Dr John Scott, wherein the Danger of the Passions Leading in Religion is Strongly Described* (London: J. Noon, 1744), pp. 3-4.

32. Anderson, *Imagining Methodism*, p. 153.
33. *Memoirs of Samuel Foote Esq., With a Collection of his Genuine Bon-Mots, Anecdotes, Opinions, etc., and Three of his Dramatic Pieces*, ed. William Cooke, 2 vols (New York: Peter A. Mesier, 1806), ii. 229; see Anderson, *Imagining Methodism*, pp. 130, 151.
34. Ireland, *Supplement to Hogarth Illustrated*, pp. 196–7.
35. 'Fashionable World', *Morning Post* (London), 3 July 1807, p. 3.
36. 'Exhibition of Old Masters at The Royal Academy', *Pall Mall Gazette*, 4 Feb. 1870, p. 6; for a similarly positive appraisal, see also 'Hogarth at the National Gallery', *The Standard* (London), 25 Dec. 1880, p. 2.
37. 'The National Gallery', *The Standard* (London), 3 June 1879, p. 2.
38. Lionel Johnson, 'Eighteenth Century Vignettes', *The Academy*, 10 Dec. 1892, pp. 531–3 (p. 532).

Chapter 7. The Man of Feeling

1. Henry Mackenzie, *The Man of Feeling*, ed. with an introduction by Maureen Harkin (Peterborough, Ontario: Broadview Press, 2005); originally published anonymously in London in 1771.
2. Janet Todd, *Sensibility: An Introduction* (London: Methuen, 1986); John Mullan, *Sentiment and Sociability: The Language of Feeling in the Eighteenth Century* (Oxford: Clarendon Press, 1988); Anne Vincent-Buffault, *The History of Tears: Sensibility and Sentimentality in France* (Basingstoke: Macmillan, 1991); G. J. Barker-Benfield, *The Culture of Sensibility: Sex and Society in Eighteenth-Century Britain* (Chicago: University of Chicago Press, 1992); Markman Ellis, *The Politics of Sensibility: Race, Gender and Commerce in the Sentimental Novel* (Cambridge: Cambridge University Press, 1996); Paul Goring, *The Rhetoric of Sensibility in Eighteenth-Century Culture* (Cambridge: Cambridge University Press, 2005); Jonathan Lamb, *The Evolution of Sympathy in the Long Eighteenth Century* (London: Pickering and Chatto, 2009).
3. Emma Barker, 'Reading the Greuze Girl: The Daughter's Seduction', *Representations* 117 (2012): 86–119; Philip Shaw, *Suffering and Sentiment in Romantic Military Art* (Farnham: Ashgate, 2013).
4. Shaw dates the incident to the winter of 1786–7, while it seems that Adam Ferguson moved into Sciennes House in 1787. Shaw, *Suffering and Sentiment*, pp. 43–4; James Ballantine (ed.), *Chronicle of the Hundredth Birthday of Robert Burns* (Edinburgh: A. Fullarton, 1859), p. 427; Fania Oz-Salzberger, 'Ferguson, Adam (1723–1816)', *Oxford Dictionary of National Biography* (Oxford University Press, 2004; online edn, Oct. 2009), doi:10.1093/ref:odnb/9315; Clark McGinn, 'The Tears of Robert Burns', Electric Scotland, <http://www.electricscotland.com/familytree/frank/burns_lives96.htm>.
5. The 'heaven-taught ploughman' was a sobriquet affixed to Burns by Henry Mackenzie himself in an unsigned review in *The Lounger* in December 1786,

reprinted in Donald A. Low (ed.), *Robert Burns; The Critical Heritage* (London: Routledge and Kegan Paul, 1974), pp. 70–1. See also Robert Crawford, 'Robert Fergusson's Robert Burns', in Robert Crawford (ed.), *Robert Burns and Cultural Authority* (Edinburgh: Edinburgh University Press, 1996), pp. 1–22 (p. 2).

6. Quoted in Shaw, *Suffering and Sentiment*, pp. 43–4.
7. *The Works of Robert Burns; With Dr Currie's Memoir of the Poet, and an Essay on his Genius and Character by Professor Wilson*, 2 vols (Glasgow: Blackie and Son, 1853–4), i. clxvii; Shaw, *Suffering and Sentiment*, pp. 43–4.
8. Joseph Wright of Derby, *The Dead Soldier* (1789); see Shaw, *Suffering and Sentiment*, ch. 2 for a discussion of the painting and its context, and p. 100 n. 2 for information about the extant versions; see also Bernard Nicholson, *Joseph Wright of Derby: Painter of Light*, 2 vols (London: Routledge and Kegan Paul, 1968).
9. Letter from Hayley to his wife, 5 May 1789; *Memoirs of the Life and Writings of William Hayley, Esq.*, ed. John Johnson, 2 vols (London: Henry Colburn, 1823), i. 387; Shaw, *Suffering and Sentiment*, p. 79.
10. Barry produced two versions of this image, in 1774 and 1786–7 respectively; Sebastian Mitchell, *Visions of Britain, 1730–1830: Anglo-Scottish Writing and Representation* (Basingstoke: Palgrave Macmillan, 2013), pp. 146–7.
11. [Gilbert West], *A Canto of the Fairy Queen, Written by Spenser* (London: G. Hawkins, 1739), stanza 53, p. 11. On gender and manly tears in the early modern period more broadly, see Julie Ellison, *Cato's Tears and the Making of Anglo-American Emotion* (Chicago: University of Chicago Press, 1999); Philip Carter, 'Tears and the Man', in Sarah Knott and Barbara Taylor (eds), *Women, Gender and Enlightenment* (Basingstoke: Palgrave Macmillan, 2005), pp. 156–73; Jennifer C. Vaught, *Masculinity and Emotion in Early Modern English Literature* (Aldershot: Ashgate, 2008); Bernard Capp, ' "Jesus Wept" but Did the Englishman? Masculinity and Emotion in Early Modern England', *Past and Present* 224 (2014): 75–108.
12. *Man of Feeling*, ch. 20, pp. 70–1.
13. Ibid., ch. 35, p. 115. This passage was one of several quoted in disbelief in 1907 by Mary Howarth in 'Retrospective Review: "The Man of Feeling"–A Hero of Old-Fashioned Romance', *Gentleman's Magazine*, Jan.–June 1907, pp. 290–5; see Ch. 15.
14. John Mullan (*Sentiment and Sociability*, p. 123) writes that contemporary reviewers who admired the tearful responses to Mackenzie's novel were 'advocating a reaction which seems ludicrous now, and what was to seem odd by the 1790s'. Janet Todd (*Sensibility*, p. 3) contrasts the intellectually and emotionally complex responses elicited by tragedy with the tear-jerking techniques of sentimental novels, which 'seem ridiculous' after they fall out of fashion.
15. Harkin, 'Introduction', *Man of Feeling*, p. 10.
16. 'The Man of Feeling', *Monthly Review* 44 (May 1771): 418.
17. Louisa Stuart to Walter Scott, 4 Sept. 1826; *The Private Letter-Books of Sir Walter Scott*, ed. Wilfred Partington (London: Hodder and Stoughton, 1930), p. 273.

18. Robert Crawford, 'Burns, Robert (1759–1796)', *Oxford Dictionary of National Biography* (Oxford University Press, 2004; online edn, May 2011), doi:10.1093/ref:odnb/4093.

19. Ibid.

20. Letter to John Murdoch, 15 Jan. 1783; *The Letters of Robert Burns*, ed. J. de Lancey Ferguson, 2nd edn, ed. G. Ross Roy, 2 vols (Oxford: Clarendon Press, 1985), i. 17.

21. Denis Diderot, 'Éloge de Richardson' (1762), quoted in Colin Jones, *The Smile Revolution in Eighteenth-Century Paris* (Oxford: Oxford University Press, 2014), p. 64.

22. David Hume, 'The Stoic' (1742), in *David Hume: Selected Essays*, ed. with an introduction and notes by Stephen Copley and Andrew Edgar (Oxford: Oxford University Press, 1993), pp. 83–91.

23. See, for instance, the tears of gratitude of Old Edwards in *Man of Feeling*, ch. 34, pp. 104–12.

24. *The Lounger*, No. 61, 1 Apr. 1786, pp. 232–40. Burns wrote that this particular story had 'cost me more honest tears than any thing I have read of a long time'; letter to Mrs Dunlop, 10 Apr. 1790; *The Letters of Robert Burns, Chronologically Arranged from Dr Currie's Collection*, 2 vols (London: John Sharpe, 1819), i. 164.

25. Crawford, 'Burns'.

26. 'The Fornicator. A New Song', in *Burns: Poems and Songs*, ed. James Kinsley (London: Oxford University Press, 1969), pp. 79–80, lines 17–18; *The Lounger*, No. 61, p. 232.

27. *Man of Feeling*, chs 28–9, pp. 84–97.

28. [Jonas Hanway], *Thoughts on the Plan for a Magdalen-House for Repentant Prostitutes* (London: James Waugh, 1758), p. 30; quoted in Ellis, *Politics of Sensibility*, p. 173.

29. John Langhorne, *Sermons Preached Before the Honourable Society of Lincoln's Inn*, 3rd edn, 2 vols (London: T. Becket, 1773), pp. 219–20; Shaw, *Suffering and Sentiment*, pp. 59–60.

30. *The Life and Adventures of Bampfylde-Moore Carew, The Noted Devonshire Stroller and Dog-Stealer as Related by Himself* (Exon: Joseph Drew, 1745); Tim Hitchcock, 'Tricksters, Lords and Servants: Begging, Friendship and Masculinity in Eighteenth-Century England', in Laura Gowing, Michael Hunter, and Miri Rubin (eds), *Love, Friendship and Faith in Europe, 1300–1800* (Basingstoke: Palgrave Macmillan, 2005), pp. 177–96.

31. Ellis, *Politics of Sensibility*, p. 176; Ann Jessie van Sant, *Eighteenth-Century Sensibility and the Novel: The Senses in Social Context* (Cambridge: Cambridge University Press, 2004), pp. 32–5; Philip Rawlings, 'Dodd, William (1729–1777)', *Oxford Dictionary of National Biography* (Oxford University Press, 2004; online edn, Jan. 2008), doi:10.1093/ref:odnb/7744.

32. *Man of Feeling*, ch. 40, p. 121.

33. V. A. C. Gattrell, *The Hanging Tree: Execution and the English People 1770–1868* (Oxford: Oxford University Press, 1996), pp. 284–92.

34. All surviving published accounts are available online; see Clive Emsley, Tim Hitch-cock, and Robert Shoemaker, 'The Proceedings: Ordinary of Newgate's Accounts', *Old Bailey Proceedings Online*, <http://www.oldbaileyonline.org, version 7.0>.
35. As reported in *The General Advertiser*, 19 Aug. 1746. See also James Foster, *An Account of the Behaviour of the Late Earl of Kilmarnock, After his Sentence, and on the Day of his Execution* (London: J. Noon, 1746), p. 35; James Montagu, *The Old Bailey Chronicle, Containing a Circumstantial Account of the Lives, Trials, and Confessions of the Most Notorious Offenders*, 4 vols (London: S. Smith, 1788), iii. 5–6; Horace Bleackley, *The Hangmen of England: How They Hanged and Whom They Hanged* (London: Taylor and Francis, 1929), pp. 82–3.
36. Andrea McKenzie, 'Maclaine, James (1724–1750)', *Oxford Dictionary of National Biography* (Oxford University Press, 2004; online edn, May 2006), doi:10.1093/ref:odnb/17637.
37. All references to the *Ordinary of Newgate's Accounts* are to *Old Bailey Proceedings Online*, <http://www.oldbaileyonline.org> (version 7.0). *Ordinary of Newgate's Account*, 10 June 1685; see also 13 June 1690.
38. *Ordinary of Newgate's Account*, 8 Feb. 1721.
39. John Stevens, *Christ Made Sin for his People, and They Made the Righteousness of God in Him: Explained in a Sermon Occasioned by the Remarkable Conversion and Repentance of Robert Tilling* (London: George Keith, 1760), pp. 30–1.
40. *Ordinary of Newgate's Account*, 28 Apr. 1760; the biblical quotation is from Ezekiel 33: 11 (King James Version).
41. *Ordinary of Newgate's Account*, 15 June 1763.
42. John Vilette, *A Genuine Account of the Behaviour and Dying Words of Willam Dodd LLD*, 2nd edn (London: Printed for the Author, 1777); a high-society fencing master, Henry Angelo, recorded his recollection of the event, fifty years after it happened, in *Reminiscences of Henry Angelo*, 2 vols (London: Henry Colburn, 1828–30), i. 456; see also Gatrell, *Hanging Tree*, pp. 292–4.
43. Todd, *Sensibility*, p. 3; although the same work does go on to give a brief explanation of the roots of the culture of sensibility in seventeenth-century religious philosophy (pp. 21–3).
44. Genesis 45: 14 (King James Version). In his journal entry for 20 Feb. 1763, Boswell wrote, 'This forenoon I read the history of Joseph and his brethren, which melted my heart and drew tears from my eyes. It is simply and beautifully told in the Sacred Writings. It is a strange thing that the Bible is so little read. I am reading it regularly at present'; Frederick A. Pottle (ed.), *Boswell's London Journal, 1762–1763* (London: Futura, 1982), p. 211; Reading Experience Database (record ID 24094), <http://www.open.ac.uk/arts/reading/UK>. On Boswell as a man of feeling, see van Sant, *Eighteenth-Century Sensibility*, pp. 54–9; Philip Carter, *Men and the Emergence of Polite Society: Britain 1660–1800* (Harlow: Longman, 2000), especially pp. 183–97.
45. Romans 12: 15, Revelation 7: 17; for more on the biblical resonances of Mack-enzie's *Man of Feeling*, and its Christian context, see R. S. Crane, 'Suggestions

Toward a Genealogy of the "Man of Feeling"', *ELH* 1 (1934): 205–30; Donald Greene, 'Latitudinarianism and Sensibility: The Genealogy of the "Man of Feeling" Reconsidered', *Modern Philology* 75 (1977): 159–83; Frans De Bruyn, 'Latitudinarianism and its Importance as a Precursor to Sensibility', *Journal of English and Germanic Philology* 80 (1981): 349–68; Barker-Benfield, *Culture of Sensibility*, pp. 65–77; Jeremy Gregory, '*Homo Religiosus*: Masculinity and Religion in the Long Eighteenth Century', in Tim Hitchcock and Michèle Cohen (eds), *English Masculinities 1660–1800* (London: Longman, 1999), pp. 85–110; Goring, *Rhetoric of Sensibility*, pp. 70–90; William Van Reyk, 'Christian Ideals of Manliness in the Eighteenth and Early Nineteenth Centuries', *Historical Journal* 52 (2009): 1053–73; Thomas Dixon, 'Enthusiasm Delineated: Weeping as a Religious Activity in Eighteenth-Century Britain', *Litteraria Pragensia* 22 (2012): 59–81.

46. Dixon, 'Enthusiasm Delineated'.
47. Marjory E. Lange, *Telling Tears in the English Renaissance* (Leiden: Brill, 1996), p. 173.
48. Henry Mackenzie, 'The Effects of Religion on Minds of Sensibility: The Story of La Roche', first published in *The Mirror*, 19 June 1779; included in appendix C of Mackenzie, *Man of Feeling*, ed. Harkin, pp. 179–90.
49. Philip Doddridge, *Meditations on the Tears of Jesus over the Grave of Lazarus: A Funeral Sermon Preached at St Alban's, 16 December 1750, on Occasion of the Much Lamented Death of the Reverend Samuel Clark D.D.* (London: James Waugh, 1751).
50. Vicesimus Knox, *Christian Philosophy, or An Attempt to Display the Evidence and Excellence of Revealed Religion*, 2 vols (London: C. Dilly, 1795), ii. 363.
51. 'John xi.35. "Jesus Wept". On Christian Compassion. Preached before his Present Majesty at St James's Chapel, 26 September 1762', in *The Works of William Mason*, 4 vols (London: T. Cadell and W. Davies, 1811), iv. 55–67 (p. 57).

Chapter 8. The French Revolution

1. See Ch. 2.
2. See Chs 13 and 14.
3. Thomas Rowlandson, 'The Contrast 1792. British Liberty. French liberty. Which is best?' (London: H. Humphrey, 1792); British Museum, registration no. J.4.50.
4. On the impact of the French Revolution on British political debates, see Marilyn Butler (ed.), *Burke, Paine, Godwin, and the Revolution Controversy* (Cambridge: Cambridge University Press, 1984); H. T. Dickinson (ed.), *Britain and the French Revolution, 1789–1815* (Basingstoke: Macmillan, 1989); Gregory Claeys, 'The French Revolution Debate and British Political Thought', *History of Political Thought* 11 (1990): 59–80; Mark Philp (ed.), *The French Revolution and British Popular Politics* (Cambridge: Cambridge University Press, 1991); Gareth Stedman Jones, *An End to Poverty? A Historical Debate* (London: Profile, 2004).

5. For an introductory overview of the causes and course of the French Revolution, see William Doyle, *The French Revolution: A Very Short Introduction* (Oxford: Oxford University Press, 2001).

6. G. J. Barker-Benfield, *The Culture of Sensibility: Sex and Society in Eighteenth-Century Britain* (Chicago: University of Chicago Press, 1992), ch. 7; Markman Ellis, *The Politics of Sensibility: Race, Gender and Commerce in the Sentimental Novel* (Cambridge: Cambridge University Press, 1996), ch. 6.

7. See below, and also Daniel O'Quinn, 'Fox's Tears: The Staging of Liquid Politics', in Alexander Dick and Angela Esterhammer (eds), *Spheres of Action: Speech and Performance in Romantic Culture* (Toronto: University of Toronto Press, 2009), pp. 194–221 (p. 210).

8. Anne Vincent-Buffault, *The History of Tears: Sensibility and Sentimentality in France* (Basingstoke: Macmillan, 1991); Nicholas Paige, 'Rousseau's Readers Revisited: The Aesthetics of *La Nouvelle Héloïse*', *Eighteenth-Century Studies* 42 (2008): 131–54; Colin Jones, *The Smile Revolution in Eighteenth-Century Paris* (Oxford: Oxford University Press, 2014), ch. 2.

9. Quoted in Irving Babbitt, *Rousseau and Romanticism*, with a new introduction by Claes G. Ryn (New Brunswick, NJ: Transaction, 1991), p. 136; original publication 1919.

10. Thomas Carlyle, *The French Revolution: A History* (1837), ch. 3.6.I, in *The Works of Thomas Carlyle*, ed. Henry Duff Traill, 30 vols (London: Chapman and Hall, 1896–9), iv. 248.

11. Henry Mackenzie, *The Man of Feeling*, ed. Henry Morley (London: Cassell and Co., 1886), pp. iv–v.

12. [Laurence Sterne], *A Sentimental Journey Through France and Italy, by Mr Yorick*, 2 vols (London: T. Becket and P. A. De Hondt, 1768), i. 123–8. Lord Melbourne alluded to this scene when explaining the eighteenth-century culture of sensibility to Queen Victoria in the 1830s; see Ch. 11.

13. Babbitt, *Rousseau and Romanticism*, p. 144.

14. See Ch. 7.

15. *Reflections on the Revolution in France* (1790), in Edmund Burke, *Revolutionary Writings*, ed. Iain Hampsher-Monk (Cambridge: Cambridge University Press, 2014), pp. 77–8.

16. *The Correspondence of Edmund Burke, vi: July 1789–December 1791*, ed. Alfred Cobban and Robert A. Smith (Cambridge: Cambridge University Press, 1967), pp. 86–7, 91.

17. Mary Wollstonecraft, *A Vindication of the Rights of Men, and A Vindication of the Rights of Woman*, ed. Sylvana Tomaselli (Cambridge: Cambridge University Press, 1995), p. 62; original publication 1790.

18. Thomas Paine, *The Rights of Man, Part I*, in *Political Writings*, ed. Bruce Kuklick (Cambridge: Cambridge University Press, 2000), pp. 70–1, 72; original publication 1791.

19. Isaac Cruikshank, *A New French Bussing Match* (London: S. W. Fores, 16 July 1790); British Museum, registration no. 1868,0808.6223.
20. 'Parliamentary Intelligence', *Lloyd's Evening Post*, 6–9 May 1791, number 5282, p. 436. For several other reports and responses, see O'Quinn, 'Fox's Tears'.
21. William Dent, *Charley Boy Crying for the Loss of his Political Father* (London: W. Dent, 12 May 1791); British Museum, registration no. 1990,1109.89.
22. Isaac Cruikshank, *The Wrangling Friends, or Opposition in Disorder* (London: S. W. Fores, 1791); British Museum, registration no. 1868,0808.6049.
23. 'How to Cry!', *St James's Chronicle or the British Evening Post*, 10–12 May 1791, p. 4; O'Quinn, 'Fox's Tears', p. 210.
24. Major John Cartwright, *A Letter to the Duke of Newcastle, with some Remarks Touching the French Revolution* (London: J. S. Jordan, 1792), pp. 81–2.
25. Isaac Cruikshank, *The Gallant Nellson [sic] Bringing Home Two Uncommon Fierce French Crocodiles from the Nile* (London: S. W. Fores, 7 Oct. 1798); British Museum, registration no. 1867,0511.64.
26. G. Canning, J. H. Frere, G. Ellis, et al., *Poetry of the Anti-Jacobin* (London: J. Wright, 1799), p. 225; James Gillray, *New Morality;–or–The promis'd Installment of the High-Priest of the Theophilanthropes, with the Homage of Leviathan and his Suite* (London: John Wright for the Anti-Jacobin Review, 1 Aug. 1798). See also Ellis, *Politics of Sensibility*, pp. 192–7; Emma Barker, 'Reading the Greuze Girl: The Daughter's Seduction', *Representations* 117 (2012): 86–119.
27. Barker-Benfield, *Culture of Sensibility*, especially chs 1 and 4; Ellis, *Politics of Sensibility*, chs 1 and 6; Goring, *Rhetoric of Sensibility*, ch. 1.
28. *The Diary and Letters of Madame D'Arblay* [Fanny Burney], ed. by her niece [Charlotte Barrett], 7 vols (London: Henry Colburn, 1842–6), i. 218–22; Barker-Benfield, *Culture of Sensibility*, p. 346; Scott Paul Gordon, *The Power of the Passive Self in English Literature, 1640–1770* (Cambridge: Cambridge University Press, 2002), p. 212.
29. Mr Cresswick [Mary Wollstonecraft], *The Female Reader* (London: J. Johnson, 1789); see also Vivien Jones, 'Mary Wollstonecraft and the Literature of Advice and Instruction', in Claudia L. Johnson (ed.), *The Cambridge Companion to Mary Wollstonecraft* (Cambridge: Cambridge University Press, 2002), pp. 119–40. On Burns, see Ch. 7.
30. Mary Wollstonecraft, *A Vindication of the Rights of Woman* (1792), chs 2 and 3, in *A Vindication of the Rights of Men, and A Vindication of the Rights of Woman*, ed. Sylvana Tomaselli (Cambridge: Cambridge University Press, 1995), pp. 87–125. For an authoritative and wide-ranging analysis of Wollstonecraft's philosophical, religious, and political ideas, see Barbara Taylor, *Mary Wollstonecraft and the Feminist Imagination* (Cambridge: Cambridge University Press, 2003).
31. Wollstonecraft, *Vindication*, ch. 12, p. 269.
32. Coleridge wrote this in 1796 in connection with the slave trade and sugar production; quoted in Janet Todd, *Sensibility: An Introduction* (London: Methuen, 1986), p. 141; see also Ellis, *Politics of Sensibility*, ch. 3.

NOTES TO PP. 118-126

33. On Wollstonecraft's life and career, see Janet Todd, *Mary Wollstonecraft: A Revolutionary Life* (London: Weidenfeld and Nicolson, 2000); Taylor, *Feminist Imagination*; Barbara Taylor, 'Wollstonecraft, Mary (1759–1797)', *Oxford Dictionary of National Biography* (Oxford University Press, 2004; online edn, Sept. 2014), doi:10.1093/ref:odnb/10893.

34. Mary Wollstonecraft to Joseph Johnson, Paris, 26 Dec. 1792, in *The Collected Letters of Mary Wollstonecraft*, ed. Janet Todd (London: Allen Lane, 2003), pp. 216–17. See also Tom Furniss, 'Mary Wollstonecraft's French Revolution', in Claudia L. Johnson (ed.), *The Cambridge Companion to Mary Wollstonecraft* (Cambridge: Cambridge University Press, 2002), pp. 59–81.

35. See Ch. 10.

36. William Wordsworth, 'Sonnet on seeing Miss Helen Maria Williams Weep at a Tale of Distress', *European Magazine* 40 (1787): 202.

37. Helen Maria Williams, *Letters Written in France*, ed. Neil Fraistat and Susan S. Lanser (Peterborough, Ontario: Broadview Press, 2001), pp. 67, 69.

38. Helen Maria Williams, *Letters from France: Containing a Great Variety of Original Information Concerning the Most Important Events that have Occurred in that Country*, 2 vols (Dublin: J. Chambers, 1794), i. 181. An earlier edition of this publication was reviewed in the *English Review* 20 (1792): 57–60; and in the *Monthly Review* 9 (1792): 93–8. Both reviews quoted this particular passage, the former noting (p. 59) that it demonstrated the 'enthusiasm of our fair writer'.

39. Adam Smith, *The Theory of Moral Sentiments* (Edinburgh: A. Kincaid and J. Bell, 1759), part V, section II, pp. 404–5. A similar contrast was made in a novel of the 1790s which suggested that, according to conventional wisdom, Frenchmen were volatile and romantic while Englishmen were stoical and phlegmatic, but that recently the nations had exchanged characters: Charlotte Smith, *The Banished Man: A Novel*, 4 vols (London: T. Cadell, Jun. and W. Davies, 1794), ii. 81. The English were variously considered plain-speaking, taciturn, reserved, and unfriendly in earlier centuries, but the emphasis on active emotional repression only gradually emerged after the 1790s, and especially later in the nineteenth century. See also Paul Langford, *Englishness Identified: Manners and Character 1650–1850* (Oxford: Oxford University Press, 2000); Peter Mandler, *The English National Character: The History of an Idea from Edmund Burke to Tony Blair* (New Haven: Yale University Press, 2006); Victoria E. Thompson, 'An Alarming Lack of Feeling: Urban Travel, Emotions, and British National Character in Post-Revolutionary Paris', *Urban History Review* 42 (2014): 8–17; and Chs 3 and 14.

Chapter 9. The Sanity of George III

1. For tabloid reports of Diana's tears, both before and during her marriage to Prince Charles, see Liz Gill and Danny McGrory, 'My Hopes by Lady Di', *Daily Express*, 27 July 1981, pp. 1, 3; James Whitaker, 'Riddle of Di's Tears: She Breaks Down in Top Restaurant', *Daily Mirror*, 9 Apr. 1988, p. 3; Robert Jobson, 'Diana

Quits Royal Stage', *Daily Express*, 4 Dec. 1993, pp. 1–2; on the public tears shed in reaction to Diana's death, see Ch. 20.

2. Ida Macalpine and Richard Hunter, *George III and the Mad-Business* (London: Allen Lane, 1969), pp. 52–5; the original sources include the diaries of Queen Charlotte's lady-in-waiting, the novelist Fanny Burney, later Madame D'Arblay, and the King's Equerry, Robert Fulke Greville.

3. Macalpine and Hunter, *George III*, especially chs 3 and 4; Roy Porter, *A Social History of Madness: Stories of the Insane* (London: Phoenix, 1996), ch. 3; Alan Bennett, *The Madness of George III* (London: Faber, 1992); Nicholas Hynter (dir.), *The Madness of King George* (Samuel Goldwyn and Channel Four Films, 1994).

4. On the politics of sentiment and emotion, both in the eighteenth century and the late twentieth, see Julie Ellison, *Cato's Tears and the Making of Anglo-American Emotion* (Chicago: University of Chicago Press, 1999).

5. Macalpine and Hunter, *George III*, pp. 75–6.

6. On Queen Victoria's reaction to a performance of *King Lear* with William Macready in the title role in 1839, see Ch. 11.

7. 'The Examination of the King's Physicians', *The Times*, 16 Jan. 1789, especially pp. 3–4.

8. On the tears of Charles James Fox and Edmund Burke, see Ch. 8.

9. Thomas Erskine had defended radical revolutionary sympathizers charged with sedition in the 1790s, including Thomas Paine and Thomas Hardy, and was Lord Chancellor from to 1807; David Lemmings, 'Erskine, Thomas, First Baron Erskine (1750–1823)', *Oxford Dictionary of National Biography* (Oxford University Press, 2004; online edn, Jan. 2008), doi:10.1093/ref:odnb/8873.

10. 'Trial of James Hadfield', *Morning Chronicle* (London), 27 June 1800, p. 1; on the place of the Hadfield case in the histories of psychiatry and the criminal law, see Richard Moran, 'The Origin of Insanity as a Special Verdict: The Trial for Treason of James Hadfield (1800)', *Law and Society Review* 19 (1985): 487–519; Joel Peter Eigen, *Witnessing Insanity: Madness and Mad-doctors in the English Court* (New Haven: Yale University Press, 1995), ch. 2; Arlie Loughnan, *Manifest Madness: Mental Incapacity in the Criminal Law* (Oxford: Oxford University Press, 2012), ch. 5.

11. On 'excrementitious humours', see Ch. 3. On 'emotional incontinence' and 'expression of emotion', see Ch. 13.

12. Thomas Dixon, *From Passions to Emotions: The Creation of a Secular Psychological Category* (Cambridge: Cambridge University Press, 2003); Thomas Dixon, 'Revolting Passions', *Modern Theology* 27 (2011): 298–312; Thomas Dixon, ' "Emotion": The History of a Keyword in Crisis', *Emotion Review* 4 (2012): 338–44.

13. I have written at greater length about the medical meanings of 'passions' and 'affections' in this period in Thomas Dixon, 'Patients and Passions: Languages of Medicine and Emotion, 1790–1850', in Fay Bound Alberti (ed.), *Medicine, Emotion, and Disease, 1750–1950* (Basingstoke: Palgrave, 2006), pp. 22–52; on

medical dimensions of eighteenth-century sensibility, see also John Mullan, *Sentiment and Sociability* (Oxford: Clarendon Press, 1988), ch. 5.

14. Cogan, who received his MD from Leyden for a dissertation on the passions, wrote three books on the subject, which were widely cited in the first half of the nineteenth century: Thomas Cogan, *An Ethical Treatise on the Passions* (Bath: Hazard and Binns, 1807); *A Philosophical Treatise on the Passions* (Bath: S. Hazard, 1802); *Theological Disquisitions; or an Enquiry into those Principles of Religion, which are Most Influential in Directing and Regulating the Passions and Affections of the Mind* (Bath: Hazard and Binns, 1812); the quotation is from Cogan, *A Philosophical Treatise*, pp. 7–8.

15. See Ch. 3.

16. Thomas Reid, *Essays on the Active Powers of Man* (Edinburgh: Bell, 1788), p. 191.

17. Ludmilla Jordanova, 'The Art and Science of Seeing in Medicine: Physiognomy 1780–1820', in William Bynum and Roy Porter (eds), *Medicine and the Five Senses* (Cambridge: Cambridge University Press, 1993), pp. 122–33; John Cule, 'The Enigma of Facial Expression: Medical Interest in Metoposcopy', *Journal of the History of Medicine and Allied Sciences* 48 (1993): 302–19; Lucy Hartley, *Physiognomy and the Meaning of Expression* (Cambridge: Cambridge University Press, 2001), ch. 2. On the relationship between Bell and Darwin, see Dixon, *From Passions to Emotions*, ch. 5; and Ch. 13 in this volume.

18. See Ch. 7.

19. L. S. Jacyna, 'Bell, Sir Charles (1774–1842)', *Oxford Dictionary of National Biography* (Oxford University Press, 2004; online edn, Jan. 2008), doi:10.1093/ref:odnb/1999; Philip Shaw, *Suffering and Sentiment in Romantic Military Art* (Farnham: Ashgate, 2013), pp. 184–207.

20. Shaw, *Suffering and Sentiment*, pp. 190, 194.

21. Charles Bell, *The Anatomy and Philosophy of Expression as Connected with the Fine Arts*, 3rd edn (London: John Murray, 1844), pp. 148–9.

22. Ibid. 150; on Hogarth's *Sigismunda*, see Ch. 6.

23. Bell, *Expression*, p. 150n.

24. Timothy Webb, 'Tears: An Introduction', *Litteraria Pragensia: Studies in Literature and Culture* 22 (2012): 1–25 (pp. 14–15); Timothy Webb, 'Tears: An Anthology', *Litteraria Pragensia: Studies in Literature and Culture* 22 (2012): 26–45 (pp. 28, 33–5); Henry Power, 'Homeric Tears and Eighteenth-Century Weepers', *Litteraria Pragensia: Studies in Literature and Culture* 22 (2012): 46–58 (p. 48); *The Iliad of Homer*, trans. Alexander Pope, 6 vols (London: W. Bowyer, 1715–20), v. 1362; Robert Steele (ed.), *Medieval Lore: An Epitome of the Science, Geography, Animal and Plant Folklore and Myth of the Middle Age* (London: Elliot Stock, 1893), p. 125; Albert the Great, *Man and the Beasts (De Animalibus, Books 22–26)*, ed. and trans. James J. Scanlan (New York: Medieval and Renaissance Texts, 1987); Monsieur de Blainville, *Travels through Holland, Germany, Switzerland and Italy*, 3 vols (London: J. Johnson and B. Davenport, 1767), i. 257–8; Thomas Dixon, 'Emotional Animals No. 1: A Weeping Horse in Augsburg, 1705', History

of Emotions Blog, 2 June 2011, <https://emotionsblog.history.qmul.ac.uk/2011/
06/emotional-animals-no-1-2>; on St Francis and his donkey, see Ch. 1.

25. William Shakespeare, *As You Like It*, ed. Juliet Dusinberre (London: Arden
Shakespeare, 2006), 2.1.36–43, p. 193; Peter Ackroyd, *Albion: The Origins of
the English Imagination* (London: Vintage, 2004), p. 6; Todd A. Borlik, *Ecocriti-
cism and Early Modern English Literature: Green Pastures* (New York: Routledge,
2011), pp. 180–5.

26. Alexandre de Pontaymeri, *A Woman's Worth, Defended Against All the Men in
the World* (London: John Wolfe, 1599), p. 41; Edward Topsell, *The History of
Four-Footed Beasts and Serpents* (London: E. Cotes, 1658), p. 578.

27. Laurent Joubert, *Traité du ris* (1579); Marjory E. Lange, *Telling Tears in the
English Renaissance* (Leiden: Brill, 1996), pp. 27, 31; Matthew Steggle, *Laughing
and Weeping in Early Modern Theatres* (Aldershot: Ashgate, 2007), p. 16.

28. Peter Harrison, 'Descartes on Animals', *Philosophical Quarterly* 42 (1992):
219–27.

29. Thomas Willis, *Two Discourses Concerning the Soul of Brutes*, trans. S. Pordage
(London: Thomas Dring, 1683), p. 81.

30. James Parsons, *Human Physiognomy Explain'd* (London: C. Davis, 1747),
pp. 78–82; [Peter Shaw], *Man: A Paper for Ennobling the Species*, no. 43, 22
Oct. 1755; for attribution to Peter Shaw MD, see *Catalogue of a Collection of
Early Newspapers and Essayists, Formed by the Late John Thomas Hope and
Presented to the Bodleian Library by the Late Rev. Frederick William Hope*
(Oxford: Clarendon Press, 1865), p. 83; on Shaw's career, see Jan Golinski,
'Shaw, Peter (1694–1763)', *Oxford Dictionary of National Biography* (Oxford
University Press, online edn, 2004), doi:10.1093/ref:odnb/25264; John Gregory,
*A Comparative View of the State and Faculties of Man with Those of the Animal
World*, 3rd edn (London: J. Dodsley, 1766), p. 11.

31. See Ch. 13.

32. *The Journal of James Yonge (1647–1721), Plymouth Surgeon*, ed. F. N. L. Poynter
(London: Longmans, Green & Co., 1963), p. 86; I am grateful to Dr Joanne
McEwan and the late Professor Philippa Maddern for drawing my attention to
this source.

33. 'The Value of Tears in the Progress of the Diseases of Children', *British Mothers'
Magazine* (1 Sept. 1849): 206. The author and title of the much-cited French
treatise were never named, but the most likely candidate for the original
dissertation is a work entitled *Considérations générales sur les larmes et les pleurs*,
presented to the Paris medical faculty by one P. H. Prévencher in May 1818.
This dissertation, in turn, seems to rely very heavily (in some cases, word for
word) on a dissertation submitted to the Paris faculty on the same subject by
another medical student in 1812; Thomas Dixon, 'Never Repress your Tears',
Wellcome History (Spring 2012): 9–10. On other French approaches to tears in
this period, see Anne Vincent-Buffault, *The History of Tears: Sensibility and
Sentimentality in France* (Basingstoke: Macmillan, 1991); Marco Menin,

'"Who Will Write the History of Tears?" History of Ideas and History of Emotions from Eighteenth-Century France to the Present', *History of European Ideas* 40 (2014): 516–32.

34. Hugh Tours, *The Life and Letters of Emma Hamilton* (London: Victor Gollancz, 1963), pp. 219–21; Tom Pocock, 'Hamilton, Emma, Lady Hamilton (bap. 1765, d. 1815)', *Oxford Dictionary of National Biography* (Oxford University Press, 2004; online edn, Oct. 2007), doi:10.1093/ref:odnb/12063. James Gillray, *The Death of Admiral Lord Nelson in the Moment of Victory* (London: H. Humphrey, 1805); National Maritime Museum, Greenwich, Object ID PAF3866,<http://collections.rmg.co.uk>.

35. On the mourning of Diana, see Ch. 20.

36. Terry Coleman, *The Nelson Touch: The Life and Legend of Horatio Nelson* (Oxford: Oxford University Press, 2002), pp. 317, 351.

37. Timothy Jenks, 'Contesting the Hero: The Funeral of Admiral Lord Nelson', *Journal of British Studies* 39 (2000): 422–53; Tom Pocock (ed.), *Trafalgar: An Eyewitness History* (London: Penguin, 2005), pp. 206–8.

38. 'Addenda to the Biographical Memoir of the Late Right Honourable Horatio Lord Viscount Nelson', *Naval Chronicle* 15 (1806): 37–52 (p. 52).

39. Pocock, *Trafalgar*, pp. 207–8.

40. Anon., 'Weeping', *The Spirit of the Public Journals for 1801: Being an Impartial Selection of the Most Exquisite Essays and Jeux d'Esprits, Principally Prose, that Appear in the Newspapers and Other Publications, Volume 5* (London: James Ridgway, 1802), pp. 136–8. The piece had appeared in several newspapers, including *Jackson's Oxford Journal*, 18 July 1801; and *The Morning Post and Gazetteer*, 21 July 1801.

41. William Godwin, *Fleetwood*, ed. Gary Handwerk and A. A. Markley (Peterborough, Ontario: Broadview Press, 2001), ch. 7, p. 111; original publication 1805; on Sophy Streatfield, see Ch. 8 in this volume.

42. Letter to Walter Scott dated 4 Sept. 1826; *The Private Letter-Books of Sir Walter Scott*, ed. Wilfred Partington (London: Hodder and Stoughton, 1930), pp. 272–3; this is discussed also by Maureen Harkin in her introduction to Henry Mackenzie, *The Man of Feeling* (Peterborough, Onatrio: Broadview Press, 2005), pp. 19–20; and in Ildiko Csengei, '"I Will Not Weep": Reading through the Tears of Henry Mackenzie's *Man of Feeling*', *Modern Language Review* 103 (2008): 952–68 (p. 952).

Chapter 10. Strange Blessing on the Nation

1. 'Royal Procession from Kensington to St James's', *The Standard* (London), 22 June 1837, p. 3.

2. 'Court Circular', *The Times*, 22 June 1837, p. 3.

3. Philip Kelley and Ronald Hudson (eds), *The Brownings' Correspondence*, iii: *January 1832–December 1837* (Winfield: Wedgestone Press, 1985), pp. 261–3.

4. 'The Young Queen' and 'Victoria's Tears', in *The Poetical Works of Elizabeth Barrett Browning* (London: Henry Frowde, 1904), pp. 315–16; original publication Elizabeth B. Barrett, *The Seraphim, and Other Poems* (London: Saunders and Otley, 1838), pp. 323–31. On tears in Browning's poetry, see Dorothy Mermin, *Elizabeth Barrett Browning: The Origins of a New Poetry* (Chicago: University of Chicago Press, 1989), pp. 68–9; and Claire Knowles, *Sensibility and Female Poetic Tradition, 1780–1860: The Legacy of Charlotte Smith* (Farnham: Ashgate, 2009), pp. 143–5.

5. On the Romantics' rethinking and reworking of eighteenth-century ideas about enthusiasm, sensibility, and emotion see Jon Mee, *Romanticism, Enthusiasm, and Regulation: Poetics and the Policing of Culture in the Romantic Period* (Oxford: Oxford University Press, 2003); Andrew M. Stauffer, *Anger, Revolution, and Romanticism* (Cambridge: Cambridge University Press, 2005); Joel Shaflak and Richard C. Sha (eds), *Romanticism and the Emotions* (Cambridge: Cambridge University Press, 2014).

6. Caspar David Friedrich, *Wanderer above the Sea of Fog* (1818), Kunsthalle, Hamburg.

7. Dorothy Wordsworth noted in her journal on 2 Feb. 1802, 'After tea I read aloud the eleventh book of Paradise Lost. We were much impressed, and also melted into tears'; *Home at Grasmere: Extracts from the Journal of Dorothy Wordsworth and from the Poems of William Wordsworth* (London: Penguin, 1986), p. 137. For an analysis of Wordsworth's 'Ode: Intimations of Immortality', first published in 1807, see Marjorie Levinson, *Wordsworth's Great Period Poems* (Cambridge: Cambridge University Press, 1986), ch. 3. On Helen Maria Williams, see Ch. 8.

8. See Ch. 8.

9. 'The Tear' (1806), *The Poetical Works of Lord Byron, Complete in One Volume* (London: John Murray, 1847), pp. 399–400.

10. Lord Byron to Mr Murray, 12 Aug. 1819, *The Life, Letters and Journals of Lord Byron* (London: John Murray, 1866), p. 404.

11. On Mary Wollstonecraft, see Ch. 8.

12. Entries for 2 Oct. 1822 and 15 Dec. 1823, *The Journals of Mary Shelley 1814–1844*, ed. Paula R. Feldman and Diana Scott-Kilvert (Baltimore: Johns Hopkins University Press, 1995), pp. 429, 469; see also Mary Shelley's 'Journal of Sorrow', Shelley's Ghost: Reshaping the Image of a Literary Family, Bodleian Libraries and New York Public Library, 2010, <http://shelleysghost.bodleian.ox.ac.uk/journal-of-sorrow>.

13. 'Tears' (1844) and 'Grief' (1844), in *Poetical Works*, p. 330; original publication, Elizabeth Barrett, *Poems*, 2 vols (London: Edward Moxon, 1844), pp. 128–9. On Barrett Browning's rejection of the culture of sensibility, see Knowles, *Sensibility and Female Poetic Tradition*, ch. 5.

14. James Smetham, *Thoughts Too Deep for Tears* (1844), Ashmolean Museum, Oxford; WA1947.314, <http://www.ashmolean.org>.

15. See Introduction.

16. 'The Grey Monk' (c.1803), in *The Complete Prose and Poetry of William Blake*, newly revised edn, ed. David V. Erdman, with commentary by Harold Bloom (Berkeley and Los Angeles: University of California Press, 2008), pp. 489–90; John Beer, 'Influence and Independence in Blake', in Michael Phillips (ed.), *Interpreting Blake* (Cambridge: Cambridge University Press, 1978), pp. 196–261 (especially pp. 220–2); Robert N. Essick, 'Blake, William (1757–1827)', *Oxford Dictionary of National Biography* (Oxford University Press, 2004; online edn, Oct. 2005), doi:10.1093/ref:odnb/2585; Steven Goldsmith, 'William Blake and the Future of Enthusiasm', *Nineteenth-Century Literature* 63 (2009): 439–60; Paul Miner, 'Blake's Enemies of Art', *Notes and Queries* 58 (2011): 537–40. For more on the cultural and political context of Blake and his work, see Jon Mee, *Dangerous Enthusiasm: William Blake and the Culture of Radicalism in the 1790s* (Oxford: Clarendon Press, 1994).
17. On this cognitive, neo-Stoic view of the emotions in philosophy, see Jerome Neu, *A Tear is an Intellectual Thing: The Meaning of Emotions* (Oxford: Oxford University Press, 2000); Martha C. Nussbaum, *Upheavals of Thought: The Intelligence of Emotions* (Cambridge: Cambridge University Press, 2001); Robert C. Solomon, *Not Passion's Slave: Emotions and Choice* (Oxford: Oxford University Press, 2003).
18. [Peter Shaw], *Man: A Paper for Ennobling the Species*, no. 43, 22 Oct. 1755, pp. 1–2; for attribution to Peter Shaw MD, see *Catalogue of a Collection of Early Newspapers and Essayists, Formed by the Late John Thomas Hope and Presented to the Bodleian Library by the Late Rev. Frederick William Hope* (Oxford: Clarendon Press, 1865), p. 83; on Shaw's career, see Jan Golinski, 'Shaw, Peter (1694–1763)', *Oxford Dictionary of National Biography* (Oxford University Press, online edn, 2004), doi:10.1093/ref:odnb/25264.
19. Susan Hoecker-Drysdale, *Harriet Martineau, First Woman Sociologist* (New York: Berg, 1992); Elaine Freedgood, 'Banishing Panic: Harriet Martineau and the Popularization of Political Economy', *Victorian Studies* 39 (1995): 33–53; Caroline Roberts. *The Woman and the Hour: Harriet Martineau and Victorian Ideologies* (Buffalo, NY: University of Toronto Press, 2002).
20. Harriet Martineau, *Ella of Garveloch: A Tale* (London: Charles Fox, 1832); Harriet Martineau, *Autobiography, With Memorials by Maria Weston*, 3 vols (London: Smith, Elder, 1877), ii. 118–19.
21. Martineau, *Autobiography*, ii. 119.
22. Ibid. 124–8; on Martineau's observations of the behaviour of Queen Victoria and her party, attending a performance of *King Lear* in 1839, see Ch. 11.
23. On her childhood doubts, see Martineau, *Autobiography*, i. 39–44; on her later atheism, see Roberts, *The Woman and the Hour*, ch. 7.
24. On the impact of Comte's philosophy on British culture and religion in the Victorian period, see Thomas Dixon, *The Invention of Altruism: Making Moral Meanings in Victorian Britain* (Oxford: Oxford University Press for the British Academy, 2008), ch. 2; on its significance to Martineau, see Susan Hoecker-

Drysdale, 'Harriet Martineau and the Positivism of Auguste Comte', in Michael R. Hill and Susan Hoecker-Drysdale (eds), *Harriet Martineau: Theoretical and Methodological Perspectives* (New York: Routledge, 2001), pp. 169–89.

25. Martineau, *Autobiography*, ii. 389–91.
26. John W. Burrow, *Evolution and Society: A Study in Victorian Social Theory* (Cambridge: Cambridge University Press, 1966), p. 107n.
27. Martineau, *Autobiography*, i. 42–3.
28. Ibid. ii. 132.
29. See Ch. 7.
30. Martineau, *Autobiography*, ii. 390–1.
31. Auguste Comte, *The Positive Philosophy of Auguste Comte, Freely Translated and Condensed by Harriet Martineau*, 2 vols (London: John Chapman 1853), i. 469.
32. John Stuart Mill, *Autobiography* (London: Longmans, Green, Reader, and Dyer), pp. 49, 52; on the comparison with Mr Gradgrind in Charles Dickens's *Hard Times* (1854), see K. J. Fielding, 'Mill and Gradgrind', *Nineteenth-Century Fiction* 11 (1956): 148–51; Thomas Dixon, 'Educating the Emotions from Gradgrind to Goleman', *Research Papers in Education* 27 (2012): 481–95. On the significance and value of tears for Mill, see Helen Small, '"Letting Oneself Go": John Stuart Mill and Helmuth Plessner on Tears', *Litteraria Pragensia: Studies in Literature and Culture* 22 (2012): 112–27.
33. Mill, *Autobiography*, pp. 140–52.
34. Ibid. 141, 143–4.
35. Ibid. 59, 152.
36. Byron, *Poetical Works*, p. 399.
37. 'Tears, Idle Tears', from *The Princess*, Alfred Tennyson, *The Poems*, ed. Christopher Ricks, 2nd edn, 3 vols (Harlow: Longman, 1987), ii. 232–3.

Chapter 11. Little Nell Without Laughing

1. 'Charles Dickens in Westminster Abbey', *Reynolds Newspaper*, 19 June 1870, p. 1.
2. For a sceptical take on several stories about readers weeping over Little Nell, see Madeline House and Graham Storey, 'Preface', *The Pilgrim Edition of the Letters of Charles Dickens*, ii: *1840–1841* (Oxford: Oxford University Press, 1969), especially pp. ix–xii.
3. Leon Litvack, 'The Politics of Perception: Dickens, Ireland and the Irish', in Neil McCaw (ed.), *Writing Irishness in Nineteenth-Century British Culture* (Aldershot: Ashgate, 2004), pp. 34–80 (p. 69 n. 53); House and Storey, 'Preface', pp. ix–x.
4. Philip Collins (ed.), *Charles Dickens: The Critical Heritage* (London: Routledge and Kegan Paul, 1971), p. 100.
5. See Ch. 7.
6. Charles Dickens, *The Old Curiosity Shop*, ed. with an introduction by Elizabeth M. Brennan (Oxford: Oxford University Press, 1999), pp. 1–6; see also Fred Kaplan, *Sacred Tears: Sentimentality in Victorian Literature* (Princeton: Princeton

University Press, 1987); Marie Banfield, 'From Sentiment to Sentimentality: A Nineteenth-Century Lexicographical Search', *19: Interdisciplinary Studies in the Long Nineteenth Century* 4 (2007), <http://19.bbk.ac.uk/index.php/19/article/viewFile/459/319>; Valerie Purton, *Dickens and the Sentimental Tradition: Fielding, Richardson, Sterne, Goldsmith, Sheridan, Lamb* (London: Anthem Press, 2012).

7. Philip Collins, *From Manly Tear to Stiff Upper Lip: The Victorians and Pathos* (Wellington, New Zealand: Victoria University Press, n.d. [1975]); Kaplan, *Sacred Tears*; Gesa Stedman, *Stemming the Torrent: Expression and Control in the Victorian Discourses on Emotion, 1830–1872* (Aldershot: Ashgate, 2002); Richard Walsh, 'Why We Wept for Little Nell: Character and Emotional Involvement', *Narrative* 5 (1997): 306–21; Nicola Bown, 'Introduction: Crying Over Little Nell' and Sally Ledger, '"Don't be so melodramatic!" Dickens and the Affective Mode', both in *19: Interdisciplinary Studies in the Long Nineteenth Century* 4 (2007), 'Rethinking Victorian Sentimentality', <http://www.19.bbk.ac.uk/index.php/19/issue/view/67>; Carolyn Burdett, 'Introduction' to *New Agenda: Sentimentalities, Journal of Victorian Culture* 16 (2011): 187–94.

8. This famous remark was ascribed to Wilde by his friend Ada Leverson in her account of the time Wilde spent staying with her and husband after his first, inconclusive trial for 'gross indecency' and before the retrial at which he was convicted, in 1895; Ada Leverson, *Letters to the Sphinx from Oscar Wilde, with Reminiscences of the Author* (London: Duckworth, 1930), p. 42; see also Richard Ellmann, *Oscar Wilde* (London: Hamish Hamilton, 1987), p. 441.

9. *The Complete Works of Oscar Wilde*, ii: *De Profundis*, 'Epistola: In Carcere et Vinculis', ed. Ian Small (Oxford: Oxford University Press, 2005), p. 140.

10. Thomas Hood, 'A Sentimental Journey from Islington to Waterloo Bridge', first published in the *London Magazine* in 1821, in Alan B. Howes (ed.), *Laurence Sterne: The Critical Heritage* (London: Routledge and Kegan Paul, 1974), pp. 367–8 (p. 368).

11. Thomas Carlyle, *The French Revolution: A History* (1837), chs 1.2.III, 1.2.VII, and 3.3.I, in *The Works of Thomas Carlyle*, ed. Henry Duff Traill, 30 vols (London: Chapman and Hall, 1896–9), ii. 36, 55, iv. 119.

12. On Carlyle, see John Drew, 'Reviewing Dickens in the Victorian Periodical Press', in Sally Ledger and Holly Furneaux (eds), *Charles Dickens in Context* (Cambridge: Cambridge University Press, 2011), pp. 35–42 (p. 36); Ledger, 'Dickens and the Affective Mode'. Thomas Hood wrote an appreciative review of *Master Humphrey's Clock*—the original title of the work that became *The Old Curiosity Shop*—in the *Athenaeum* in 1840. Dickens made particular mention of this review and his pleasure on discovering it was by Thomas Hood in the Preface to the 1848 and subsequent editions of the novel; Collins, *Critical Heritage*, pp. 94–8; Dickens, *The Old Curiosity Shop*, p. 6.

13. My own experience of reading 'The Happy Prince' featured in 'Margaret Are You Grieving? A Cultural History of Weeping', BBC Radio 3, 27 Jan. 2013, <http://www.bbc.co.uk/programmes/b01pz96d>. On the eighteenth-century propensity for weeping over dead birds, see Ch. 8.

14. P. D. Edwards, 'Marsh, Anne (bap. 1791, d. 1874)', *Oxford Dictionary of National Biography* (Oxford University Press, 2004, online edn) doi:10.1093/ref:odnb/18117; 'Obituary of Mrs Marsh', *The Athenaeum*, 17 Oct. 1874, pp. 512–13.

15. Margaret Oliphant, writing about *Hard Times* in *Blackwoods Magazine* in 1855; Collins, *Critical Heritage*, p. 331.

16. Vyvyan Holland, *Son of Oscar Wilde* (London: Rupert Hart-Davis, 1954), pp. 53–4.

17. 'The Happy Prince', in Oscar Wilde, *Complete Shorter Fiction*, ed. Isobel Murray (Oxford: Oxford University Press, 2008), p. 103.

18. A review of the Royal Academy sculpture gallery in 1841 admired the 'exceeding tenderness and mournful beauty' of E. G. Papworth's *Poor Little Nell*, comparing it with Francis Chantrey's *The Sleeping Children* which 'drew together young mothers to weep' at the Academy some years previously; 'Royal Academy', *The Athenaeum*, 22 May 1841, pp. 406–7. One of the very first paintings exhibited by William Holman Hunt—later a central member of the Pre-Raphaelite Brotherhood—was *Little Nell and her Grandfather* (1845), now in the collection of Museums Sheffield; Richard D. Altick, *Paintings from Books: Art and Literature in Britain 1760–1900* (Columbus: Ohio State University Press, 1985), p. 466. A review of a concert in 1849 reported that Miss Eliza Lyon had 'rendered a ballad called "Little Nell" with the deepest pathos and expression, and won a unanimous encore'; 'Music', *The Critic*, 15 Jan. 1849, p. 41. Also in 1849, nearly a decade after her first appearance, *The Athenaeum* was complaining about the 'second-hand pathos' of all the 'excellent children who have died in emulation of Little Nell' in popular fiction; 'Our Library Table', *The Athenaeum*, 10 Mar. 1849, p. 251.

19. Bown, 'Crying Over Little Nell' and Ledger, 'Dickens and the Affective Mode' both analyse Dickens's ability to elicit sentimental tears. Kaplan, *Sacred Tears*, p. 71, quotes from an account by Jane Frith of a public reading by Dickens, where she saw 'everyone in the hall in floods of tears', but did not herself feel moved to join in. Collins, *Manly Tear*, pp. 5–7 gives examples of Thackeray, Eliot, Tennyson, and Clough, as well as Dickens, all being moved to tears by reading their own work.

20. In 1869, the *Spectator* drew a contrast between the 'true pathos' of the death of Paul Dombey and the 'maudlin emotionalism' of the end of Little Nell; 'Mr Dickens's Moral Services to Literature', *The Spectator*, 17 Apr. 1869, pp. 10–11. On Dickens's public readings of the death scene of Paul Dombey as one of his most successful public performances, see Philip Collins (ed.), *Charles Dickens: The Public Readings* (Oxford: Clarendon Press, 1975); Charles Dickens, *The Story of Little Dombey and Other Performance Fictions* (Peterborough, Ontario: Broadview Press, 2013).

21. Charles Dickens, *Dombey and Son*, ed. with an introduction and notes by Dennis Walder (Oxford: Oxford University Press, 2001), ch. 16, pp. 240–1; first published in instalments 1846–8, and as a single volume in 1848.

22. Elizabeth Barrett Browning, 'Grief' (1844), in *The Poetical Works of Elizabeth Barrett Browning* (London: Henry Frowde, 1904), p. 330.

23. Pat Jalland, *Death in the Victorian Family* (Oxford: Oxford University Press, 1996), p. 5.

24. 'Mortality Statistics: Deaths Registered in England and Wales (Series DR), 2012', Office for National Statistics, 22 Oct. 2013, <http://www.ons.gov.uk>.

25. When the Leader of the Opposition David Cameron's son Ivan died in February 2009, the Prime Minister Gordon Brown, who himself had lost an infant daughter in 2002, told the House of Commons: 'Every child is precious and irreplaceable, and the death of a child is an unbearable sorrow that no parent should ever have to endure'; 'Country's Prayers with Camerons', BBC News, 25 Feb. 2009, <http://news.bbc.co.uk/1/hi/uk_politics/7910125.stm>. See also Ch. 19.

26. While Jalland, *Death in the Victorian Family*, focuses on highly educated upper-middle-class families, others have tried to recover working-class experiences of death and expressions of grief, notably Julie-Marie Strange, *Death, Grief and Poverty in Britain, 1870–1914* (Cambridge: Cambridge University Press, 2005).

27. Jalland, *Death in the Victorian Family*; Laurence Lerner, *Angels and Absences: Child Deaths in the Nineteenth Century* (Nashville and London: Vanderbilt University Press, 1997); on Charles Darwin's grief over his daughter Annie's death, see Ch. 13.

28. On James Mill, father of John Stuart Mill, and both men's attitudes to emotion, see Ch. 10.

29. Peter T. Marsh, 'Tait, Archibald Campbell (1811–1882)', *Oxford Dictionary of National Biography* (Oxford University Press, 2004; online edn, Jan. 2008), doi:10.1093/ref:odnb/26917.

30. Jalland, *Death in the Victorian Family*, pp. 127–30; Lerner, *Angels and Absences*, pp. 14–17; Catherine and Craufurd Tait, *A Memoir*, ed. William Benham (London: Macmillian & Co., 1879).

31. Tait and Tait, *Memoir*, p. 443n.

32. Ibid. 383.

33. Ibid. 358.

34. Michael Slater, *Dickens and Women* (London: Dent, 1983), pp. 95–6; Brennan, 'Introduction', in Dickens, *The Old Curiosity Shop*, pp. xxiv–xxv.

35. Macready to Dickens, 25 Jan. 1841, *The Pilgrim Edition of the Letters of Charles Dickens*, ii: *1840–1841* (Oxford: Oxford University Press, 1969), p. 193; cited in Bown, 'Crying Over Little Nell' and Lerner, *Angels and Absences*, p. 176. For an account of Macready (and others) sobbing in 1844 at a private reading by Dickens of his Christmas story *The Chimes*, see Ledger, 'Dickens and the Affective Mode'.

36. 'George Acorn', Reading Experience Database (record ID 2368), <http://www. open.ac.uk/arts/reading/UK>; Jonathan Rose, *The Intellectual Life of the British Working Classes* (New Haven: Yale University Press, 2001), p. 111.

37. Paul Schlicke, 'A "discipline of feeling": Macready's *Lear* and *The Old Curiosity Shop*', *Dickensian* 76 (1980): 78–90; Philip Hobsbaum, *A Reader's Guide to Charles Dickens* (Syracuse, NY: Syracuse University Press, 1998), pp. 56–8.

38. 'Monday 18th February 1839', Lord Esher's Typescript of Queen Victoria's Journal, p. 47, <http://www.queenvictoriasjournals.org>; Harriet Martineau, *Autobiography, With Memorials by Maria Weston*, 3 vols (London: Smith, Elder, 1877), ii. 119–20.

39. Thomas Rowlandson, 'Tragedy Spectators' (London: S. W. Fores, 1789); Victoria and Albert Museum, Museum no. S.57-2008, <http://collections.vam.ac.uk>.

40. Peter Mandler, 'Lamb, William, Second Viscount Melbourne (1779–1848)', *Oxford Dictionary of National Biography* (Oxford University Press, 2004; online edn, Jan. 2008), doi:10.1093/ref:odnb/15920; Karen Chase and Michael Levenson, '"I never saw a man so frightened": The Young Queen and the Parliamentary Bedchamber', in Margaret Homans and Adrienne Munich (eds), *Remaking Queen Victoria* (Cambridge: Cambridge University Press, 1997), pp. 200–18.

41. A search for 'tears' in the online version of Victoria's journal in the very early years of her reign, from 1837 to 1839, brings up dozens of examples of Lord Melbourne's eyes filling and overflowing; Queen Victoria's Journal, <http://www.queenvictoriasjournals.org>.

42. 'Thursday 16th November 1837', p. 19; 'Friday 19th January 1838', p. 28; Queen Victoria's Journal.

43. 'Monday 10th February 1840', p. 345, Queen Victoria's Journal.

44. 'Monday 18th March 1839', p. 149, Queen Victoria's Journal. The reference to donkeys was an allusion to the scene involving a dead donkey in Laurence Sterne's *Sentimental Journey*; see Ch. 8.

45. 'Sunday 19th August 1838', p. 37; 'Monday 18th March 1839', p. 153; Queen Victoria's Journal.

46. On English anti-Catholicism and representations of excessive mourning, in Ireland and elsewhere, during the Reformation, see Ch. 2.

47. See Ch. 13.

48. James H. Murphy, *Abject Loyalty: Nationalism and Monarchy in Ireland during the Reign of Queen Victoria* (Crosses Green: Cork University Press, 2001), p. 20.

49. 'Royal Procession from Kensington to St James's', *The Standard* (London), 22 June 1837, p. 3.

50. Murphy, *Abject Loyalty*, ch. 2.

51. The account of this affecting scene was quoted at length from a Whig newspaper by the disapproving *Spectator* writer; 'Ireland', *The Spectator*, 10 July 1841, pp. 9–10, <http://archive.spectator.co.uk>.

52. Ecclesiastes 4: 1.

53. Litvack, 'Dickens, Ireland and the Irish', pp. 43–6.

Chapter 12. Damp Justice

1. See Ch. 7.
2. Michael Fry, 'Jeffrey, Francis, Lord Jeffrey (1773–1850)', *Oxford Dictionary of National Biography* (Oxford University Press, 2004; online edn, Sept. 2013), doi:10.1093/ref:odnb/14698.
3. Letters from Francis Jeffrey to Charles Dickens, 31 Jan. 1847 and 5 July 1847, quoted in Henry Cockburn, *Life of Lord Jeffrey: With a Selection from his Correspondence*, 2nd edn, 2 vols (Edinburgh: Adam and Charles Black, 1852), ii. 406, 425–6; Philip Collins (ed.), *Charles Dickens: The Critical Heritage* (London: Routledge, 2001), pp. 217, 222; see also Sally Ledger, '"Don't be so melodramatic!" Dickens and the Affective Mode', *19: Interdisciplinary Studies in the Long Nineteenth Century* 4 (2007), <http://19.bbk.ac.uk/index.php/19/article/viewFile/456/316>.
4. On the lengthy afterlife of the 'stiff upper lip' as an object of sentimental nostalgia, see Ch. 20.
5. On the scandal and its effects see Alexandra Kelso, 'Parliament on its Knees: MPs' Expenses and the Crisis of Transparency at Westminster', *Political Quarterly* 80 (2009): 329–38; Charles Pattie and Ron Johnston, 'The Electoral Impact of the UK 2009 MPs' Expenses Scandal', *Political Studies* 60 (2012): 730–50. The £1,645 claimed by Sir Peter Viggers for a duck house became symbolic of the whole episode; Martin Beckford, 'MPs' Expenses: "Duck House" MP Sir Peter Viggers Keeps up Spending on Garden', *Daily Telegraph*, 10 Dec. 2009, <http://www.telegraph.co.uk>.
6. Karen McVeigh, 'Former Tory Peer in Courtroom Outburst During Expenses Trial', *The Guardian*, 20 Jan. 2011, <http://www.theguardian.com>; see also, on Eliot Morley's tears, Chris Greenwood, 'Tears of Ex-MP Jailed for Lying over £31,000 Expenses', *Daily Mail*, 21 May 2011, <http://www.dailymail.co.uk>.
7. On witchcraft trials and public executions, see Chs 4 and 7.
8. The image is by Honoré Daumier, in his *Gens de Justice* series; 'Lawyer Advises Defendant to Shed a Few Tears', Cartoon Stock, uploaded 10 Oct. 2008, ID csl4172, <http://www.cartoonstock.com>.
9. George Cruikshank, *The Drunkard's Children*, coloured etching (1848), Wellcome Library, London, ref. 19824, <http://wellcomeimages.org>.
10. 'Court Sees Mother's TV Appeal', BBC News, 12 Nov. 2008, <http://news.bbc.co.uk/1/hi/uk/7725251.stm>; 'Shannon Matthews Trial: Karen Matthews in Tears Giving Evidence', *Daily Telegraph*, 27 Nov. 2008, <http://www.telegraph.co.uk>.
11. For a fuller discussion and further examples, see Thomas Dixon, 'The Tears of Mr Justice Willes', *Journal of Victorian Culture* 17 (2012): 1–23.
12. In April 1851, Levi Harwood and Samuel Jones were hanged in front of Horsemonger Lane Jail for the murder of a clergyman. The 'stoical indifference' of Harwood eventually gave way, under the influence of the chaplain and the

prison governor, to confession, tears, and reconciliation with his fellow-prisoner; *The Lady's Newspaper*, 19 Apr. 1851, p. 217.

13. 'The Murder on the North London Railway', *The Times*, 31 Oct. 1864, p. 7; the report noted that as he left the dock, the condemned man's resolve finally left him, and he dissolved in tears. It was by then too late for his weeping to have any effect.

14. William Roughead, 'Dr Pritchard', in James H. Hodge (ed.), *Famous Trials 4* (London: Penguin, 1954), pp. 143-75 (pp. 166-7); 'Reflections on the Pritchard Trial', *Reynolds's Newspaper*, 16 July 1865, p. 6.

15. This was in a Dublin newspaper, *Freeman's Journal and Daily Commercial Advertiser*, 12 Apr. 1850, p. 3. A few years earlier a Dublin case was reported involving a girl who had been seduced, had miscarried, and whose family had forcibly removed her from the house of her seducer: 'the learned Judge shed tears, and many present were deeply affected'; *Standard*, 7 Oct. 1844, p. 3.

16. The fullest source on Willes's life and career is R. F. V. Heuston, 'James Shaw Willes', *Northern Ireland Legal Quarterly* 16 (1965): 193-214. See also A. W. B. Simpson, 'Willes, Sir James Shaw (1814-1872)', *Oxford Dictionary of National Biography* (Oxford University Press, online edn, 2004), doi:10.1093/ref:odnb/29442; Dixon, 'The Tears of Mr Justice Willes', p. 2.

17. Dixon, 'The Tears of Mr Justice Willes'.

18. Abraham Solomon, *Waiting for the Verdict* (1857), oil on canvas, Tate Collection, <http://www.tate.org.uk>. See also *Solomon: A Family of Painters* (London: Inner London Education Authority, 1985), the catalogue of an exhibition held at the Geffrye Museum, London, 8 Nov.-31 Dec. 1985.

19. *The Works of Lord Macaulay, Complete*, edited by his sister, Lady Trevelyan, 8 vols (London: Longmans, Green, and Co., 1866), i. 548.

20. Michael Lobban, 'Brougham, Henry Peter, First Baron Brougham and Vaux (1778-1868)', *Oxford Dictionary of National Biography* (Oxford University Press, 2004; online edn, Jan. 2008), doi:10.1093/ref:odnb/3581.

21. Timothy Webb, 'Tears: An Anthology', *Litteraria Pragensia: Studies in Literature and Culture* 22 (2012): 26-45 (p. 39).

22. 'A Touching Scene at the Old Bailey', *Punch*, 10 Nov. 1855, p. 185.

23. 'Northern Circuit. Liverpool, March 26', *The Times*, 28 Mar. 1859, p. 11.

24. Kate Summerscale, *The Suspicions of Mr Whicher, or The Murder at Road Hill House* (London: Bloomsbury, 2009), especially pp. 248-54.

25. 'News of the Day', *Birmingham Daily Post*, 22 July 1865, p. 2; 'The Road Murder', *Bristol Mercury*, 22 July 1865, p. 8; 'The Trial of Constance Kent', *Caledonian Mercury*, 22 July 1865, p. 3; Charles Kingston, *The Judges and the Judged* (London: John Lane, 1926), p. 256; *Wiltshire and Somerset Journal*, quoted in June Sturrock, 'Murder, Gender, and Popular Fiction by Women in the 1860s: Braddon, Oliphant, Yonge', in Andrew Maunder and Grace Moore (eds), *Victorian Crime, Madness and Sensation* (Aldershot: Ashgate, 2004), pp. 73-88 (p. 78).

26. 'Latest News', *Dundee Courier and Argus*, Saturday, 22 July 1865, p. 3; 'News of the Day', *Birmingham Daily Post*, 27 July 1865, pp. 4, 8; 'Summary of This Morning's News', *Pall Mall Gazette*, 27 July 1865, p. 5; 'Miss Constance Kent', *The Standard* (London), 27 July 1865, p. 3.
27. See Chs 8 and 10.
28. See also Chs 11 and 13.
29. 'Sir James Shaw Willes', *The Times*, 4 Oct. 1872, p. 8, quoting from the obituary for Willes in the *Law Times*, which referred to Willes's 'kind and almost womanly disposition'.
30. E. P. Whipple, writing in the *Atlantic Monthly*, Feb. 1873, p. 238, quoted in Philip Collins, *From Manly Tear to Stiff Upper Lip: The Victorians and Pathos* (Wellington, New Zealand: Victoria University Press, n.d. [1975]), p. 14; see also Carolyn Burdett, 'Introduction' to *New Agenda: Sentimentalities*, *Journal of Victorian Culture* 16 (2011): 187–94.
31. 'Weeping Plays', *The Era*, 8 Apr. 1882, p. 14. Later in the 1880s a substantial further aesthetic, psychological, and medical discussion about the production of tears in the theatre, especially by actors themselves, was initiated by William Archer's *Masks or Faces? A Study in the Psychology of Acting* (London: Longmans, Green and Co., 1888).
32. 'The Road Murder', *Bristol Mercury*, 22 July 1865, p. 8.
33. Heuston, 'James Shaw Willes'; Dixon, 'The Tears of Mr Justice Willes', pp. 19–20.
34. The details of the suicide were reported in the pages of many newspapers including *The Standard* (London), 4 Oct. 1872, p. 3; *Glasgow Herald*, 4 Oct. 1872, p. 5; *Western Daily Press*, 5 Oct. 1872, p. 2.
35. 'Serious Charge of Arson Against a Policeman', *Birmingham Daily Post*, 18 Dec. 1888, p. 7; 'A Divided Duty', *York Herald*, 19 Dec. 1888; p. 5.
36. Keith Surridge, 'Warren, Sir Charles (1840–1927)', *Oxford Dictionary of National Biography* (Oxford University Press, 2004; online edn, May 2006), doi:10.1093/ref:odnb/36753.
37. 'Robert Emotional. A Play of the Period', *Funny Folks*, 29 Dec. 1888, p. 418.

Chapter 13. Old Ladies and Other Animals

1. On Darwin's life and achievements, see Adrian Desmond and James Moore, *Darwin* (London: Penguin, 1992); Janet Browne, *Darwin: A Biography*, 2 vols (London: Jonathan Cape, 1995, 2002).
2. For more on the history of the 'stiff upper lip' as both a phrase and an ideal, see Ch. 14.
3. Charles Darwin, *The Expression of the Emotions in Man and Animals* (London: John Murray, 1872), p. 155. The original text of this and all Charles Darwin's other publications are available at Darwin Online, edited by John van Wyhe, <http://darwin-online.org.uk>.

4. Darwin, *Expression*, pp. 195–7.
5. Charles Darwin, The Autobiography of Charles Darwin, ed. Nora Barlow (London: Collins, 1958), pp. 131–2; Charles Darwin, 'A Biographical Sketch of an Infant', *Mind* 2 (1877): 285–94 (p. 292); both available at Darwin Online, edited by John van Wyhe, <http://darwin-online.org.uk>.
6. Darwin, *Expression*, pp. 153–4.
7. See Ch. 1.
8. Darwin, *Expression*, p. 154.
9. 'Tears, Idle Tears', from *The Princess*, Alfred Tennyson, *The Poems*, ed. Christopher Ricks, 2nd edn, 3 vols (Harlow: Longman, 1987), ii. 232–3.
10. William James, 'What is an Emotion?', *Mind* 9 (1884): 188–205 (pp. 189–90); on James's theory of emotions and its place in the history of psychology, see Thomas Dixon, *From Passions to Emotions: The Creation of a Secular Psychological Category* (Cambridge: Cambridge University Press, 2003), ch. 7, and '"Emotion": The History of a Keyword in Crisis', *Emotion Review* 4 (2012): 338–44.
11. On Darwin's theory of weeping and the history of Victorian science and culture, see Paul White, 'Darwin Wept: Science and the Sentimental Subject', *Journal of Victorian Culture* 16 (2011): 195–213; Thomas Dixon, 'The Tears of Mr Justice Willes', *Journal of Victorian Culture* 17 (2012): 1–23. An authoritative and comprehensive recent scientific book about crying begins with an assessment of Darwin's approach to tears and his theory that they were purposeless from an evolutionary point of view: Ad Vingerhoets, *Why Only Humans Weep: Unravelling the Mysteries of Tears* (Oxford: Oxford University Press, 2013), pp. 1–3.
12. On Charles Bell's contributions to the histories of tears, science, and medicine, see Ch. 9 and, in relation to Darwin's theories, Dixon, *From Passions to Emotions*, ch. 5; White, 'Darwin Wept'.
13. Some at least partially dissented from the orthodoxy, for example the veterinary surgeon William Youatt who wrote in the 1830s that deer, horses, and dogs were known to weep in a way that he compared with the secretion of tears from 'mental emotion' in humans; 'Mr Youatt's Veterinary Lectures Delivered at the University of London', *The Veterinarian* 7 (1834): 461–75 (p. 474).
14. Darwin, *Expression*, pp. 135–7, 163, 167–8. One of Darwin's many correspondents wrote to him, having read his accounts of weeping elephants in the *Expression*, to add further testimony—an account from Gordon Cumming, *The Lion Hunter of South Africa* (London: John Murray, 1856), p. 227, describing an African elephant with large tears trickling from its eyes after it was shot; William Gregory Walker to Charles Darwin, 21 Aug. 1873, Darwin Correspondence Project, <http://www.darwinproject.ac.uk/entry-9020>; I am very grateful to Dr Paul White of the Darwin Correspondence Project in Cambridge, for giving me access to the text of this and other letters to Darwin on the subjects of tears and weeping, some of which are not yet fully available online.
15. Darwin, *Expression*, pp. 135–7.

16. Ibid. 163.
17. On the substance and significance of Darwin's arguments about emotions in the *Expression*, see Dixon, *Passions to Emotions*, pp. 159–79; White, 'Darwin Wept'; Paul White, 'Darwin's Emotions: The Scientific Self and the Sentiment of Objectivity', *Isis* 100 (2009): 811–26; Gregory Radick, 'Darwin's Puzzling *Expression*', *Comptes rendus biologies* 333 (2010): 181–7; Tiffany Watt-Smith, *On Flinching: Theatricality and Scientific Looking from Darwin to Shell Shock* (Oxford: Oxford University Press, 2014), ch. 1.
18. On Darwin's science in the context of Victorian racial attitudes, see Charles Darwin, *The Descent of Man, and Selection in Relation to Sex*, ed. James Moore and Adrian Desmond (London: Penguin, 2004), 'Introduction'; Adrian Desmond and James Moore, *Darwin's Sacred Cause: Race, Slavery and the Quest for Human Origins* (London: Allen Lane, 2009); Robert Kenny, 'From the Curse of Ham to the Curse of Nature: The Influence of Natural Selection on the Debate on Human Unity Before the Publication of *The Descent of Man*', *British Journal for the History of Science* 40 (2007): 367–88; Douglas Lorimer, 'Science and the Secularisation of Victorian Images of Race', in Bernard Lightman (ed.), *Victorian Science in Context* (Chicago: University of Chicago Press, 1997), pp. 212–35.
19. Darwin, *Expression*, pp. 154–5.
20. Thomas W. Higginson to Charles Darwin, 30 Mar. 1873, Darwin Correspondence Project, <http://www.darwinproject.ac.uk/entry-8830>.
21. This was one of the themes of Mandell Creighton's 1896 Romanes Lecture, *The English National Character* (London: Henry Frowde, 1896), reviewed in *The Spectator*, 20 June 1896, pp. 8–9, <http://http://archive.spectator.co.uk>. See also Peter Mandler, *The English National Character: The History of an Idea from Edmund Burke to Tony Blair* (New Haven: Yale University Press, 2006), chs 3 and 4.
22. Thomas S. Clouston, *Clinical Lectures on Mental Diseases* (London: J. and A. Churchill, 1883), pp. 90–1.
23. Darwin, *Expression*, p. 155.
24. 'Darwin on the Expression of the Emotions', *The Graphic*, 16 Nov. 1872, pp. 462–3.
25. See Ch. 2.
26. Darwin, *Expression*, p. 155.
27. See Ch. 1.
28. Darwin, *Expression*, pp. 155–6; on Darwin's collaboration with Crichton-Browne, see Alison M. Pearn, '"This excellent observer . . .": The Correspondence between Charles Darwin and James Crichton-Browne, 1869–75', *History of Psychiatry* 21 (2010): 160–75.
29. John Charles Bucknill and Daniel Hack Tuke, *A Manual of Psychological Medicine*, 4th edn (London: J. and A. Churchill, 1879), p. 140; for more on Victorian medicine, psychology, and tears see Dixon, 'The Tears of Mr Justice Willes'.

30. One early use of the phrase comes in a book by the physician and specialist in mental pathology Henry Maudsley, *Natural Causes and Supernatural Seemings* (London: Kegan Paul, Trench and Co., 1886), pp. 300–1, in a passage where Maudsley describes the ecstatic enthusiasm of the Unitarian writer Dr James Martineau (brother of Harriet Martineau), as evidenced in his descriptions of union with the divine, as 'streams of emotional incontinence'.

31. Richard Littlejohn quoted in James Thomas, *Diana's Mourning: A People's History* (Cardiff: University of Wales Press, 2002), p. 17; Toby Young, 'When Did Tears Become Compulsory?', *The Spectator*, 14 July 2012, p. 60. Responses to the new tearful sensibility, from the 1990s onwards, are discussed in Ch. 20.

32. Desmond and Moore, *Darwin*, pp. 375–87; Randal Keynes, *Annie's Box: Charles Darwin, his Daughter and Human Evolution* (London: Fourth Estate, 2001); White, 'Darwin Wept', pp. 196–9; 'Death of Anne Elizabeth Darwin', Darwin Correspondence Project, <http://www.darwinproject.ac.uk/death-of-anne-darwin>. On Darwin's expressions of sympathy for his grieving friend Joseph Hooker, when he too lost a much-loved daughter, see Jim Endersby, 'Sympathetic Science: Charles Darwin, Joseph Hooker, and the Passions of Victorian Naturalists', *Victorian Studies* 51 (2009): 299–320 (pp. 306–9).

33. Desmond and Moore, *Darwin*, p. 651.

34. Darwin, *Expression*, pp. 195–7.

35. See Ch. 11.

36. Darwin, *Expression*, p. 153.

Chapter 14. The 'If' Upper Lip

1. 'Wilde and Taylor: Close of the Re-Trial', *Portsmouth Evening News*, 27 May 1895, p. 2, and *Hampshire Telegraph*, 1 June 1895, p. 2.

2. *The Complete Works of Oscar Wilde*, ii: *De Profundis*, 'Epistola: In Carcere et Vinculis', ed. Ian Small (Oxford: Oxford University Press, 2005), pp. 127–8.

3. Freud refers to the woman in connection with the case of Fräulein Elisabeth von R., in Josef Breuer and Sigmund Freud, *Studies on Hysteria: The Standard Edition of the Complete Psychological Works of Sigmund Freud*, ii: *1893–1895*, trans. James Strachey and Anna Freud (London: The Hogarth Press and the Institute of Psycho-Analysis, 1955), pp. 162–3.

4. Wilde, *De Profundis*, p. 128.

5. The poem was first published in 1898 with the author given as 'C.3.3.', the number of Wilde's cell. From 1899 onwards, Wilde was identified as the author on the title page. Oscar Wilde, 'The Ballad of Reading Gaol', *The Complete Works of Oscar Wilde*, i: *Poems and Poems in Prose*, ed. Bobby Fong and Karl Beckson (Oxford: Oxford University Press, 2000), pp. 195–216 (pp. 203, 216, lines 269–70, 633–6).

6. As a child, Wilde was baptized both into the Anglican Church of Ireland and, in secret and at his mother's request, into the Roman Catholic Church. He seriously

considered converting to Roman Catholicism during his student years in Oxford in the 1870s, and retained a sincere interest in the figure of Christ and in Catholic liturgy and theology throughout his life. He received the last rites of the Catholic Church on his deathbed in Paris in 1900, at the request of his friend Robbie Ross. On Wilde's religious life and ideas, see Stephen Arata, 'Oscar Wilde and Jesus Christ', in Joseph Bristow (ed.), *Wilde Writings: Contextual Conditions* (Toronto: University of Toronto Press, 2003), pp. 254–72; Jarlath Killeen, *The Faiths of Oscar Wilde: Catholicism, Folklore and Ireland* (Basingstoke: Palgrave Macmillan, 2005); Patrick R. O'Malley, 'Religion', in Frederick S. Roden (ed.), *Palgrave Advances in Oscar Wilde Studies* (Basingstoke: Palgrave Macmillan, 2004), pp. 167–88.

7. Catherine Robson, *Heart Beats: Everyday Life and the Memorized Poem* (Princeton: Princeton University Press, 2012), pp. 230–4. Liz Bury, 'Robert Frost's Snowy Walk Tops Radio 4 Count of Nation's Favourite Poems', *The Guardian*, 26 Sept. 2013, <http://www.theguardian.com>. Kipling was Margaret Thatcher's favourite poet; her fascination with his work went back to her childhood. Thatcher remembered Kipling's verses, along with Hollywood movies, as offering her a glimpse of romance and exoticism beyond the confines of her relatively drab provincial, Methodist upbringing; Margaret Thatcher, *The Path to Power* (London: HarperCollins, 1995), p. 17. 'If—' was reportedly Thatcher's favourite poem, and she was presented with a first edition of Kipling's verses by her Downing Street staff when resigning as Prime Minister in 1990; Jonathan Aitken, *Margaret Thatcher: Power and Personality* (London: Bloomsbury, 2013), pp. 214, 647–8; see also Ch. 19.

8. Rudyard Kipling, *Something of Myself: For my Friends Known and Unknown* (London: Macmillan and Co., 1937), p. 191.

9. Bruce Tarran, *George Hillyard: The Man Who Moved Wimbledon* (Kibworth Beauchamp: Matador, 2013), p. 104.

10. Rudyard Kipling, 'If—', in *Rewards and Fairies* (London: Macmillan and Co., 1910), pp. 175–6.

11. Kipling, *Something of Myself*, ch. 6, 'South Africa'; Thomas Pinney, 'Kipling, (Joseph) Rudyard (1865–1936)', *Oxford Dictionary of National Biography* (Oxford University Press, 2004; online edn, Jan. 2011), doi:10.1093/ref:odnb/34334.

12. On Victorian and Edwardian models of masculinity, including the father–son relationship, see John Tosh, *A Man's Place: Masculinity and the Middle-Class Home in Victorian England* (New Haven: Yale University Press, 1999), ch. 4; Claudia Nelson, *Invisible Men: Fatherhood in Victorian Periodicals, 1850–1910* (Athens, Ga: University of Georgia Press, 1995); Angus McLaren, *The Trials of Masculinity: Policing Sexual Boundaries, 1870–1930* (Chicago: University of Chicago Press, 1997); Martin Francis, 'The Domestication of the Male? Recent Research on Nineteenth- and Twentieth-Century British Masculinity', *Historical Journal* 45 (2002): 637–52; Stephen Heathorn, 'How Stiff were their Upper Lips? Research on Late-Victorian and Edwardian Masculinity', *History Compass* 2 (2004), doi: 10.1111/j.1478-0542.2004.00093.x.

13. 'Popular American Phrases', *All the Year Round*, 18 Feb. 1871, p. 273.

14. A handbook of physiognomy and phrenology published in America in 1849 used the phrase to mean 'self-esteem'; J. W. Redfield, *Outline of a New System of Physiognomy* (New York: J. S. Redfield, 1849), p. 75. For other uses with American connections from the 1860s onwards, see: 'Small But Interesting', *Fun*, 17 Dec. 1864, p. 137; 'Erema; or, My Father's Sin', *Cornhill Magazine* 34 (Nov. 1876), p. 534; T. Baron Russell, 'The American Language', *Gentleman's Magazine* 275 (Nov. 1893), pp. 529–33 (p. 532).

15. For examples of a 'stiff upper lip' denoting an attitude of isolationism and self-sufficiency in foreign affairs, and in military contexts, see Alfred Simmons, 'The Ideas of the New Voters', *Fortnightly Review* 37 (Feb. 1885), p. 153; 'Dramatis Personae: Sir Claude MacDonald', *Outlook*, 21 May 1898, pp. 488–9; 'A Week of Empire', *Outlook*, 16 Dec. 1899, p. 640; 'Notes of the Week', *Saturday Review of Politics, Literature, Science and Art*, 23 Aug. 1902, pp. 221–4 (p. 222); J. W. Fortescue, 'Some Blunders and a Scapegoat', *Nineteenth Century and After* 52 (Sept. 1902), p. 353.

16. On Victorian sentimentalism and its decline, see Chs 11–13, and also Carolyn Burdett, 'Introduction' to *New Agenda: Sentimentalities, Journal of Victorian Culture* 16 (2011): 187–94; Nicola Bown, 'Introduction: Crying over Little Nell', in 'Rethinking Victorian Sentimentality', *19: Interdisciplinary Studies in the Long Nineteenth Century* 4 (2007), <http://19.bbk.ac.uk/index.php/19/article/viewFile/453/313>; Philip Collins, *From Manly Tear to Stiff Upper Lip: The Victorians and Pathos* (Wellington, New Zealand: Victoria University Press, n.d. [1975]).

17. Louise Joy, '"Snivelling like a kid": Edith Nesbit and the Child's Tears', *Litteraria Pragensia: Studies in Literature and Culture* 22 (2012): 128–42 (pp. 130, 132).

18. E.C.F., 'A Day School Seventy Years Ago', *Church Times*, 15 Feb. 1946, p. 104.

19. See Chs 17–20. In 1932, *The Times* reported on a visit of the Prince of Wales to the Belgrave Hospital for Children, where he expressed sympathy with the patients, including a 5-year-old boy called Peter Garvie, who told the prince he hoped to join the Life Guards regiment when he grew up. Before the royal visit, the boy had shed tears of pain when having stitches removed, at which the nurse told him, 'Life Guards don't cry. Perhaps if you're very brave the Prince of Wales will make you one of his Life Guards'; 'The Prince's Gift to Boy Patient', *The Times*, 13 May 1932, p. 11.

20. Elizabeth Gargano, *Reading Victorian Schoolrooms: Childhood and Education in Nineteenth-Century Fiction* (New York: Routledge, 2008), pp. 101–7.

21. Harriet Martineau, *The Crofton Boys: A Tale* (London: Charles Knight, 1841), pp. 34, 164.

22. 'The Third Boy at Beechycombe. Chapter II: The Third Boy Becomes a Mystery', in S. O. Beeton (ed.), *Beeton's Boy's Annual: A Volume of Fact, Fiction, History, and Adventure* (London: Ward, Lock, and Tyler, 1868), pp. 447–54 (p. 450). For further examples of early uses of 'blub' meaning 'weep' from the 1860s to the

1890s, see the *Oxford English Dictionary*, online edn (Oxford: Oxford University Press).

23. According to David Newsome, there was a change of tone in Victorian public school education in the later nineteenth century: 'excessive displays of emotions came in time to be regarded as bad form: patriotism and doing one's duty to country and Empire became the main sentiments which the new system sought to inculcate'; David Newsome, *Godliness and Good Learning: Four Studies on a Victorian Ideal* (London: John Murray, 1961), p. 26. On later Victorian education and imperialism, see also Pamela Horn, 'English Elementary Education and the Growth of the Imperial Ideal: 1880–1914', in J. A. Mangan (ed.), *Benefits Bestowed? Education and British Imperialism* (Manchester: Manchester University Press, 1988), pp. 39–55; Tosh, *A Man's Place*, ch. 8; Claudia Nelson, 'Growing Up: Childhood', in Herbert F. Tucker (ed.), *A Companion to Victorian Literature and Culture* (Oxford: Blackwell, 1999), pp. 69–81.

24. Geoffrey Gorer, *Death, Grief, and Mourning in Contemporary Britain* (London: The Cresset Press, 1965), pp. 2–3; Pat Jalland, *Death in War and Peace: Loss and Grief in England, 1914–1970* (Oxford: Oxford University Press, 2010), p. 101.

25. Ivor Brown, 'The Best Game to Watch', *Saturday Review of Politics, Literature, Science and Art*, 14 Nov. 1925, p. 563.

26. 'Bigger and Wetter Tears', *The Times*, 15 Feb. 1936, p. 13.

27. E. M. Forster, 'Notes on the English Character' (1920), in *Abinger Harvest* (London: Edward Arnold & Co., 1936), pp. 3–14 (p. 5).

28. See Ch. 17.

29. George Gershwin (music) and Ira Gershwin (lyrics), 'Stiff Upper Lip', in George Stevens (dir.), *A Damsel in Distress* (RKO Pictures, 1937). On ideas of Britishness in the Gershwins' works of the 1920s and 1930s see James Ross Moore, 'The Gershwins in Britain', *New Theatre Quarterly* 10 (1994): 33–48.

30. Abel Stevens, *The History of the Religious Movement of the Eighteenth Century Called Methodism*, vol. ii (New York: Carlton and Porter, 1859), p. 89. On tears and Methodism, see Ch. 5.

31. On Cromwell's tears, see Ch. 4.

32. 'Lloyd George in Tears at his Carnarvon Meeting', *Dundee Evening Telegraph*, 10 Dec. 1909, p. 2.

33. 'Tears!', *Hull Daily Mail*, 10 Dec. 1909, p. 4.

34. Peter Simkins, *Kitchener's Army: The Raising of the New Armies 1914–1916* (Barnsley: Pen and Sword Military, 2007), pp. 96–7.

35. For more on Cavell and her stiff upper lip, see Ch. 15.

36. 'Not Emotional: A Character Sketch of our Tommies', *Liverpool Echo*, 25 Oct. 1915, p. 4.

37. Frederic Manning, *The Middle Parts of Fortune: Somme and Ancre 1916*, ed. Paul Fussell (London: Penguin, 1990), p. 15; original publication 1929. For further insights into the sensations, feelings, and emotions of men fighting in the Great War, see also Joanna Bourke, *Dismembering the Male: Men's Bodies, Britain and*

the Great War (London: Reaktion Books, 1996); Santanu Das, *Touch and Intimacy in First World War Literature* (Cambridge: Cambridge University Press, 2008); Michael Roper, *The Secret Battle: Emotional Survival in the Great War* (Manchester: Manchester University Press, 2009).

38. 'Soldiers in Tears', *Daily Mirror*, 17 June 1916, p. 11.

39. For a study of the 'military man of feeling' in both fiction and reality in the Victorian and Edwardian periods, with particular reference to William Make-peace Thackeray's much-loved character of Colonel Newcome, see Holly Fur-neaux, 'Victorian Masculinities, or Military Men of Feeling: Domesticity, Militarism, and Manly Sensibility', in Juliet John (ed.), *The Oxford Handbook of Victorian Literary Culture* (Oxford: Oxford University Press, forthcoming).

40. W. Graham Robertson, *Time Was: The Reminiscences of W. Graham Robertson* (London: Hamish Hamilton, 1931), p. 321. I am grateful to Nicola Bown for alerting me to this source. See also Tracy C. Davis, 'What are Fairies For?', in Tracy C. Davis and Peter Holland (eds), *The Performing Century: Nineteenth-Century Theatre's History* (Basingstoke: Palgrave Macmillan, 2007), pp. 32–59.

41. 'The Theatre Royal', *Portsmouth Evening News*, 23 Oct. 1909, p. 3; for Woolwich performance see Figure 17.

42. Anthony Glyn, *Elinor Glyn: A Biography* (London: Hutchinson, 1955), p. 104; J. Lee Thompson, *Forgotten Patriot: A Life of Alfred, Viscount Milner of St. James's and Cape Town, 1854–1925* (Madison: Fairleigh Dickinson University Press, 2007), p. 228; I first found the account of Lord Milner reading aloud to Elinor Glyn in 1903 through the Reading Experience Database (record ID 5601), which uses thousands of sources to chart the experience of reading in the UK between 1450 and 1945: <http://www.open.ac.uk/arts/reading/UK>.

43. See Chs 16 and 20.

44. Vyvyan Holland, *Son of Oscar Wilde* (London: Rupert Hart-Davis, 1954), p. 53.

45. Rudyard Kipling, 'Thrown Away', in *Plain Tales from the Hills* (London: Mac-millan and Co., 1915), pp. 15–26 (pp. 22–3); original publication 1888. I am grateful to Susie Paskins and to Holly Furneaux for directing me towards this early story by Kipling as an example of his more sentimental side.

46. Daniel Pick, *Faces of Degeneration: A European Disorder, c.1848–1918* (Cambridge: Cambridge University Press, 1989), pp. 24–6; Thomas Dixon, *The Invention of Altruism: Making Moral Meanings in Victorian Britain* (Oxford: Oxford University Press for the British Academy, 2008), ch. 8, especially pp. 332–3.

47. Max Nordau, *Degeneration* (New York: D. Appleton and Co., 1895), ch. 3, p. 19.

48. Nellie Melba, *Melodies and Memories* (London: Thornton Butterworth, 1925), pp. 260–2.

49. Holland, *Son of Oscar Wilde*, pp. 139–45, 152–3; 'Cyril Holland (E Social 1899–1903): Son of Oscar Wilde', *The Old Radleian* (2011), pp. 8–19, <http://www.radley.org.uk/2011OldRadleian.aspx>.

50. Holland, *Son of Oscar Wilde*, p. 140. See also George Robb, *British Culture and the First World War* (Basingstoke: Palgrave, 2002), pp. 33–4; Michael Roper,

'Between Manliness and Masculinity: The "War Generation" and the Psychology of Fear in Britain, 1914–1950', *Journal of British Studies* 44 (2005): 343–62 (p. 348).

51. Oscar Wilde, 'Lady Windermere's Fan', in *The Importance of Being Earnest, and Other Plays*, ed. Peter Raby (Oxford: Oxford University Press, 1995), Act 3, p. 44.
52. Holland, *Son of Oscar Wilde*, p. 144.
53. The story has been dramatized in a 1997 stage play by David Haig, *My Boy Jack*, which in 2007 was produced as a film for television, directed by Brian Kirk.
54. *The Private Diaries of Sir H. Rider Haggard, 1914–1925*, ed. D. S. Higgins (London: Cassell, 1980), pp. 41–5.

Chapter 15. Patriotism is not Enough

1. On Nelson and his death, see Ch. 9.
2. *Aberdeen Journal*, 18 Mar. 1920, p. 5.
3. 'Miss Earhart—British Pathé News', first released 25 June 1928, <http://www.britishpathe.com/video/miss-earhart>.
4. *Gloucestershire Echo*, 21 Mar. 1932, p. 4. See also Juliet Gardiner, *The Thirties: An Intimate History* (London: HarperPress, 2010), p. 694, which cites the *Daily Mirror* for 14 Mar. 1932.
5. 'Edith Cavell', *British Journal of Nursing*, 30 Oct. 1915, p. 346. See also Claire Daunton, 'Cavell, Edith Louisa (1865–1915)', *Oxford Dictionary of National Biography*, online edn (Oxford University Press, 2004), doi:10.1093/ref:odnb/32330.
6. Daunton, 'Cavell, Edith Louisa (1865–1915)'.
7. 'Life and Letters', *The Academy*, 13 Nov. 1915, p. 211.
8. Helen Key, 'Edith Cavell', *The Cornishman and Cornish Telegraph*, 2 Dec. 1915, p. 3. On *The Man of Feeling*, see Ch. 7.
9. Jacqueline Banerjee, 'Frampton's Monument to Edith Cavell', The Victorian Web, 26 May 2009, <http://www.victorianweb.org/sculpture/frampton/28.html>.
10. 'The Cavell Memorial', *Lancashire Evening Post*, 7 Sept. 1929, p. 4.
11. Virginia Woolf, 'Professions for Women', in *The Crowded Dance of Modern Life: Selected Essays*, vol. ii, edited with an introduction and notes by Rachel Bowlby (London: Penguin, 1993), pp. 102–3.
12. On the emotional relationships between mothers and sons during the First World War, including experiences of separation, love, and loss, and the gendering of grief, see Michael Roper, *The Secret Battle: Emotional Survival and the Great War* (Manchester: Manchester University Press, 2009), especially pp. 205–42. On women and the grieving process in the twentieth century, including the impact of the First World War on their practices of mourning, see also Julie-Marie Strange, *Death, Grief and Poverty in Britain, 1870–1914* (Cambridge: Cambridge University Press, 2005); Pat Jalland, *Death in War and Peace: Loss and Grief in England, 1914–1970* (Oxford: Oxford University

Press, 2010); Lucy Noakes, *Death, Grief and Mourning in Second World War Britain* (Manchester: Manchester University Press, forthcoming).

13. Barclay wrote under several pseudonyms. On her career and writings, including these 'Billet Notes' during the Great War, see her autobiography: Oliver Sandys (pseud.), *Full and Frank: The Private Life of a Woman Novelist* (London: Hurst and Blackett, 1941).

14. 'Billet Notes: Being Casual Pencillings from a Fighting Man to his Mother', *Nash's and Pall Mall Magazine*, Jan. 1915, pp. 35–42.

15. Edith Talbot, 'The Soldier's Wife', *Evening Despatch*, 21 June 1915, p. 4.

16. An early example of the genre was published as an advice column in 1895: Deborah Primrose, 'Tears, Idle Tears', *Hearth and Home*, 18 July 1895, p. 356.

17. Thomas Dixon, 'Never Repress your Tears', *Wellcome History* (Spring 2012): 9–10. On earlier ideas about tears and health, and the figure of the French physician, see also Ch. 9.

18. 'Tears, Idle Tears', *Daily Mirror*, 20 May 1908, p. 7.

19. 'Weeping Wives', *Daily Mirror*, 6 Jan. 1909, p. 10.

20. 'Women Who Never Cry: Business Girl's Grit Replaces Victorian Tears and Hysterics', *Daily Mirror*, 31 Oct. 1911, p. 5.

21. Dorothy Brunton, 'How Good Looks Suffer: You Mustn't Cry if You Would be Beautiful', *Daily Mirror*, 27 Apr. 1929, p. 16. See also Mary Manners, 'Be Hard-Hearted and Happy', *Daily Mirror*, 26 Sept. 1929, p. 7.

22. Leatham was discussing the Representation of the People Bill, in its committee stage. *Hansard*, 12 June 1884, vol. 209, column 103, <http://hansard.millbanksystems.com/commons/1884/jun/12/committee-progress-10th-june-eighth-night#column_103>.

23. For a flavour of these attitudes and the lives of those who lived with them and struggled against them, see Leonore Davidoff and Belinda Westover (eds), *Our Work, our Lives, our Words: Women's History and Women's Work* (Basingstoke: Macmillan Education, 1986); Carolyn Christensen Nelson (ed.), *Literature of the Women's Suffrage Campaign in England* (Peterborough, Ontario: Broadview Press, 2004); June Purvis and Sandra Stanley Holton (eds), *Votes for Women* (London: Routledge, 2000). One British institution which perpetuated the idea that women were naturally more emotional than men was the Foreign Office, where this supposed difference was used as a reason to exclude women from diplomatic careers in the 1930s and 1940s; Helen McCarthy, *Women of the World: The Rise of the Female Diplomat* (London: Bloomsbury, 2014), pp. 235–6, 345–6.

24. Maria Braden, *Women Politicians and the Media* (Lexington: University of Kentucky Press, 1996), p. 24.

25. 'The Human Touch in Parliament', *Daily Mirror*, 13 Apr. 1917, p. 5.

26. *Dundee Courier*, 19 Sept. 1922, p. 4.

27. *Nottingham Evening Post*, 3 Oct. 1913, p. 7.

28. *Manchester Evening News*, 3 Dec. 1914, p. 7.

29. *Hull Daily Mail*, 1 Nov. 1926, p. 7.

30. *North Devon Journal*, 3 Feb. 1938, p. 3.
31. Dorothy L. Sayers, *Murder Must Advertise*, with a new introduction by Elizabeth George (London: Hodder and Stoughton, 2003), ch. 17, p. 312; first published in 1933 by Victor Gollancz Ltd.
32. See Ch. 8.
33. See Ch. 10.
34. Woolf's essay on Mary Wollstonecraft was first published in *The Nation and Athenaeum* in 1929, and was reprinted in 1932 with three other studies as part of Woolf's 'Four Figures'. Woolf's view of Wollstonecraft is discussed in: Cora Kaplan, 'Mary Wollstonecraft's Reception and Legacies', in Claudia L. Johnson (ed.), *The Cambridge Companion to Mary Wollstonecraft* (Cambridge: Cambridge University Press, 2002), pp. 246-70 (pp. 251-2).
35. Mary Howarth was, briefly, the first editor of the *Daily Mirror*, in 1903, when the paper was launched, initially with an almost entirely female staff and aimed at female readers. The experiment was short-lived and the paper was relaunched, with a male editor, as an illustrated paper aimed at both sexes. See Patricia Holland, 'The Politics of the Smile: "soft news" and the Sexualisation of the Popular Press', in Cynthia Carter, Gill Branston, and Stuart Allen (eds), *News, Gender and Power* (London: Routledge, 1998), pp. 17-32 (p. 21).
36. Mary Howarth, 'Retrospective Review: "The Man of Feeling"—A Hero of Old-Fashioned Romance', *Gentleman's Magazine*, Jan.-June 1907, pp. 290-5.
37. *The Listener*, 28 Oct. 1936, p. 829.
38. Father Thurston reviewed the book in *The Month* in 1936, and his comments were later quoted in George Burns, 'Margery Kempe Reviewed', *The Month* 171, no. 885 (Mar. 1938): 238-44 (p. 241).
39. Sanford Brown Meech and Hope Emily Allen (eds), *The Book of Margery Kempe: The Text from the Unique MS Owned by Colonel W. Butler Bowdon* (London: Published for the Early English Text Society by Humphrey Milford, Oxford University Press, 1940), pp. lxiv-lxv.
40. Virginia Woolf also alluded to the Kingsley poem in the title of her anti-war essay 'Women Must Weep', published in 1938. See Naomi Black, *Virginia Woolf as Feminist* (Ithaca, NY: Cornell University Press, 2004), pp. 134, 145.
41. *The Times*, 31 May 1929; quoted in Pat Thane, 'What Difference Did the Vote Make?', in Amanda Vickery (ed.), *Women, Privilege, and Power: British Politics, 1750 to the Present* (Stanford, Calif.: Stanford University Press, 2001), pp. 253-88 (p. 262).
42. On the gains and losses of independence and agency experienced by women during the twentieth century, with reference to both political participation and wartime opportunities, see Penny Summerfield, 'Approaches to Women and Social Change in the Second World War', in Brian Brivati and Harriet Jones (eds), *What Difference Did the War Make?* (Leicester: Leicester University Press, 1995), pp. 63-79; Penny Summerfield, *Reconstructing Women's Wartime Lives* (Manchester: Manchester University Press, 1998); Thane, 'What Difference Did

the Vote Make?'; Virginia Nicholson, *Millions Like Us: Women's Lives in War and Peace 1939–1949* (London: Penguin, 2011).

43. See Ch. 4.
44. Again, actual change has not lived up to the predictions of the inter-war period. Women in the twenty-first century still worry about the risk and effects of shedding tears in the workplace, as revealed in newspaper and broadcast pieces such as a discussion on BBC Radio 4's *Woman's Hour* on the topic of 'Crying at Work', broadcast on 20 June 2011, <http://www.bbc.co.uk/programmes/poohp7f7>.
45. 'Women Who Forget How to Cry', 13 Oct. 1926, p. 7. See also a letter to the *Mirror* from a male correspondent the following year, noting that he had never seen one of his female friends cry, and expressing his own preference for 'the unromantic sensible type of woman' over the 'sobbing, simpering and clinging type'. 'Through "The Mirror"', *Daily Mirror*, 22 May 1927, p. 7.
46. 'Dorothy Dix's Love Bureau', *Daily Mirror*, 31 Aug. 1937, p. 22.
47. 'Women's Tears', *Daily Mail*, 27 Oct. 1936, p. 10.
48. 'Are You One of the Hard-Faced Hussies?', *Daily Mirror*, 15 Dec. 1936, p. 12.

Chapter 16. Thank You for Coming Back to Me

1. On the implied location of Milford, whether the north of England as suggested by various signposts and exteriors in the film, or the Home Counties, which would be consistent with the accents of most of the characters, see Richard Dyer, *Brief Encounter* (London: British Film Institute, 1993), p. 57; Antonia Lant, *Blackout: Reinventing Women for Wartime British Cinema* (Princeton: Princeton University Press, 1991), p. 169. On the place of the film in relation to works by David Lean and other directors working in British film in the 1940s, see Charles Drazin, *The Finest Years: British Cinema of the 1940s* (London: I.B.Tauris, 2007), especially pp. 55–70.
2. François Truffaut, *The Films in my Life* (New York: Simon and Schuster, 1978), p. 160.
3. Dyer, *Brief Encounter*, pp. 41–68, reflects on the Britishness of the film, and the nostalgic appeal that its contained and awkward emotional style creates.
4. Mass Observation was founded in 1937 as a new attempt to create an 'anthropology of ourselves', charting various aspects of British social and cultural life; Nick Hubble, *Mass Observation and Everyday Life: Culture, History, Theory* (Basingstoke: Palgrave Macmillan, 2006); James Hinton, *Nine Wartime Lives: Mass Observations and the Making of the Modern Self* (Oxford: Oxford University Press, 2010). The Mass Observation project connected with a rich and varied sample of the 'ordinary' British public, albeit one by no means fully representative of the whole population. For a useful discussions of the value and limitations of Mass Observation as a source for cultural and social history, including an example of a newly married man who was so happy that he cried on Christmas day 1940,

see Claire Langhamer, *The English in Love: The Intimate Story of an Emotional Revolution* (Oxford: Oxford University Press, 2013), pp. xv–xxi.

5. The replies to directives are held at the Mass Observation Archive (hereafter MOA), which is one of the Special Collections of the University of Sussex. The responses quoted in this chapter are all taken from the August 1950 Directive Replies (hereafter DR), and are identified by their index number and/or basic biographical information such as sex, age, and occupation. The answers to the question about crying at the pictures have also been analysed in Sue Harper and Vincent Porter, *Weeping in the Cinema in 1950: A Reassessment of Mass-Observation Material* (Brighton: Mass-Observation Archive, University of Sussex Library, 1995); and Sue Harper and Vincent Porter, 'Moved to Tears: Weeping in the Cinema in Postwar Britain', *Screen* 37 (1996): 152–73.

6. These figures are based on an analysis of 100 male and 100 female respondents to the MOA August 1950 directive included in a separate folder labelled 'Directive Replies: August 1950. Analysis', held with the replies themselves.

7. Kate Fox, *The Kleenex for Men Crying Game Report: A Study of Men and Crying* (Oxford: Social Issues Research Centre, 2004), <http://www.sirc.org/publik/crying_game.pdf>, pp. 10–12.

8. 'Dorothy Drew's Show Talk', *Hastings and St Leonards Observer*, 15 Jan. 1938, p. 9.

9. MOA, DR, Aug. 1950, 'Analysis'.

10. MOA, DR, Aug. 1950, participant index numbers 0177, 814, 3034.

11. Harper and Porter, 'Moved to Tears'.

12. MOA, DR, Aug. 1950, married male participant, age 53, index number 3842, occupation given as 'Sales Organizer'.

13. MOA, DR, Aug. 1950, single female participant, age 45, index number 1313, occupation given as 'Artist and Teacher'.

14. Harper and Porter, *Weeping in the Cinema*, p. 3; Harper and Porter, 'Moved to Tears', p. 154; although both these publications seem to me to overstate somewhat the extent to which stereotyped gender differences prevail in the responses.

15. See, for instance, MOA, DR, Aug. 1950, male participants with index numbers 732, 1351, and 4507.

16. MOA, DR, Aug. 1950, married male participant, age 43, index number 4322, occupation given as 'Warehouseman'.

17. Harper and Porter, *Weeping in the Cinema*, p. 26.

18. In 1949, in a talk for BBC Radio's *Woman's Hour*, G. B. Stern spoke about her own tendency to cry at weddings, happy endings in books, the cheering of returning soldiers, and any transition from bad news to good news in real life (transmitted Wednesday 6 July 1949; transcript held at the BBC Written Archives Centre, Caversham Park, Reading). For more on the phenomenon of crying at the happy ending, see Ch. 18.

19. MOA, DR, Aug. 1950, participant index number 1008.

20. On the broader history and theory of 'weepies', women's pictures, melodrama, and movie audiences, see the recommended works on tears and the cinema in the 'Further Reading' section.
21. *Yorkshire Evening Post*, 26 Feb. 1930, p. 8.
22. 'Dorothy Drew's Show Talk', *Hastings and St Leonards Observer*, 15 Jan. 1938, p. 9.
23. Suzanna Danuta Walters, *Lives Together/Worlds Apart: Mothers and Daughters in Popular Culture* (Berkeley and Los Angeles: University of California Press, 1992), pp. 24–34.
24. *Aberdeen Journal*, 1 Mar. 1938, p. 8.
25. *Portsmouth Evening News*, 5 Mar. 1938, p. 7.
26. *Grantham Journal*, 12 Aug. 1939, p. 6; Margaret Thatcher, *The Path to Power* (London: HarperCollins, 1995), pp. 14–15.
27. Cecil Parkinson interviewed on *Newsnight*, BBC Two, 8 Apr. 2013. For more on Margaret Thatcher's tears, see Ch. 19.
28. Barbara Gunnell, 'Tears—No Longer a Crying Shame', *New Statesman*, 22 Nov. 1999, <http://www.newstatesman.com/node/136193>.
29. Winston S. Churchill, *The Second World War*, ii: *Their Finest Hour* (New York: Houghton Mifflin, 1949), pp. 307–8.
30. *The Spectator*, 11 July 1940, p. 3, <http://archive.spectator.co.uk>. See also Richard Toye, *The Roar of the Lion: The Untold Story of Churchill's World War II Speeches* (Oxford: Oxford University Press, 2013), p. 63; Kevin Matthews, review of *The Roar of the Lion: The Untold Story of Churchill's World War II Speeches* (review no. 1542), <http://www.history.ac.uk/reviews/review/1542>; Martin Francis, 'Tears, Tantrums, and Bared Teeth: The Emotional Economy of Three Conservative Prime Ministers, 1951–1963', *Journal of British Studies* 41 (2002): 354–87 (p. 373).
31. D. J. Wenden and K. R. M. Short, 'Winston S. Churchill: Film Fan', *Historical Journal of Film, Radio and Television* 11(1991): 197–214 (pp. 204–5); Charles Barr, '"Much Pleasure and Relaxation in These Hard Times": Churchill and Cinema in The Second World War', *Historical Journal of Film, Radio and Television* 31 (2011): 561–86 (pp. 566–7). I am grateful to Mark Glancy for drawing my attention to the subject of Churchill's own responses to films. On the tears of Emma Hamilton, and many others, in response to the death of Nelson in 1805, see Ch. 9.
32. A London Clergyman, 'Dry Those Tears', *Seven: Magazine of People's Writings* 2, no. 2, July–Aug. 1941, pp. 3–5; accessed via the *Mass Observation Online* database. For an account of the responses of parents and press to the bombing of a South London school in 1943, see Lucy Noakes, 'Gender, Grief and Bereavement in Second World War Britain', *Journal of War and Culture Studies* 8 (2015): forthcoming.
33. Noakes, 'Gender, Grief and Bereavement'.
34. Stephen H. Roberts, 'Why Hitler Backs his Hunches', *Daily Express*, 14 Mar. 1938, p. 12.

35. Quentin J. Reynolds, *The Wounded Don't Cry* (London: Cassell and Co., 1941).
36. Joe Illingworth, 'Confident Yorkshiremen in Holland', *Yorkshire Post*, 25 Sept. 1944, p. 1.
37. See Introduction.
38. 'Surrender in Holland, Denmark, and North-West Germany', *Yorkshire Post*, 5 May 1945, p. 1; Victor Lewis, 'Jap "Never Surrender" General Weeps Again', *Press and Journal*, 12 Sept. 1945, p. 1; see also Christopher Bayly and Tim Harper, *Forgotten Wars: The End of Britain's Asian Empire* (London: Allen Lane, 2007), p. 50.
39. The liberation of the Channel Islands was a particularly dramatic, and tearful, example: see *Yorkshire Post*, 11 May 1945, p. 1.
40. 'Laughter and Tears', *Western Morning News*, 20 Sept. 1945, p. 3.
41. 'Ronald Neame on *Brief Encounter*'s Ending', The Criterion Collection, 29 Mar. 2012, <http://www.criterion.com/current/posts/2227>.
42. Jeffrey Richards, *Films and British National Identity: From Dickens to Dad's Army* (Manchester: Manchester University Press, 1997), pp. 123–4. The film had even provoked derision in the 1940s, at least among one working-class audience in Kent at an early test screening; it would always find its most sentimentally responsive viewers among the middle classes. See Kevin Brownlow, *David Lean: A Biography* (London: Faber and Faber, 1997), p. 203; Melanie Williams, '*Brief Encounter* (1945)', in Sarah Barrow and John White (eds), *Fifty Key British Films* (London: Routledge, 2008), pp. 55–60 (p. 56).
43. See Ch. 9.
44. The moment comes after a trip on a boating lake. Alec has fallen into the water, and as he dries off in the boatman's hut he and Laura declare their feelings for the first time.
45. 'It Could Happen to Anybody', *Derby Daily Telegraph*, 12 Mar. 1946, p. 2.
46. On this and other resonances of the film with its first audiences in 1945, see Lant, *Blackout*, p. 187.
47. Jeffrey Richards and Dorothy Sheridan (eds), *Mass-Observation at the Movies* (London: Routledge and Kegan Paul, 1987), 'Introduction', p. 15.
48. On psychoanalysis and tears see Ch. 17; and Thomas Dixon, 'The Waterworks', Aeon Magazine, 22 Feb. 2013, <http://aeon.co/magazine/psychology/thomas-dixon-tears>. On the idea that in *Brief Encounter* Laura displays the symptoms of a Freudian hysteric, see Dyer, *Brief Encounter*, p. 21; and Lant, *Blackout*, pp. 181–3.
49. Harper and Porter, 'Moved to Tears', pp. 169–70.
50. Richards and Sheridan, *Mass-Observation at the Movies*, p. 13.
51. John Pudney, 'For Johnny' (1942), in *The Oxford Dictionary of Quotations*, new edn, ed. Elizabeth M. Knowles (Oxford: Oxford University Press, 1999), p. 616; see also Brian Murdoch, *Fighting Songs and Warring Words: Popular Lyrics of Two World Wars* (London: Routledge, 1990), pp. 167–8; Noakes, 'Gender, Grief and Bereavement'.

52. Richards, *Films and British National Identity*, pp. 87-9.
53. A 36-year-old schoolmaster, quoted in Harper and Porter, 'Moved to Tears', p. 171.
54. MOA, DR, Aug. 1950, male participant, age 34, civil servant, index number 0175.
55. Dyer, *Brief Encounter*, pp. 32-3, 48-53; Lant, *Blackout*, pp. 163-7, 183-92. A 33-year-old male journalist (MOA, DR, Aug. 1950, index number 83) wrote: 'I seem to get back to 1946 and "Brief Encounter" before I find one which was really tear-making. That, I suppose, because it is closest to real (middle class) life than any other film yet made.'
56. On the culture of emotional containment, concealment, and restraint, see Ch. 17, and Noakes, 'Gender, Grief, and Bereavement'; Pat Jalland, *Death in War and Peace: Loss and Grief in England, 1914-1970* (Oxford: Oxford University Press, 2010); Sonya O. Rose, *Which People's War? National Identity and Citizenship in Britain, 1939-1945* (Oxford: Oxford University Press, 2003), ch. 5, pp. 151-96.
57. Michael Pointer, *Charles Dickens on the Screen: The Film, Television, and Video Adaptations* (Lanham, Md: Scarecrow Press, 1996).
58. John 11: 25.
59. MOA, 'Fade Out (Film)', File Report 393, Sept. 1940. The ending of the 1939 film *Nurse Edith Cavell*, directed by Herbert Wilcox and starring Anna Neagle in the title role, also featured among respondents' favoured 'fade-outs'; Richards and Sheridan, *Mass-Observation at the Movies*, p. 207. On Cavell, see Ch. 15. On Neagle, see Ch. 17.
60. *A Tale of Two Cities*, dir. Ralph Thomas, Rank, 1958.
61. '50 Films That Make Men Cry', *GQ Magazine*, 26 Apr. 2011, <http://www.gq-magazine.co.uk>.

Chapter 17. Grief Observed

1. Brian Hession, 'Healing Tears', a talk for 'The Silver Lining' programme, broadcast Tuesday 8 July 1958, 4.45-5.00 p.m., Home Service. Transcript held at the BBC Written Archives Centre, Caversham Park, Reading.
2. Pat Jalland has surveyed the evolution of British attitudes to death during the nineteenth and twentieth centuries. In her judgement, the Second World War marked the final break with lost traditions of mourning, which were now replaced by 'a pervasive model of suppressed privatized grieving which became deeply entrenched in the nation's social psychology' and dominated until the mid-1960s. Pat Jalland, *Death in War and Peace: Loss and Grief in England, 1914-1970* (Oxford: Oxford University Press, 2010), p. 10, and *passim*. See also the list of recommended works on death and mourning in modern Britain in the 'Further Reading' section.

3. On tearful responses to the coronation in 1953, see Ch. 20, and Wendy Webster, *Englishness and Empire, 1939–1965* (Oxford: Oxford University Press, 2005). On the history of *Coronation Street*, see Richard Dyer et al., *Coronation Street* (London: BFI Publishing, 1981) and, on the broader history of British television in this period, Joe Moran, *Armchair Nation: An Intimate History of Britain in Front of the TV* (London: Profile, 2013), ch. 4.
4. 'In Memoriam: Brian Hession', *Church Times*, 13 Oct. 1961, p. 17.
5. Matthew 5: 4.
6. Hession 'Healing Tears'.
7. 'Catholic Ceremonial', *Church Times*, 11 Oct. 1957, p. 12.
8. See Chs 1–4 for the earlier history of that tradition.
9. Jenna Bailey, *Can Any Mother Help Me?* (London: Faber and Faber, 2007), pp. 246–8; see also Jenna Bailey, 'Can Any Mother Help Me?', History of Emotions Blog, 20 Mar. 2014, <https://emotionsblog.history.qmul.ac.uk/2014/03/can-any-mother-help-me>.
10. 'Co-Operative Correspondence Club', BBC Radio 4, *Woman's Hour*, 6 Aug. 2007, <http://www.bbc.co.uk/radio4/womanshour/04/2007_32_mon.shtml>.
11. Jalland, *Death in War and Peace*, pp. 236–7. See also J. A. W. Bennett, 'Lewis, Clive Staples (1898–1963)', rev. Emma Plaskitt, *Oxford Dictionary of National Biography* (Oxford University Press, 2004), online edn, May 2008, doi: 10.1093/ref:odnb/34512. Lewis's recollections of his childhood, including learning to treat emotion as something dangerous and embarrassing, are to be found in C. S. Lewis, *Surprised by Joy: The Shape of my Early Life* (London: Geoffrey Bles, 1955), especially chs 1–2.
12. On 'Maudlin' tears, see Ch. 2.
13. C. S. Lewis, *A Grief Observed* (London: Faber & Faber, 1964), pp. 8, 14, 31; original publication N. W. Clerk, *A Grief Observed* (London: Faber & Faber, 1961). On Lewis's book and its place in the literature of loss and grief in the 1960s and 1970s, see Jalland, *Death in War and Peace*, ch. 12.
14. Lewis, *A Grief Observed*, pp. 11–13.
15. Mothers sending their young sons away to boarding school also had to learn not to shed public tears at the moment of parting. This was something Marjorie Proops wrote about in 1957, when the queen had the experience of sending the young Prince Charles away to school for the first time; Marjorie Proops, 'You Can't Kiss a Schoolboy Goodbye!', *Daily Mirror*, 18 Sept. 1957, p. 11.
16. Douglas H. Gresham, 'Introduction' to C. S. Lewis, *A Grief Observed* (Harper-Collins e-book, 2009), pp. xix–xx. See Ch. 14, on the inculcation of a stiff upper lip in British schools from the nineteenth century onwards.
17. Douglas H. Gresham, *Lenten Lands* (New York: Macmillan, 1988), p. 127.
18. Gresham, 'Introduction', p. xx.
19. Lewis, *A Grief Observed*, p. 47.
20. See, for instance, Frank Furedi, *Therapy Culture: Cultivating Vulnerability in an Uncertain Age* (London: Routledge, 2003).

21. Josef Breuer and Sigmund Freud, *Studies on Hysteria: The Standard Edition of the Complete Psychological Works of Sigmund Freud*, ii: *1893–1895*, trans. James Strachey and Anna Freud (London: The Hogarth Press and the Institute of Psycho-Analysis, 1955), pp. 3–11. See also Thomas Dixon, 'The Waterworks', Aeon Magazine, 22 Feb. 2013, <http://aeon.co/magazine/psychology/thomas-dixon-tears>.

22. On Churchill's tears, see Ch. 16. Churchill's famous speech was referred to along with further examples of the association of tears with other bodily fluids in Robert L. Sadoff, 'On the Nature of Crying and Weeping', *Psychiatric Quarterly* 40 (1966): 490–503 (p. 493).

23. Phyllis Greenacre, 'Urination and Weeping', *American Journal of Orthopsychiatry* 15 (1945): 81–8 (p. 81). See also Phyllis Greenacre, 'Pathological Weeping', *Psychoanalytic Quarterly* 16 (1945): 62–75.

24. Mass Observation, File Report 290, *Women in Wartime* (June 1940), accessed via Mass Observation Online.

25. Mass Observation, Directive Response, Aug. 1950, male participant in his forties, index number 1120. For more on Mass Observation and the August 1950 directive, see Ch. 16.

26. 'So Get Weeping, Dad!', *Daily Mirror*, 11 Aug. 1954, p. 2.

27. Eve Perrick, 'TV Tears Wash Those Wisecracks Away', *Daily Express*, 26 Nov. 1953, p. 4.

28. *Southern Daily Echo*, 18 Jan. 1957. See also 'The Reverend Brian Hession', The Big Red Book: Celebrating Television's This is your Life, <http://www.bigredbook.info/brian_hession.html>.

29. Neagle's appearance features in an essay about the history of emotional expression on television, from the 1950s onwards, by the film-maker and cultural critic Adam Curtis: 'The Curse of Tina Part Two: Learning to Hug', The Medium and the Message Blog, 4 Oct. 2011, <http://www.bbc.co.uk/blogs/adamcurtis/posts/the_curse_of_tina_part_two>.

30. 'Anna Neagle Weeps Before TV Millions', *Daily Express*, 18 Feb. 1958, p. 7.

31. Charles Drazin, *The Finest Years: British Cinema of the 1940s* (London: I.B.Tauris, 2007), p. 219; on Cavell and her stiff upper lip, see Ch. 15.

32. James Thomas, 'The Cruel Keyhole', *Daily Express*, 19 Feb. 1958, p. 6.

33. Ibid. See also 'Anna Neagle—Press Reactions', The Big Red Book: Celebrating Television's This is your Life, <http://www.bigredbook.info/article3.05.html>.

34. 'Unshed Tears', *Daily Mirror*, 8 Feb. 1961, p. 8.

35. 'It's the Show that Balances on a Tightrope', The Big Red Book: Celebrating Television's This is your Life, <http://www.bigredbook.info/article10.02.html>.

36. Clifford Davis, 'Mr Harding is Near to Tears', *Daily Mirror*, 19 Sept. 1960, p. 18.

37. *Southern Daily Echo*, 18 Jan. 1957; 'The Reverend Brian Hession', The Big Red Book: Celebrating Television's This is your Life, <http://www.bigredbook.info/brian_hession.html>. On the mythology surrounding Harding's tears on *Face to Face*, see Moran, *Armchair Nation*, pp. 136–8.

38. Sheila Duncan, 'Crying Might Help', *Daily Mirror*, 12 Sept. 1961, p. 16. The repressed Suttons reminded Sheila Duncan of the scene in the 1950 movie *Blue Lamp* in which a policeman's wife's immediate reaction to the news of her husband's death was silently to place some flowers into a vase. The film was mentioned as an especially moving one by some of the respondents to the August 1950 Mass Observation Directive asking about crying at the pictures. See Sue Harper and Vincent Porter, 'Moved to Tears: Weeping in the Cinema in Postwar Britain', *Screen* 37 (1996): 152–73 (pp. 160–1).
39. See Ch. 14.
40. Geoffrey Gorer, *Death, Grief, and Mourning in Contemporary Britain* (London: The Cresset Press, 1965); Jalland, *Death in War and Peace*, ch. 11, quotations at pp. 217, 218, 224.
41. Sara Robson, 'Grief Has Real Meaning for a Child', *Daily Mirror*, 18 Feb. 1965, p. 15.

Chapter 18. Ha'way the Lads!

1. This is an allusion to Virginia Woolf's famous assertion that 'on or about December 1910 human character changed'. Virginia Woolf, 'Mr. Bennett and Mrs. Brown' (1924), in *The Virginia Woolf Reader*, ed. Mitchell A. Leaska (San Diego: Harcourt Brace Jovanovic, 1984), p. 194. See also Peter Stansky, *On or About December 1910: Early Bloomsbury and its Intimate World* (Cambridge, Mass.: Harvard University Press, 1996), pp. 2–4, 243.
2. Art historian James Elkins suggests that Mark Rothko, who committed suicide in 1970, was unique among modern painters in setting out to produce tears. In an interview in 1957, Rothko commented that people who wept in front of his pictures were 'having the same religious experience I had when I painted them'; James Elkins, *Pictures and Tears: A History of People Who Have Cried in Front of Paintings* (New York: Routledge, 2001), pp. 12–13. For more on weeping over paintings in the eighteenth century, see Ch. 6. The example of a man weeping over Joan Baez singing 'Kumbaya' comes from Dalbir Bindra, 'Weeping: A Problem of Many Facets', *Bulletin of the British Psychological Society* 25 (1972): 281–4 (p. 283).
3. James Booth, *Philip Larkin: Life, Art, and Love* (London: Bloomsbury, 2014), pp. 423–5. On the aesthetics of sensibility in the eighteenth century, see Chs 6–9.
4. Lance Hardy, *Stokoe, Sunderland and '73: The Story of the Greatest FA Cup Final Shock of All Time* (London: Orion Books, 2009), pp. 13–22, 86–8.
5. Geoffrey Whitten, 'Revivalist Has More Than Blind Faith', *The Times*, 6 Apr. 1973, p. 13. See also Hardy, *Stokoe, Sunderland and '73*, p. 98.
6. Posted by a fan using the name 'Laeotaekhun' on the Sunderland Message Board, in a discussion thread entitled 'What's the Most Emotion You Felt at a Match?', 8 Aug. 2014, <http://www.readytogo.net/smb>.

7. From Les Murray's 'An Absolutely Ordinary Rainbow', first published in his 1969 collection *The Weatherboard Cathedral*; Les Murray, *Collected Poems* (Melbourne: Black Inc, 2006), pp. 28–30. On the emotional responses of players and fans, as well as their manager, at the end of the Hillsborough semi-final see Hardy, *Stokoe, Sunderland and '73*, pp. 187–9; and Desmond Hackett, 'Sunderland Grab the Glory', *Daily Express*, 9 Apr. 1973, p. 23.
8. Gerald Sinstadt, 'The Cup Final: Inspiration versus Hardened Skill', *The Times*, 4 May 1973, p. 12.
9. 'Leeds Again Too Busy for Civic Reception at Home', *The Times*, 3 May 1973, p. 8.
10. Derek Dougan, 'David and Goliath in Football Boots', *The Times*, 5 May 1973, p. 12.
11. *Sunderland vs Leeds Utd: 1973 FA Cup Final*, Ilc Media, 2004, DVD.
12. Quoted in Hardy, *Stokoe, Sunderland, and '73*, p. 266.
13. *Sunderland vs Leeds Utd*, DVD. The *Sunday Mirror* described Stokoe's 'beaming, tearful face' at the end of the Wembley final; quoted in Hardy, *Stokoe, Sunderland and '73*, p. 296.
14. *Sunderland vs Leeds Utd*, DVD; also quoted in Hardy, *Stokoe, Sunderland and '73*, pp. 264–5.
15. On more recent sporting and athletic tears, see Ch. 20.
16. Gerald Sinstadt, 'The Cup Final: Inspiration versus Hardened Skill', *The Times*, 4 May 1973, p. 12. The *Mirror* took a similarly approving tone in writing of Stokoe's unexpected but touching display of emotion, describing the scene as tears rolled down Stokoe's cheeks as he embraced his wife at Hillsborough; Frank McGhee, 'Messiah and Miracle', *Daily Mirror*, 9 Apr. 1973, pp. 30–1.
17. Marje Proops, 'My Quality Street Gang', *Daily Mirror*, 1 May 1973, p. 17.
18. Marje Proops, 'He's Ashamed of Weeping', *Daily Mirror*, 4 May 1978, p. 9.
19. The circulation of the *Daily Mirror* fell from 4.7 to 3.8 million between 1970 and 1979; Matthias M. Matthijs, *Ideas and Economic Crises in Britain from Attlee to Blair, 1945-2005* (Abingdon: Routledge, 2011), p. 120.
20. Rebecca Rolfe's research into the behaviour of Academy Award recipients demonstrates that there was a marked increase in tearful acceptance speeches starting around 1993 when Tom Hanks and Steven Spielberg both wept (the latter becoming the only winner of the Best Director Oscar to date to have choked up or wept with emotion). Prior to the 1990s, men had been slightly more likely to weep than women when receiving Oscars, but Helen Hunt's tears when accepting the Best Actress award in 1997 started a fifteen-year run in which only three leading actress recipients did not cry. Rebecca Rolfe, 'How They Behaved', Thank the Academy, 2013, <http://www.rebeccarolfe.com/projects/thanktheacademy>.
21. Bel Mooney, 'Sit Right Down and CRY', *Daily Mirror*, 19 Apr. 1979, p. 9.
22. 'Where Have All the He-Men Gone?', *Daily Mirror*, 17 May 1973, p. 33.
23. Frank Taylor, 'Room at the Top', *Daily Mirror*, 17 Apr. 1973, p. 30.
24. Letter published in the sports pages of the *Daily Mirror*, 4 Mar. 1976, p. 27. Later the same year, one Mrs R. W. Husband of Ashtead, Surrey, wrote to *The*

Times, with reference to American politicians and TV shows, asking, 'What has happened to the tradition that Strong Men Don't Cry (at least not in public)?'; *The Times*, 13 Nov. 1976, p. 13. Jeffrey Bernard complained about the effete and spoiled nature of modern footballers in his column entitled 'Cup Fever', which also mentioned the emotional tears of the players, in the *Spectator*, 7 May 1976, p. 14, The Spectator Archive, <http://archive.spectator.co.uk>.

25. Matt Cook et al., *A Gay History of Britain: Love and Sex Between Men Since the Middle Ages* (Oxford: Greenwood World Publishing, 2007), chs 5 and 6.

26. Marje Proops, 'The Night He Cried', *Daily Mirror*, 19 Dec. 1971, p. 13.

27. Marje Proops, 'Anguish Over their Cry-Baby Son', *Daily Mirror*, 13 July 1978, p. 9.

28. Ronald Bedford, 'Go On and Cry, You Big He-Men', *Daily Mirror*, 11 July 1974, p. 5.

29. Stan Hawkins, *The British Pop Dandy: Masculinity, Popular Music and Culture* (Farnham: Ashgate, 2009), pp. 81–4.

30. The Cure, 'Boys Don't Cry', written by Robert Smith, Laurence Tolhurst, and Michel Dempsey (Fiction Records, 1979).

31. Tears for Fears, 'I Believe', written by Roland Orzabal, 'Shout', written by Roland Orzabal and Ian Stanley, *Songs From the Big Chair* (Phonogram/Mercury, 1985).

32. Arthur Janov, *Prisoners of Pain: Unlocking the Power of the Mind to End Suffering* (New York: Anchor Press, 1980).

33. See Ch. 17.

34. Ad Vingerhoets, *Why Only Humans Weep: Unravelling the Mysteries of Tears* (Oxford: Oxford University Press, 2013), pp. 220–1. A similar form of crying-based therapy from the same period is described in Ben C. Finney, 'Say It Again: An Active Therapy Technique', *Psychotherapy: Theory, Research and Practice* 9 (1972): 157–65.

35. In 1969, Don Short wrote with some cynicism about the ability of the American pop singer Vikki Carr to turn on her tears while performing: 'Tears—For the Millions', *Daily Mirror*, 8 Feb. 1969, p. 9. The most famously lachrymose American performer of the 1950s was Johnnie Ray. When Ray performed in Britain in 1976, Geoffrey Wansell reviewed the event for *The Times*, writing, 'The time warp war in action last night as one of the first singers to make dreams wet with tears for teenage audiences returned to London after 18 years.' The event, for Wansell, was not a success. It was like 'watching a waxwork' and neither Ray nor his audience was moved to tears; 'Johnnie Ray: The London Palladium', *The Times*, 3 Aug. 1976, p. 7.

36. Jann S. Wenner, *Lennon Remembers* (London: Verso Books, 2000), pp. 1–4; John Wyse Jackson, *We All Want to Change the World: The Life of John Lennon* (London: Haus Publishing Limited, 2005), p. 132. A psychological study of 70 British men and 70 British women published in 1982 found that the men recalled their crying behaviour reduced around the age of 11, on average; for

women the onset of less tearful behaviour was placed at the age of 16; D. G. Williams, 'Weeping by Adults: Personality Correlates and Sex Differences', *Journal of Psychology* 110 (1982): 217–26.

37. Ivor Davies, 'When Adults Cry on Santa's Knee', *Daily Express*, 21 Dec. 1970, p. 2.
38. Ross Benson, 'If You Want to Grow Up, Be a Cry Baby', *Daily Express*, 3 May 1978, p. 11.
39. Jack O. Balswick and Charles W. Peek, 'The Inexpressive Male: A Tragedy of American Society', *Family Co-Ordinator* 20 (1971): 363–8.
40. Veronica Papworth, 'Stiff Upper Lips Can Harm your Health', *Sunday Express*, 3 Feb. 1980, p. 19.
41. See Ch. 17.
42. On the figure of the French physician, see Thomas Dixon, 'Never Repress your Tears', *Wellcome History* (Spring 2012): 9–10; and Ch. 9 in this volume. On the influence of American films and television on British culture, see Ch. 17.
43. 'For Crying Out Loud', What Larks Productions for BBC Four, first broadcast 14 Feb. 2011, <http://www.bbc.co.uk/programmes/booymhqz>.
44. See Chs 1 and 5.
45. For some examples of crying at the happy endings of films, see Ch. 16.
46. Sandor S. Feldman, 'Crying at the Happy Ending', *Journal of the American Psychoanalytic Association* (1956): 477–85 (p. 479); see also Vingerhoets, *Why Only Humans Weep*, pp. 87–8.
47. Jay S. Efran and Timothy J. Spangler, 'Why Grown-Ups Cry', *Motivation and Emotion* 3 (1979): 63–72.
48. Frank McGhee, 'Messiah and Miracle', *Daily Mirror*, 9 April 1973, p. 30.
49. Quoted in Hardy, *Stokoe, Sunderland and '73*, p. 226.
50. Judith Kay Nelson, *Seeing Through Tears: Crying and Attachment* (New York: Routledge, 2005), pp. 47–8.
51. Veronica Papworth, 'Stiff Upper Lips Can Harm your Health', *Sunday Express*, 3 Feb. 1980, p. 19; Marje Proops, 'A Tough Guy's Crying Shame', *Daily Mirror*, 6 Dec. 1983, p. 9.
52. 'If You Have Tears to Shed', *Daily Express*, 14 July 1980, p. 8.
53. Hardy, *Stokoe, Sunderland, and '73*, pp. 175–6, 185, 187–8.

Chapter 19. The Thatcher Tears

1. See Ch. 15.
2. Mark Brown, 'Spitting Image Exhibition Allows Margaret Thatcher Centre Stage—Again', The Guardian Online, 25 Feb. 2014, <http://www.theguardian.com>.
3. Leo Abse, *Margaret, Daughter of Beatrice: A Politician's Psycho-Biography of Margaret Thatcher* (London: Jonathan Cape, 1989), e.g. pp. 61, 250.
4. Hilary Mantel, 'The Assassination of Margaret Thatcher: August 6th 1983', and author interview with Damian Barr, *The Guardian*, Review Section, 20 Sept.

2014, pp. 2–5; also available at The Guardian Online, 19 Sept. 2014, <http://www.theguardian.com>.

5. Wendy Webster, *Not a Man to Match Her: The Marketing of a Prime Minister* (London: The Women's Press, 1990), pp. 78–87; Margaret Scammell, 'The Phenomenon of Political Marketing: The Thatcher Contribution', *Contemporary British History* 8 (1994): 23–43.

6. Webster, *Not a Man to Match Her*, p. 85; Douglas Keay interview with Margaret Thatcher, 'Whatever I Go Through Now, Can't Be as Terrible', *Woman's Own*, 28 Aug. 1982, Margaret Thatcher Foundation, <http://www.margaretthatcher.org/document/123130>.

7. Webster, *Not a Man to Match Her*, p. 85; 'Interview for London Weekend Television (LWT) Aspel and Company', Broadcast 21 Aug. 1984, Margaret Thatcher Foundation, <http://www.margaretthatcher.org/document/105507>.

8. A possible partial exception to these generalizations is Harold Macmillan, Conservative Prime Minister from 1957 to 1963, who was described as having a voice 'heavy with emotion' and a tear 'in the corner of his eye', and as 'fighting back the tears' somewhat theatrically, in the context of two television interviews, but Thatcher's performance in 1985 is the first clear-cut and well-documented case of actual weeping. Macmillan himself said of the new medium of television that those watching it in their homes 'were not subject to any of the emotions which can be stirred in a great political gathering'. See Martin Francis, 'Tears, Tantrums, and Bared Teeth: The Emotional Economy of Three Conservative Prime Ministers, 1951–1963', *Journal of British Studies* 41 (2002): 354–87 (pp. 367, 379); John Turner, *Macmillan* (London: Longman, 1994), p. 173; Mike Featherstone, *Undoing Culture: Globalization, Postmodernism, and Identity* (London: Sage, 1995), p. 106.

9. On Edmund Muskie and the gendering of politicians' tears, see Stephanie A. Shields, *Speaking from the Heart: Gender and the Social Meaning of Emotion* (Cambridge: Cambridge University Press, 2002), pp. 161–5.

10. 'The Crying Game: When Politicians Get Teary', Channel 4 News, 12 Apr. 2012, <http://www.channel4.com/news>.

11. 'Anders Behring Breivik Weeps in Oslo Court', BBC News, 16 Apr. 2012, <http://www.bbc.co.uk/news/world-europe-17727993>.

12. 'Gordon Brown Weeps Recalling Daughter's Death', *Sunday Telegraph*, 7 Feb. 2010, <http://www.telegraph.co.uk/news/politics/gordon-brown/7179967/Gordon-Brown-weeps-recalling-daughters-death.html>; Simon Walter, 'Gordon Brown Weeps on TV as he Talks about Death of Jennifer', *Mail on Sunday*, 7 Feb. 2010, <http://www.dailymail.co.uk/news/article-1249089>.

13. Tim Shipman, 'Another Day, Another Emotional Party Leader: After Gordon Brown's Tears, David Cameron Breaks Down on TV', *Daily Mail*, 16 Feb. 2010, <http://www.dailymail.co.uk/news/article-1251069>. Toby Young, 'David Cameron: Talked from the Heart about Ivan in Tonight's ITV interview',

Telegraph Blog, 12 Apr. 2010, <http://blogs.telegraph.co.uk/news/tobyyoung/100034036/david-cameron-itv-interview>.

14. Fraser Nelson, 'Cameron Steps Up his Game', Spectator Coffeehouse Blog, 14 Feb. 2010, <http://blogs.spectator.co.uk/coffeehouse/2010/02/cameron-steps-up-his-game>.

15. 'Prime Minister David Cameron's Tears for Late Son Ivan on Emotional Visit to Former School', Daily Record, 19 Nov. 2010, <http://www.dailyrecord.co.uk/news/uk-world-news/prime-minister-david-camerons-tears-1076220>.

16. Ben Wright, 'Cameron Frames Election Choice With Tax Cuts Pledge', BBC News, 1 Oct. 2014, <http://www.bbc.co.uk/news/uk-politics-29448836>.

17. On Churchill's tears, see Ch. 16.

18. Cristina Odone, 'A Blubbing Politician? It's Enough to Make You Weep', Telegraph Blog, 7 Apr. 2011, <http://blogs.telegraph.co.uk/news/cristinaodone/100082936/a-blubbing-politician-nick-clegg>. In the interview for the New Statesman, with Jemima Khan, Clegg had said 'I'm not a punch-bag' and 'I've of course got feelings', revealing that at home in the evenings he liked to read novels and 'cries regularly to music', New Statesman, 7 Apr. 2011, <http://www.newstatesman.com/uk-politics/2011/04/clegg-interview-coalition-life>. The front page of the Sun newspaper, the day after Margaret Thatcher's resignation in 1990, also mistakenly implied that her tears on that day were the first of her entire premiership: 'Mrs T-ears', The Sun, 23 Nov. 1990, p. 1.

19. Andy McSmith, 'It's my Party and I'll Cry if I Want to', The Independent, 23 Nov. 2011, <http://www.independent.co.uk/news/uk/politics/its-my-party-and-ill-cry-if-i-want-to-6266291.html>.

20. Martin Francis has argued for an approach to political history which recognizes that 'the world of politics is a part of, and not apart from, the realm of private feeling'; Francis, 'Tears, Tantrums, and Bared Teeth', p. 387.

21. The emotions and tears of several of Thatcher's predecessors as Tory leader are analysed in Francis, 'Tears, Tantrums, and Bared Teeth'.

22. Michael Cockerell, 'How to Be a Tory Leader', Daily Telegraph, 1 Dec. 2005, <http://www.telegraph.co.uk/culture/3648425/How-to-be-a-Tory-leader.html>.

23. Geoffrey Howe, Conflict of Loyalty (London: Macmillan, 1994), p. 94. For a similar account of Thatcher's election in 1975 bringing tears to male eyes, see Patrick Cosgrave, Margaret Thatcher: Prime Minister (London: Arrow, 1979), p. 13. I am grateful to Robert Saunders for these references.

24. John Ezard, 'Mrs Thatcher's Emotional Side', The Guardian, 21 Sept. 1978, p. 2.

25. On the problems experienced by the Labour Party in appealing to female voters in the 1950s and 1960s, see Amy Black and Stephen Brooke, 'The Labour Party, Women, and the Problem of Gender, 1951–1966', Journal of British Studies 36 (1997): 419–52.

26. Michael Evans, 'Why I Cry by Maggie', Daily Express, 21 Sept. 1978, p. 7.

27. Patricia Clough, 'Thatcher Moved to Tears by the Berlin Wall', The Times, 30 Oct. 1982, p. 1; Ian Black, 'Holocaust Images Move Thatcher to Tears', The

NOTES TO PP. 287–291

Guardian, 26 May 1986, p. 1; Charles Powell, interviewed for the PBS Documentary *Commanding Heights: The Battle for the World Economy*, Episode 2: 'The Agony of Reform' (dir. William Cran, Heights Productions Inc., 2002), described Thatcher's tears during her visit to Gdańsk, and I am grateful to Robert Saunders for drawing my attention to this example.

28. 'Fears Grow for Mark', *Daily Express*, 14 Jan. 1982, p. 1. See also Penny Chorlton, 'Thatcher Weeps for her Missing Son', *The Guardian*, 14 Jan. 1982, <http://www.theguardian.com/theguardian/1982/jan/14/fromthearchive>.

29. Dominic Lawson, 'Believe it or Not, Thatcher Was a Woman Who Cared', *The Independent*, 8 Apr. 2013, <http://www.independent.co.uk/voices/comment/dominic-lawson-believe-it-or-not-thatcher-was-a-woman-who-cared-8564896.html>. See also John Campbell, *Margaret Thatcher*, ii: *The Iron Lady* (London: Vintage, 2008), pp. 140, 150–1; Jonathan Aitken, *Margaret Thatcher: Power and Personality* (London: Bloomsbury, 2013), p. 361.

30. Douglas Keay interview with Margaret Thatcher, 'Whatever I Go Through Now, Can't Be as Terrible', *Woman's Own*, 28 Aug. 1982, Margaret Thatcher Foundation, <http://www.margaretthatcher.org/document/123130>.

31. John Ezard, 'Thatcher Honours Falklands War Dead', *The Guardian*, 11 Jan. 1983, p. 1; Webster, *Not a Man to Match Her*, pp. 84–5.

32. On the role of Frey and other American psychiatrists in British media stories about the benefits of weeping from the 1970s onwards, see Ch. 18. The recollection of being called 'Mama Thatcher' in Italy came in a 1984 speech in Finchley as well as in the 1985 television interview with Miriam Stoppard quoted below; 'Silver Anniversary for "Mama Thatcher"', Margaret Thatcher Foundation, 28 January 1984, <http://www.margaretthatcher.org/document/105607>; I am grateful to Helen McCarthy for drawing this to my attention.

33. William H. Frey II, with Muriel Langseth, *Crying: The Mystery of Tears* (Minneapolis: Winston Press, 1985), pp. 48–52.

34. Peter Jones (dir.), 'Woman to Woman', Yorkshire Television, broadcast on ITV, 19 Nov. 1985, Margaret Thatcher Foundation, <http://www.margaretthatcher.org/document/105830>; 'Miriam Stoppard Talks to Margaret Thatcher', BFI Archive Collection, London, Reference number 326007, <http://collections-search.bfi.org.uk/web>.

35. 'Tears and Resolution in Candid Thatcher Interview', *The Times*, 19 Nov. 1985, p. 2.

36. Abse, *Margaret, Daughter of Beatrice*.

37. Judith Kay Nelson, *Seeing Through Tears: Crying and Attachment* (New York: Routledge, 2005), especially pp. 47–8.

38. See Ch. 16.

39. Nicholas Shakespeare, 'Television: Unity in Diversity', *The Times*, 20 Nov. 1985, p. 10.

40. This theme of authenticity and reality returns in Ch. 20, and the Conclusion.

41. On early televised tears, including Harding's, see Ch. 17.

42. 'Dear Bill' and 'Maggie in TV Tears Shocker', *Private Eye*, No. 625, 29 Nov. 1985, pp. 17, 18. See also Benny Green, 'Television: Hanky-Panky', *Punch*, 27 Nov. 1985, p. 86.
43. '1983–1987 Polls', UK Polling Report, <http://ukpollingreport.co.uk/voting-intention-1983-1987>; 'General Election Results 11 June 1987', Guides to Parliament (Factsheets), <http://www.parliament.uk/about/how/guides/factsheets/members-elections/m11>.
44. Sally Potter (dir.), 'Tears', Channel 4, broadcast 19 Sept. 1987. The four programmes were produced by Sarah Radclyffe for Working Title Productions in 1986 and were broadcast weekly on Channel 4 in September and October 1987, starting with 'Tears'; BFI Archive Collection, London, Reference numbers 299385–299388, <http://collections-search.bfi.org.uk/web>.
45. John Dugdale, 'Guidelines', *The Listener*, 17 Sept. 1987, p. 29.
46. 'The Rt Hon. Paul Yaw Boateng, Doctor of Laws', Bristol University Honorary Degrees, 18 July 2007, <http://www.bristol.ac.uk/pace/graduation/honorary-degrees/hondeg07/boateng.html>. In 2000, Boateng wrote of the experience of seeing a bronze sculpture of the crucifixion made by a craftsman in the Congo, depicting Christ, his mother, and Mary Magdalene with the features of black Africans. The image, representing for Boateng the way that Christ had been wrested away from 'the colonial master' to become the African's own, moved him 'almost to the point of tears'; 'Behold the Lamb of God', *Church Times*, 20 Apr. 2000, p. 15. On Thatcher's Methodism, see Eliza Filby, *God and Mrs Thatcher: Conviction Politics in Britain's Secular Age* (London: Biteback, 2015).
47. See Chs 5 and 12.
48. Francis, 'Tears, Tantrums, and Bared Teeth', p. 364.
49. Norman Hare, 'Most are Christian "in some sense"', *Church Times*, 19 Aug. 1988, p. 5.
50. Potter, 'Tears'.
51. See Ch. 13.
52. Aitken, *Margaret Thatcher*, p. 291.
53. Douglas Keay Interview for *Woman's Own*, 23 Sept. 1987, Margaret Thatcher Foundation, <http://www.margaretthatcher.org/document/106689>, including a subsequent explanatory statement made to the *Sunday Times* in 1988 stating on Mrs Thatcher's behalf: 'She prefers to think in terms of the acts of individuals and families as the real sinews of society rather than of society as an abstract concept. Her approach to society reflects her fundamental belief in personal responsibility and choice. To leave things to "society" is to run away from the real decisions, practical responsibility and effective action.'
54. Louisa Hadley, *Responding to Margaret Thatcher's Death* (Basingstoke: Palgrave Macmillan, 2014), ch. 1.
55. Cecil Parkinson interviewed on *Newsnight*, BBC Two, 8 Apr. 2013; see also Kenneth Baker's recollection of the occasion in Iain Dale (ed.), *Memories of*

Maggie: A Portrait of Margaret Thatcher (London: Politico's, 2000), p. 154, reprinted from Kenneth Baker, *The Turbulent Years* (London: Faber & Faber, 1993). Thatcher herself also recalled being moved to tears on several occasions during the final days of her premiership; Margaret Thatcher, *The Downing Street Years* (London: HarperCollins, 1993), pp. 856, 857, 861.

56. 'George Osborne on "welling up" at Margaret Thatcher Funeral', BBC News, 23 Apr. 2013, <http://www.bbc.co.uk/news/uk-politics-22263810>.

57. John Humphrys, *Devil's Advocate* (London: Hutchinson, 1999), ch. 4, 'Sentimentality'. For further responses to the mourning for Diana, see Ch. 20.

Chapter 20. Sensibility Regained

1. 'Victoria's Tears', in Elizabeth B. Barrett, *The Seraphim, and Other Poems* (London: Saunders and Otley, 1838), pp. 328–31; see also Ch. 10.

2. Anne Watts, *Always the Children: A Nurse's Story of Home and War* (London: Simon & Schuster, 2010), ch. 7.

3. Wendy Webster, *Englishness and Empire, 1939–1965* (Oxford: Oxford University Press, 2005), p. 97.

4. For an example of how the changes in emotional style seemed to one commentator reviewing the 1990s at the end of the decade, see Barbara Gunnell, 'Tears— No Longer a Crying Shame', *New Statesman*, 22 Nov. 1999, <http://www. newstatesman.com/node/136193>.

5. Robert Jobson and Sean Rayment, 'True Grief' and 'For Britannia, Tears that the Royals Couldn't Hide', *Daily Express*, 12 Dec. 1997, pp. 1, 3; Adrian Lee, 'Why the Royals Can Never Forgive Blair and Brown', *Daily Express*, 17 May 2011, pp. 28–9.

6. Ross Benson, 'It All Ends in Tears', *Daily Express*, 1 July 1997, pp. 1, 5; Stephen Vines, 'Hong Kong Handover: Patten Wipes a Tear as Last Post Sounds', *Independent*, 1 July 1997, <http://www.indpendent.co.uk>.

7. 'Blair Pays Tribute to Diana', BBC News, 1 Sept. 1997, <http://www.bbc.co.uk/ news/special/politics97/diana/blairreact.html>. See also Jim McGuigan, 'British Identity and "the People's Princess"', *Sociological Review* 48 (2000): 1–18; James Thomas, *Diana's Mourning: A People's History* (Cardiff: University of Wales Press, 2002), ch. 1.

8. 'Express Opinion: The Queen Must Lead Us in our Grief', and Ludovic Kennedy, 'Thanks to Diana, Wills is our Ray of Hope', both in *Daily Express*, 4 Sept. 1997, p. 14. On 8 Sept. 1997, the *Independent* published a survey and analysis of the previous week's coverage, paying attention to questions of emotion and media representation, with contributions by Virginia Ironside, Thomas Sutcliffe, and Ann Treneman: 'Diana: How We Saw It', *Independent*, 8 Sept. 1997, <http:// www.independent.co.uk/news/media/diana-how-we-saw-it-1238054.html>.

9. Queen Elizabeth II, 'Tribute to Diana, Princess of Wales', 5 Sept. 1997, C-Span Cable TV Archive, <http://www.c-span.org/video/?90552-1/death-princess-diana>;

see also 'Speech Following the Death of Diana, Princess of Wales', 5 Sept. 1997, The Official Website of the British Monarchy, <http://www.royal.gov.uk>.

10. The *Express* observed that 'stiff upper lips were forgotten' as both the queen and Prince Philip were reduced to tears, noting that three months earlier, ahead of Diana's funeral, 'the Royal Family stood accused of not showing enough emotion in public' but that the decommissioning of the royal yacht *Britannia* had witnessed 'a Royal Family transformed'; *Express*, 12 Dec. 1997, p. 3.

11. James Thomas, 'Beneath the Mourning Veil: Mass-Observation and the Death of Diana', *Mass-Observation Archive Occasional Paper No. 12* (Brighton: University of Sussex Library, 2002), p. 3; Thomas, *Diana's Mourning*, ch. 5.

12. Thomas, 'Beneath the Mourning Veil', p. 1; Thomas, *Diana's Mourning*, pp. 1–3; Jenny Kitzinger, 'Image', part of a 'Special Debate' on 'Flowers and Tears: The Death of Diana, Princess of Wales', *Screen* 38 (1998): 73–9; Robert Turnock, *Interpreting Diana: Television Audiences and the Death of a Princess* (London: British Film Institute, 2000), p. 81; Peter Mandler, *The English National Character: The History of an Idea from Edmund Burke to Tony Blair* (New Haven: Yale University Press, 2006), pp. 236–7; Kate Fox, *Watching the English: The Hidden Rules of English Behaviour*, updated edn (London: Hodder & Stoughton, 2014), pp. 255–6.

13. John Humphrys, *Devil's Advocate* (London: Hutchinson, 1999), ch. 4; Turnock, *Interpreting Diana*, p. 83. On the association of fascists with tears and emotionalism, see also Ch. 16.

14. Boris Johnson, 'Politics', *The Spectator*, 7 Oct. 1995, p. 8, <http://archive.spectator.co.uk>.

15. Boris Johnson, 'Where is This, Argentina?', *Daily Telegraph*, 3 Sept. 1997; quoted in Thomas, *Diana's Mourning*, p. 111; and Mandler, *The English National Character*, p. 237.

16. See Ch. 18.

17. John Wragg, 'Heartbreak!', *Daily Express*, 5 July 1990, p. 56.

18. 'Cry Gazza Cry', *Spitting Image*, Central Television, 1990, clip available on YouTube, <http://www.youtube.com/watch?v=-cWzY2oVyMA>. On the cultural symbolism of Gazza in the 1990s, see also Ian Hamilton, 'Gazza Agonistes', *Granta* 45 (1993): 9–125.

19. See Ch. 19.

20. Peter McKay, 'Hankies Ready, It's the Crying Games', *Mail on Sunday*, 5 Aug. 2012, <http://www.dailymail.co.uk>; Tim Rayment, 'Win or Lose, It's the Crying Games', *Sunday Times* (News), 5 Aug. 2012, p. 11.

21. The 17-year-old British swimmer Judy Grinham wept when presented with her gold medal for the 100 metres backstroke at the Melbourne Olympics in 1956, setting a new world record and becoming the first British swimmer to win an Olympic gold since 1924; Peter Wilson, 'Gold Day for Pride of London', *Daily Mirror*, 6 Dec. 1956, p. 21. In 1964, at the Tokyo games, the only Japanese swimmers to win a medal, the

four-man 200 metres relay team, shed tears of joy when taking bronze; 'Americans End with 16 of the Twenty-Two Gold Medals', *The Times*, 19 Oct. 1964, p. 4.

22. Richard Williams, 'The Crying Games', *The Guardian*, 5 Aug. 1996, p. A1.

23. Robert Philip, 'Sobbing Giant With a Dry Eye on Another Hero's Record', *Daily Telegraph*, 23 Aug. 2004, <http://www.telegraph.co.uk>.

24. Rod Liddle, 'Big Girls Don't Cry. Nor Do Conservatives', *The Spectator*, 26 Aug. 2004, p. 22, <http://archive.spectator.co.uk/article>.

25. See Ch. 19.

26. 'Boris Johnson: Ceremony left me "crying like a baby"', BBC News, 28 July 2012, <http://www.bbc.co.uk/news/uk-19027643>; Peter Dominiczak, 'Boris Johnson Left in Floods of Tears by "stupefyingly brilliant" Opening Ceremony', *London Evening Standard*, 28 July 2012, <http://www.standard.co.uk>; 'Johnson: "The final tear-sodden juddering climax of London 2012"', BBC News, 10 Sept. 2012, <http://www.bbc.co.uk/news/uk-19549553>.

27. See Ch. 7.

28. Jim White's comment was typical: 'Murray won something few had expected yesterday: the nation's heart'; *Telegraph*, 9 July 2012, p. 1; the Sport section of the same paper carried a picture of an emotional Murray on its front page, with the headline, 'Murray the Brave: Tearful Scot Wins Hearts and Minds as He Falls to Supreme Federer'.

29. Toby Young, 'When Did Tears Become Compulsory?', *The Spectator*, 14 July 2012, p. 60. Jenny Diski voiced a similar distaste for Murray's capitulation to the prevailing 'sentimental sadism'; 'Please Don't Cry', London Review of Books Blog, 9 July 2012, <http://www.lrb.co.uk/blog/2012/07/09/jenny-diski/please-dont-cry>. Contributors to Jeremy Vine's radio show on 9 July 2012 expressed a range of views, ranging from disgust and dismay to admiration and new-found affection for Murray. The journalist Patrick Hayes, expressing the minority view, complained that Murray was indulging in an 'emotional, therapeutic, circle-time sort of experience' and should have kept his emotions private; 'Jeremy Vine', BBC Radio 2, 9 July 2012, <http://www.bbc.co.uk/programmes/b01kjgtb>.

30. On Kipling's 'If–', see Ch. 14.

31. Martin Hodgson, 'Murray Describes Fight to Cope with Trauma of Dunblane School Killings', *The Guardian*, 5 June 2008, <http://www.theguardian.com/sport>; 'Andy Murray Breaks Down in Tears as He Remembers Dunblane Massacre', *Telegraph*, 28 June 2013, <http://www.telegraph.co.uk>; Tara Brady, 'Making of Murray: How Andy Survived the Dunblane Massacre to Grow into a Sporting Superstar', *Daily Mail*, 7 July 2013, <http://www.dailymail.co.uk>; 'Andy Murray in Tears at Freedom of Stirling Award', BBC News, 23 Apr. 2014, <http://www.bbc.co.uk/news/uk-scotland-27130166>.

32. Mary Howarth, 'Retrospective Review: "The Man of Feeling"—A Hero of Old-Fashioned Romance', *Gentleman's Magazine*, Jan.–June 1907, pp. 290–5 (p. 294); see also Chs 7 and 15 of this volume.

33. Anon., 'Weeping', *The Spirit of the Public Journals for 1801: Being an Impartial Selection of the Most Exquisite Essays and Jeux d'Esprits, Principally Prose, that Appear in the Newspapers and Other Publications, Volume 5* (London: James Ridgway, 1802), pp. 136–8; see also Ch. 9.

34. On Willes, see Ch. 12 and Thomas Dixon, 'The Tears of Mr Justice Willes', *Journal of Victorian Culture* 17 (2012): 1–23.

35. Jo Brand, 'For Crying Out Loud', What Larks Productions for BBC Four, first broadcast 14 Feb. 2011, <http://www.bbc.co.uk/programmes/booymhqz>.

36. Kay Withers, 'Cry Baby', *Woman's Hour*, Monday 29 Jan. 1968; transcript held at the BBC Written Archives Centre, Caversham Park, Reading.

37. *The Diary and Letters of Madame D'Arblay* [Fanny Burney], ed. by her niece [Charlotte Barrett], 7 vols (London: Henry Colburn, 1842–6), i. 218–22; G. J. Barker-Benfield, *The Culture of Sensibility: Sex and Society in Eighteenth-Century Britain* (Chicago: University of Chicago Press, 1992), p. 346; Scott Paul Gordon, *The Power of the Passive Self in English Literature, 1640–1770* (Cambridge: Cambridge University Press, 2002), p. 212; see also Ch. 8 of this volume.

38. Charlie Brooker, *The Hell of it All* (London: Faber and Faber, 2009), pp. 29–30; originally published in 'Charlie Brooker's Screen Burn', *The Guardian*, 1 Sept. 2007, <http://www.theguardian.com>.

39. 'Crying Now Meaningless', *The Daily Mash*, 7 Oct. 2013, <http://www.thedailymash.co.uk>.

40. 'Anne Edwards Traces the Start of a Stiff Upper Lip', *Daily Express*, 12 Oct. 1953, p. 3. Marjorie Proops wrote in similar vein a few years later about the pain of mothers who had to repress their feelings and their tears when sending their sons off to boarding school for the first time: Marjorie Proops, 'You Can't Kiss a Schoolboy Goodbye!', *Daily Mirror*, 18 Sept. 1957, p. 11.

41. See Chs 17–19.

42. Margaret Driscoll, 'Goodbye Stiff Upper Lip', *Sunday Times*, 16 Nov. 1997, p. 6. In the same year, the Samaritans' chief executive Simon Armson, commenting about rising suicide rates among the young, and a lack of sympathy for depression among their peers, said, 'Sadly it seems the stiff upper lip is not yet a thing of the past. We need to do all we can to help the young realise the importance of talking about difficult feelings'; John Chapman, 'Anguish of the Young as Suicide Rates Rocket', *Daily Express*, 17 May 1997, p. 25.

43. Kate Fox, *The Kleenex-for-Men Crying Game Report: A Study of Men and Crying* (Oxford: Social Issues Research Centre, 2004), <http://www.sirc.org/publik/crying_game.pdf>.

44. Sally Guyoncourt, '30% of Men Have Cried This Month', *Daily Express*, 18 Sept. 2004, p. 51. The report also prompted a discussion asking 'Is it Alright for Men to Cry?' on *Woman's Hour*, BBC Radio 4, 29 Sept. 2004, <http://www.bbc.co.uk/radio4/womanshour/2004_39_wed_03.shtml>.

45. Laura Holland, 'We've Kissed Goodbye to the Stiff Upper Lip', *Daily Express*, 26 Mar. 2010, p. 3; 'The British Stiff Upper Lip Finally Wobbles', Warburtons

Bakery Press Release, 26 Mar. 2010, <http://www.warburtons.co.uk/press/latest_news.php?p=27&id=861>.

46. 'Why the Stiff Upper Lip Has Gone Soggy as Men Become Happy to Show their Emotions', *Daily Mail*, 8 Feb. 2011, <http://www.dailymail.co.uk>; William Leith, 'All Cried Out—Whatever Happened to our Stiff Upper Lip?', *Sunday Telegraph*, 6 Nov. 2011, Magazine, pp. 16–17; Lauren Paxman, 'What Stiff Upper Lip?', *Daily Mail*, 25 Nov. 2011, <http://www.dailymail.co.uk>.

47. Harris MacLeod, 'Do Brits Still Have Stiff Upper Lips?', YouGov, 4 Oct. 2012, <http://yougov.co.uk>.

48. Virginia Woolf, 'Professions for Women', in *The Crowded Dance of Modern Life: Selected Essays*, volume ii, ed. with an introduction and notes by Rachel Bowlby (London: Penguin, 1993), pp. 102–3; see also Ch. 15 in this volume.

49. See Ch. 16.

50. Sam Taylor-Wood, *Crying Men* (Göttingen: Steidl, 2004); Anthony Holden and Ben Holden (eds), *Poems that Make Grown Men Cry: 100 Men on the Words that Move Them* (London: Simon & Schuster, 2014).

51. Ad Vingerhoets, *Why Only Humans Weep: Unravelling the Mysteries of Tears* (Oxford: Oxford University Press, 2013), ch. 10.

52. See Ch. 18.

53. Eileen Fairweather, 'The Feminist Backlash: We're Waving, Not Drowning', *Cosmopolitan* (London: National Magazine Company Limited), Jan. 1985, pp. 88–9, 135.

54. Mark Mason, 'Get a Grip, Chaps. There's Too Much Male Blubbing in Public Life', *The Spectator*, 28 Apr. 2012, p. 24.

55. Kate Fox, in the detailed Kleenex study of 2004, reported that 'the politically correct, New Man views of our male focus-group participants seemed to have little or no influence on their actual behaviour: the majority still did not report crying anywhere near as much as the female participants, and their comments and anecdotes indicated that they were still clearly reluctant to be seen crying'; Fox, *The Kleenex-for-Men Crying Game Report*, p. 6.

56. *Woman's Hour*, BBC Radio 4, 29 Sept. 2004, <http://www.bbc.co.uk/radio4/womanshour/2004_39_wed_03.shtml>.

57. Ally Fogg, 'We Tell Boys Not to Cry, Then Wonder About Male Suicide', *The Guardian*, Comment is Free Blog, 17 Jan. 2012, <http://www.theguardian.com>.

58. See Chs 14, 17, and 19.

59. 'Ian Hislop's Stiff Upper Lip: An Emotional History of Britain', Wingspan Productions for BBC Two, first broadcast Oct. 2012, <http://www.bbc.co.uk/programmes/b01n7rh4>.

60. On crying over not crying in films of the 1940s see Ch. 16.

61. 'Shadow Theatre of Attraction with a Great British Montage. Britain's Got Talent Final, 2013', YouTube, 8 June 2013, <http://www.youtube.com/watch?v=x1r9qNVqSrk>; Fiona Keating, 'Attraction Win Britain's Got Talent as Eggs Fly at Simon Cowell', *International Business Times*, 9 June 2013, <http://www.ibtimes.co.uk>.

Conclusion

1. David Hume, *A Treatise of Human Nature*, ed. L. Selby-Bigge and P. Nidditch (Oxford: Clarendon Press, 1978), p. 415; first published 1739–40. See also Chs 5 and 10 in this volume.
2. Edmund Burke, *Reflections on the Revolution in France* (1790), in *Burke: Revolutionary Writings*, ed. Iain Hampsher-Monk (Cambridge: Cambridge University Press, 2014), p. 82.
3. Thomas Paine, *The Rights of Man* (1791), in *Paine: Political Writings*, ed. Bruce Kuklick (Cambridge: Cambridge University Press, 2000), p. 129.
4. For some recommended works on the history of emotions see the 'Further Reading' section.
5. Paxman appeared on the show in January 2006. 'Jeremy Paxman', Who Do You Think You Are Past Stories, BBC Website, <http://www.bbc.co.uk/whodoyouthinkyouare/past-stories/jeremy-paxman.shtml>.
6. Jo Brand, 'For Crying Out Loud', What Larks Productions for BBC Four, first broadcast 14 Feb. 2011, <http://www.bbc.co.uk/programmes/booymhqz>.
7. 'No Coward Soul is Mine' (1846), in Emily Jane Brontë, *The Complete Poems*, ed. Janet Gezari (London: Penguin, 1992), p. 182; on Brontë's engagement with the Stoic philosophy of Epictetus, see Margaret Maison, 'Emily Brontë and Epictetus', *Notes and Queries* 223 (1978): 230–1.
8. 'Brian Blessed', *Who Do You Think You Are?*, BBC One, 14 Aug. 2014, <http://www.bbc.co.uk/programmes/b04dw11r>. 'How Who Do You Think You Are? Silenced Brian Blessed', *Yorkshire Post*, 4 Aug. 2014, <http://www.yorkshirepost.co.uk>.
9. 'Who Do You Think You Are? Brian Blessed Silenced and Brought to Tears as he Discovers his "adventurous roots"', *Hull Daily Mail*, 13 Aug. 2014, <http://www.hulldailymail.co.uk>.
10. Alison Graham, 'Why Must Social History Documentaries Invariably Lead to the "Crying Shot"', *Radio Times*, 14 July 2012, <http://www.radiotimes.com>.
11. For an interesting analysis see James Thomas, *Diana's Mourning: A People's History* (Cardiff: University of Wales Press, 2002), ch. 5.
12. 'Public Calamities and the Public Bearing', *The Spectator*, 16 Dec. 1871, pp. 9–10, <http://archive.spectator.co.uk>.
13. Letter from Descartes of 18 May 1645, *The Correspondence Between Princess Elisabeth of Bohemia and René Descartes*, ed. and trans. Lisa Shapiro (Chicago: University of Chicago Press, 2007), p. 87.
14. David Hume, 'The Stoic' (1742), in *David Hume: Selected Essays*, ed. with an introduction and notes by Stephen Copley and Andrew Edgar (Oxford: Oxford University Press, 1993), pp. 83–91 (pp. 87–8).
15. On the production history of *Titus Andronicus*, see Jonathan Bate, 'Introduction', in William Shakespeare, *Titus Andronicus*, ed. Jonathan Bate (London: Arden Shakespeare, 1995), pp. 37–69.

16. Plato's views featured in the classicist Professor Simon Goldhill's contributions to a radio feature I presented in 2013: 'Margaret Are You Grieving? A Cultural History of Weeping', BBC Radio 3, 27 Jan. 2013, <http://www.bbc.co.uk/programmes/b01pz96d>.

17. Shakespeare, *Titus Andronicus*, ed. Bate, Act III, Scene 1, pp. 194, 195, 201. For more on *Titus Andronicus*, see Ch. 3.

18. Anthony Sher and Gregory Doran, *Woza Shakespeare! Titus Andronicus in South Africa* (London: Methuen Drama, 1996), p. 166.

19. Fiona Shaw, 'Playing Electra in Derry Helped Me See the Power of Tragedy', *The Guardian*, 29 Apr. 2014, <http://www.guardian.com>; Jane Montgomery Griffiths, 'Remembering Derry: Sophocles' Electra and the Space of Memory', *Didaskalia* 7.2 (2009), <http://www.didaskalia.net/issues/vol7no2/griffiths.html>. Fiona Shaw also contributed to 'Margaret Are You Grieving?', BBC Radio 3.

20. Sher and Doran, *Woza Shakespeare!*, pp. 200, 238, 261, 262.

21. Ibid. 238.

22. See Ch. 3.

23. See Ch. 17 for a discussion of Freudian theorists, including Phyllis Greenacre.

24. Alvin Borgquist, 'Crying', *American Journal of Psychology* 17.2 (1906): 149–205 (pp. 152–3).

25. Ad Vingerhoets, *Why Only Humans Weep: Unravelling the Mysteries of Tears* (Oxford: Oxford University Press, 2013), pp. 51–2, 91–2, 105–12. See also Jerome Neu, *A Tear is an Intellectual Thing: The Meanings of Emotion* (Oxford: Oxford University Press, 2000), ch. 2, especially pp. 35–6; Thomas Dixon, 'The Waterworks', Aeon Magazine, 22 Feb. 2013, <http://aeon.co/magazine/psychology/thomas-dixon-tears>. On Darwin, see Ch. 13.

26. Sandor S. Feldman, 'Crying at the Happy Ending', *Journal of the American Psychoanalytic Association* 4 (1956): 477–85.

27. Feldman, 'Crying at the Happy Ending', pp. 481–2, 484–5.

28. Anna Laetitia Barbauld, *Hymns in Prose for Children*, 6th edn (London: J. Johnson, 1794), p. 88.

29. C. S. Lewis, *A Grief Observed* (London: Faber & Faber, 1964), p. 34.

30. 'The Doer of Good', in Oscar Wilde, *Complete Shorter Fiction*, ed. Isobel Murray (Oxford: Oxford University Press, 2008), pp. 253–5.

31. John Donne, 'John 11.35. Jesus Wept' (1622/3), in *The Sermons of John Donne*, ed. with introductions and critical apparatus by George R. Potter and Evelyn M. Simpson, 10 vols (Berkeley and Los Angeles: University of California Press, 1959), iv. 324–44 (p. 341).

32. On the manly, Anglo-Saxon tears and kisses of King Cnut and his friends and family, see Tracey-Anne Cooper, 'The Shedding of Tears in Late Anglo-Saxon England', in Elina Gertsman (ed.), *Crying in the Middle Ages: Tears of History* (New York: Routledge, 2012), pp. 175–92 (pp. 177–81).

33. David Cesarani, *Arthur Koestler: The Homeless Mind* (London: William Heinemann, 1998).

34. Arthur Koestler, *The Act of Creation* (London: Hutchinson, 1964), book i, ch. 12, 'The Logic of the Moist Eye', pp. 271–84 (p. 273).

35. Charles Dickens, *Dombey and Son*, ed. with an introduction and notes by Dennis Walder (Oxford: Oxford University Press, 2001), ch. 16, p. 240; first published in instalments 1846–8, and as a single volume in 1848.

36. 'Time', in *Posthumous Poems of Percy Bysshe Shelley* (London: John and Henry L. Hunt, 1824), p. 215.

37. Donne, 'Elegie on the Lady Markham' (1609), quoted in Marjory E. Lange, *Telling Tears in the English Renaissance* (Leiden: E. J. Brill, 1996), p. 196; Donne, 'John 11.35. Jesus Wept', pp. 331, 337, 339.

ONLINE RESOURCES

I have divided the online archives, publications, and databases used in researching this book into two categories—those with publicly accessible content at the time of writing, and those accessed through an institutional or individual subscription. For publicly accessible sites I have included a web address.

Publicly Available

BBC Genome Project: Radio Times Listings, 1923–2009
   http://genome.ch.bbc.co.uk
Big Red Book Online: Celebrating Television's This is your Life
   http://www.bigredbook.info
British Film Institute Collection Search
   http://collections-search.bfi.org.uk/web
British Museum Collection Online
   https://www.britishmuseum.org/research/collection_online/search.aspx
Complete Works of Charles Darwin Online
   http://darwin-online.org.uk
Darwin Correspondence Project
   http://www.darwinproject.ac.uk
Google Books
   http://books.google.com
Hansard Online: Official Reports of Debates in Parliament, 1803–2005
   http://hansard.millbanksystems.com
Internet Archive
   https://archive.org
Margaret Thatcher Foundation
   http://www.margaretthatcher.org
The Modernist Journals Project
   http://modjourn.org
Old Bailey Proceedings Online
   http://www.oldbaileyonline.org
OTA: The University of Oxford Text Archive
   http://ota.ahds.ac.uk
Project Gutenberg
   https://www.gutenberg.org

Queen Victoria's Journals
   http://www.queenvictoriasjournals.org
The Spectator Archive, 1828–2008
   http://archive.spectator.co.uk
Thank the Academy, by Rebecca Rolfe
   http://www.rebeccarolfe.com/projects/thanktheacademy
The UK Reading Experience Database
   http://www.open.ac.uk/arts/reading/UK

Available Through Subscription

17th–18th-Century Burney Collection Newspapers
19th-Century British Newspapers
The British Newspaper Archive
British Periodicals
Early English Books Online (EEBO)
Eighteenth-Century Collections Online (ECCO)
JISC Historic Books
JSTOR
Nineteenth-Century UK Periodicals
Oxford Dictionary of National Biography, Online Edition
Oxford English Dictionary Online
The Times Digital Archive, 1785–1985
UK Press Online

FURTHER READING

The endnotes cite the primary and secondary sources for each chapter. In creating the list below, I have chosen articles and books that could serve as useful starting points for further research into some of the topics and historical themes explored in this book.

Theories of Weeping

Gary L. Ebersole, 'The Function of Ritual Weeping Revisited: Affective Expression and Moral Discourse', *History of Religions* 39 (2000): 211–46.

Sandor S. Feldman, 'Crying at the Happy Ending', *Journal of the American Psychoanalytic Association* 4 (1956): 477–85.

William H. Frey II, with Muriel Langseth, *Crying: The Mystery of Tears* (Minneapolis: Winston Press, 1985).

Arthur Koestler, *The Act of Creation* (London: Hutchinson, 1964), 'The Logic of the Moist Eye', pp. 271–84.

Jeffrey A. Kottler, *The Language of Tears* (San Francisco: Jossey-Bass, 1996).

Tom Lutz, *Crying: The Natural and Cultural History of Tears* (New York: Norton, 1999).

Judith Kay Nelson, *Seeing Through Tears: Crying and Attachment* (New York: Routledge, 2005).

Jerome Neu, *A Tear is an Intellectual Thing: The Meanings of Emotion* (Oxford: Oxford University Press, 2000).

Michael R. Trimble, *Why Humans Like to Cry: Tragedy, Evolution, and the Brain* (Oxford: Oxford University Press, 2012).

Ad Vingerhoets, *Why Only Humans Weep: Unravelling the Mysteries of Tears* (Oxford: Oxford University Press, 2013).

Tears in History

Sheila Page Bayne, *Tears and Weeping: An Aspect of Emotional Climate Reflected in Seventeenth-Century French Literature* (Tübingen: Narr, 1981).

Bernard Capp, ' "Jesus Wept" But Did the Englishman? Masculinity and Emotion in Early Modern England', *Past and Present* 224 (2014): 75–108.

Thomas Dixon, 'The Tears of Mr Justice Willes', *Journal of Victorian Culture* 17 (2012): 1–23.

James Elkins, *Pictures and Tears: A History of People Who Have Cried in Front of Paintings* (New York: Routledge, 2001).

Julie Ellison, *Cato's Tears and the Making of Anglo-American Emotion* (Chicago: University of Chicago Press, 1999).

Thorsten Fögen (ed.), *Tears in the Graeco-Roman World* (Berlin: Walter de Gruyter, 2009).

Elina Gertsman (ed.), *Crying in the Middle Ages: Tears of History* (New York: Routledge, 2012).

Marjory E. Lange, *Telling Tears in the English Renaissance* (Leiden: E. J. Brill, 1996).

Marco Menin, ' "Who Will Write the History of Tears?" History of Ideas and History of Emotions from Eighteenth-Century France to the Present', *History of European Ideas* 40 (2014): 516–32.

Anne Vincent-Buffault, *The History of Tears: Sensibility and Sentimentality in France* (Basingstoke: Macmillan, 1991).

Timothy Webb (ed.), *Towards a Lachrymology: Tears in Literature and Cultural History, Litteraria Pragensia: Studies in Literature and Culture* 22:43 (2012).

History of Emotions

Fay Bound Alberti (ed.), *Medicine, Emotion, and Disease, 1750–1950* (Basingstoke: Palgrave, 2006).

Joanna Bourke, 'Fear and Anxiety: Writing about Emotion in Modern History', *History Workshop Journal* 55 (2003): 111–33.

Peter Burke, 'Is There a Cultural History of the Emotions?', in Penelope Gouk and Helen Hills (eds), *Representing Emotions: New Connections in the Histories of Art, Music and Medicine* (Aldershot: Ashgate, 2005), pp. 35–48.

Elena Carrera (ed.), *Emotions and Health, 1200–1700* (Leiden: Brill, 2013).

Thomas Dixon, *From Passions to Emotions: The Creation of a Secular Psychological Category* (Cambridge: Cambridge University Press, 2003).

Thomas Dixon, ' "Emotion": The History of a Keyword in Crisis', *Emotion Review* 4 (2012): 338–44.

Lucien Febvre, 'La Sensibilité et l'histoire: comment reconstituer la vie affective d'autrefois?' *Annales d'histoire sociale* 3 (1941): 5–20.

Ute Frevert, *Emotions in History: Lost and Found* (Budapest: Central European University Press, 2011).

Johan Huizinga, *The Autumn of the Middle Ages*, trans. Rodney J. Payton and Ulrich Mammitzsch (Chicago: University of Chicago Press, 1996). First published 1919.

Claire Langhamer, *The English in Love: The Intimate Story of an Emotional Revolution* (Oxford: Oxford University Press, 2013).

Susan J. Matt and Peter N. Stearns (eds), *Doing Emotions History* (Urbana: University of Illinois Press, 2014).

Gail Kern Paster, Katherine Rowe, and Mary Floyd-Wilson (eds), *Reading the Early Modern Passions: Essays in the Cultural History of Emotion* (Philadelphia: University of Pennsylvania Press, 2004).

Jan Plamper, *The History of Emotions: An Introduction* (Oxford: Oxford University Press, 2015).

William M. Reddy, *The Navigation of Feeling: A Framework for the History of Emotions* (Cambridge: Cambridge University Press, 2001).

Michael Roper, *The Secret Battle: Emotional Survival and the Great War* (Manchester: Manchester University Press, 2009).

Barbara Rosenwein, *Emotional Communities in the Early Middle Ages* (Ithaca, NY: Cornell University Press, 2006).

Ulinka Rublack (trans. Pamela Selwyn), 'Fluxes: The Early Modern Body and the Emotions', *History Workshop Journal* 53 (2002): 1–16.

Religion and Feeling

Misty G. Anderson, *Imagining Methodism in Eighteenth-Century Britain: Enthusiasm, Belief and the Borders of the Self* (Baltimore: Johns Hopkins University Press, 2012).

Raymond A. Anselment, 'Mary Rich, Countess of Warwick, and the Gift of Tears', *Seventeenth Century* 22 (2007): 336–57.

Eamon Duffy, *The Stripping of the Altars: Traditional Religion in England, c.1400–c.1580* (New Haven and London: Yale University Press, 1992).

Katherine Harvey, 'Episcopal Emotions: Tears in the Life of the Medieval Bishop', *Historical Research* 87 (2014): 591–610.

David Hempton, *The Religion of the People: Methodism and Popular Religion c.1750–1900* (London: Routledge, 1996).

Susan C. Karant-Nunn, *The Reformation of Feeling: Shaping the Religious Emotions in Early Modern Germany* (Oxford: Oxford University Press, 2010).

Sandra McEntire, *The Doctrine of Compunction in Medieval England: Holy Tears* (Lewiston, NY: Edwin Mellen Press, 1990).

Phyllis Mack, *Visionary Women: Ecstatic Prophecy in Seventeenth-Century England* (Berkeley and Los Angeles: University of California Press, 1992).

Sarah McNamer, *Affective Meditation and the Invention of Medieval Compassion* (Philadelphia: University of Pennsylvania Press, 2010).

Emma Major, *Madam Britannia: Women, Church, and Nation 1712–1812* (Oxford: Oxford University Press, 2011).

Piroska Nagy, *Le Don des larmes au Moyen Âge: un instrument spirituel en quête d'institution, V^e–XIIIe siècle* (Paris: Albin Michel, 2000).

Kimberley Christine Patton and John Stratton Hawley (eds), *Holy Tears: Weeping in the Religious Imagination* (Princeton: Princeton University Press, 2005).

Miri Rubin, *Emotion and Devotion: The Meaning of Mary in Medieval Religious Cultures* (Budapest: Central European University Press, 2009).

Alec Ryrie, *Being Protestant in Reformation Britain* (Oxford: Oxford University Press, 2013).

Alison Shell, *Catholicism, Controversy and the English Literary Imagination, 1558–1660* (Cambridge: Cambridge University Press, 1999).

Richard Strier, 'Herbert and Tears', *ELH* 46 (1979): 221–47.

Sorrow and Sadness in the English Renaissance

Angus Gowland, *The Worlds of Renaissance Melancholy: Robert Burton in Context* (Cambridge: Cambridge University Press, 2006).

Elizabeth Hodgson, *Grief and Women Writers in the English Renaissance* (Cambridge: Cambridge University Press, 2014).

Gary Kuchar, *The Poetry of Religious Sorrow in Early Modern England* (Cambridge: Cambridge University Press, 2008).

G. W. Pigman III, *Grief and English Renaissance Elegy* (Cambridge: Cambridge University Press, 1985).

Jeremy Schmidt, *Melancholy and the Care of the Soul: Religion, Moral Philosophy and Madness in Early Modern England* (Aldershot: Ashgate, 2007).

Erin Sullivan, *Beyond Melancholy: Sadness and Selfhood in Renaissance England* (Oxford: Oxford University Press, forthcoming).

Margo Swiss and David A. Kent (eds), *Speaking Grief in English Literary Culture: Shakespeare to Milton* (Pittsburgh: Duquesne University Press, 2002).

Drama and Theatre

William Archer, *Masks or Faces? A Study in the Psychology of Acting* (London: Longmans, Green and Co., 1888).

Bridget Escolme, *Emotional Excess on the Shakespearean Stage: Passion's Slaves* (London: Bloomsbury Arden Shakespeare, 2013).

Mary Floyd-Wilson, *English Ethnicity and Race in Early Modern Drama* (Cambridge: Cambridge University Press, 2003).

Cora Fox, *Ovid and the Politics of Emotion in Elizabethan England* (New York: Palgrave Macmillann, 2009).

Indira Ghose, *Shakespeare and Laughter: A Cultural History* (Manchester: Manchester University Press, 2008).

Katharine Goodland, *Female Mourning in Medieval and Renaissance English Drama: From the Raising of Lazarus to King Lear* (Aldershot: Ashgate, 2005).

Allison P. Hobgood, *Passionate Playgoing in Early Modern England* (Cambridge: Cambridge University Press, 2014).

Gail Kern Paster, *The Body Embarrassed: Drama and the Disciplines of Shame in Early Modern England* (Ithaca, NY: Cornell University Press, 1993).

Joseph R. Roach, *The Player's Passion: Studies in the Science of Acting* (Newark: University of Delaware Press, 1985).

Matthew Steggle, *Laughing and Weeping in Early Modern Theatres* (Aldershot: Ashgate, 2007).

Sensibility, Sympathy, and Sentimentality

G. J. Barker-Benfield, *The Culture of Sensibility: Sex and Society in Eighteenth-Century Britain* (Chicago: University of Chicago Press, 1992).

Nicola Bown (ed.), *Rethinking Victorian Sentimentality, 19: Interdisciplinary Studies in the Long Nineteenth Century* 4 (2007), <http://www.19.bbk.ac.uk/index.php/19/issue/view/67>.

Carolyn Burdett (ed.), *New Agenda: Sentimentalities*, in *Journal of Victorian Culture* 16 (2011): 187–274.

Markman Ellis, *The Politics of Sensibility: Race, Gender and Commerce in the Sentimental Novel* (Cambridge: Cambridge University Press, 1996).

Jim Endersby, 'Sympathetic Science: Charles Darwin, Joseph Hooker, and the Passions of Victorian Naturalists', *Victorian Studies* 51 (2009): 299–320.

Paul Goring, *The Rhetoric of Sensibility in Eighteenth-Century Culture* (Cambridge: Cambridge University Press, 2005).

Fred Kaplan, *Sacred Tears: Sentimentality in Victorian Literature* (Princeton: Princeton University Press, 1987).

Jonathan Lamb, *The Evolution of Sympathy in the Long Eighteenth Century* (London: Pickering and Chatto, 2009).

John Mullan, *Sentiment and Sociability: The Language of Feeling in the Eighteenth Century* (Oxford: Clarendon Press, 1988).

Adam Phillips and Barbara Taylor, *On Kindness* (London: Hamish Hamilton, 2009).

Valerie Purton, *Dickens and the Sentimental Tradition: Fielding, Richardson, Sterne, Goldsmith, Sheridan, Lamb* (London: Anthem Press, 2012).

Philip Shaw, *Suffering and Sentiment in Romantic Military Art* (Farnham: Ashgate, 2013).

Janet Todd, *Sensibility: An Introduction* (London: Methuen, 1986).

Ann Jessie van Sant, *Eighteenth-Century Sensibility and the Novel: The Senses in Social Context* (Cambridge: Cambridge University Press, 2004).

Paul White, 'Darwin's Emotions: The Scientific Self and the Sentiment of Objectivity', *Isis* 100 (2009): 811–26.

Paul White, 'Darwin Wept: Science and the Sentimental Subject', *Journal of Victorian Culture*, 16 (2011): 195–213.

Gender

Joanna Bourke, *Dismembering the Male: Men's Bodies, Britain and the Great War* (London: Reaktion Books, 1996).

Bernard Capp, ' "Jesus Wept" But Did the Englishman? Masculinity and Emotion in Early Modern England', *Past and Present* 224 (2014): 75–108.

Philip Carter, 'Tears and the Man', in Sarah Knott and Barbara Taylor (eds), *Women, Gender and Enlightenment* (Basingstoke: Palgrave Macmillan, 2005), pp. 156–73.

Tracey-Anne Cooper, 'The Shedding of Tears in Late Anglo-Saxon England', in Elina Gertsman (ed.), *Crying in the Middle Ages: Tears of History* (New York: Routledge, 2012), pp. 175–92.

Kate Fox, *The Kleenex-for-Men Crying Game Report: A Study of Men and Crying* (Oxford: Social Issues Research Centre, 2004), <http://www.sirc.org/publik/crying_game.pdf>.

Holly Furneaux, 'Victorian Masculinities, or Military Men of Feeling: Domesticity, Militarism, and Manly Sensibility', in Juliet John (ed.), *The Oxford Handbook of Victorian Literary Culture* (Oxford: Oxford University Press, forthcoming).

Katharine Goodland, *Female Mourning in Medieval and Renaissance English Drama: From the Raising of Lazarus to King Lear* (Aldershot: Ashgate, 2005).

Kimberley-Joy Knight, '*Si puose calcina a' propi occhi*: The Importance of the Gift of Tears for Thirteenth-Century Religious Women and their Hagiographers', in Elina Gertsman (ed.), *Crying in the Middle Ages: Tears of History* (New York: Routledge, 2012), pp. 136–55.

Sarah Knott and Barbara Taylor (eds), *Women, Gender and Enlightenment* (Basingstoke: Palgrave Macmillan, 2005).

Phyllis Mack, *Heart Religion in the British Enlightenment: Gender and Emotion in Early Methodism* (Cambridge: Cambridge University Press, 2008).

Virginia Nicholson, *Millions Like Us: Women's Lives in War and Peace 1939–1949* (London: Penguin, 2011).

Patricia Phillippy, *Women, Death and Literature in Post-Reformation England* (Cambridge: Cambridge University Press, 2002).

Milette Shamir and Jennifer Travis (eds), *Boys Don't Cry? Rethinking Narratives of Masculinity and Emotion in the U.S.* (New York: Columbia University Press, 2002).

Stephanie A. Shields, *Speaking from the Heart: Gender and the Social Meaning of Emotion* (Cambridge: Cambridge University Press, 2002).

Barbara Taylor, *Mary Wollstonecraft and the Feminist Imagination* (Cambridge: Cambridge University Press, 2003).

John Tosh, *A Man's Place: Masculinity and the Middle-Class Home in Victorian England* (New Haven: Yale University Press, 1999).

Jennifer C. Vaught, *Masculinity and Emotion in Early Modern English Literature* (Aldershot: Ashgate, 2008).

Cinema

Melanie Bell and Melanie Williams (eds), *British Women's Cinema* (London: Routledge, 2009).

Stanley Cavell, *Contesting Tears: The Hollywood Melodrama of the Unknown Woman* (Chicago: University of Chicago Press, 1996).

Richard Dyer, *Brief Encounter* (London: British Film Institute, 1993).

Sue Harper and Vincent Porter, *Weeping in the Cinema in 1950: A Reassessment of Mass-Observation Material* (Brighton: Mass-Observation Archive, University of Sussex Library, 1995).

Sue Harper and Vincent Porter, 'Moved to Tears: Weeping in the Cinema in Postwar Britain', *Screen* 37 (1996): 152–73.

Antonia Lant, *Blackout: Reinventing Women for Wartime British Cinema* (Princeton: Princeton University Press, 1991).

Tom Lutz, *Crying: The Natural and Cultural History of Tears* (New York: Norton, 1999).

Kenneth MacKinnon, *Love, Tears, and the Male Spectator* (London: Associated University Presses, 2002).

Alison L. McKee, *The Woman's Film of the 1940s: Gender, Narrative, and History* (New York: Routledge, 2014).

Steve Neale, 'Melodrama and Tears', *Screen* 27 (1986): 6–23.

Jeffrey Richards, *Films and British National Identity: From Dickens to Dad's Army* (Manchester: Manchester University Press, 1997).

Jeffrey Richards and Dorothy Sheridan (eds), *Mass-Observation at the Movies* (London: Routledge & Kegan Paul, 1987).

Englishness

Mary Floyd-Wilson, *English Ethnicity and Race in Early Modern Drama* (Cambridge: Cambridge University Press, 2003).

Kate Fox, *Watching the English: The Hidden Rules of English Behaviour*, updated edition (London: Hodder and Stoughton, 2014).

Michael Kenny, *The Politics of English Nationhood* (Oxford: Oxford University Press, 2014).

Paul Langford, *Englishness Identified: Manners and Character 1650–1850* (Oxford: Oxford University Press, 2000).

Peter Mandler, *The English National Character: The History of an Idea from Edmund Burke to Tony Blair* (New Haven: Yale University Press, 2006).

Robert Tombs, *The English and their History* (London: Allen Lane, 2014).

Wendy Webster, *Englishness and Empire, 1939–1965* (Oxford: Oxford University Press, 2005).

Politics

Maria Braden, *Women Politicians and the Media* (Lexington: University of Kentucky Press, 1996).

Markman Ellis, *The Politics of Sensibility: Race, Gender and Commerce in the Sentimental Novel* (Cambridge: Cambridge University Press, 1996).

Martin Francis, 'Tears, Tantrums, and Bared Teeth: The Emotional Economy of Three Conservative Prime Ministers, 1951–1963', *Journal of British Studies* 41 (2002): 354–87.

Jonas Liliequist, 'The Political Rhetoric of Tears in Early Modern Sweden', in Jonas Liliequist (ed.), *A History of Emotions, 1200–1800* (London: Pickering and Chatto, 2012), pp. 181–205.

Daniel O'Quinn, 'Fox's Tears: The Staging of Liquid Politics', in Alexander Dick and Angela Esterhammer (eds), *Spheres of Action: Speech and Performance in Romantic Culture* (Toronto: University of Toronto Press, 2009), pp. 194–221.

Mark Philp (ed.), *The French Revolution and British Popular Politics* (Cambridge: Cambridge University Press, 1991).

Lance Price, *Where Power Lies: Prime Ministers v the Media* (London: Simon and Schuster, 2010).

Amanda Vickery (ed.), *Women, Privilege, and Power: British Politics, 1750 to the Present* (Stanford, Calif.: Stanford University Press, 2001).

Wendy Webster, *Not a Man to Match Her: The Marketing of a Prime Minister* (London: The Women's Press, 1990).

Death, Grief, and Mourning

David Cannadine, 'War and Death, Grief and Mourning in Modern Britain', in Joachim Whaley (ed.), *Mirrors of Mortality: Studies in the Social History of Death* (London: Europa, 1981), pp. 187–242.

Katharine Goodland, *Female Mourning in Medieval and Renaissance English Drama: From the Raising of Lazarus to King Lear* (Aldershot: Ashgate, 2005).

Geoffrey Gorer, *Death, Grief, and Mourning in Contemporary Britain* (London: The Cresset Press, 1965).

Pat Jalland, *Death in the Victorian Family* (Oxford: Oxford University Press, 1996).

Pat Jalland, *Death in War and Peace: Loss and Grief in England, 1914–1970* (Oxford: Oxford University Press, 2010).

Adrian Kear and Deborah Lynn Steinberg (eds), *Mourning Diana: Nation, Culture and the Performance of Grief* (London: Routledge, 1999).

Lucy Noakes, *Death, Grief and Mourning in Second World War Britain* (Manchester: Manchester University Press, forthcoming).

Patricia Phillippy, *Women, Death and Literature in Post-Reformation England* (Cambridge: Cambridge University Press, 2002).

Julie-Marie Strange, *Death, Grief and Poverty in Britain, 1870–1914* (Cambridge: Cambridge University Press, 2005).

James Thomas, 'Beneath the Mourning Veil: Mass-Observation and the Death of Diana', *Mass-Observation Archive Occasional Paper No. 12* (Brighton: University of Sussex Library, 2002).

James Thomas, *Diana's Mourning: A People's History* (Cardiff: University of Wales Press, 2002).

Robert Turnock, *Interpreting Diana: Television Audiences and the Death of a Princess* (London: British Film Institute, 2000).

Tony Walters (ed.), *The Mourning of Diana* (London: Berg, 1999).

ACKNOWLEDGEMENTS

My work on this topic—which was not initially intended to become a book—began with research undertaken in 2009 for a talk about Charles Darwin's theory of weeping, delivered at an event organized by Angelique Richardson and her colleagues at the University of Exeter to mark the bicentenary of Darwin's birth. I became intrigued by tears, and continued to explore their meaning in 2010 in the context of an AHRC-funded project at Queen Mary University of London on 'Embodied Emotions', alongside Ali Campbell, Clare Whistler, and Bhavesh Hindocha. Clare Qualmann alerted me to a talk being given by Virginia Eatough about the psychology of crying, and through Virginia I was put in touch with Claire Whalley and Charlie Sever at What Larks Productions, who were making a television programme called *For Crying Out Loud*, presented by Jo Brand, on the meaning of tears, and were looking for a historical contributor. It was through my involvement in this programme, and an associated interview alongside Jo Brand for *Woman's Hour* on BBC Radio 4, that I first started to think there was potential for a whole book, and the idea of *Weeping Britannia* began to take shape. Around the same time, I was working on my first publication on the subject, which eventually came out in the *Journal of Victorian Culture* as 'The Tears of Mr Justice Willes'. Helen Rogers was hugely encouraging and patient in helping me convert my drastically over-length submission into something publishable.

I have spoken about my research at several academic seminars and conferences, and am indebted to the organizers, hosts, and participants in those events, whose questions, criticisms, and suggestions contributed significantly to the course of my research: University of Exeter Conference on Darwin, Medicine and the Humanities (Angelique Richardson); Imperial College London, History of Science Departmental Seminar (Andrew Mendelsohn and Abigail Woods); British Society for Eighteenth-Century Studies Annual Conference, Oxford (Jeremy Gregory and Michael Burden); University of Cambridge Modern Cultural History Seminar (Peter Mandler and Laurence Klein); Netherlands Historical Association Annual Conference, The Hague (Herman Roodenburg); 'Wandering Feelings' Conference, Queen Mary and Birkbeck (Carolyn Burdett and Tiffany Watt-Smith); Birkbeck English Graduate Lecture Series (Anthony Bale); Birkbeck History Research Student Seminar (Janet Weston); British Psychological Society, History of Psychology Symposium at the Wellcome Trust (Alan Collins and Rhodri Hayward); British Society for Literature and Science Annual Conference, Cardiff (Keir Waddington, Martin Willis, and

Anthony Mandal); Institute of Historical Research Long Eighteenth Century Research Seminar (Sally Holloway); North London University of the Third Age (Derek Scott); University of Edinburgh Workshop on Loss, Grief, and Pain (Anna Groundwater); Historical Association, Bath Branch (Boyd Schlenther). In undertaking archival research, I was indebted to the following for their help and support: the Mass Observation Archive, Sussex (Jessica Scantlebury); the BBC Written Archives Centre, Caversham (Jeff Walden); the BFI Archive, London; Hertfordshire Archives and Local Studies.

Throughout my five years of researching and writing about tears and their history, I have been fortunate to work alongside inspiring and supportive colleagues at Queen Mary University of London, both in the School of History and through the interdisciplinary work of the Centre for the History of the Emotions, whose advice, expertise, and encouragement have been invaluable, including Rhodri Hayward, Colin Jones, Miri Rubin, Amanda Vickery, Barbara Taylor, Morag Shiach, Elena Carrera, Tiffany Watt-Smith, Katherine Angel, Tom Asbridge, Eleanor Betts, Fay Bound Alberti, Andrea Brady, Sarah Crook, Virginia Davis, James Ellison, Jules Evans, Mark Glancy, Liz Gray, Tristram Hunt, Julian Jackson, Åsa Jansson, Helen McCarthy, Jane Mackelworth, Chris Millard, Michael Questier, Robert Saunders, Jade Shepherd, Chris Sparks, Stephen Spencer, Miranda Stanyon, Emma Sutton, and Emma Yates. My research was further supported through a Wellcome Trust award for a project at Queen Mary on 'Medicine, Emotion, and Disease in History'. During the final stages of the project, Clare Whistler was a Leverhulme Trust Artist in Residence at the Centre for the History of the Emotions, curating a series of creative events on 'Weather, Tears, and Waterways', which provided illumination and inspiration as I completed my book.

I learned a huge amount about tears as an aesthetic response while working with audio producer Natalie Steed on a feature for BBC Radio 3, entitled 'Margaret, Are You Grieving? A Cultural History of Weeping', first broadcast in January 2013. It was thanks to Natalie that this programme was commissioned, and I had the opportunity to learn from her and from our contributors, to all of whom I am very grateful: Pete de Bolla, Ian Bostridge, Virginia Eatough, Giles Fraser, Simon Goldhill, Miri Rubin, Fiona Shaw, and Matthew Sweet. I was asked to act as a consultant for a series made by Wingspan Productions for BBC Two, *Ian Hislop's Stiff Upper Lip: An Emotional History of Britain*, after one of the producers on the series, Nick Tanner, attended the 'Wandering Feelings' conference at Queen Mary. I am grateful to Archie Baron, Debbie Lee, and Nick Tanner for this opportunity. I learned a great deal both from the historical research undertaken by Debbie, Nick, and others for the series, and from the process of thinking with them about how to construct a narrative history of British emotional identity.

One of the enjoyable things about working on this book has been the fact that everyone has some experience of tears, and some opinion about them, whether from their own lives, scholarly research, or both. Dozens of people have been kind enough to offer me ideas and examples arising from their knowledge and experience for potential inclusion in this book, and I am very grateful to them all: Joanne Bailey, Matthew Bailey, Nicola Bown, Joseph Bristow, Susan Broomhall, Polly Bull, Carolyn Burdett, Geoffrey Cantor, Bernard Capp, Louise Carter, Santanu Das, Emma Dixon, Kay Dixon, Kate Dixon Humphreys, Tom Dixon Humphreys, William Dixon Humphreys, Stephanie Downes, Jim Endersby, Matt ffytche, Catherine Fletcher, Martin Francis, Matthew Grenby, Anna Groundwater, Claudia Hammond, James Harris, Katherine Harvey, Tim Hitchcock, Stephen Hoar, Stuart Hogarth, Sally Holloway, James Humphreys, Elena Isayev, Tom Jones, Nina Queenie Kane, Matthew Klugman, Kimberley Knight, Ed Lake, Mike Levey, Toby Lichtig, Sarah Lowden Poole, Alyson Lowe, Jo Lyon, Joanne McEwan, Ross MacFarlane, Angela McShane, Philippa Maddern, Wendy Michallat, Matilda Murday, Susie Paskins, Chris Pearson, Giselle Portuondo, Rose Reynolds, Emerson Roberts, Beth Robinson, Willemijn Ruberg, Mark Seymour, Susanna Shapland, Giles Shilson, Erin Sullivan, Pam Thurschwell, Stephanie Trigg, Kate Tunstall, Keir Waddington, Tim Webb, Paul White, Gillian Williamson, and Peter Yeandle.

Material previously used in the following publications is re-used above with the kind permission of the respective publishers and journals: Thomas Dixon, 'Patients and Passions: Languages of Medicine and Emotion, 1790–1850', in Fay Bound Alberti (ed.), *Medicine, Emotion, and Disease, 1750–1950* (Basingstoke: Palgrave Macmillan, 2006), pp. 22–52; Thomas Dixon, 'Enthusiasm Delineated: Weeping as a Religious Activity in Eighteenth-Century Britain', *Litteraria Pragensia: Studies in Literature and Culture* 22 (2012): 59–81; Thomas Dixon, 'The Tears of Mr Justice Willes', *Journal of Victorian Culture* 17 (2012): 1–23.

I am also grateful for permission to reprint the following material: extracts from participants' responses to the Mass Observation's questionnaire, August 1950, reproduced by permission of Curtis Brown Group Ltd, London, on behalf of The Trustees of the Mass Observation Archive. Lines from 'An Absolutely Ordinary Rainbow' by Les Murray from *New Collected Poems* (Carcanet, 2003), reprinted by permission of the publishers. Lines from 'For Johnny' by John Pudney from *For Johnny: Poems of World War Two* (Shepheard-Walwyn, 1976), reprinted by permission of David Higham Associates Ltd for the Estate of John Pudney. Lines from the lyrics of 'Stiff Upper Lip' from *Crazy For You*, words and music by George Gershwin and Ira Gershwin, copyright © 1937, renewed by Nowaki Music, Frankie G. Songs, and Ira Gershwin Music (ASCAP), reprinted by permission of Warner Chappell and Hal Leonard Corporation. All rights for Nowaki Music administered by Imagem Sounds. All rights for Ira Gershwin Music administered by W B Music Corp. All Rights Reserved. International Copyright Secured. Lines from the lyrics of 'Boys Don't Cry' (The Cure), words by Robert James Smith, music by Robert James Smith, Laurence Andrew Tolhurst and Michael Stephen Dempsey, copyright © 1979, 1980 Fictions Songs Ltd, reprinted by permission of Music Sales Ltd, and Hal Leonard Corporation. All rights in the United States and Canada administered by Universal Music–MGB Songs. All Rights Reserved. International Copyright Secured. Lines from the lyrics of 'I Believe' (Tears for Fears), words and music by Roland

Orzabal, copyright © 1985 Roland Orzabal Ltd and BMG VM Music Ltd; and 'Shout' (Tears for Fears), words and music by Roland Orzabal and Ian Stanley, copyright © 1984 BMG 10 Music Ltd and BMG VM Music Ltd, reprinted by permission of Hal Leonard Corporation. All rights administered by BMG Rights Management (US) LLC. All Rights Reserved. International Copyright Secured. Although every effort has been made to trace and contact all copyright holders before publication this has not been possible in all cases. If notified, the publisher will rectify any errors or omissions at the earliest opportunity.

It is many years since I had my first tentative conversations with my literary agent Anna Power about possible book projects. Throughout the intervening period, Anna has been instrumental in helping me channel those ideas effectively into the physical reality of this book, gently but firmly pushing me in the right direction, with tact and a lot of patience. I am most grateful to Christopher Wheeler and Luciana O'Flaherty at Oxford University Press for supporting the book, and especially to Matthew Cotton for his attentive editorial interventions and advice. I am also grateful to the anonymous readers appointed by OUP to comment both on the initial proposal and on the final text. Sandra Assersohn provided invaluable assistance with the sourcing of illustrations, and Connie Robertson with literary permissions. As I reached the final stages of writing, several colleagues kindly read and commented on draft chapters, suggesting many improvements; for these I am grateful to Joanna Bourke, Holly Furneaux, Mark Glancy, Hetta Howes, Helen McCarthy, Lucy Noakes, Robert Saunders, and Tiffany Watt-Smith. Jackie Pritchard's eagle-eyed copy-editing and Andrew Hawkey's proofreading saved me from several errors, and ensured that the final text was prepared to the highest standards.

My wife, Emily Butterworth, read and commented on each chapter, offering insight and encouragement at every turn, and she will be as relieved as anyone to see this book finally published so that we can all have a break from weeping. I started researching the history of tears just before our first son, Caleb, was born, and finished writing the book during his first term at school. This book is dedicated with love to Caleb, who, along with his little brother Laurie, has taught me a lot about crying, of all kinds.

PICTURE CREDITS

INDEX

Bold numbers indicate references to illustrations.

Jalland, Pat 288 n. 2, 416
Jamaica 170
James VI of Scotland, and I of England 30
    Daemonologie 60
    translation of the Bible 30
James, William 189–90
Jameson, Leander Starr 200–1, 212
Janov, Arthur 272–3, 275
Jeffrey, Francis 169–70, 179
Jeffreys, George (1st Baron and judge) 176
Jerusalem 18, 20, 25, 37, 62, 105,
    107, 287
Jesus of Nazareth 18, 20–3, 28–30, 35–6,
    37, 57, 60, 76, 77, 107, 117–18,
    160–1, 251, 327, 329
    passion of 18, 20–1, 23–5, 35, 37, 398 n. 46
    tears over grave of Lazarus 23, 30, 107,
        117–18, 251, 327
    tears over Jerusalem 62, 105, 107
Joan of Arc 215
John, Elton:
    'Candle in the Wind' 316
John, St, *see* Bible
Johnson, Amy 215, 220
Johnson, Boris 281, 304, 306–7
Johnson, Joseph 119
Johnson, Lionel 95
Johnson, Samuel 103
Joubert, Laurent 133
joy:
    tears of 7, 18, 49, 78, 116, 138, 140, 239,
        251, 263, 267, 268, 274–6, 324
judges, *see* lawyers; Willes, Sir James Shaw
Julian of Norwich 25–6

Kames, Lord (Henry Home) 86
Kean, Edmund 143
Kellner, Peter 281
Kempe, Margery 15–26, 31, 73, 195–6, 227
    extreme weeping 15, 17–18, 20–1, 73
    pilgrimages 18, 19–20
    sexual temptations 16, 18–19, 322–3 n. 2
    theology of 16–17
Kennedy, Ludovic 302
Kent, Constance 177–80
Kepler, Johannes 150
Key, Helen 217
Khan, Jemima 396 n. 18
Kilmarnock, Earl of 103
Kingsley, Charles:
    'The Three Fishers' 227–8, 383 n. 40
King's Lynn 15–17, 19, 22
The King's Speech 3, 9
Kinnock, Neil 292

Kipling, John (son of Rudyard) 201, 214
    story dramatized in *My Boy Jack* 381 n. 53
Kipling, Rudyard 200–1, 203, 211–12, 214,
    235, 277, 308, 377 n. 7
    Captains Courageous 235
    'If—' 200–1, 214, 277, 308, 377 n. 7
    The Jungle Book 211
    Stalky & Co. 203
    'Thrown Away' 211–12
kissing 30, 32, 34, 49, 99, 106, 114, 117, 166,
    197, 213, 215, 225, 227, 230, 264, 267,
    269, 277, 389 n. 15, 405 n. 32
Kitchener, Horatio Herbert (Earl Kitchener of
    Khartoum) 207, 213, 214
Kleenex 232, 236, 297, 313, 402 n. 43
Knox, John 35
Knox, Vicesimus 107
Koestler, Arthur 328–9
Korda, Alexander 237
Kureishi, Hanif 293–4, 315
    My Beautiful Launderette 293
Kyd, Thomas 39, 342–3 n. 48

Labour Party politicians 268, 279, 281–2,
    285, 289, 292, 300–1, 302, 304, 306,
    396 n. 25
lachrymology, *see* tears, theories of
lamentation 21, 24, **25**, 32–7, 45, 57,
    122, 131
'Land of Hope and Glory' 234, 242, 316
Langford, Paul 340 n. 10, 359 n. 39, 415
Langhorne, John 97, 102
Lanyer, Aemilia 30, 37
Larkin, Philip:
    'The Mower' 263
Laud, William 59
laughter 43–4, 47, 53, 57, 82, 111, 131–3, 139,
    154, 167, 170, 191, 194, 212, 241, 260,
    271, 292–3, 322, 341 n. 16
Lavington, George 94
lawyers 96, 100, 103, 169–70, 171,
    174–7, 294
    barristers 128–9, 171, 175, 178
    judges 169, 171–2, 174–82
    see also courtrooms
Lazarus, *see* Bible
Lean, David 230–1, 244
Leatham, Edward 223
Le Blanc, Abbé:
    *Letters on the English and French
    Nations* 51
Leeds 172
    Leeds United Football Club 265, 269
Leigh, Vivien 238

Lemnius, Levinus:
The Touchstone of Complexions 41–2
Lennon, John 272–3
Levellers 65
Leverson, Ada 367 n. 8
Lewis, C. S. 252–5, 259, 327
A Grief Observed 252–5, 327
Liberal politicians 206, 207, 223, 282, 283,
285, 297, 396 n. 18
Liddle, Rod 305–6
Limerick 167
Littlejohn, Richard 196
Liverpool 180, 208
Livingstone, Ken 281, 206
Lloyd George, David 206–7, 283
Lollards, *see* Christianity
London 2012, *see* Olympic and Paralympic
Games
Londonderry 32, 323
London Zoo 192–3
Loos, Battle of 214
Louis XVI 108, 109, 114, 119,
179, 226
love 16–17, 21, 37, 60, 77, 78, 86–7, 94, 152,
163, 165, 228–9, 230, 244–5, 254, 270–1,
284, 302, 328
romantic 152, 163, 165, 222, 228–9,
230, 235, 240–2, 244–5, 270–1, 284,
328; *see also* Romantic movement
Lusitania, sinking of 204, 221, 260

McCaffrey, John 228
McCann, Madeleine 171
Macdonald, Malcolm 269
Mackenzie, Henry 96–8, 100, 101, 106–7,
111, 117, 130, 138–9, 149, 153–4, 165,
169, 218, 226, 307, 309
The Man of Feeling 96–107, 111, 130,
138–9, 143, 149, 153–4, 218, 309
religious views 106–7, 355–6 n. 45
responses of readers 99–100, 111, 138–9,
154, 226, 241
MacLaine, James 103–4
Macmillan, Harold 284, 395 n. 8
Macready, Charles 162–3
McSmith, Andy 283
Madam Tussaud's 215
madness, *see* insanity
Magdalene, *see* Mary Magdalene
Malleus Maleficarum 60
man of feeling, *see* masculinity
The Man of Feeling (novel), *see* Mackenzie,
Henry
Manchester 176, 225, 269

Mandler, Peter 359 n. 39, 375 n. 21, 400 n.
12, 415
Manilow, Barry 280
Manning, Frederic:
The Middle Parts of Fortune 208
Mantel, Hilary:
'The Assassination of Margaret
Thatcher' 279–80
Marie Antoinette, queen and wife of Louis
XVI 109, 113
Market Theatre (Johannesburg) 322
Marlowe, Christopher 39
Marmontel, Jean-François 151, 152
Marsh, Anne:
'The Admiral's Daughter' 155–6
Marshall, Henrietta:
Our Island Story 2
Martin, Captain William 1–2, 239
Martineau, Harriet 147–50, 152, 155,
163, 203
The Crofton Boys 203
'Ella of Garveloch' 148, 149
Martineau, James 376 n. 30
Mary Magdalene 11, 23, **28**, 30–1, 37–8, 60,
61–2, 90, 101, 106, 251, 336 n. 5, 398 n.
46; *see also* 'maudlin'; prostitutes;
Southwell, Robert
Mary, mother of Jesus 11, 18, 22–4, **25**, 26,
37, 43, 49
Mary, Queen of Scots 30, 35
masculinity 96–107, 118, 143–6, 174, 179,
181–2, 199–214, 243, 263–78, 279–80,
314–15, 334 n. 24, 413–14
'boys don't cry' 154, 268, 270–1, 315, 278
n. 19, 392–3 n. 24
fear of effeminacy 4, 8, 48, 66, 116–17,
121, 143–6, 200, 214, 233–4,
269–70, 315
'manly tear' 98–100, 137
The Man of Feeling (novel), *see* Mackenzie,
Henry
military 135–7, 207–14, 239–40,
379–80 n. 37, 380 n. 39
'new man' of 1970s onwards 4, 263–78,
314–15, 403 n. 55
see also femininity; soldiers
Masefield, John 318
Mason, Mark 315
Mason, William 107
Mass Observation 1, 231–5, 243, 256, 293,
384–5 n. 4, 415, 416
Matthews, Karen 171–2
'maudlin' 11, 38, 89–90, 243, 253, 258, 270,
368 n. 20